VOL. 1

STORY BY
PARK JIN-RYONG

ART BY
SHIN YONG-GWAN

LOS ANGELES • TOKYO • LONDON • HAMBURG

Translator - Youngiu Ryu
English Adaptation - Solina Wong
Copy Editor - Troy Lewter, Suzanne Waldman
Retouch and Lettering - Vicente Rivera, Jr.
Cover Artist - Anna Kembaum
Graphic Designer - John Lo

Editor - Nora Wong
Digital Imaging Manager - Chris Buford
Pre-Press Manager - Antonio DePietro
Production Managers - Jennifer Miller, Mutsumi Miyazaki
Art Director - Matt Alford
Managing Editor - Jill Freshney
VP of Production - Ron Klamert
President & C.O.O. - John Parker
Publisher & C.E.O. - Stuart Levy

E-mail: info@TOKYOPOP.com
Come visit us online at www.TOKYOPOP.com

A 😊 **TOKYOPOP**® Manga

TOKYOPOP Inc.
5900 Wilshire Blvd. Suite 2000
Los Angeles, CA 90036

Eternity Vol. 1

ISBN: 1-59182-788-4

First TOKYOPOP printing: July 2004

10 9 8 7 6 5 4 3 2 1

Printed in the USA

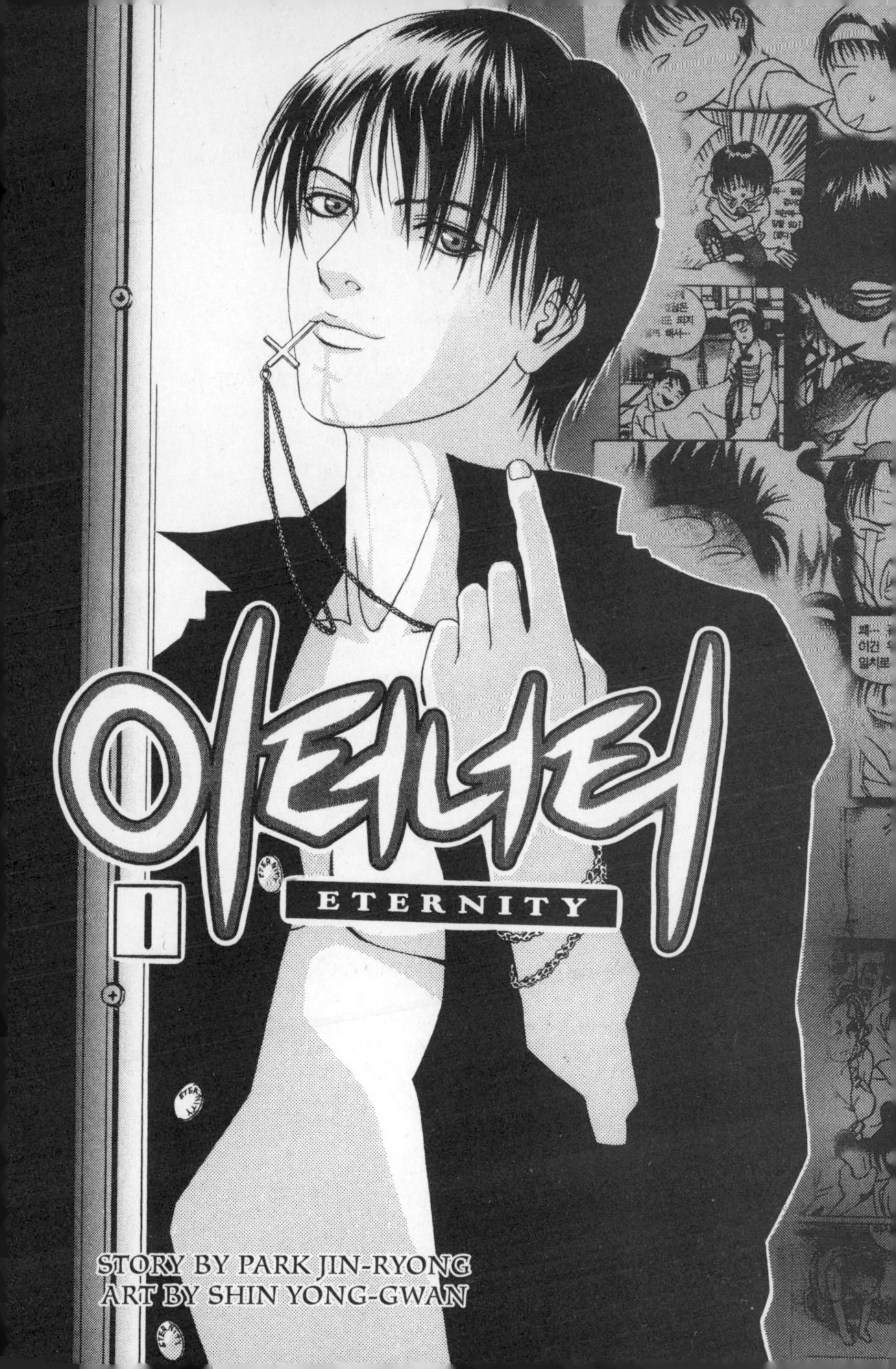
이터니티
ETERNITY
1
STORY BY PARK JIN-RYONG
ART BY SHIN YONG-GWAN

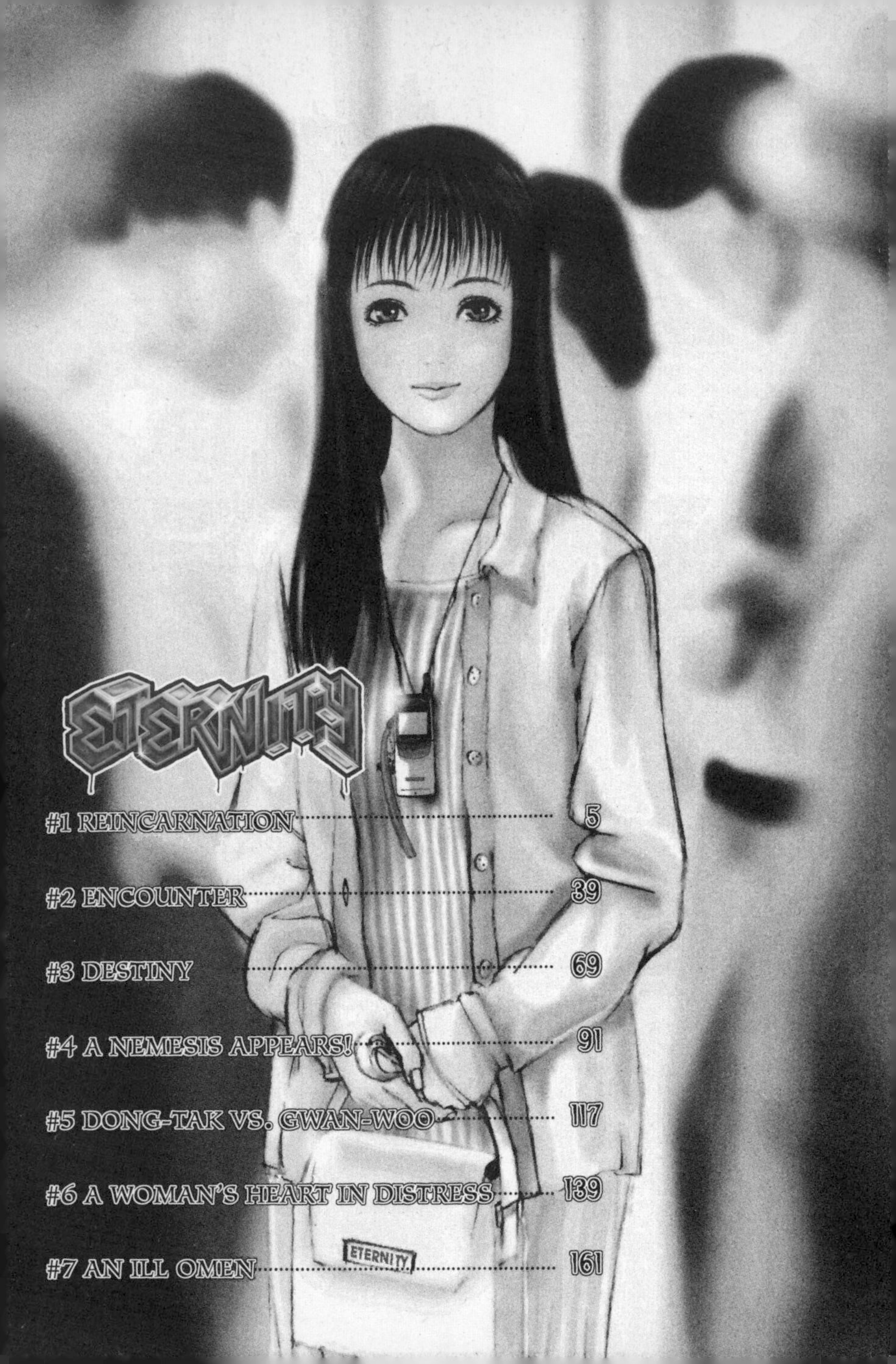
ETERNITY

ETERNITY

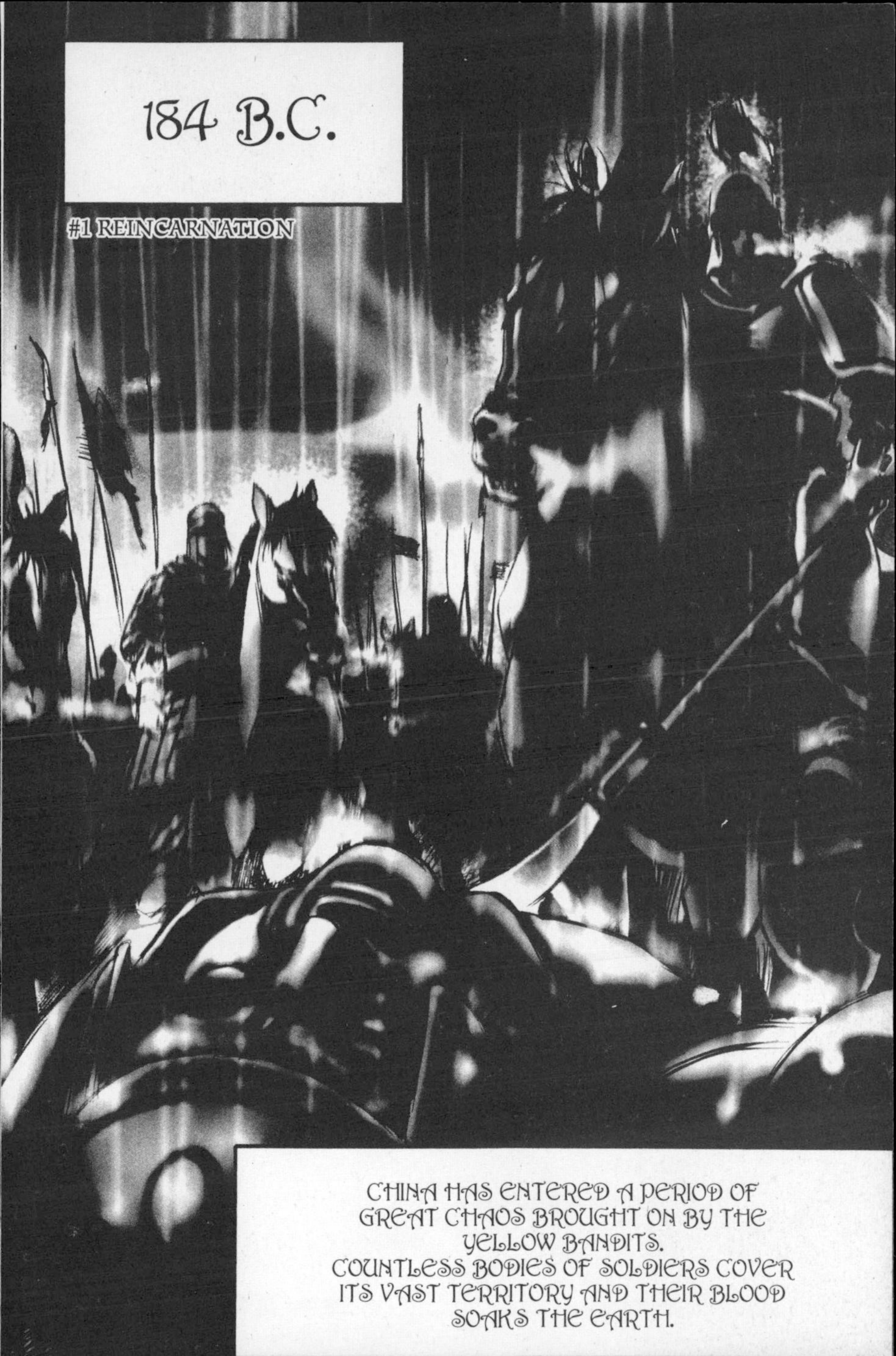
184 B.C.
#1 REINCARNATION
CHINA HAS ENTERED A PERIOD OF GREAT CHAOS BROUGHT ON BY THE YELLOW BANDITS. COUNTLESS BODIES OF SOLDIERS COVER ITS VAST TERRITORY AND THEIR BLOOD SOAKS THE EARTH.

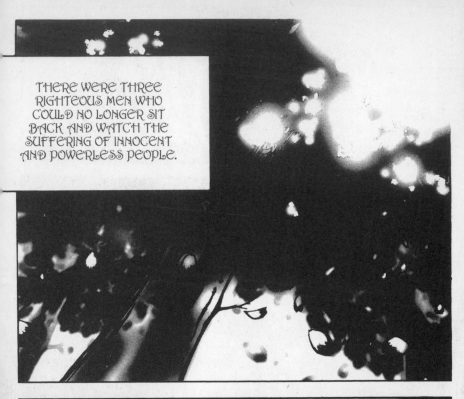

THERE WERE THREE RIGHTEOUS MEN WHO COULD NO LONGER SIT BACK AND WATCH THE SUFFERING OF INNOCENT AND POWERLESS PEOPLE.

THEY TOOK AN OATH OF BROTHERHOOD UNDER A PEACH BLOSSOM TREE THAT TRANSCENDED EVEN DEATH ITSELF. THEIR NAMES ARE...

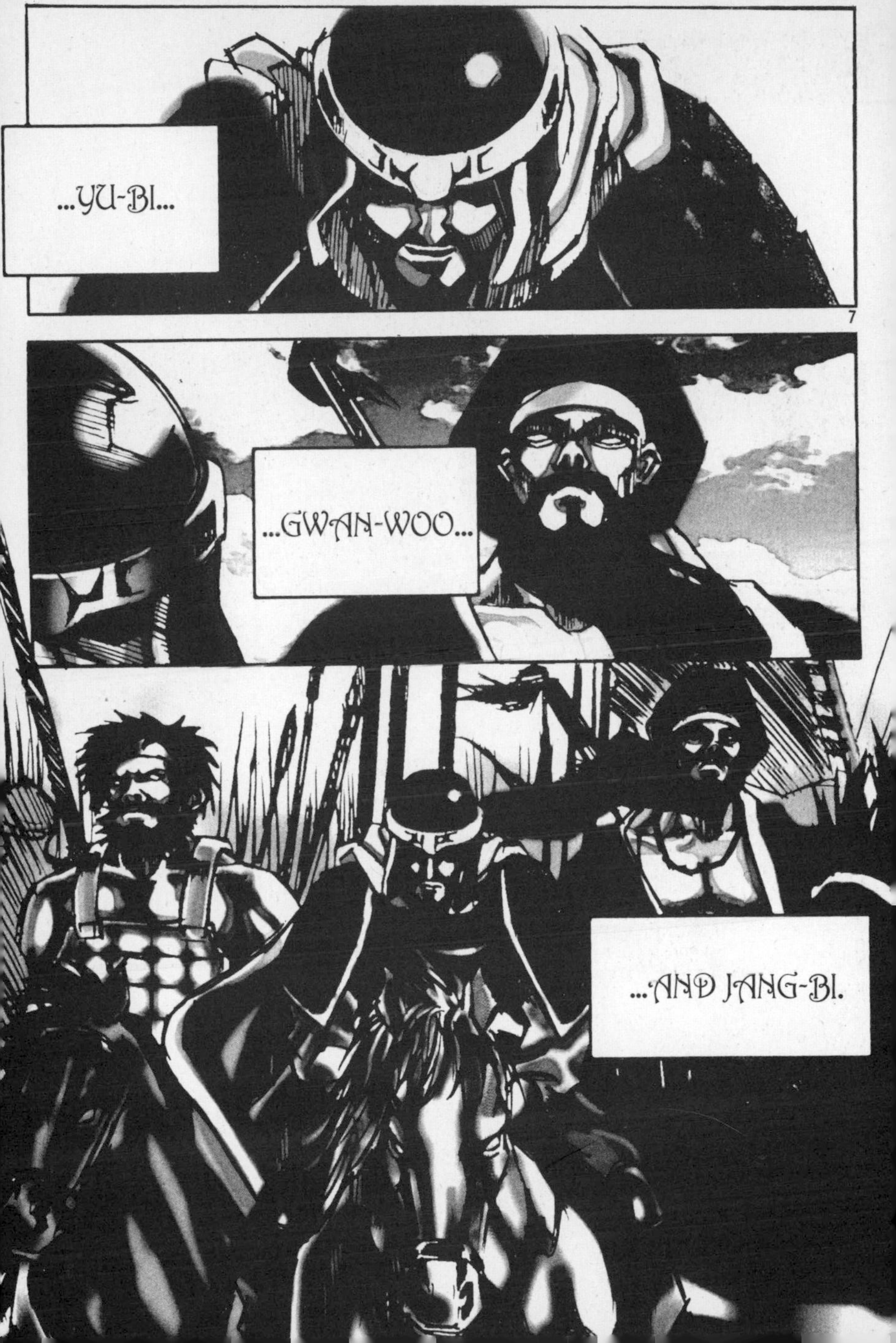
...YU-BI...
...GWAN-WOO...
...AND JANG-BI.

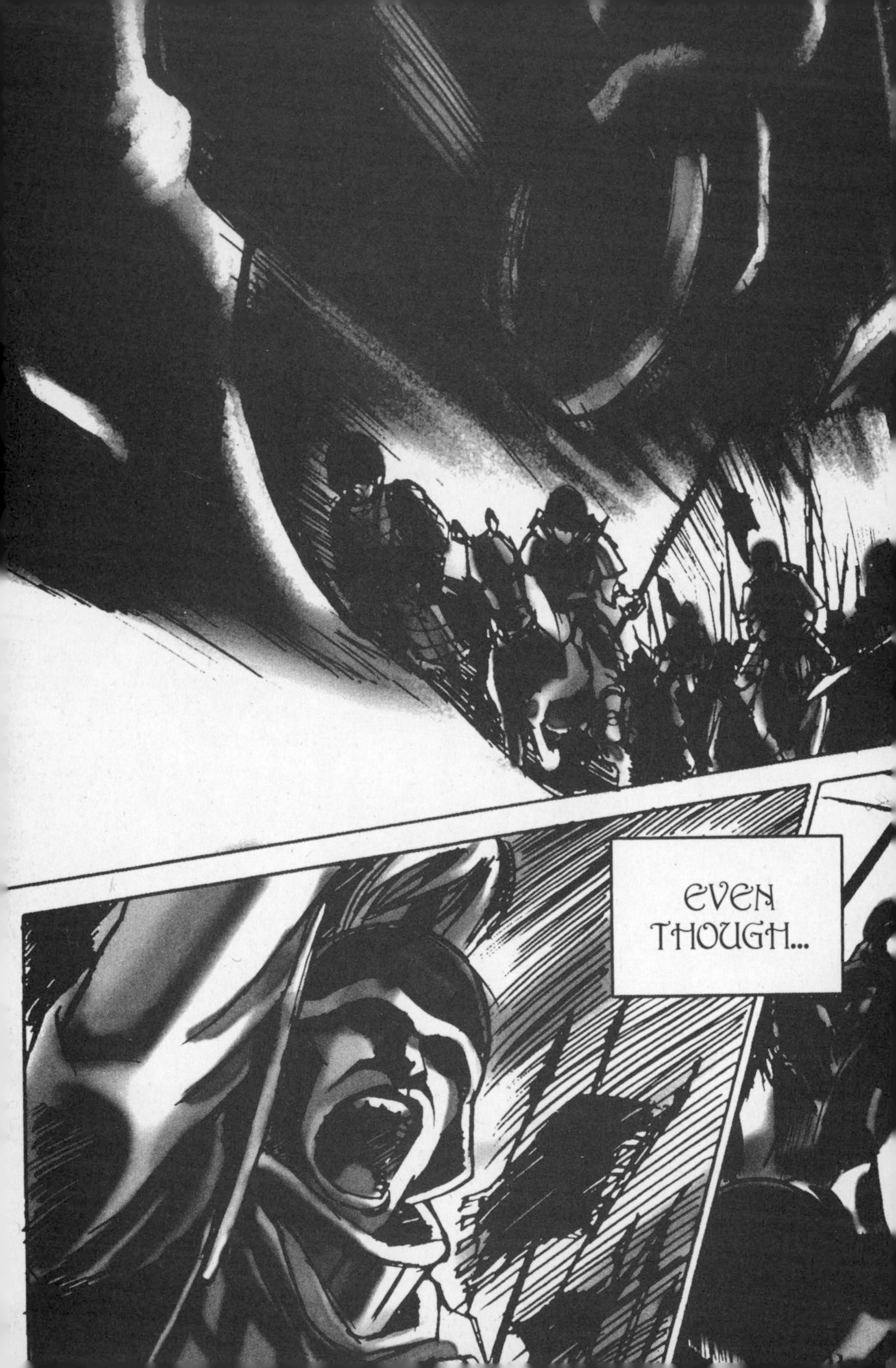
EVEN THOUGH...

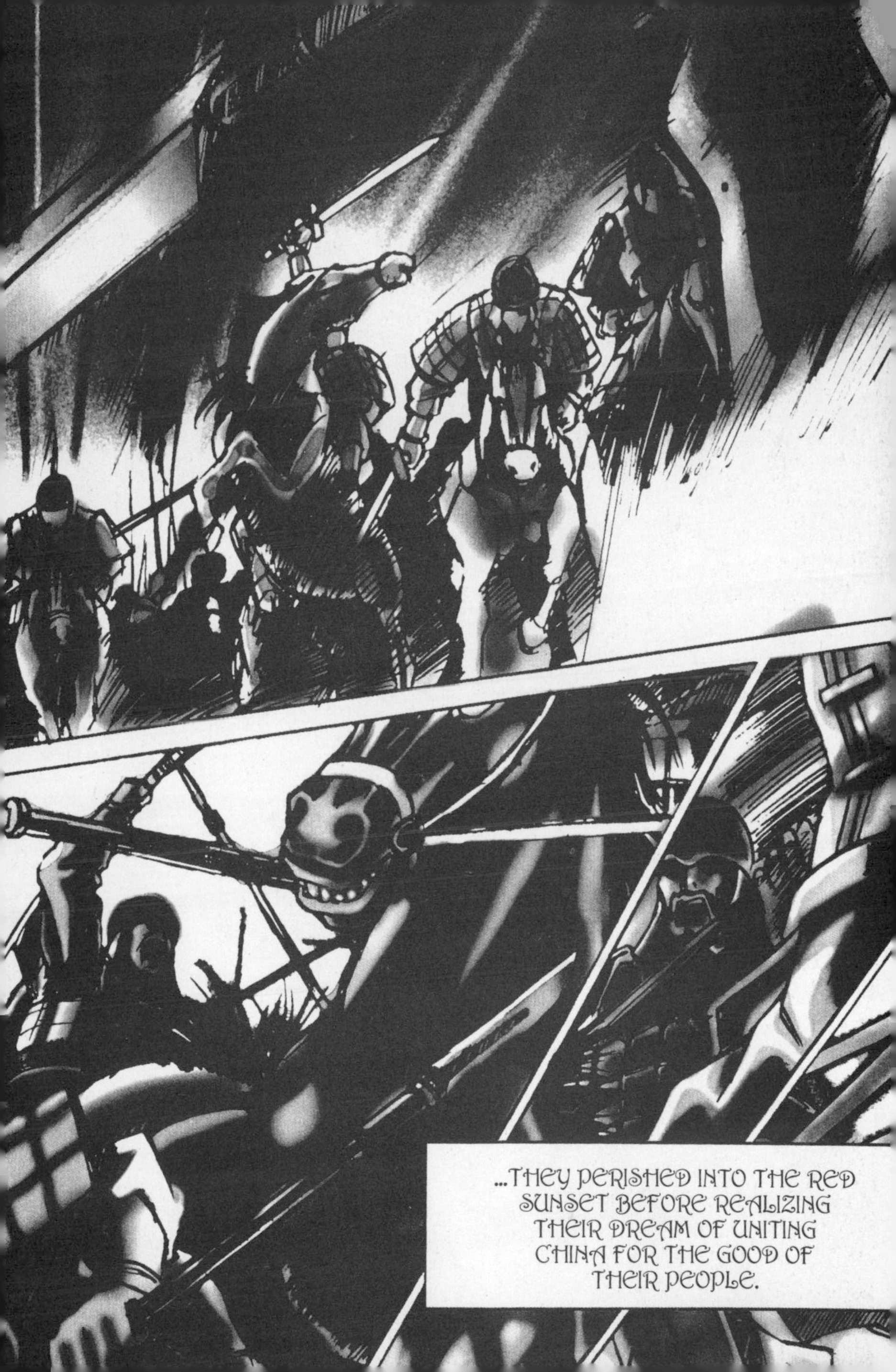
...THEY PERISHED INTO THE RED SUNSET BEFORE REALIZING THEIR DREAM OF UNITING CHINA FOR THE GOOD OF THEIR PEOPLE.

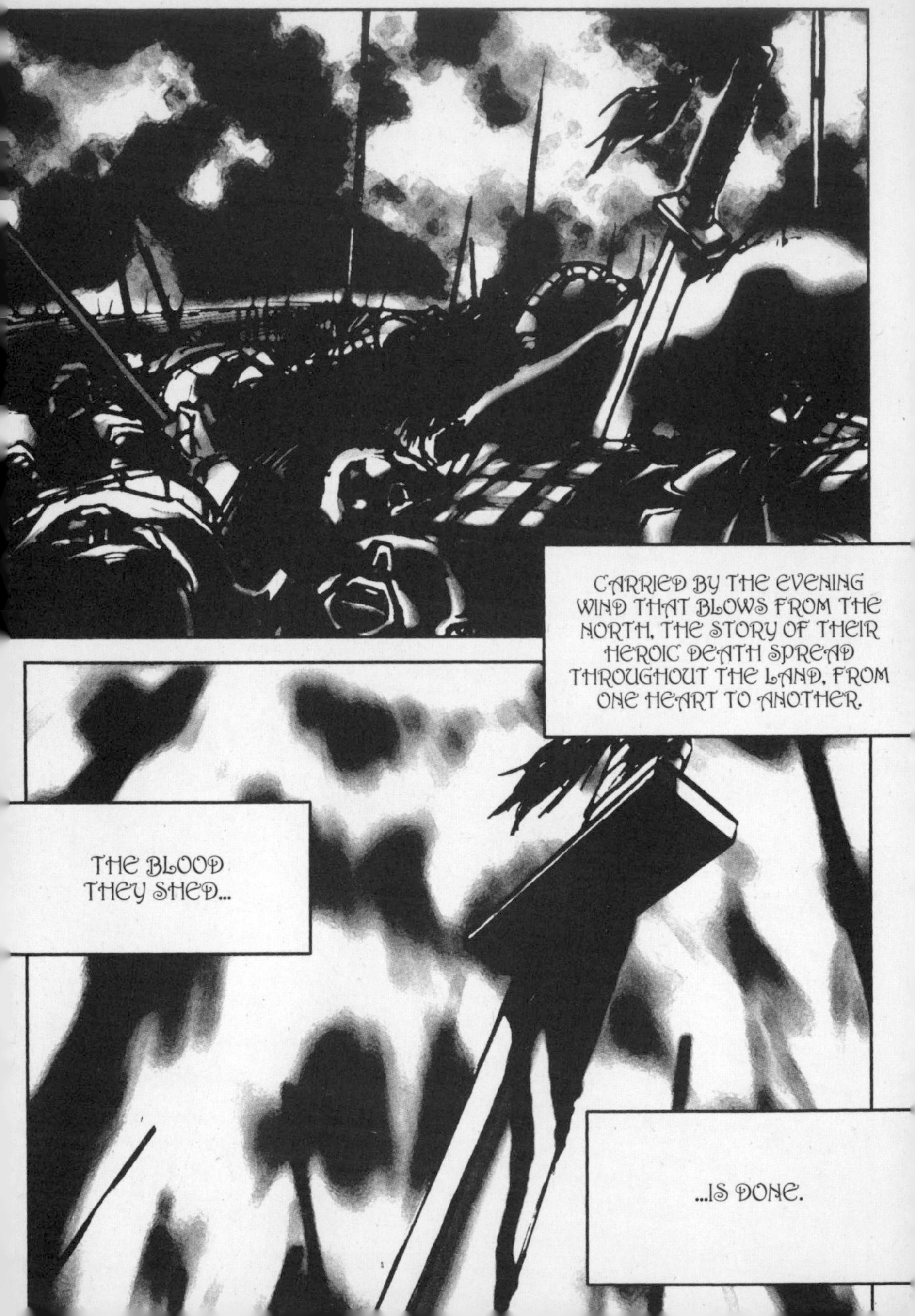
CARRIED BY THE EVENING WIND THAT BLOWS FROM THE NORTH, THE STORY OF THEIR HEROIC DEATH SPREAD THROUGHOUT THE LAND, FROM ONE HEART TO ANOTHER.
THE BLOOD THEY SHED...
...IS DONE.

ETERNITY

#1. REINCARNATION

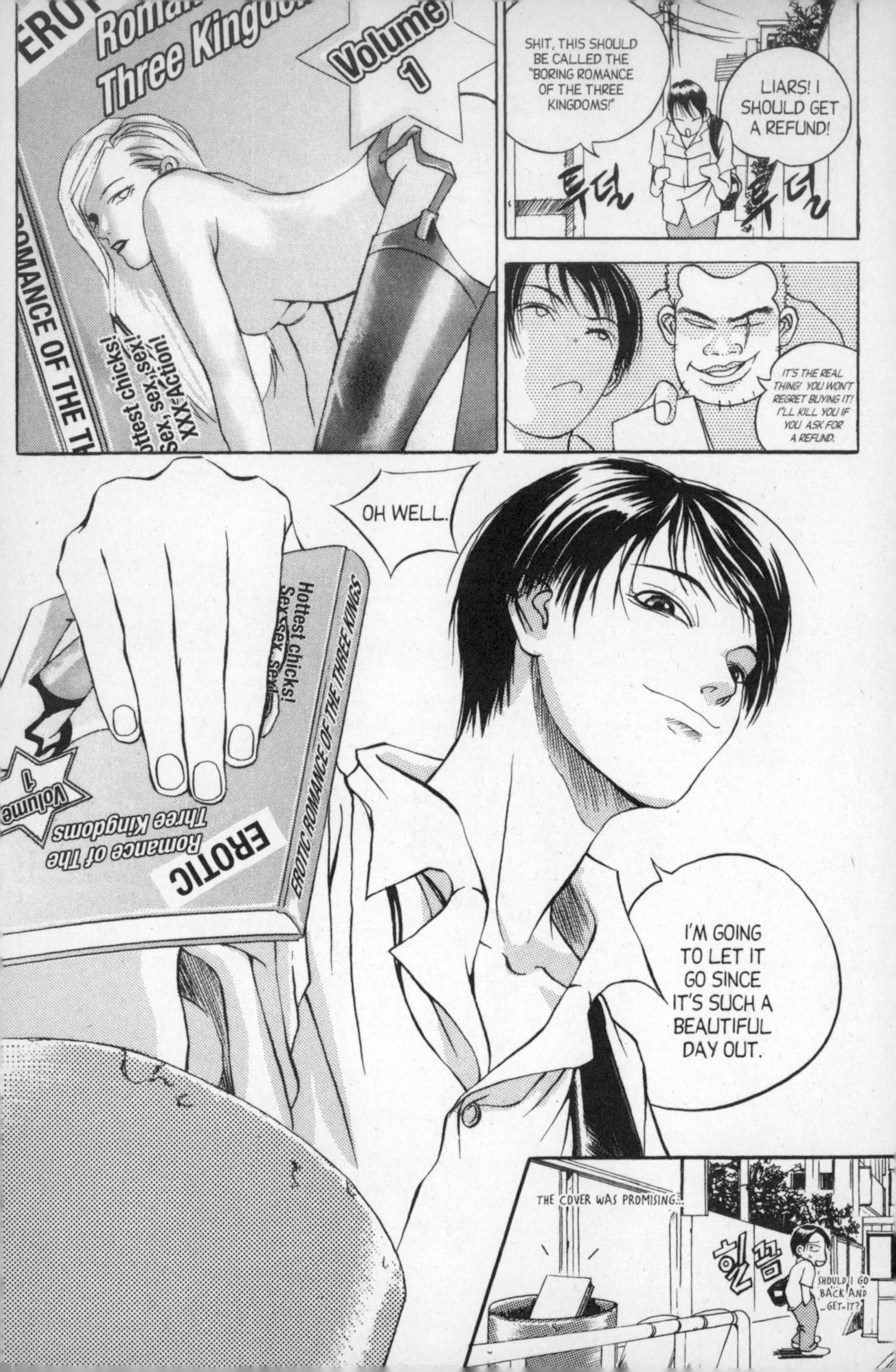
Volume 1
Hottest chicks!
Sex, sex, sex!
XXX Action!
SHIT, THIS SHOULD BE CALLED THE "BORING ROMANCE OF THE THREE KINGDOMS!"
LIARS! I SHOULD GET A REFUND!
투덜 투덜
IT'S THE REAL THING! YOU WON'T REGRET BUYING IT! I'LL KILL YOU IF YOU ASK FOR A REFUND.
OH WELL.
EROTIC
Romance of The Three Kingdoms
Volume 1
Hottest chicks! Sex, sex, sex!
EROTIC ROMANCE OF THE THREE KINGS
I'M GOING TO LET IT GO SINCE IT'S SUCH A BEAUTIFUL DAY OUT.
THE COVER WAS PROMISING...
힐끔
SHOULD I GO BACK AND GET IT?

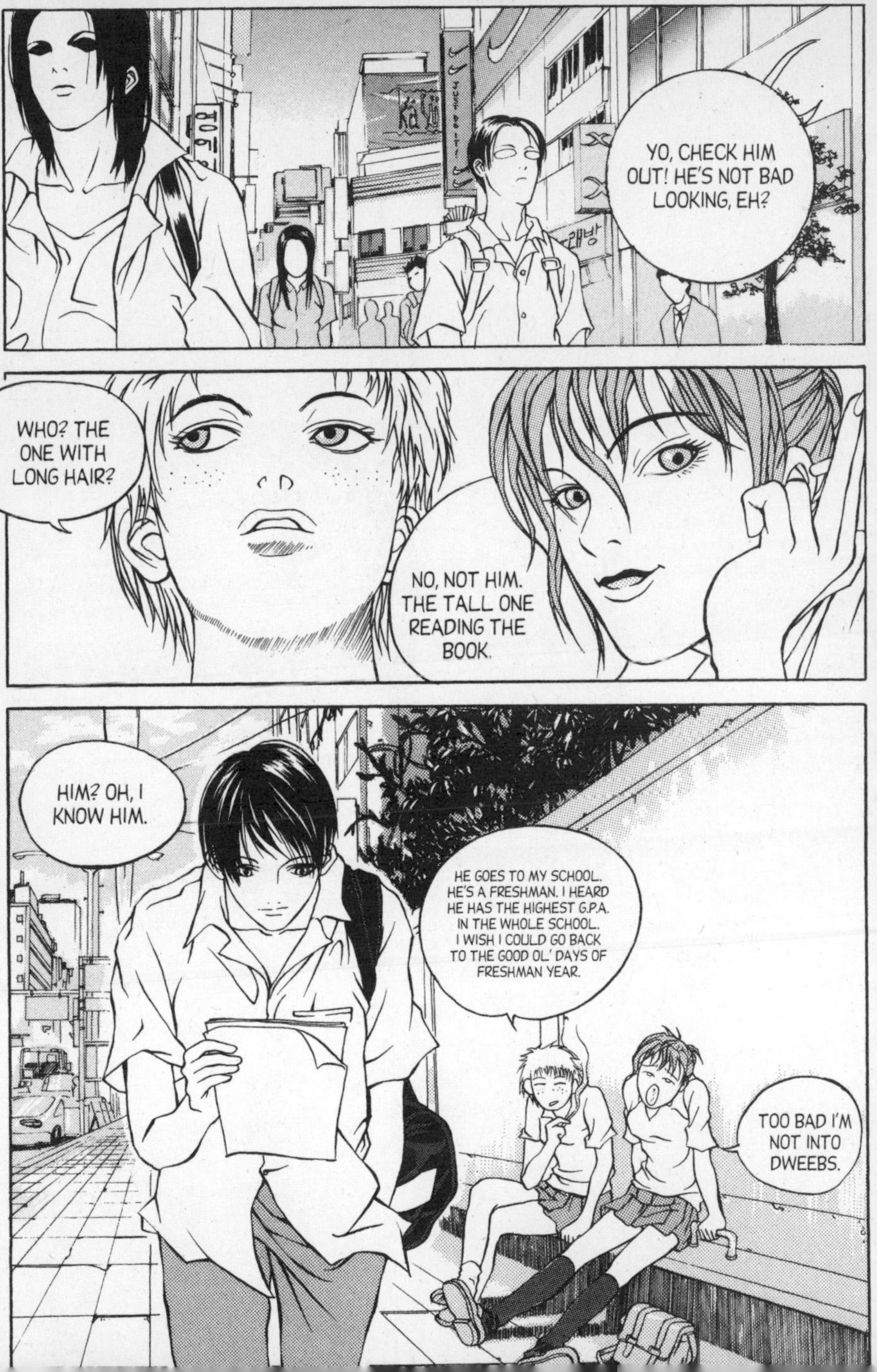
YO, CHECK HIM OUT! HE'S NOT BAD LOOKING, EH?
WHO? THE ONE WITH LONG HAIR?
NO, NOT HIM. THE TALL ONE READING THE BOOK.
HIM? OH, I KNOW HIM.
HE GOES TO MY SCHOOL. HE'S A FRESHMAN. I HEARD HE HAS THE HIGHEST G.P.A. IN THE WHOLE SCHOOL. I WISH I COULD GO BACK TO THE GOOD OL' DAYS OF FRESHMAN YEAR.
TOO BAD I'M NOT INTO DWEEBS.

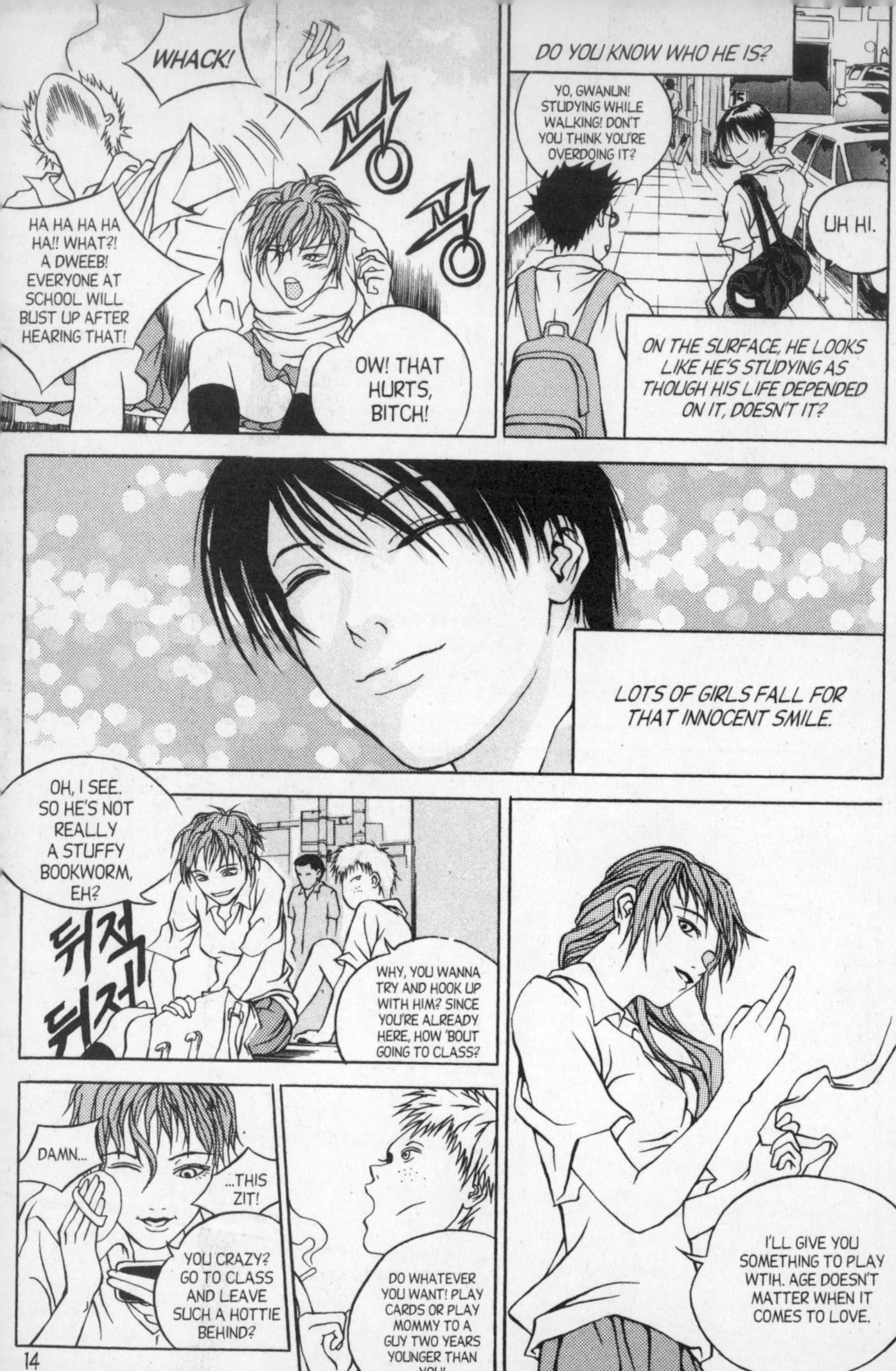
WHACK!
HA HA HA HA HA!! WHAT?! A DWEEB! EVERYONE AT SCHOOL WILL BUST UP AFTER HEARING THAT!
OW! THAT HURTS, BITCH!
DO YOU KNOW WHO HE IS?
YO, GWANUN! STUDYING WHILE WALKING! DON'T YOU THINK YOU'RE OVERDOING IT?
UH HI.
ON THE SURFACE, HE LOOKS LIKE HE'S STUDYING AS THOUGH HIS LIFE DEPENDED ON IT, DOESN'T IT?
LOTS OF GIRLS FALL FOR THAT INNOCENT SMILE.
OH, I SEE. SO HE'S NOT REALLY A STUFFY BOOKWORM, EH?
뒤적 뒤적
WHY, YOU WANNA TRY AND HOOK UP WITH HIM? SINCE YOU'RE ALREADY HERE, HOW 'BOUT GOING TO CLASS?
DAMN...
...THIS ZIT!
YOU CRAZY? GO TO CLASS AND LEAVE SUCH A HOTTIE BEHIND?
DO WHATEVER YOU WANT! PLAY CARDS OR PLAY MOMMY TO A GUY TWO YEARS YOUNGER THAN YOU!
I'LL GIVE YOU SOMETHING TO PLAY WTIH. AGE DOESN'T MATTER WHEN IT COMES TO LOVE.

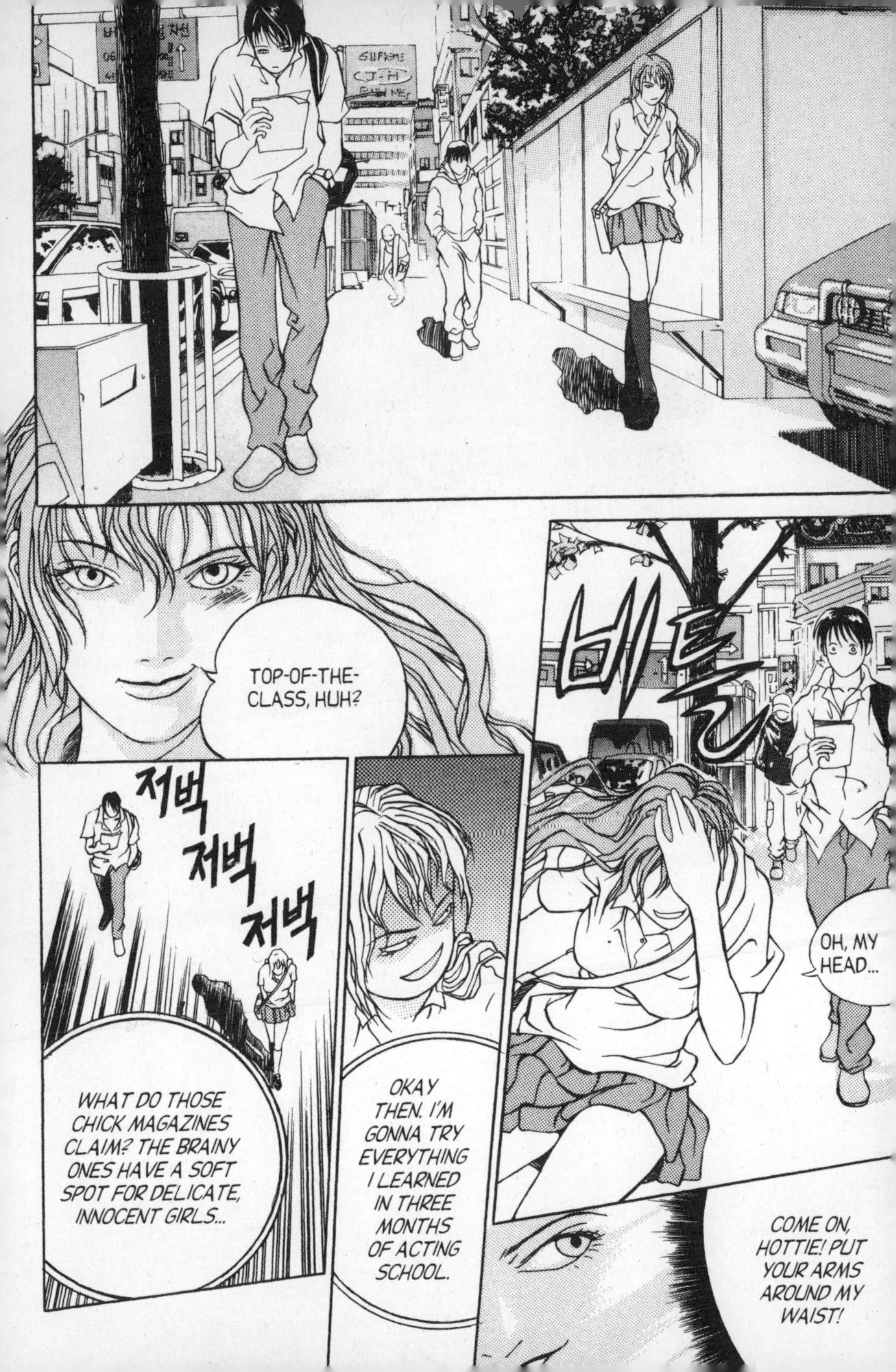
TOP-OF-THE-CLASS, HUH?
저벅 저벅 저벅
WHAT DO THOSE CHICK MAGAZINES CLAIM? THE BRAINY ONES HAVE A SOFT SPOT FOR DELICATE, INNOCENT GIRLS...
OKAY THEN. I'M GONNA TRY EVERYTHING I LEARNED IN THREE MONTHS OF ACTING SCHOOL.
비틀
OH, MY HEAD...
COME ON, HOTTIE! PUT YOUR ARMS AROUND MY WAIST!

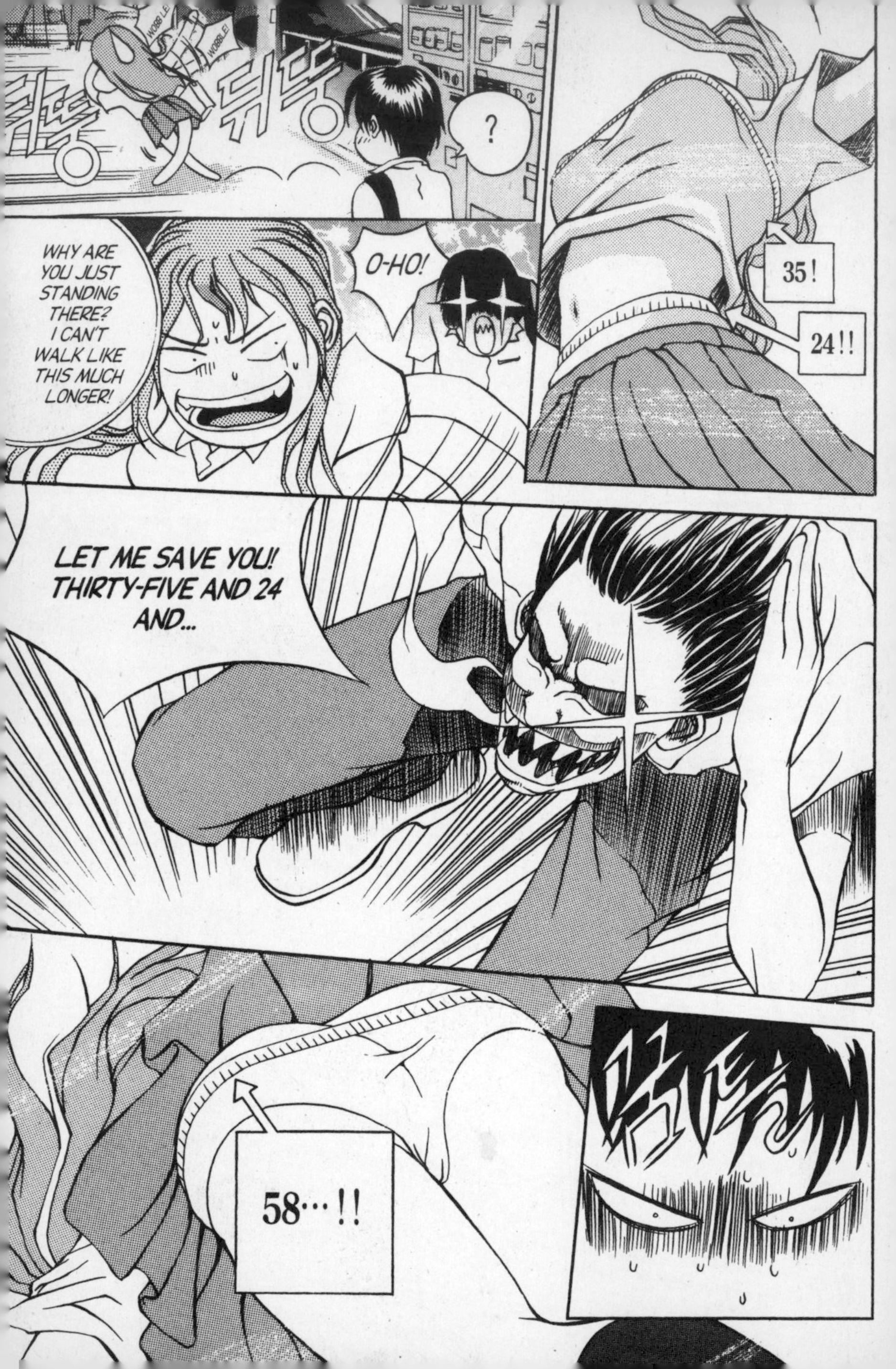
WOBBLE
WOBBLE!
뒤뚱
?
WHY ARE YOU JUST STANDING THERE? I CAN'T WALK LIKE THIS MUCH LONGER!
O-HO!
35!
24!!
LET ME SAVE YOU! THIRTY-FIVE AND 24 AND...
58…!!

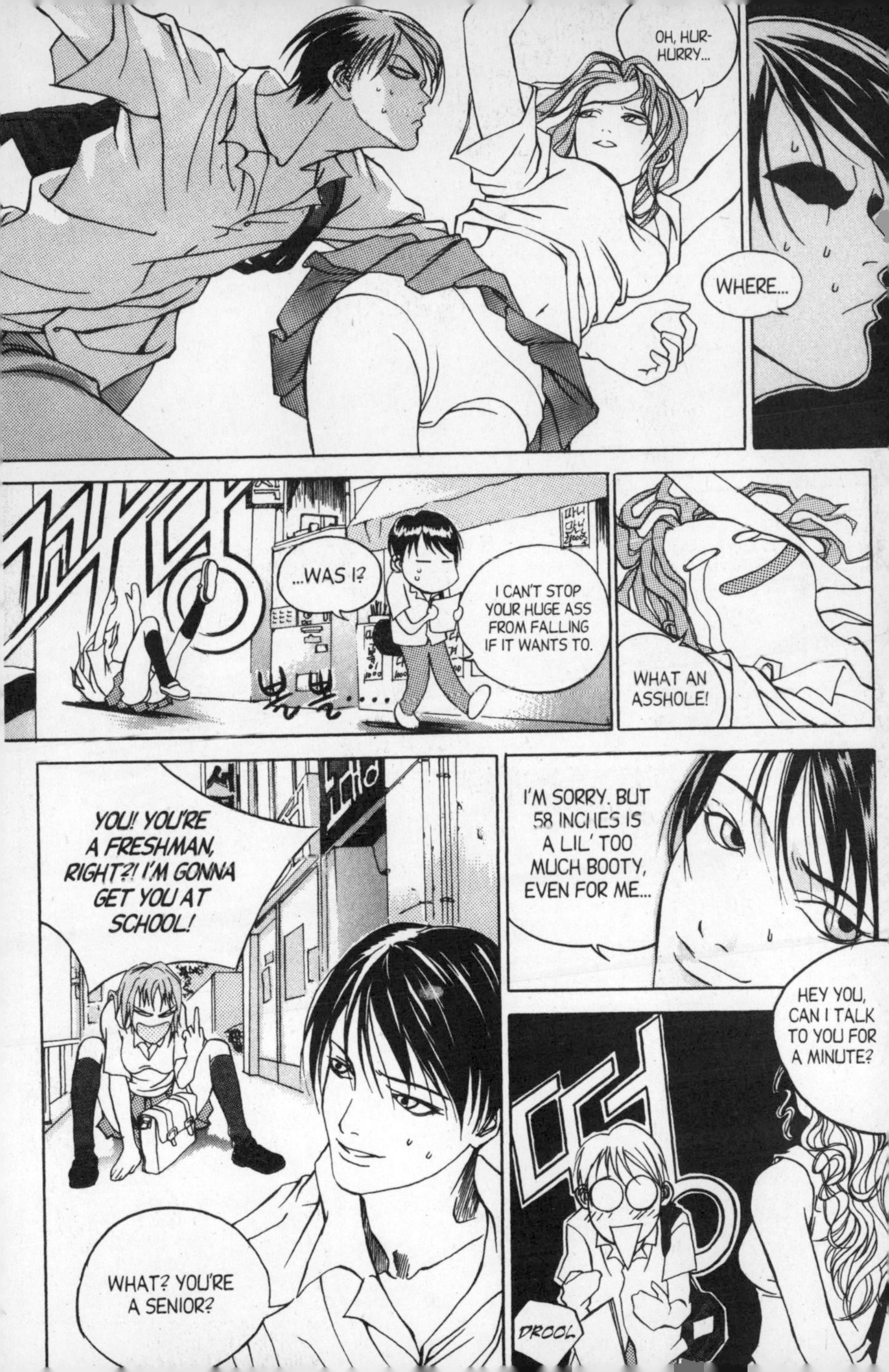
OH, HUR-HURRY...
WHERE...
...WAS I?
I CAN'T STOP YOUR HUGE ASS FROM FALLING IF IT WANTS TO.
WHAT AN ASSHOLE!
YOU! YOU'RE A FRESHMAN, RIGHT?! I'M GONNA GET YOU AT SCHOOL!
WHAT? YOU'RE A SENIOR?
I'M SORRY. BUT 58 INCHES IS A LIL' TOO MUCH BOOTY, EVEN FOR ME...
HEY YOU, CAN I TALK TO YOU FOR A MINUTE?
DROOL

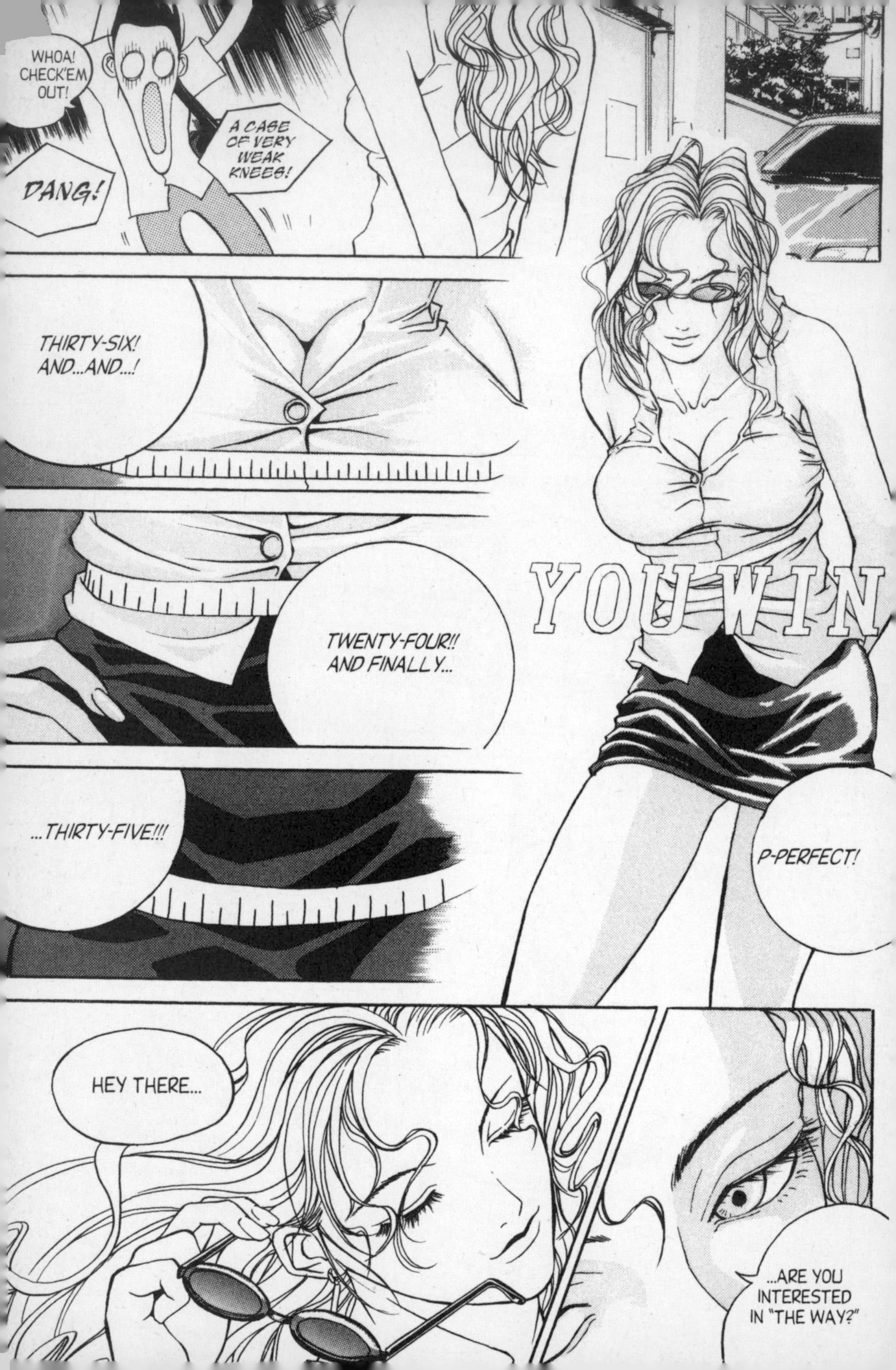
WHOA! CHECK'EM OUT!
A CASE OF VERY WEAK KNEES!
DANG!
THIRTY-SIX! AND...AND...!
TWENTY-FOUR!! AND FINALLY...
...THIRTY-FIVE!!!
YOU WIN
P-PERFECT!
HEY THERE...
...ARE YOU INTERESTED IN "THE WAY?"

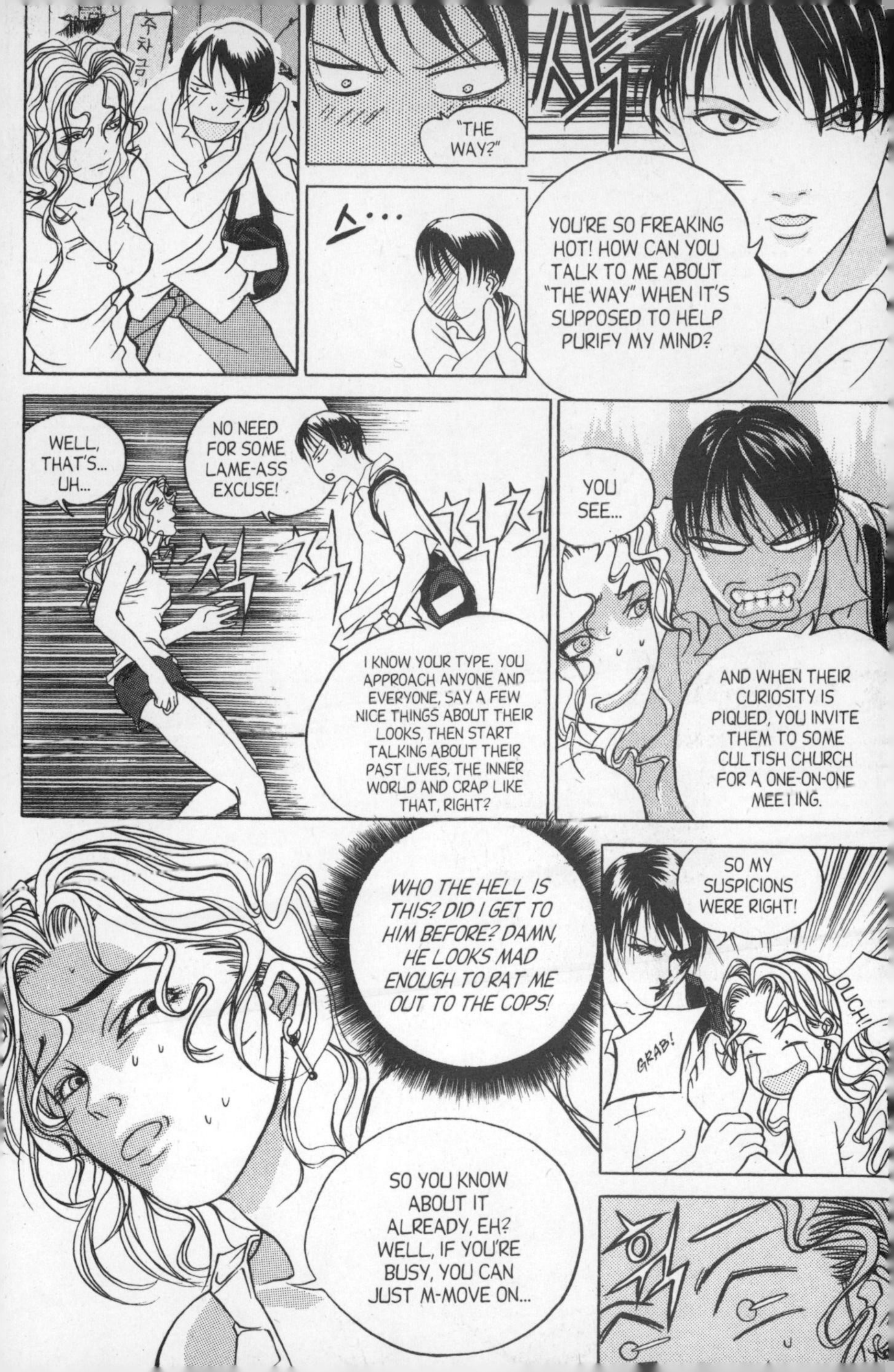
주차금지
"THE WAY?"
스...
YOU'RE SO FREAKING HOT! HOW CAN YOU TALK TO ME ABOUT "THE WAY" WHEN IT'S SUPPOSED TO HELP PURIFY MY MIND?
WELL, THAT'S... UH...
NO NEED FOR SOME LAME-ASS EXCUSE!
I KNOW YOUR TYPE. YOU APPROACH ANYONE AND EVERYONE, SAY A FEW NICE THINGS ABOUT THEIR LOOKS, THEN START TALKING ABOUT THEIR PAST LIVES, THE INNER WORLD AND CRAP LIKE THAT, RIGHT?
YOU SEE...
AND WHEN THEIR CURIOSITY IS PIQUED, YOU INVITE THEM TO SOME CULTISH CHURCH FOR A ONE-ON-ONE MEETING.
WHO THE HELL IS THIS? DID I GET TO HIM BEFORE? DAMN, HE LOOKS MAD ENOUGH TO RAT ME OUT TO THE COPS!
SO YOU KNOW ABOUT IT ALREADY, EH? WELL, IF YOU'RE BUSY, YOU CAN JUST M-MOVE ON...
SO MY SUSPICIONS WERE RIGHT!
GRAB!
OUCH!

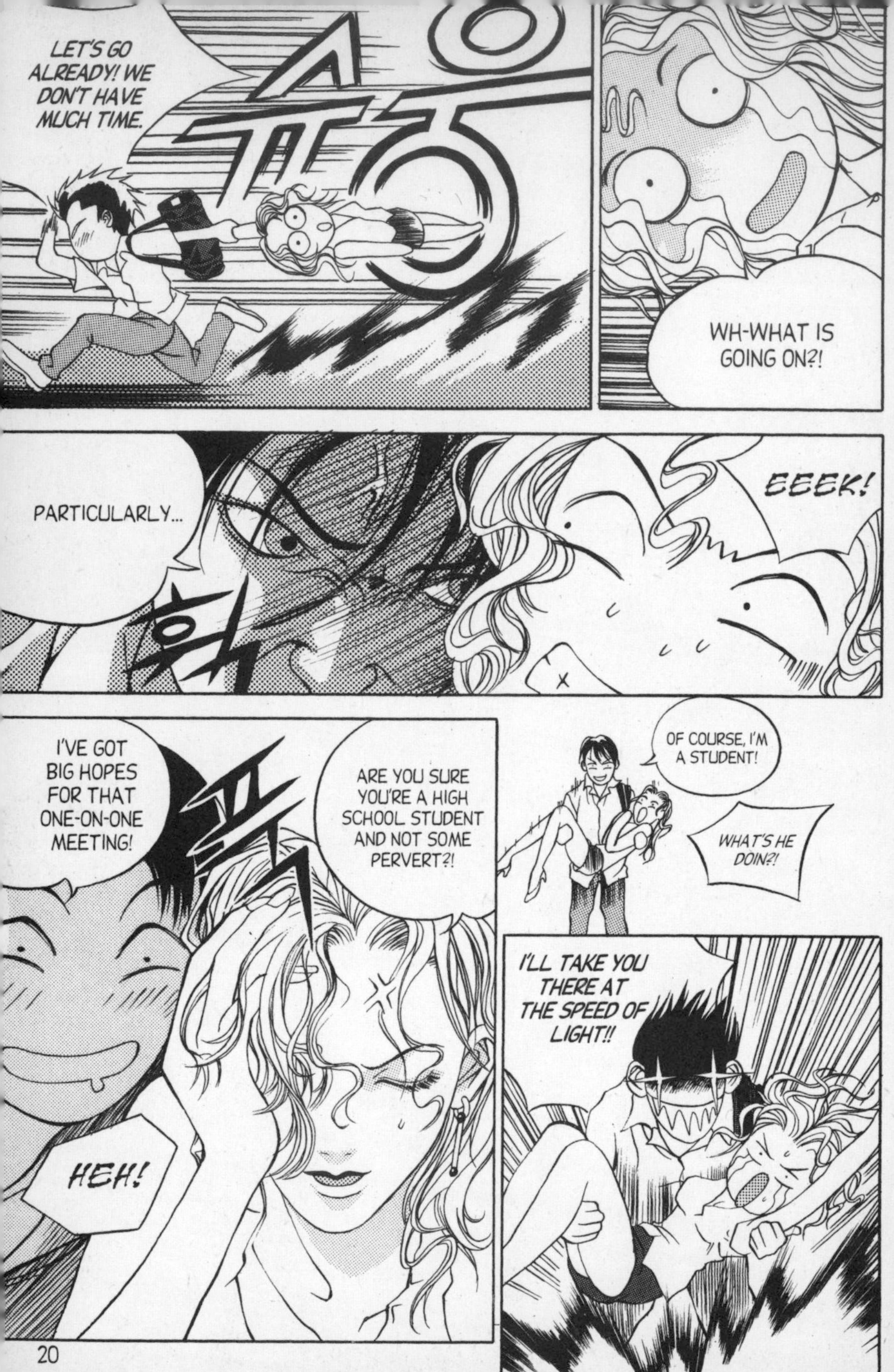
LET'S GO ALREADY! WE DON'T HAVE MUCH TIME.
WH-WHAT IS GOING ON?!
PARTICULARLY...
EEEK!
I'VE GOT BIG HOPES FOR THAT ONE-ON-ONE MEETING!
ARE YOU SURE YOU'RE A HIGH SCHOOL STUDENT AND NOT SOME PERVERT?!
HEH!
OF COURSE, I'M A STUDENT!
WHAT'S HE DOIN?!
I'LL TAKE YOU THERE AT THE SPEED OF LIGHT!!

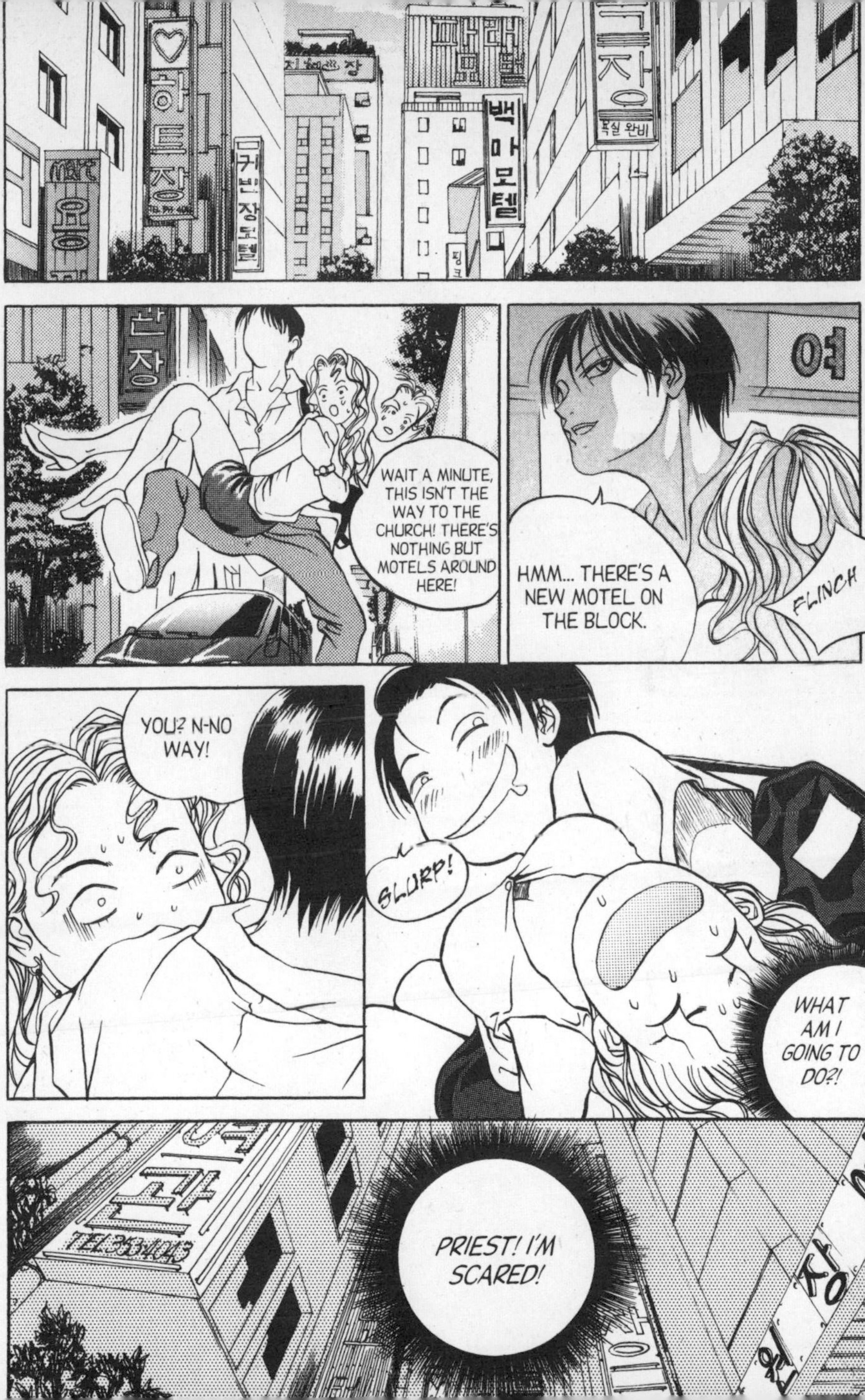

하트장
귀빈장모텔
백마모텔
욕실 완비
WAIT A MINUTE, THIS ISN'T THE WAY TO THE CHURCH! THERE'S NOTHING BUT MOTELS AROUND HERE!
HMM... THERE'S A NEW MOTEL ON THE BLOCK.
FLINCH
YOU? N-NO WAY!
SLURP!
WHAT AM I GOING TO DO?!
PRIEST! I'M SCARED!

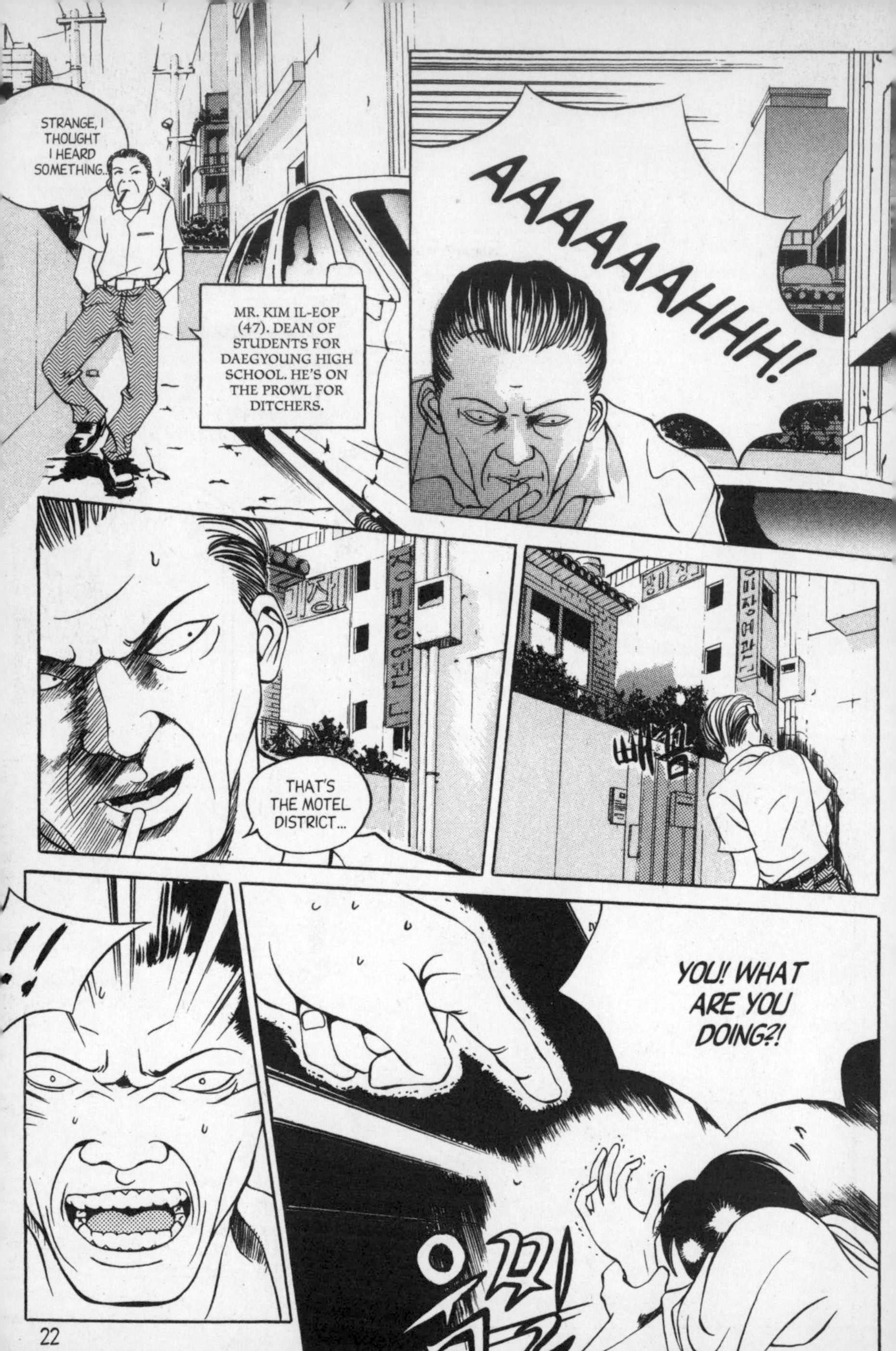
STRANGE, I THOUGHT I HEARD SOMETHING...
MR. KIM IL-EOP (47). DEAN OF STUDENTS FOR DAEGYOUNG HIGH SCHOOL. HE'S ON THE PROWL FOR DITCHERS.
AAAAAAHHH!
THAT'S THE MOTEL DISTRICT...
!!
YOU! WHAT ARE YOU DOING?!

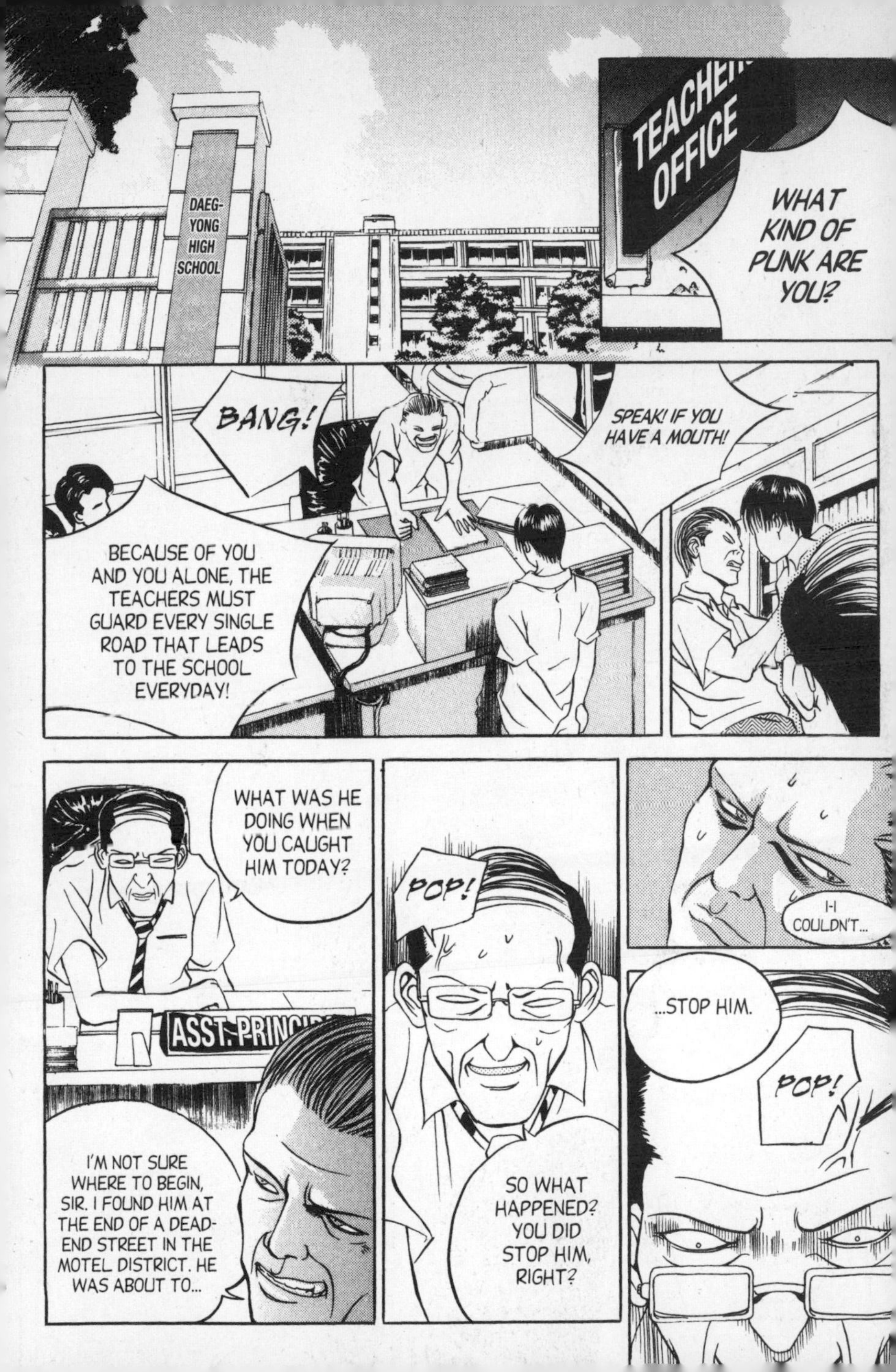
DAEG-YONG HIGH SCHOOL
TEACHER OFFICE
WHAT KIND OF PUNK ARE YOU?
BANG!
BECAUSE OF YOU AND YOU ALONE, THE TEACHERS MUST GUARD EVERY SINGLE ROAD THAT LEADS TO THE SCHOOL EVERYDAY!
SPEAK! IF YOU HAVE A MOUTH!
WHAT WAS HE DOING WHEN YOU CAUGHT HIM TODAY?
ASST. PRINCI
I'M NOT SURE WHERE TO BEGIN, SIR. I FOUND HIM AT THE END OF A DEAD-END STREET IN THE MOTEL DISTRICT. HE WAS ABOUT TO...
POP!
SO WHAT HAPPENED? YOU DID STOP HIM, RIGHT?
I-I COULDN'T...
...STOP HIM.
POP!

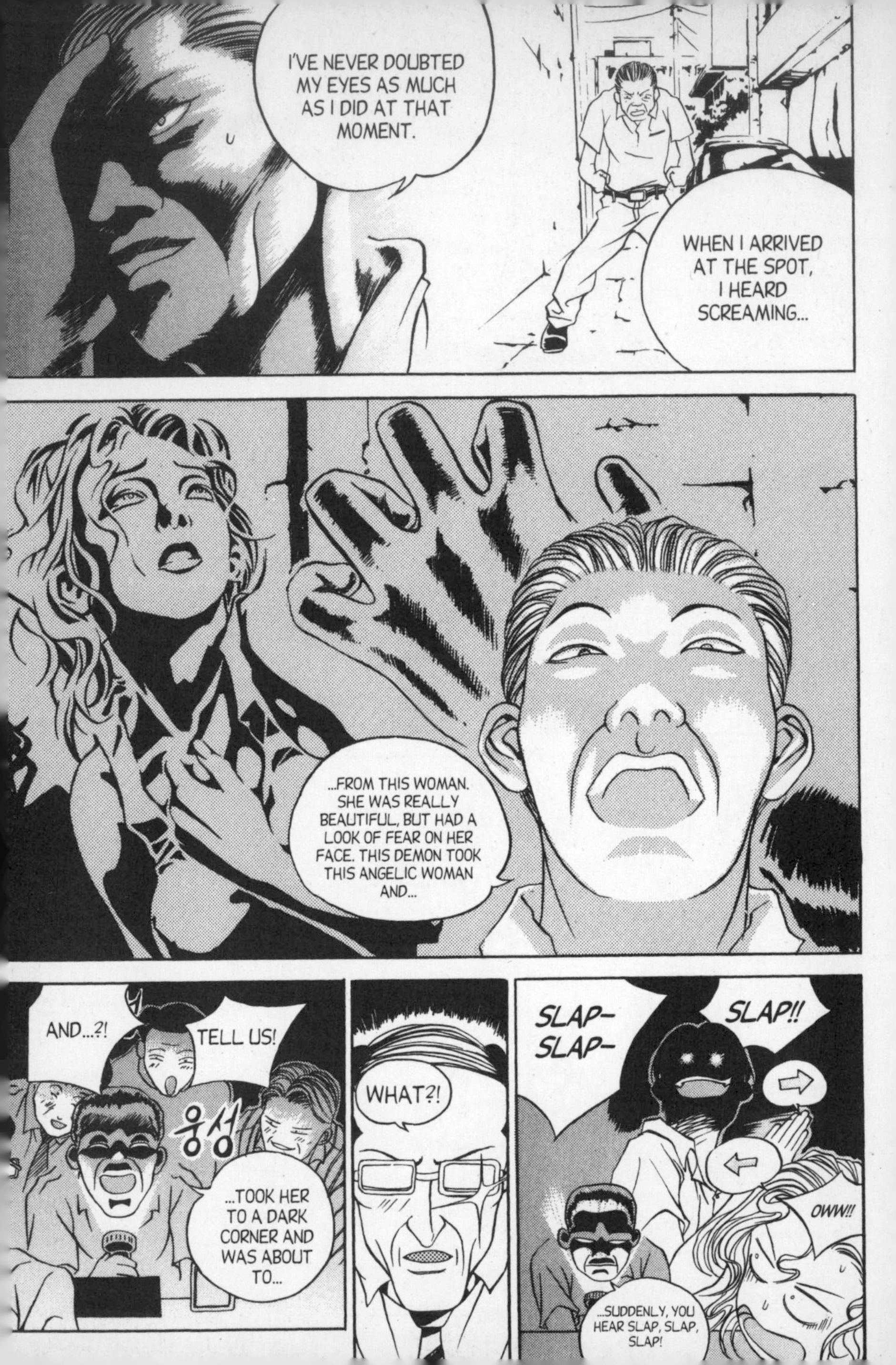
I'VE NEVER DOUBTED MY EYES AS MUCH AS I DID AT THAT MOMENT.
WHEN I ARRIVED AT THE SPOT, I HEARD SCREAMING...
...FROM THIS WOMAN. SHE WAS REALLY BEAUTIFUL, BUT HAD A LOOK OF FEAR ON HER FACE. THIS DEMON TOOK THIS ANGELIC WOMAN AND...
AND...?!
TELL US!
웅성
...TOOK HER TO A DARK CORNER AND WAS ABOUT TO...
WHAT?!
SLAP- SLAP-
SLAP!!
OWW!!
...SUDDENLY, YOU HEAR SLAP, SLAP, SLAP!

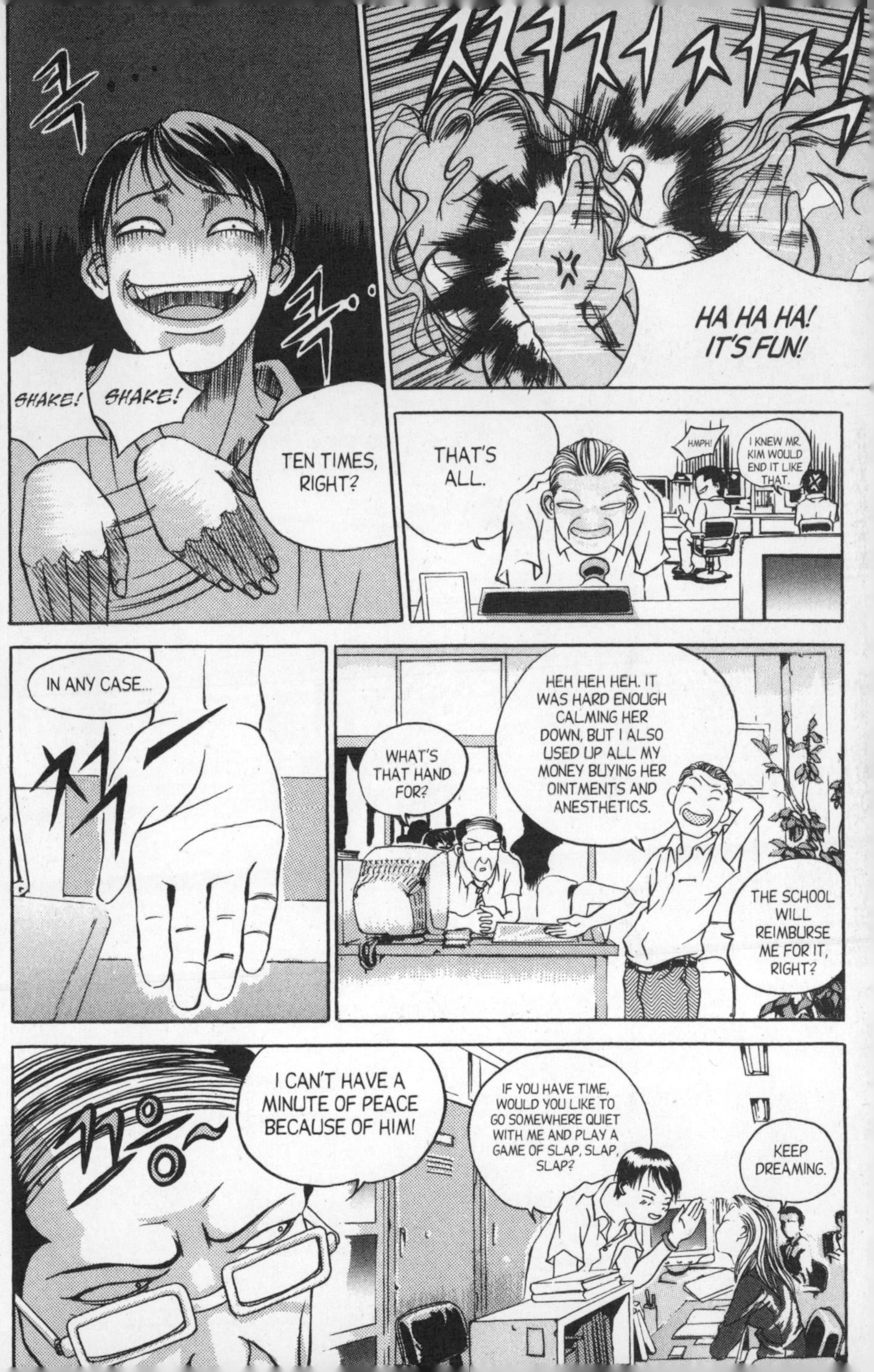
SHAKE! SHAKE!
TEN TIMES, RIGHT?
HA HA HA! IT'S FUN!
THAT'S ALL.
HMPH!
I KNEW MR. KIM WOULD END IT LIKE THAT.
IN ANY CASE...
WHAT'S THAT HAND FOR?
HEH HEH HEH. IT WAS HARD ENOUGH CALMING HER DOWN, BUT I ALSO USED UP ALL MY MONEY BUYING HER OINTMENTS AND ANESTHETICS.
THE SCHOOL WILL REIMBURSE ME FOR IT, RIGHT?
I CAN'T HAVE A MINUTE OF PEACE BECAUSE OF HIM!
IF YOU HAVE TIME, WOULD YOU LIKE TO GO SOMEWHERE QUIET WITH ME AND PLAY A GAME OF SLAP, SLAP, SLAP?
KEEP DREAMING.

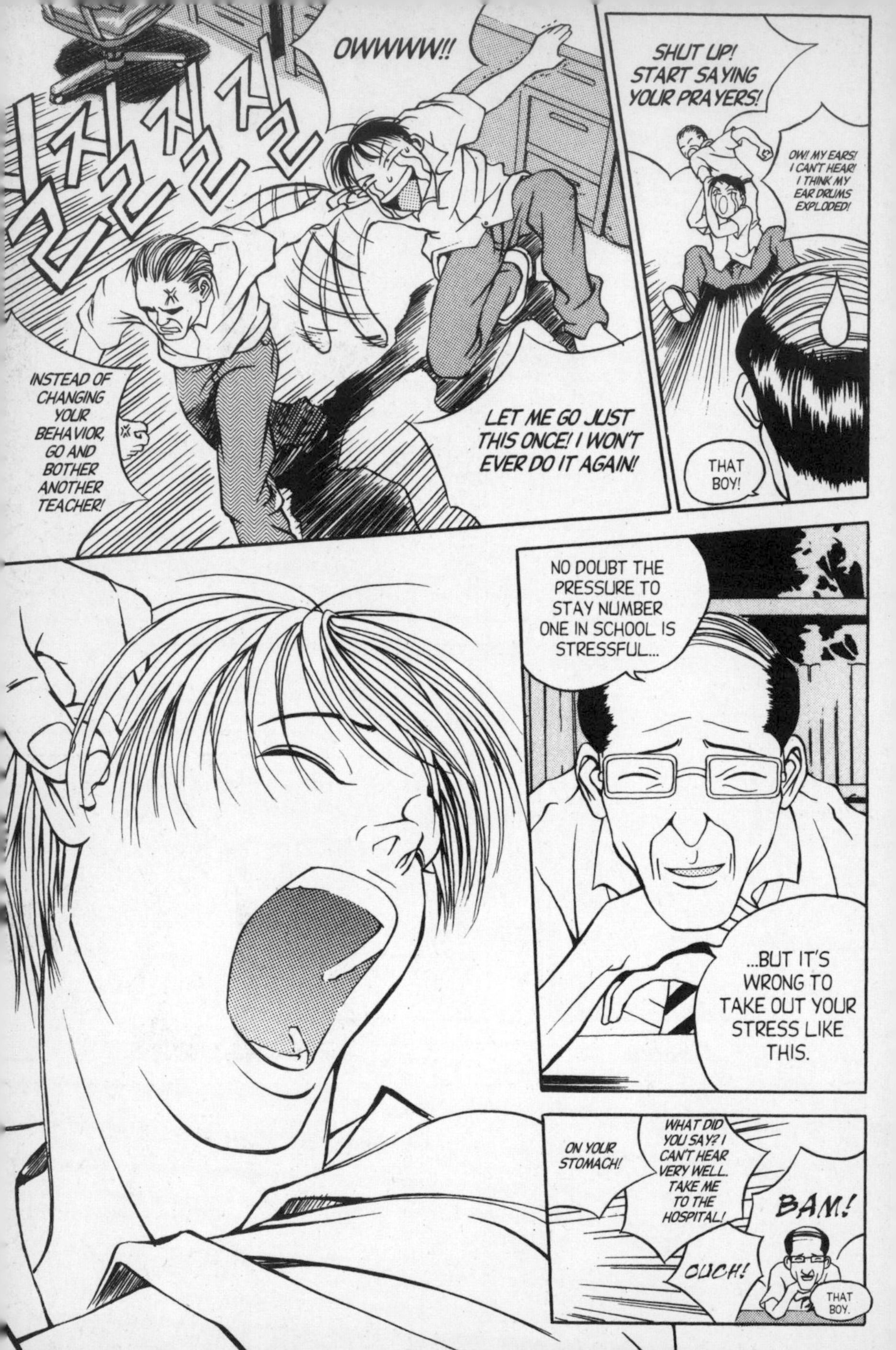
OWWWW!!
INSTEAD OF CHANGING YOUR BEHAVIOR, GO AND BOTHER ANOTHER TEACHER!
LET ME GO JUST THIS ONCE! I WON'T EVER DO IT AGAIN!
SHUT UP! START SAYING YOUR PRAYERS!
OW! MY EARS! I CAN'T HEAR! I THINK MY EAR DRUMS EXPLODED!
THAT BOY!
NO DOUBT THE PRESSURE TO STAY NUMBER ONE IN SCHOOL IS STRESSFUL...
...BUT IT'S WRONG TO TAKE OUT YOUR STRESS LIKE THIS.
ON YOUR STOMACH!
WHAT DID YOU SAY? I CAN'T HEAR VERY WELL. TAKE ME TO THE HOSPITAL!
BAM!
OUCH!
THAT BOY.

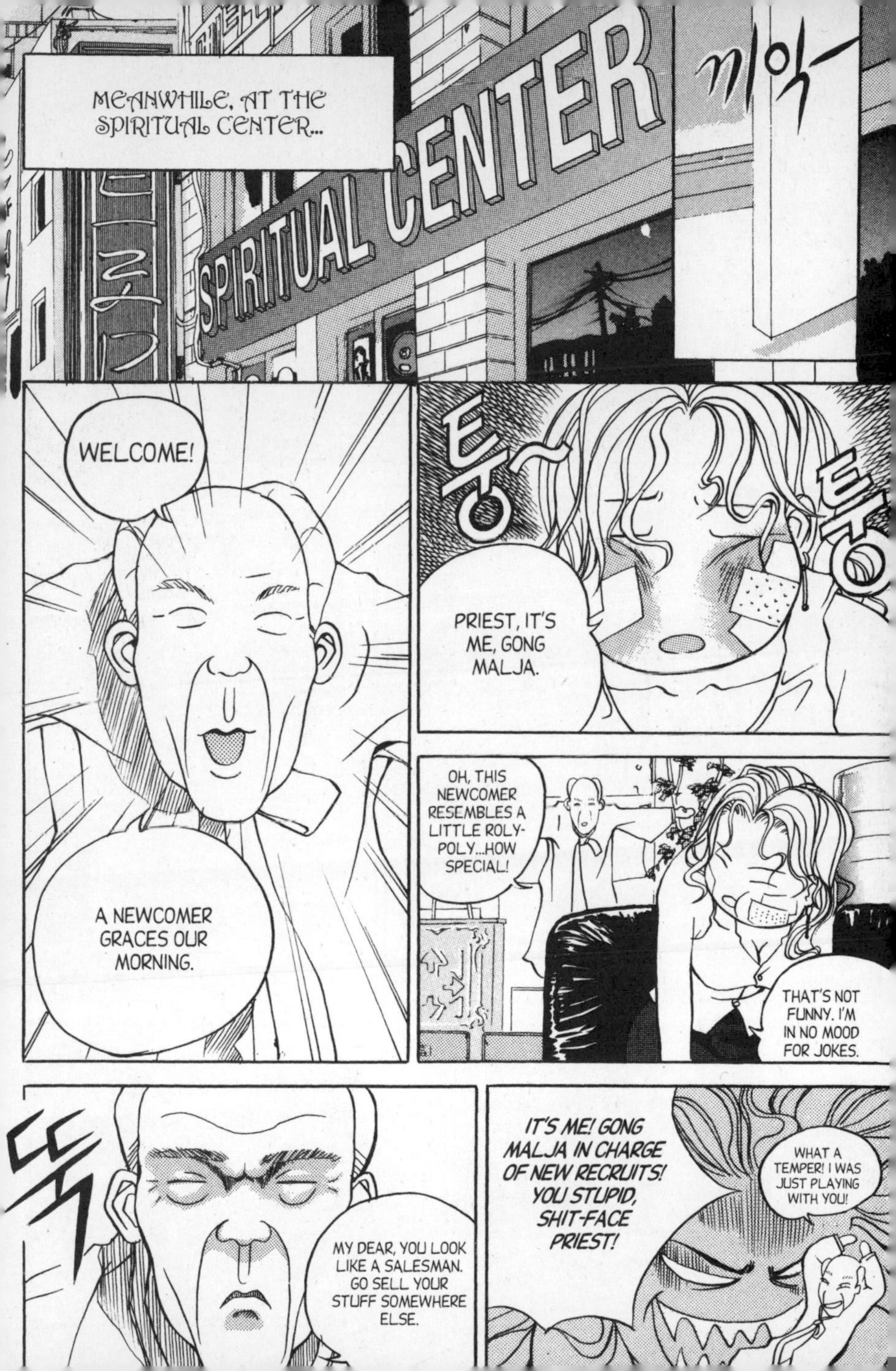

MEANWHILE, AT THE SPIRITUAL CENTER...
SPIRITUAL CENTER
끼익
WELCOME!
A NEWCOMER GRACES OUR MORNING.
탕~
탕
PRIEST, IT'S ME, GONG MALJA.
OH, THIS NEWCOMER RESEMBLES A LITTLE ROLY-POLY...HOW SPECIAL!
THAT'S NOT FUNNY. I'M IN NO MOOD FOR JOKES.
MY DEAR, YOU LOOK LIKE A SALESMAN. GO SELL YOUR STUFF SOMEWHERE ELSE.
IT'S ME! GONG MALJA IN CHARGE OF NEW RECRUITS! YOU STUPID, SHIT-FACE PRIEST!
WHAT A TEMPER! I WAS JUST PLAYING WITH YOU!

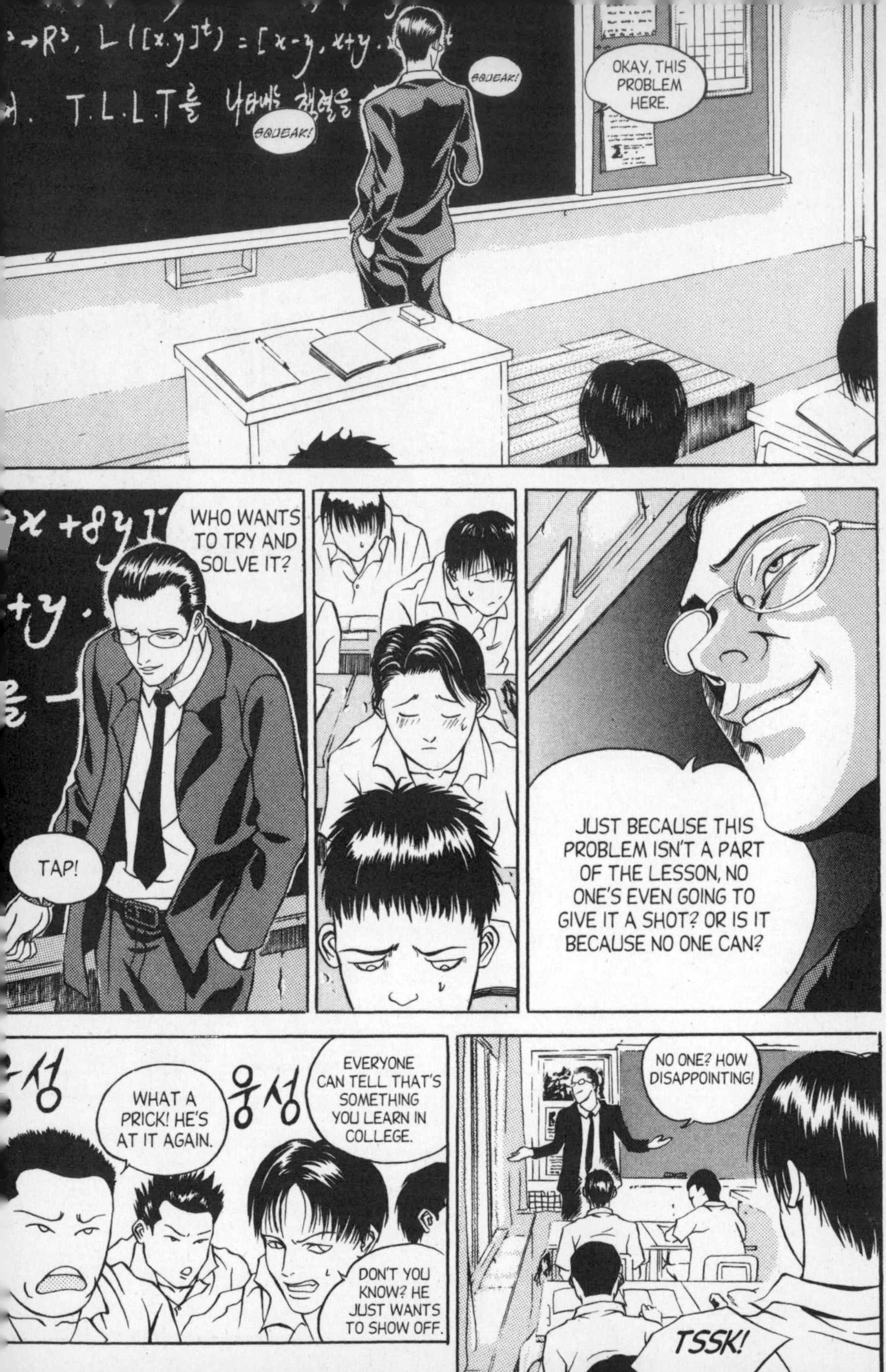
SQUEAK!
SQUEAK!
OKAY, THIS PROBLEM HERE.
WHO WANTS TO TRY AND SOLVE IT?
TAP!
JUST BECAUSE THIS PROBLEM ISN'T A PART OF THE LESSON, NO ONE'S EVEN GOING TO GIVE IT A SHOT? OR IS IT BECAUSE NO ONE CAN?
웅성
WHAT A PRICK! HE'S AT IT AGAIN.
웅성
EVERYONE CAN TELL THAT'S SOMETHING YOU LEARN IN COLLEGE.
DON'T YOU KNOW? HE JUST WANTS TO SHOW OFF.
NO ONE? HOW DISAPPOINTING!
TSSK!

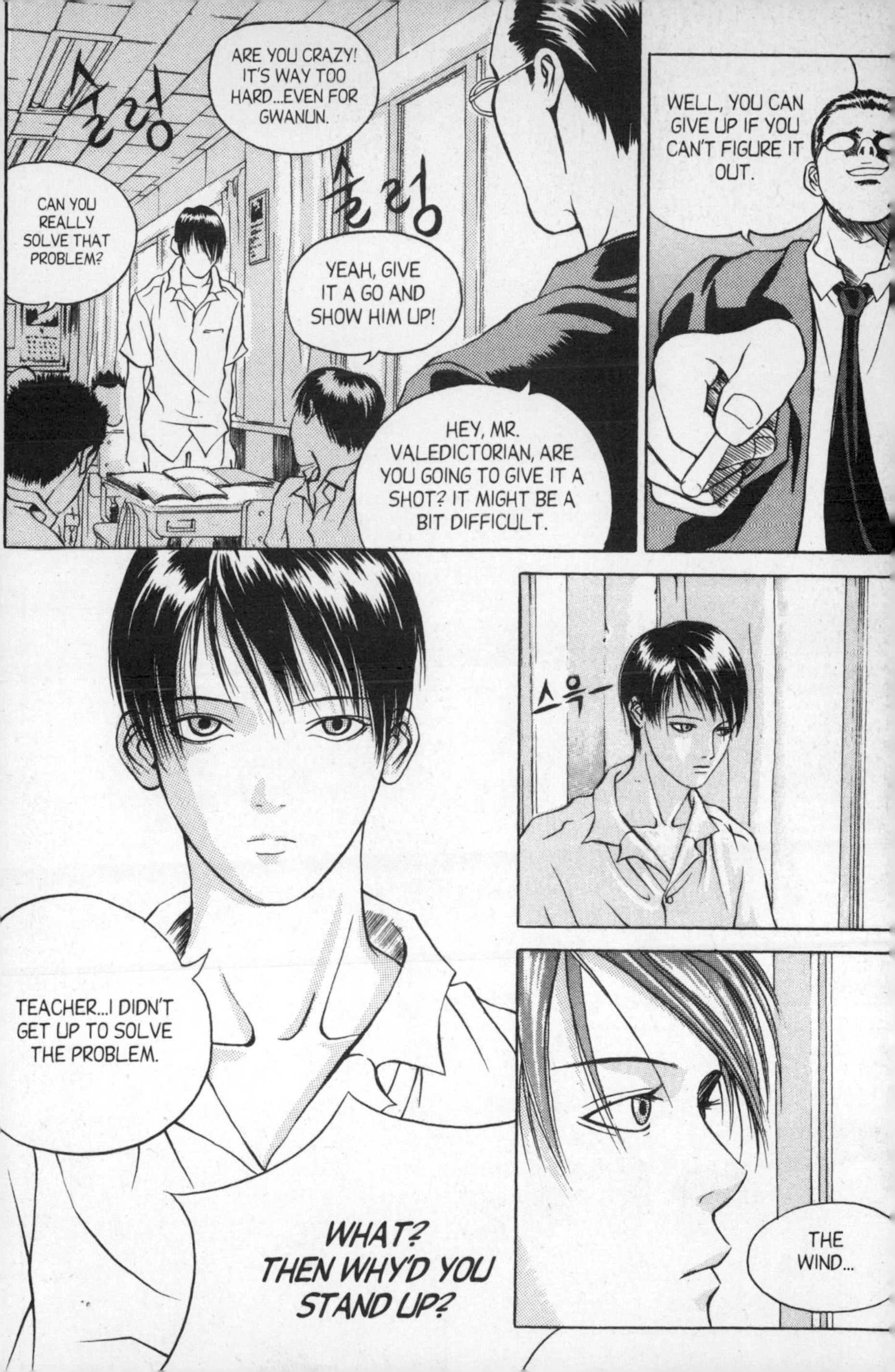
술렁
ARE YOU CRAZY! IT'S WAY TOO HARD...EVEN FOR GWANUN.
CAN YOU REALLY SOLVE THAT PROBLEM?
술렁
YEAH, GIVE IT A GO AND SHOW HIM UP!
HEY, MR. VALEDICTORIAN, ARE YOU GOING TO GIVE IT A SHOT? IT MIGHT BE A BIT DIFFICULT.
WELL, YOU CAN GIVE UP IF YOU CAN'T FIGURE IT OUT.
TEACHER...I DIDN'T GET UP TO SOLVE THE PROBLEM.
WHAT? THEN WHY'D YOU STAND UP?
스윽—
THE WIND...

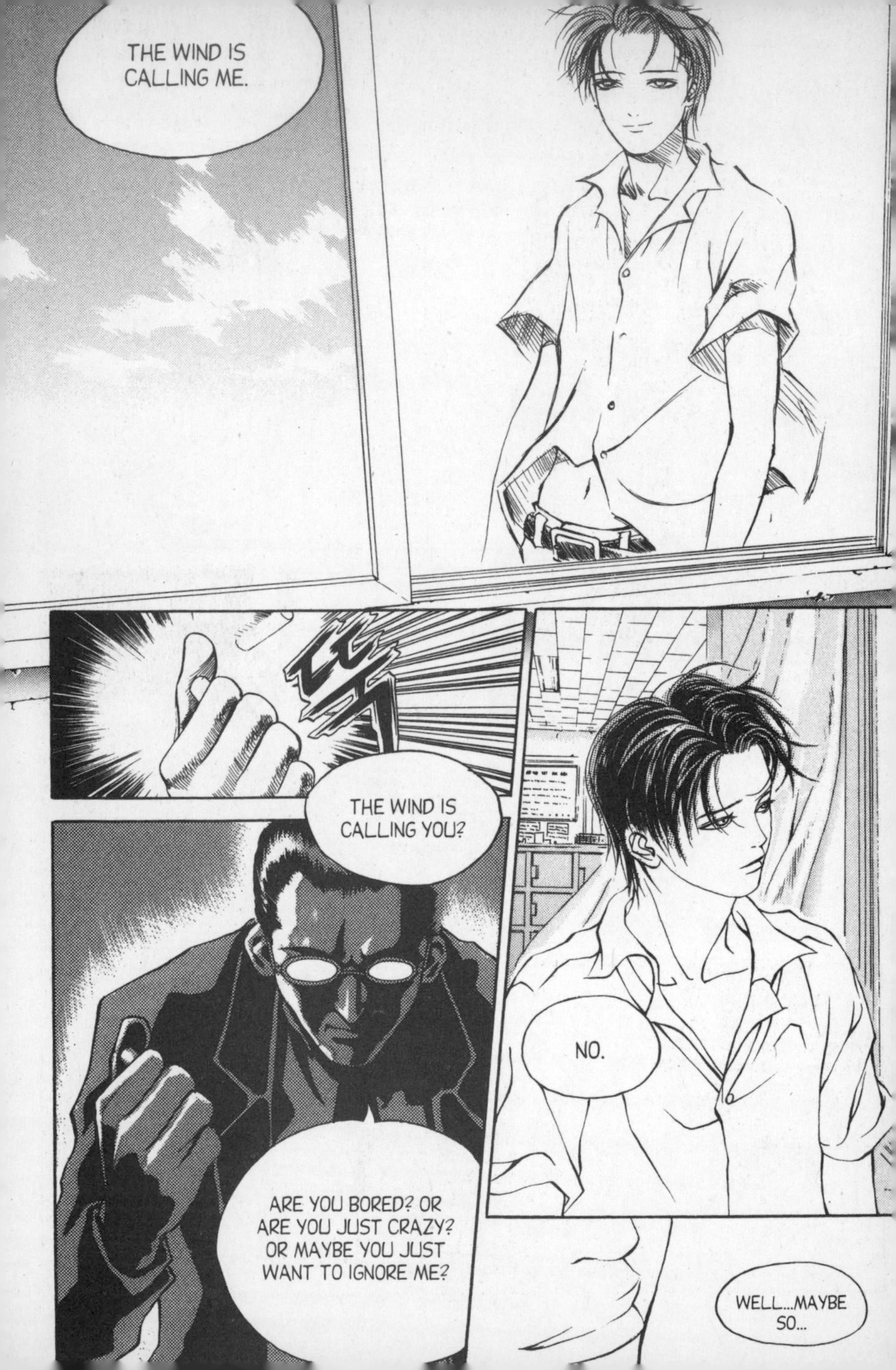
THE WIND IS CALLING ME.
THE WIND IS CALLING YOU?
ARE YOU BORED? OR ARE YOU JUST CRAZY? OR MAYBE YOU JUST WANT TO IGNORE ME?
NO.
WELL...MAYBE SO...

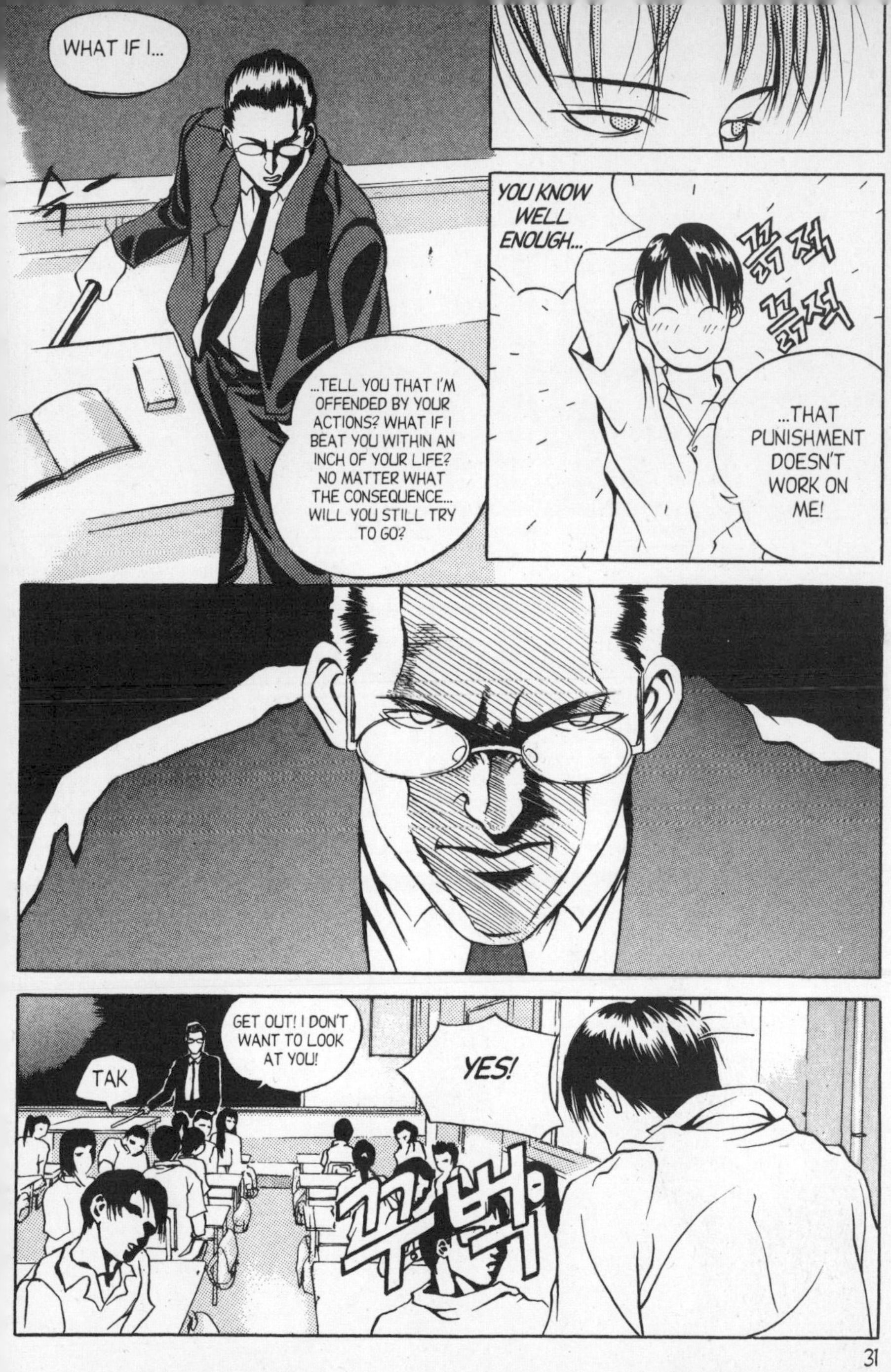
WHAT IF I...
...TELL YOU THAT I'M OFFENDED BY YOUR ACTIONS? WHAT IF I BEAT YOU WITHIN AN INCH OF YOUR LIFE? NO MATTER WHAT THE CONSEQUENCE... WILL YOU STILL TRY TO GO?
YOU KNOW WELL ENOUGH...
끄적
끄적
...THAT PUNISHMENT DOESN'T WORK ON ME!
TAK
GET OUT! I DON'T WANT TO LOOK AT YOU!
YES!
꾸벅

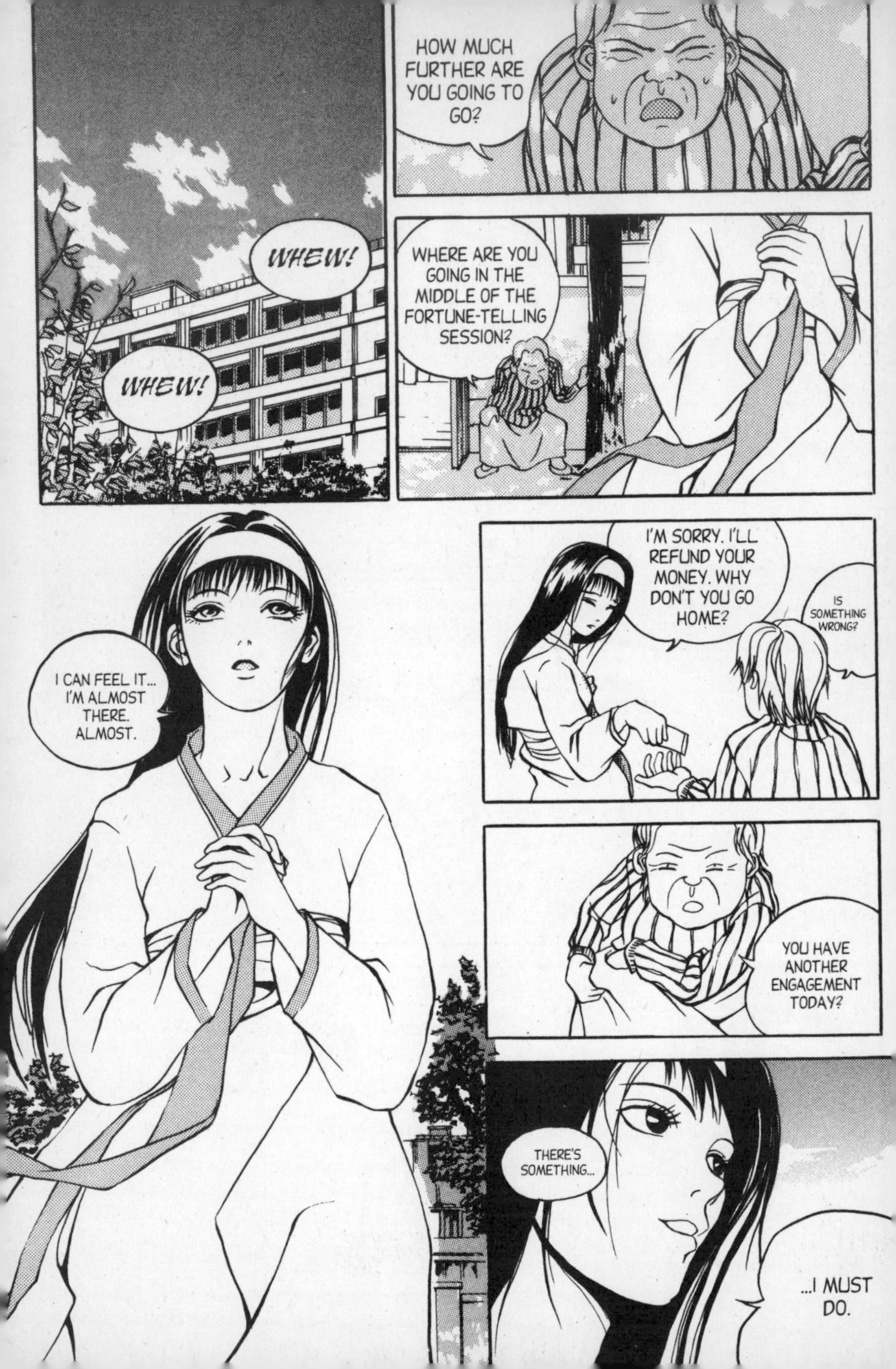
WHEW!
WHEW!
HOW MUCH FURTHER ARE YOU GOING TO GO?
WHERE ARE YOU GOING IN THE MIDDLE OF THE FORTUNE-TELLING SESSION?
I CAN FEEL IT... I'M ALMOST THERE. ALMOST.
I'M SORRY. I'LL REFUND YOUR MONEY. WHY DON'T YOU GO HOME?
IS SOMETHING WRONG?
YOU HAVE ANOTHER ENGAGEMENT TODAY?
THERE'S SOMETHING...
...I MUST DO.

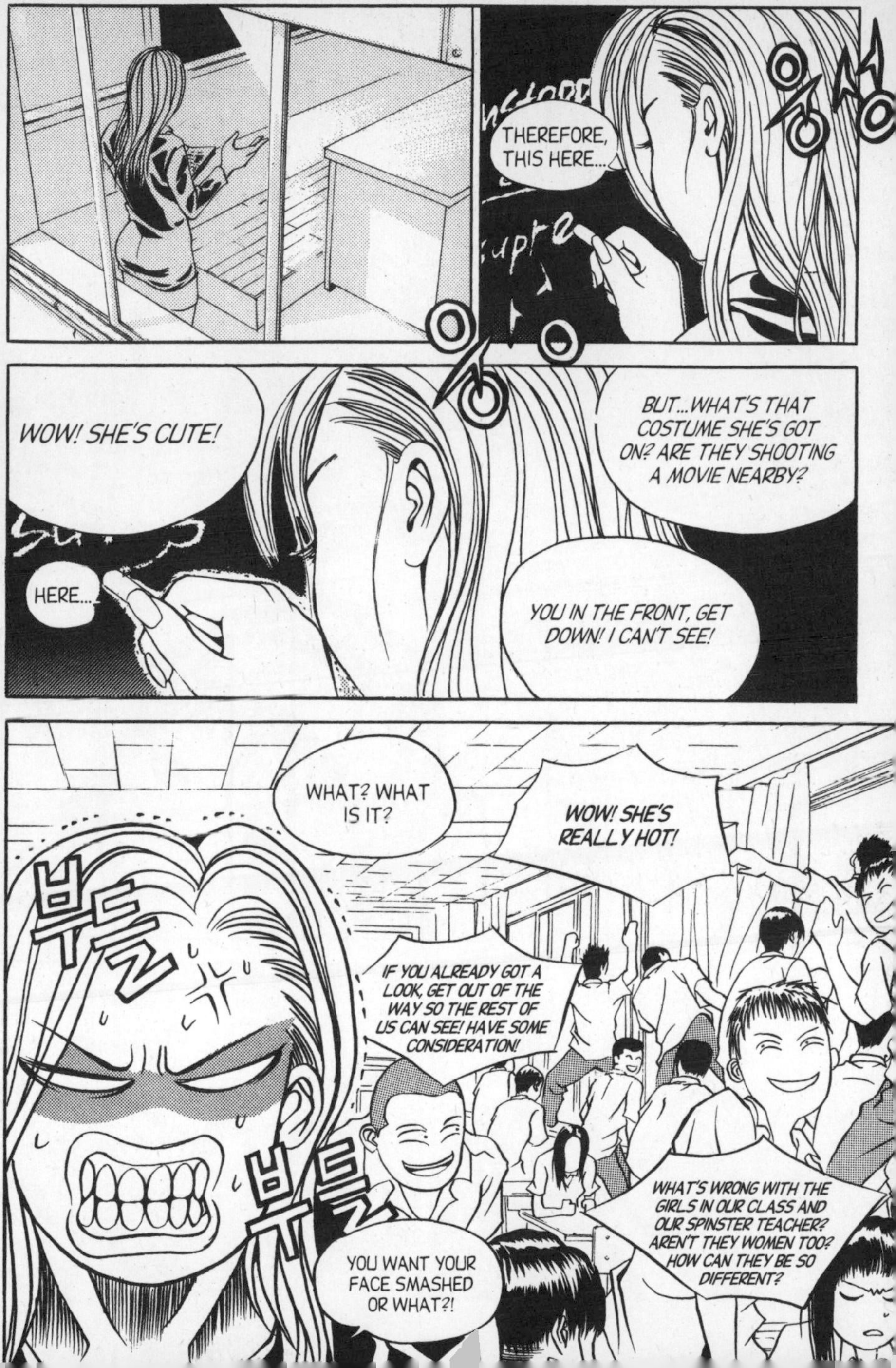
THEREFORE, THIS HERE...
WOW! SHE'S CUTE!
HERE...
BUT...WHAT'S THAT COSTUME SHE'S GOT ON? ARE THEY SHOOTING A MOVIE NEARBY?
YOU IN THE FRONT, GET DOWN! I CAN'T SEE!
부들
WHAT? WHAT IS IT?
WOW! SHE'S REALLY HOT!
IF YOU ALREADY GOT A LOOK, GET OUT OF THE WAY SO THE REST OF US CAN SEE! HAVE SOME CONSIDERATION!
부들
YOU WANT YOUR FACE SMASHED OR WHAT?!
WHAT'S WRONG WITH THE GIRLS IN OUR CLASS AND OUR SPINSTER TEACHER? AREN'T THEY WOMEN TOO? HOW CAN THEY BE SO DIFFERENT?

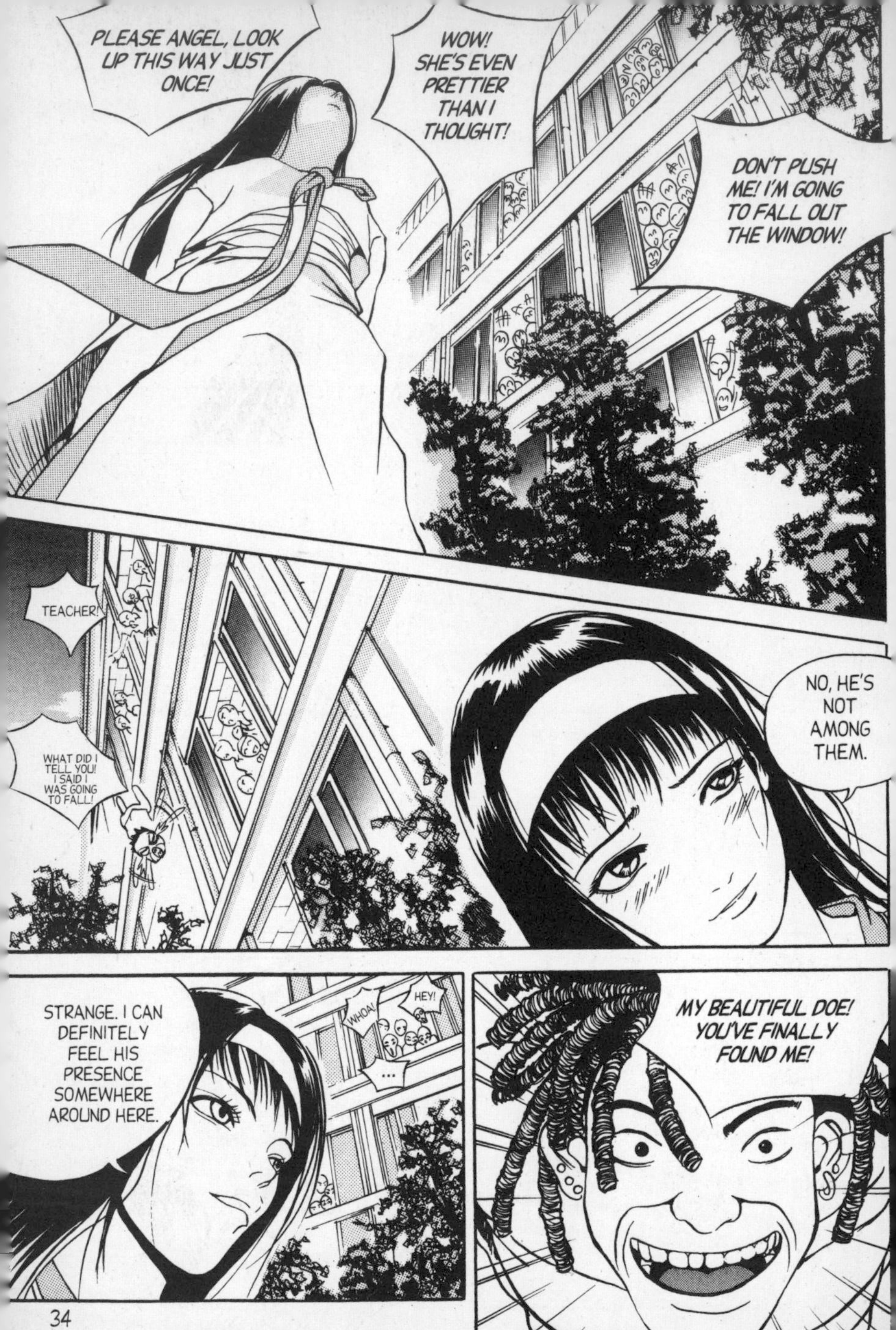

PLEASE ANGEL, LOOK UP THIS WAY JUST ONCE!
WOW! SHE'S EVEN PRETTIER THAN I THOUGHT!
DON'T PUSH ME! I'M GOING TO FALL OUT THE WINDOW!
TEACHER!
WHAT DID I TELL YOU! I SAID I WAS GOING TO FALL!
NO, HE'S NOT AMONG THEM.
STRANGE. I CAN DEFINITELY FEEL HIS PRESENCE SOMEWHERE AROUND HERE.
WHOA!
HEY!
...
MY BEAUTIFUL DOE! YOU'VE FINALLY FOUND ME!

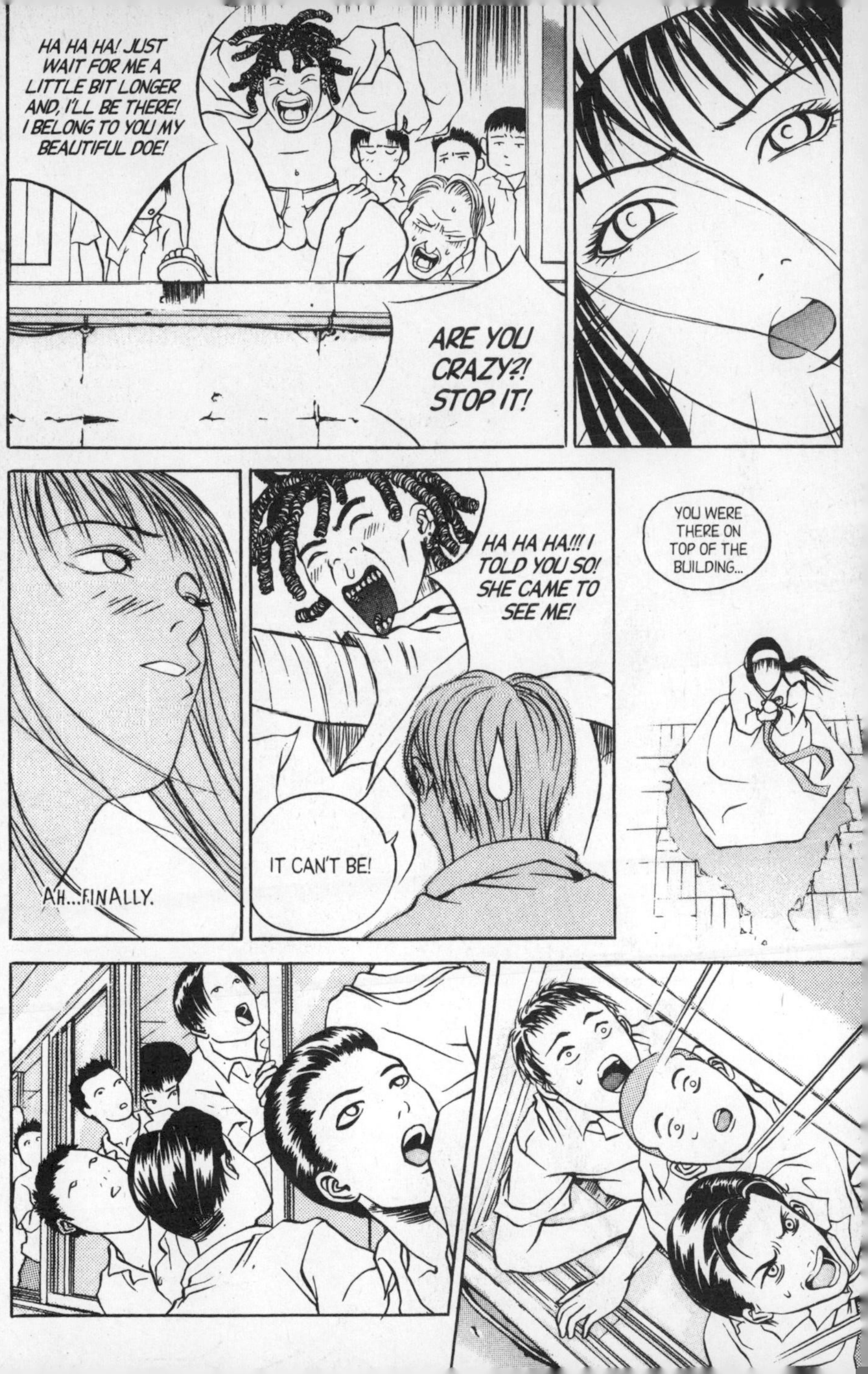
HA HA HA! JUST WAIT FOR ME A LITTLE BIT LONGER AND, I'LL BE THERE! I BELONG TO YOU MY BEAUTIFUL DOE!
ARE YOU CRAZY?! STOP IT!
AH...FINALLY.
HA HA HA!!! I TOLD YOU SO! SHE CAME TO SEE ME!
IT CAN'T BE!
YOU WERE THERE ON TOP OF THE BUILDING...

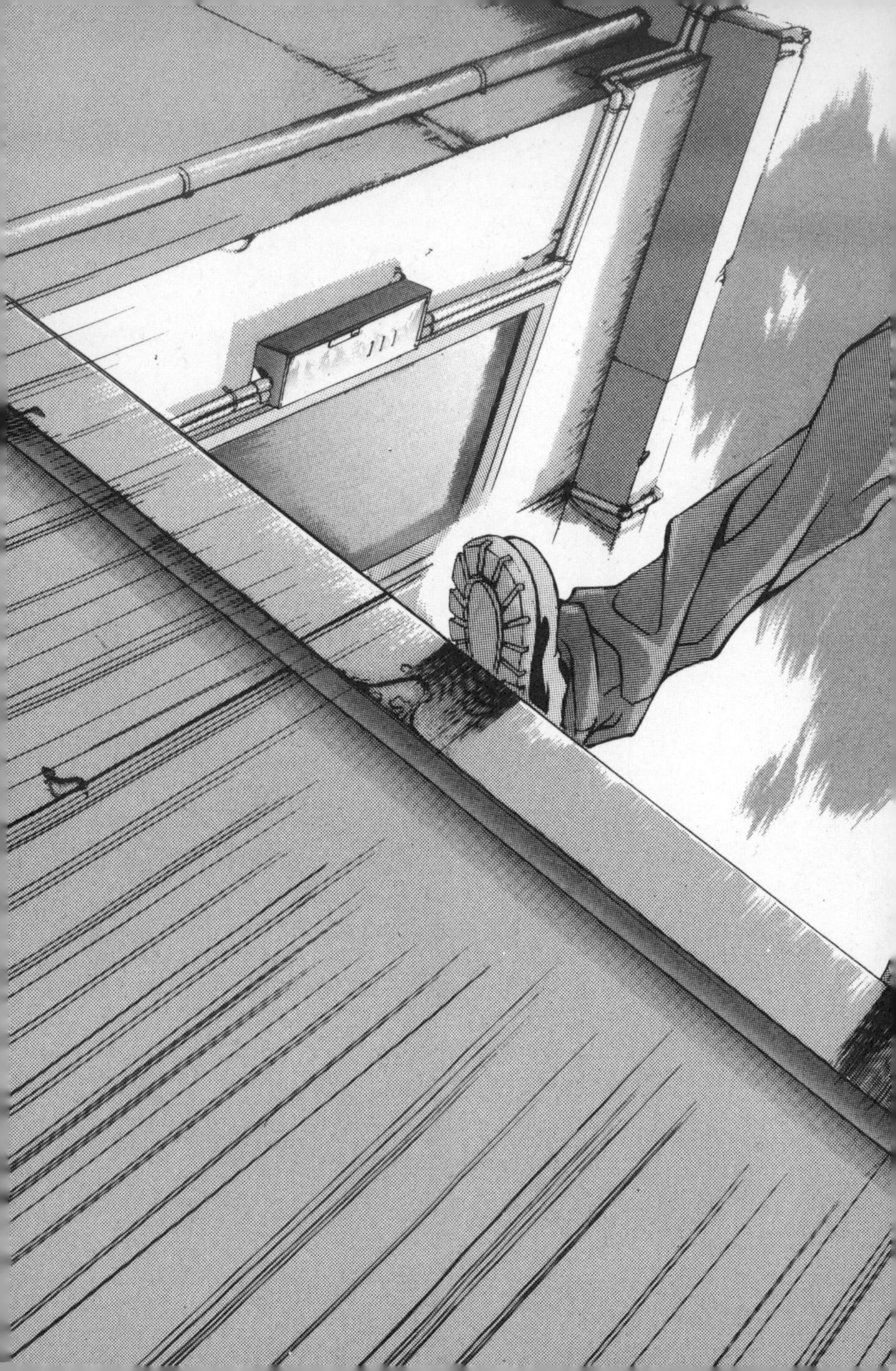

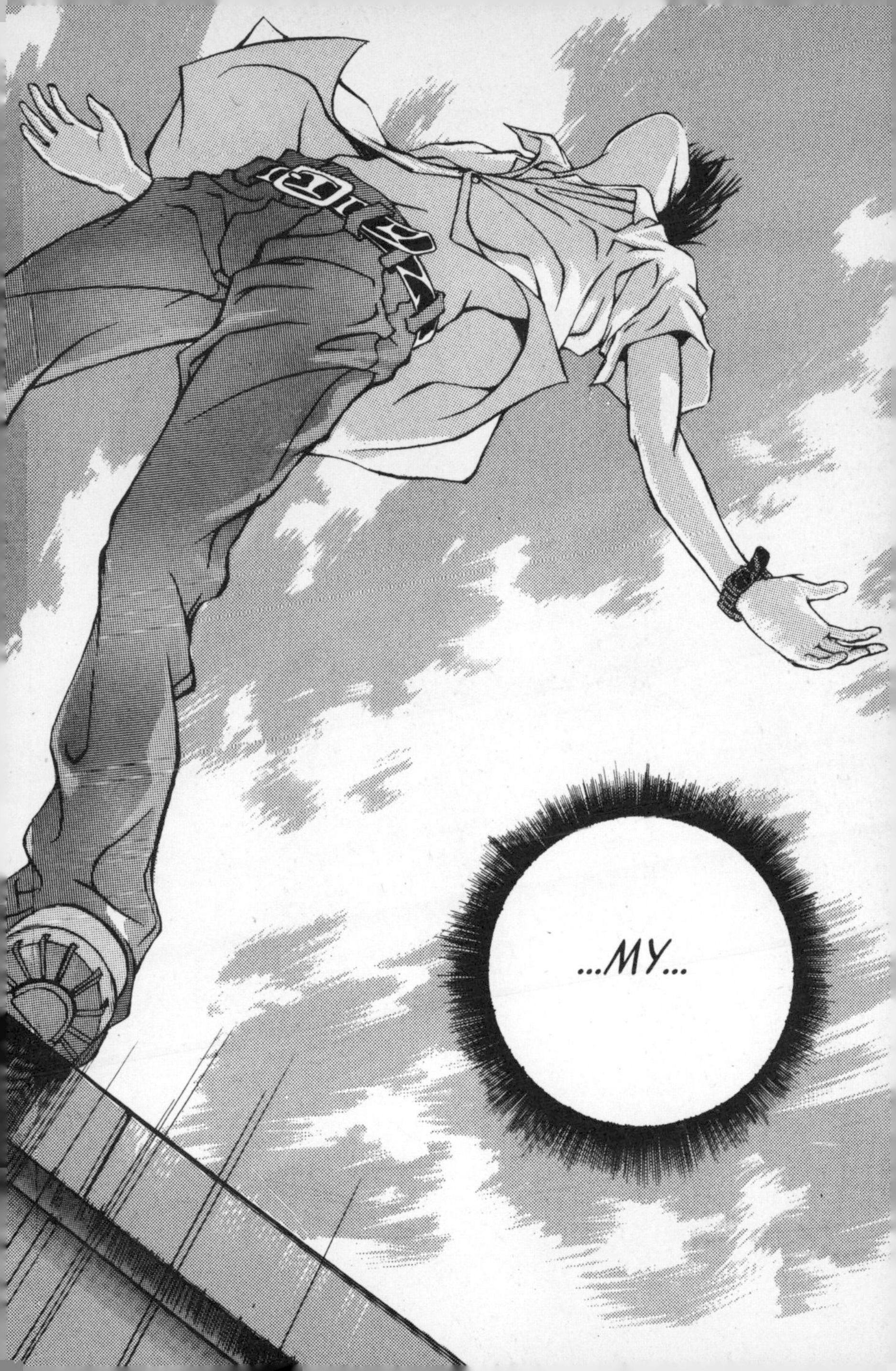
...MY...

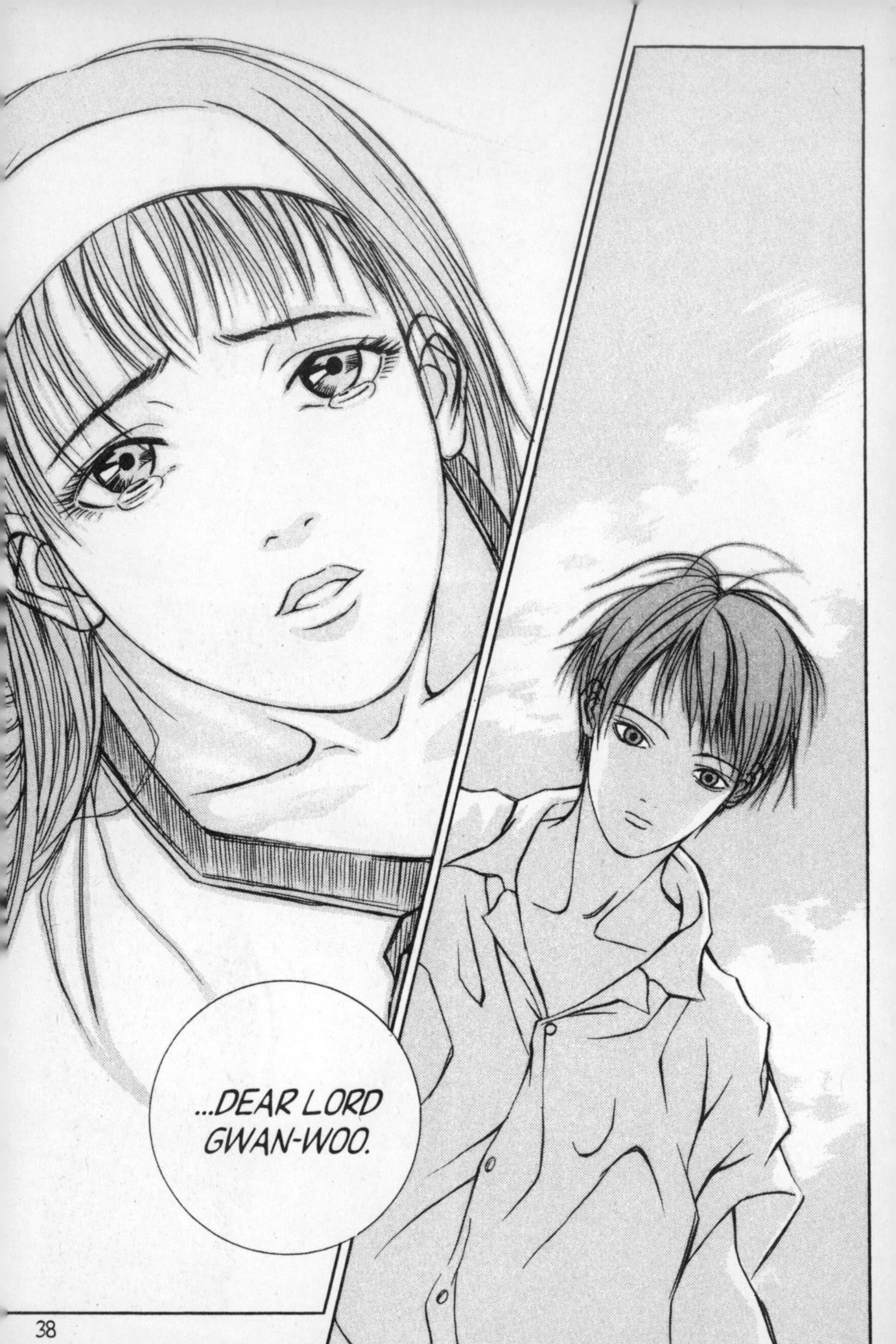
...DEAR LORD GWAN-WOO.

이터니티

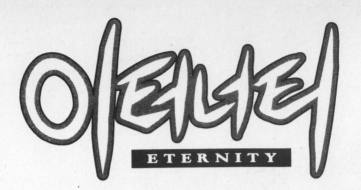

ETERNITY

#2 ENCOUNTER

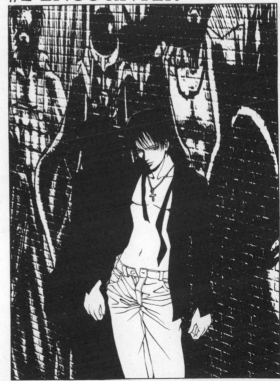

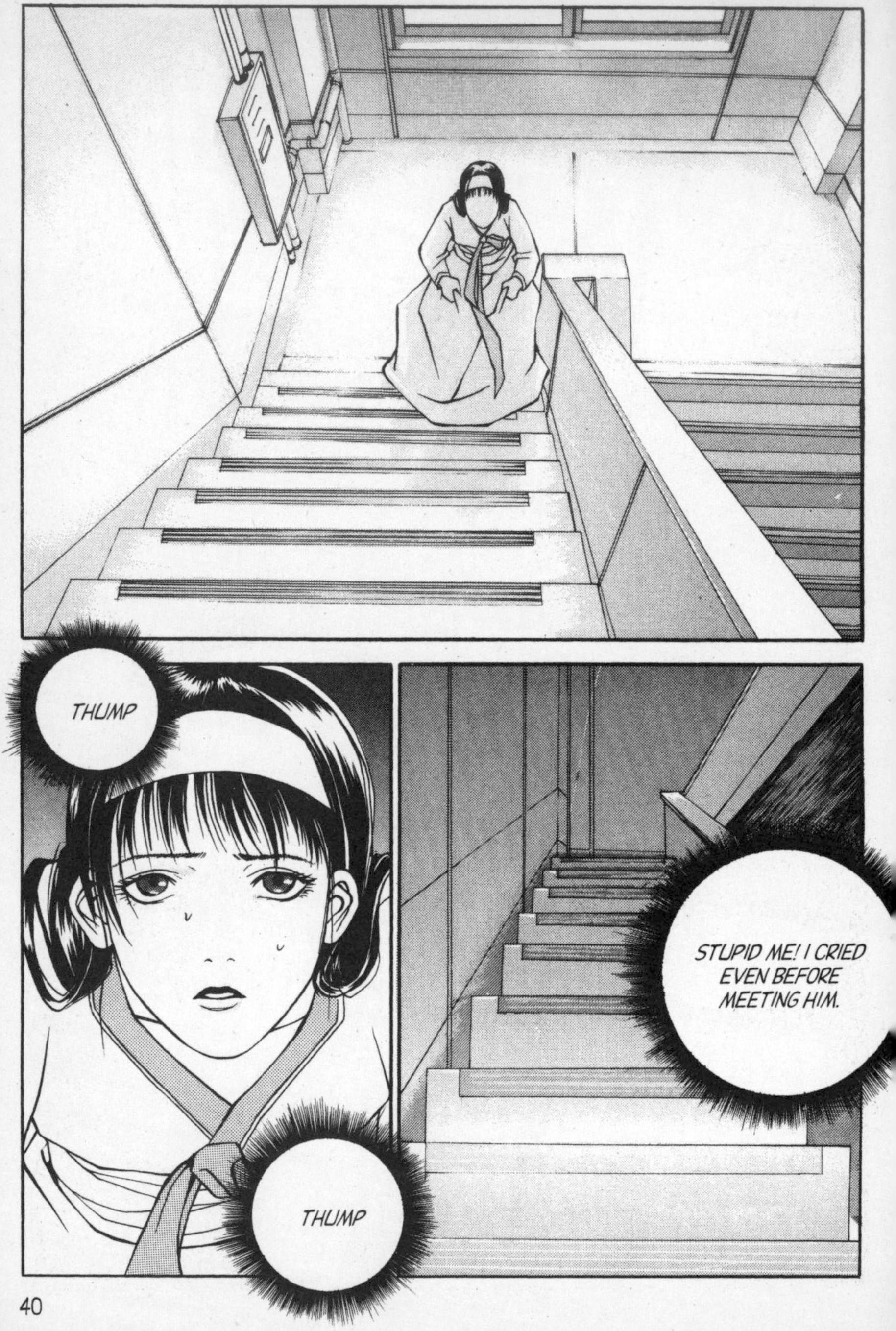
THUMP
THUMP
STUPID ME! I CRIED EVEN BEFORE MEETING HIM.

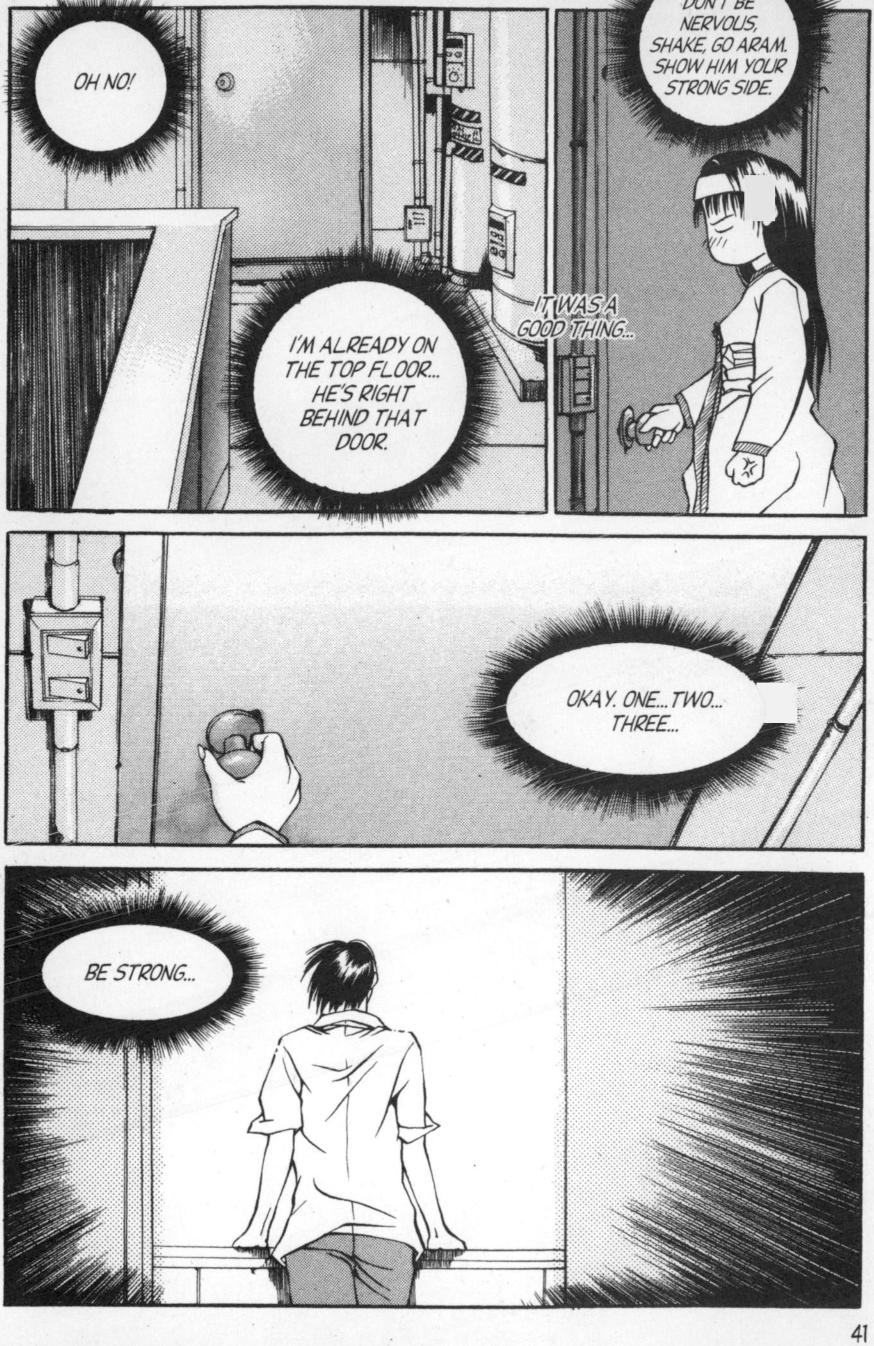
DON'T BE NERVOUS, SHAKE, GO ARAM. SHOW HIM YOUR STRONG SIDE.
IT WAS A GOOD THING...
OH NO!
I'M ALREADY ON THE TOP FLOOR... HE'S RIGHT BEHIND THAT DOOR.
OKAY. ONE...TWO... THREE...
BE STRONG...

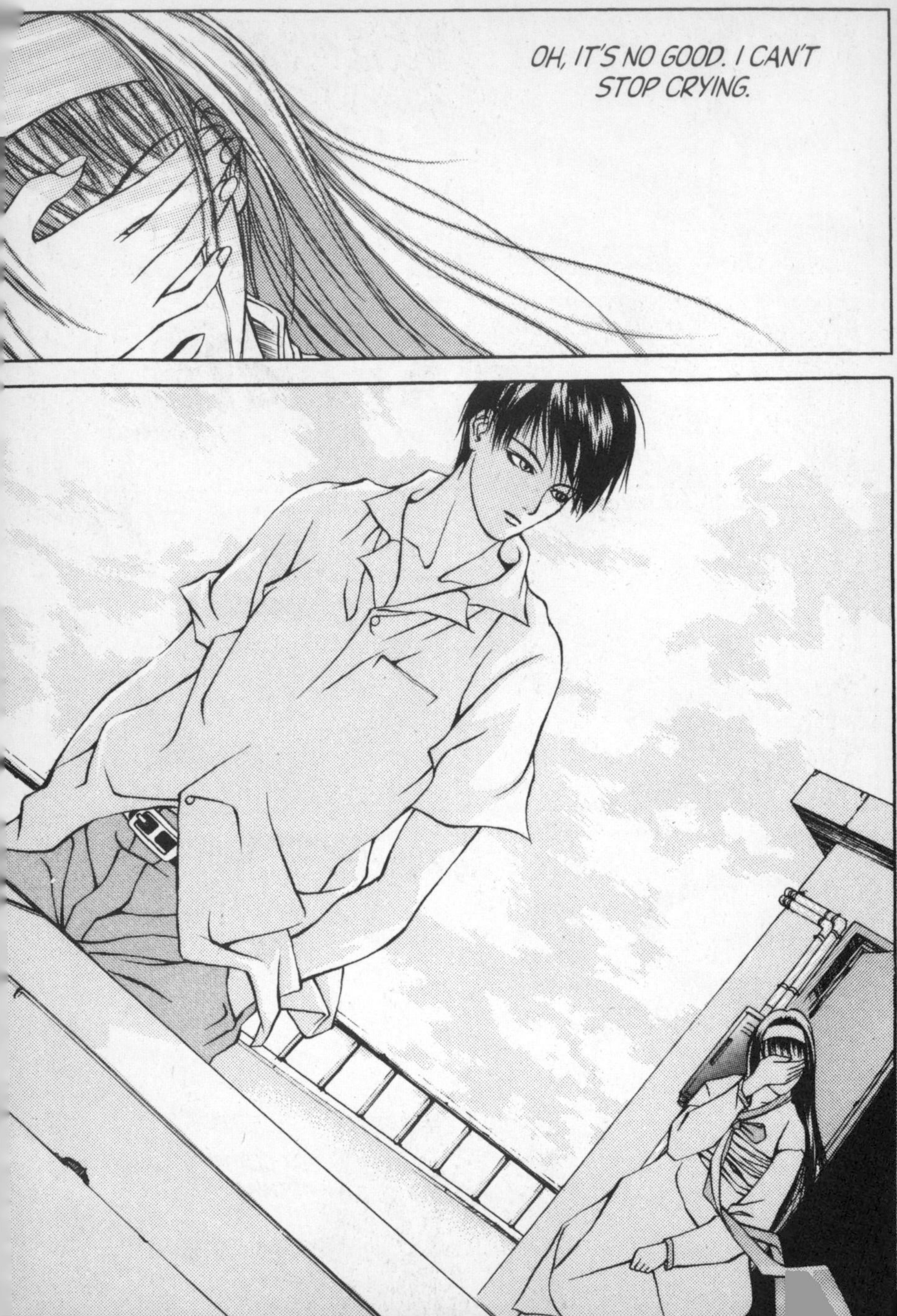
OH, IT'S NO GOOD. I CAN'T STOP CRYING.

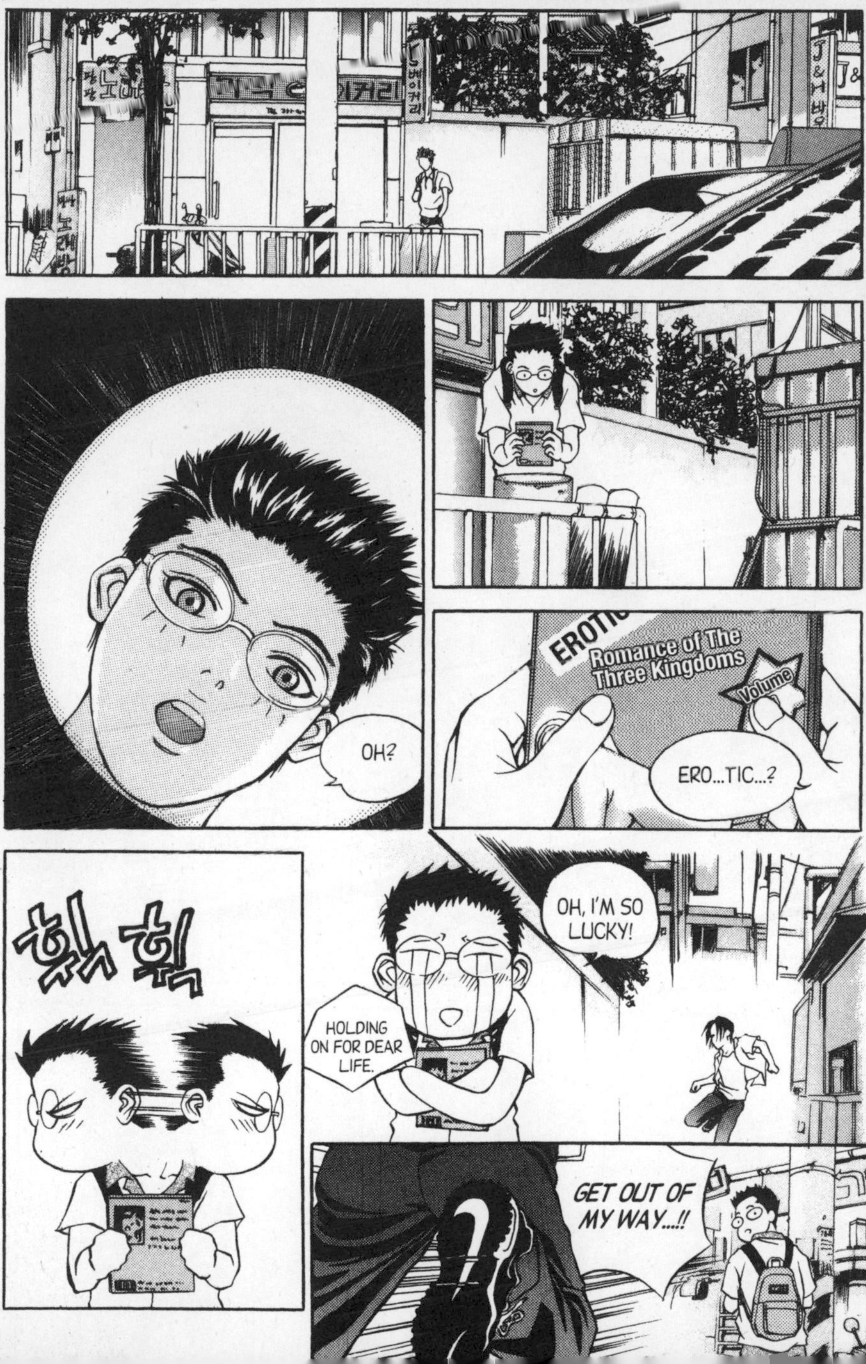
OH?
EROTI
Romance of The Three Kingdoms
Volume
ERO...TIC...?
헉 헉
HOLDING ON FOR DEAR LIFE.
OH, I'M SO LUCKY!
GET OUT OF MY WAY...!!

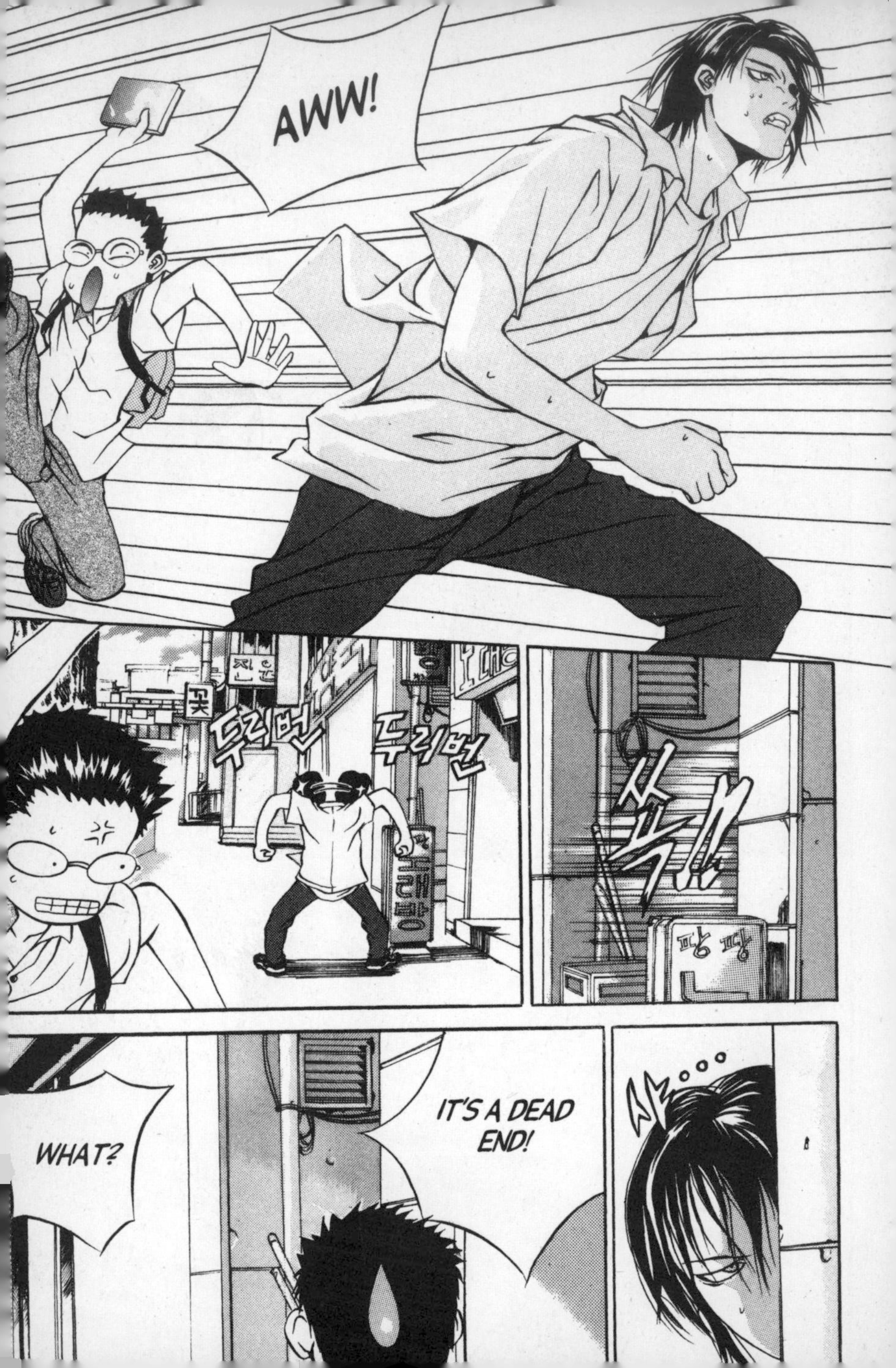
AWW!
꽃
두리번
두리번
WHAT?
IT'S A DEAD END!

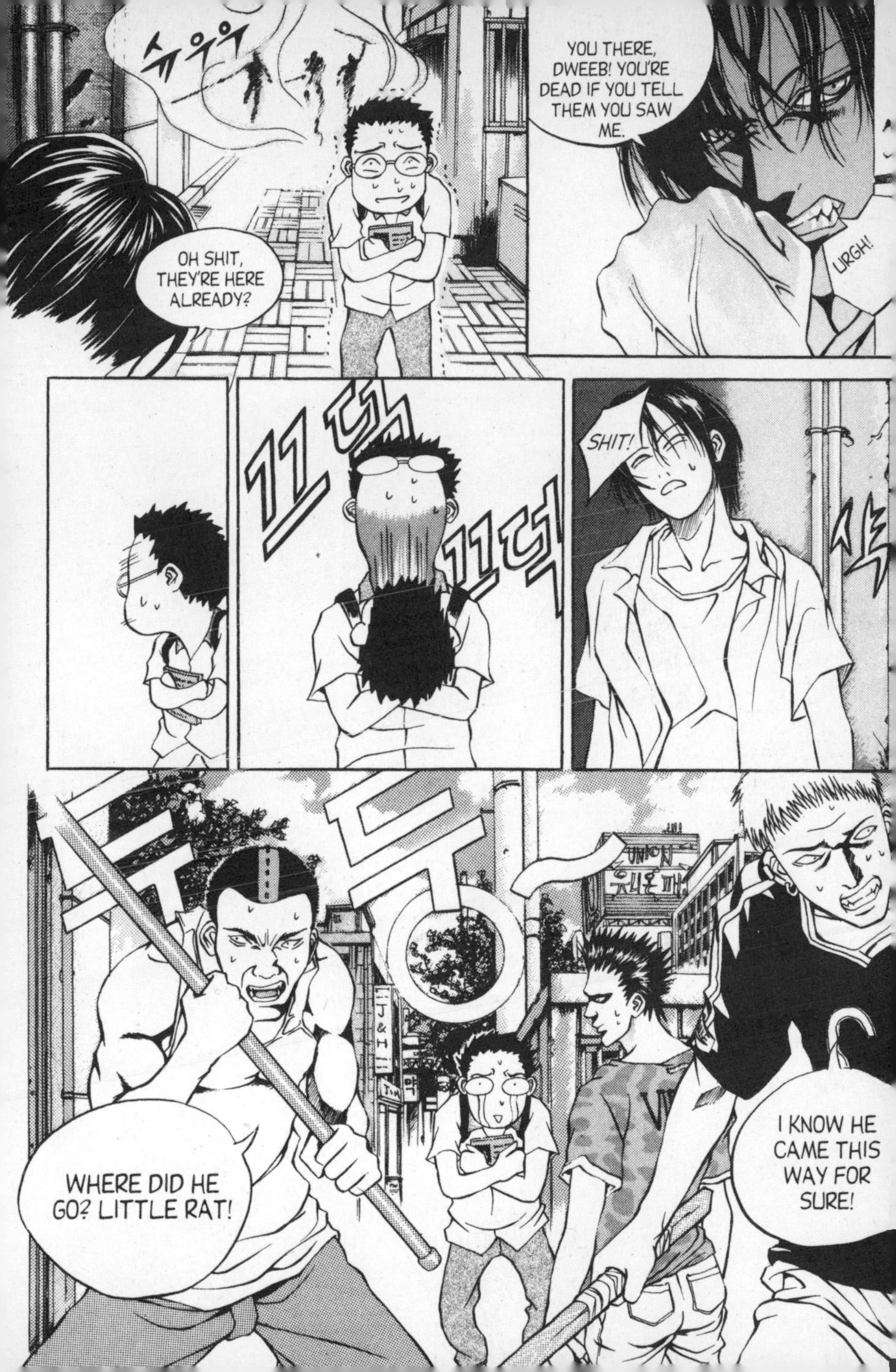
OH SHIT, THEY'RE HERE ALREADY?
YOU THERE, DWEEB! YOU'RE DEAD IF YOU TELL THEM YOU SAW ME.
URGH!
SHIT!
WHERE DID HE GO? LITTLE RAT!
I KNOW HE CAME THIS WAY FOR SURE!

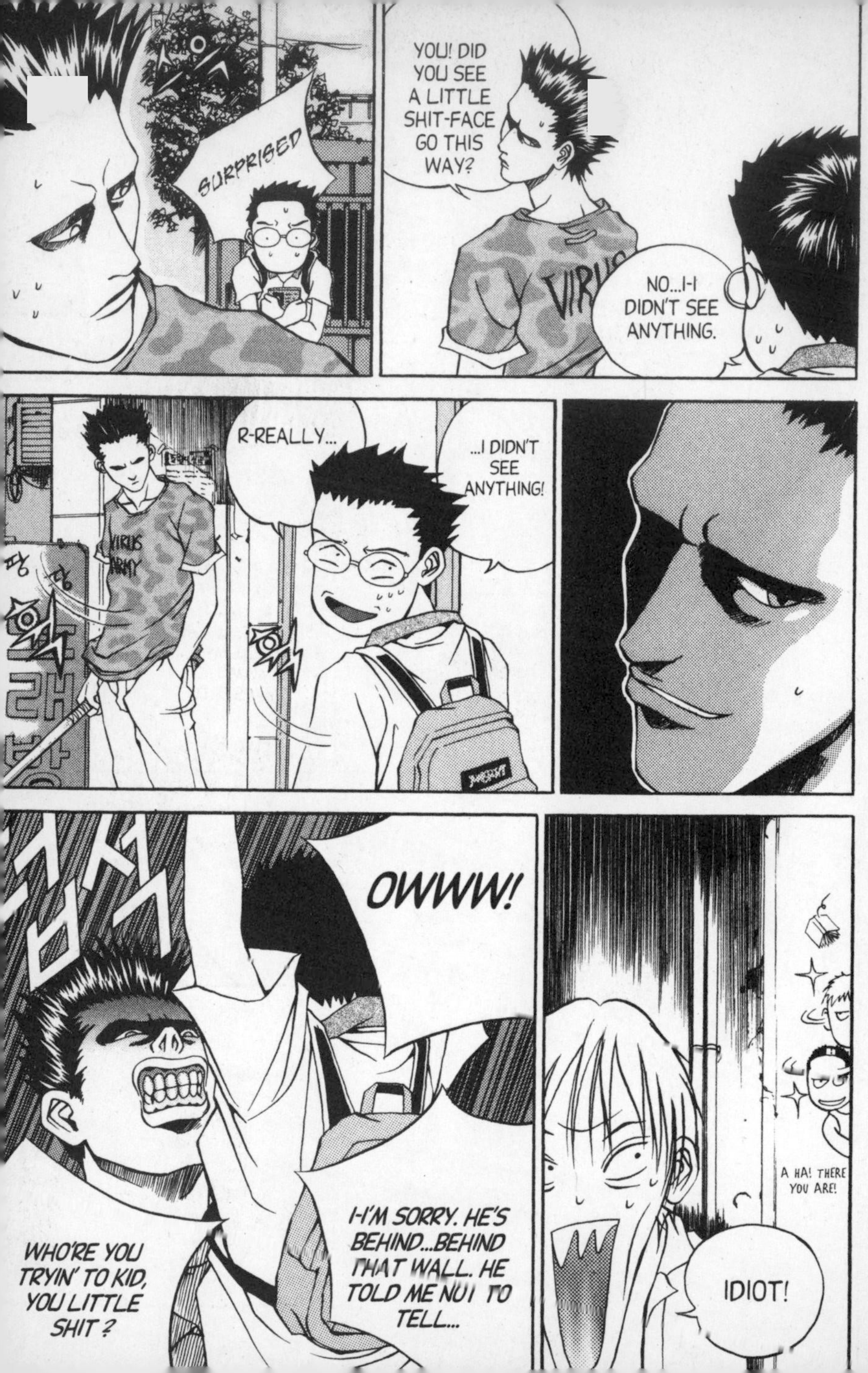
SURPRISED
YOU! DID YOU SEE A LITTLE SHIT-FACE GO THIS WAY?
NO...I-I DIDN'T SEE ANYTHING.
R-REALLY...
...I DIDN'T SEE ANYTHING!
OWWW!
WHO'RE YOU TRYIN' TO KID, YOU LITTLE SHIT?
I-I'M SORRY. HE'S BEHIND...BEHIND THAT WALL. HE TOLD ME NOT TO TELL...
A HA! THERE YOU ARE!
IDIOT!

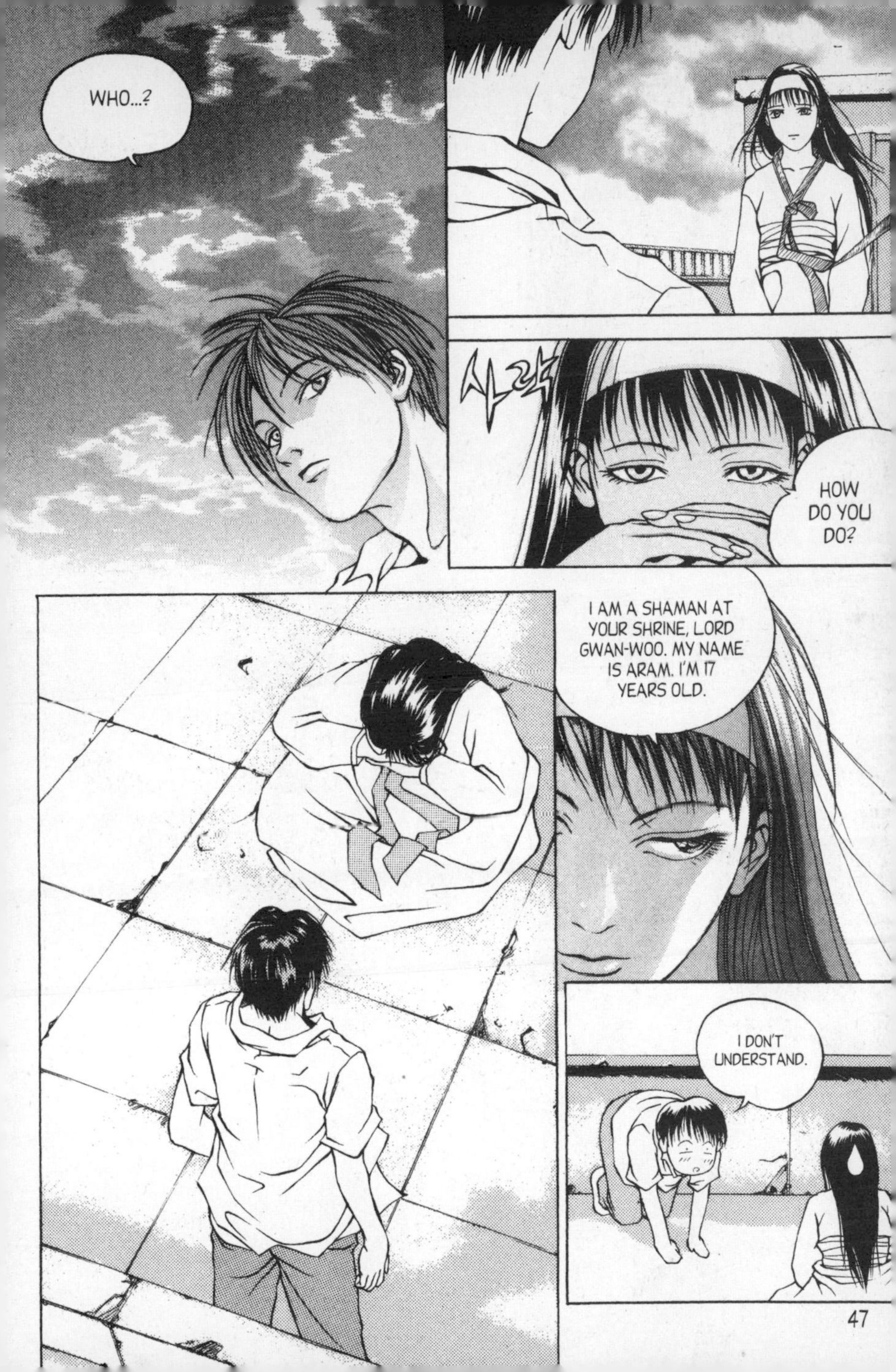
WHO...?
사락
HOW DO YOU DO?
I AM A SHAMAN AT YOUR SHRINE, LORD GWAN-WOO. MY NAME IS ARAM. I'M 17 YEARS OLD.
I DON'T UNDERSTAND.

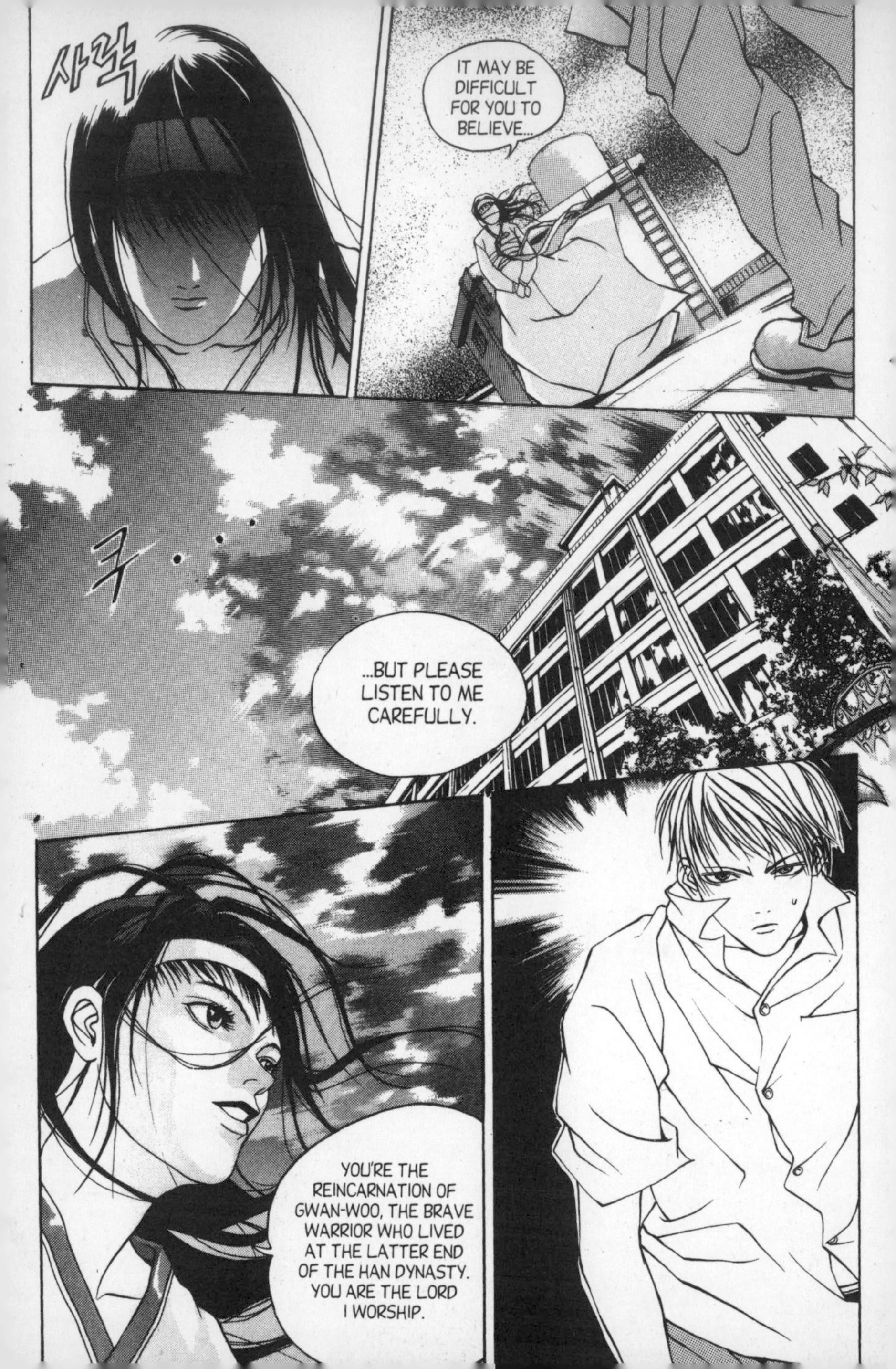
사락
IT MAY BE DIFFICULT FOR YOU TO BELIEVE...
ㅋ...
...BUT PLEASE LISTEN TO ME CAREFULLY.
YOU'RE THE REINCARNATION OF GWAN-WOO, THE BRAVE WARRIOR WHO LIVED AT THE LATTER END OF THE HAN DYNASTY. YOU ARE THE LORD I WORSHIP.

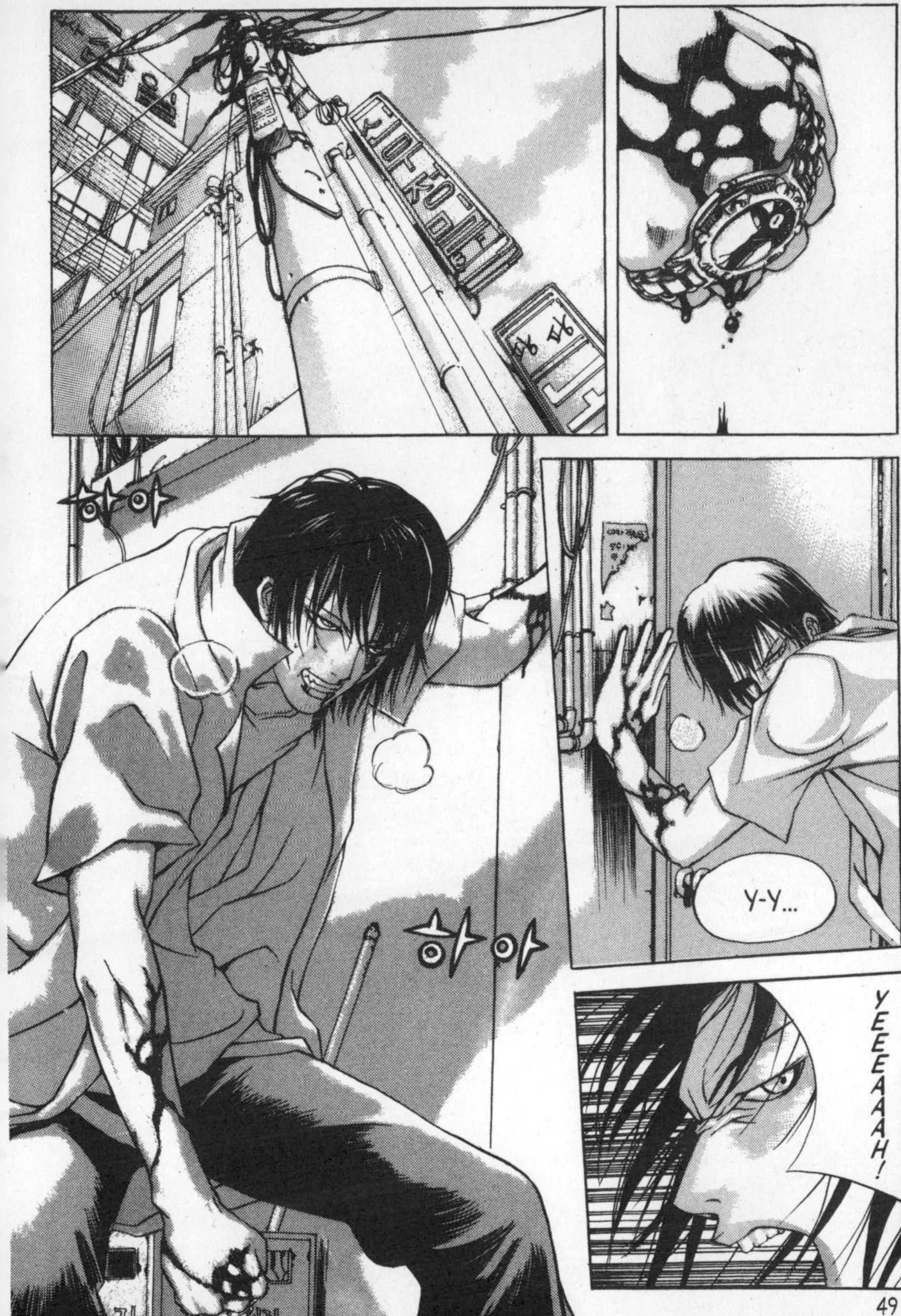
Y-Y...
YEEEAAAH!

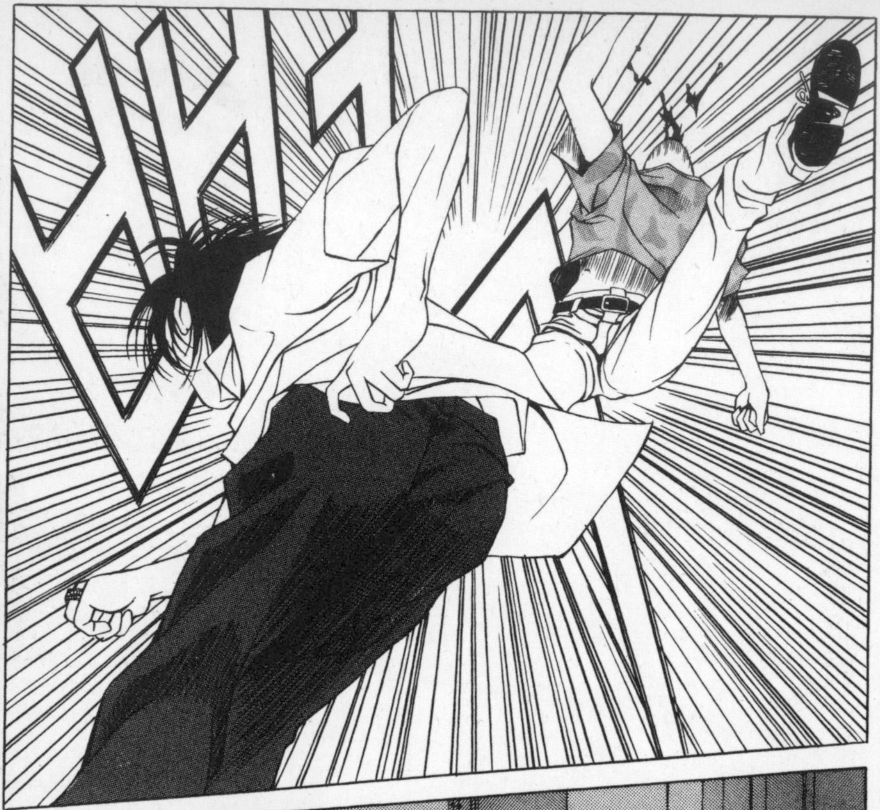

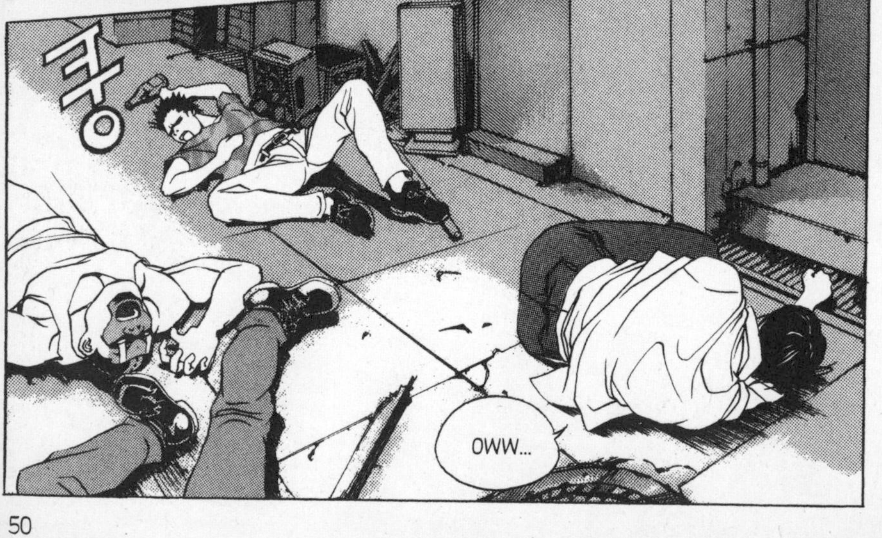
쿵
OWW...

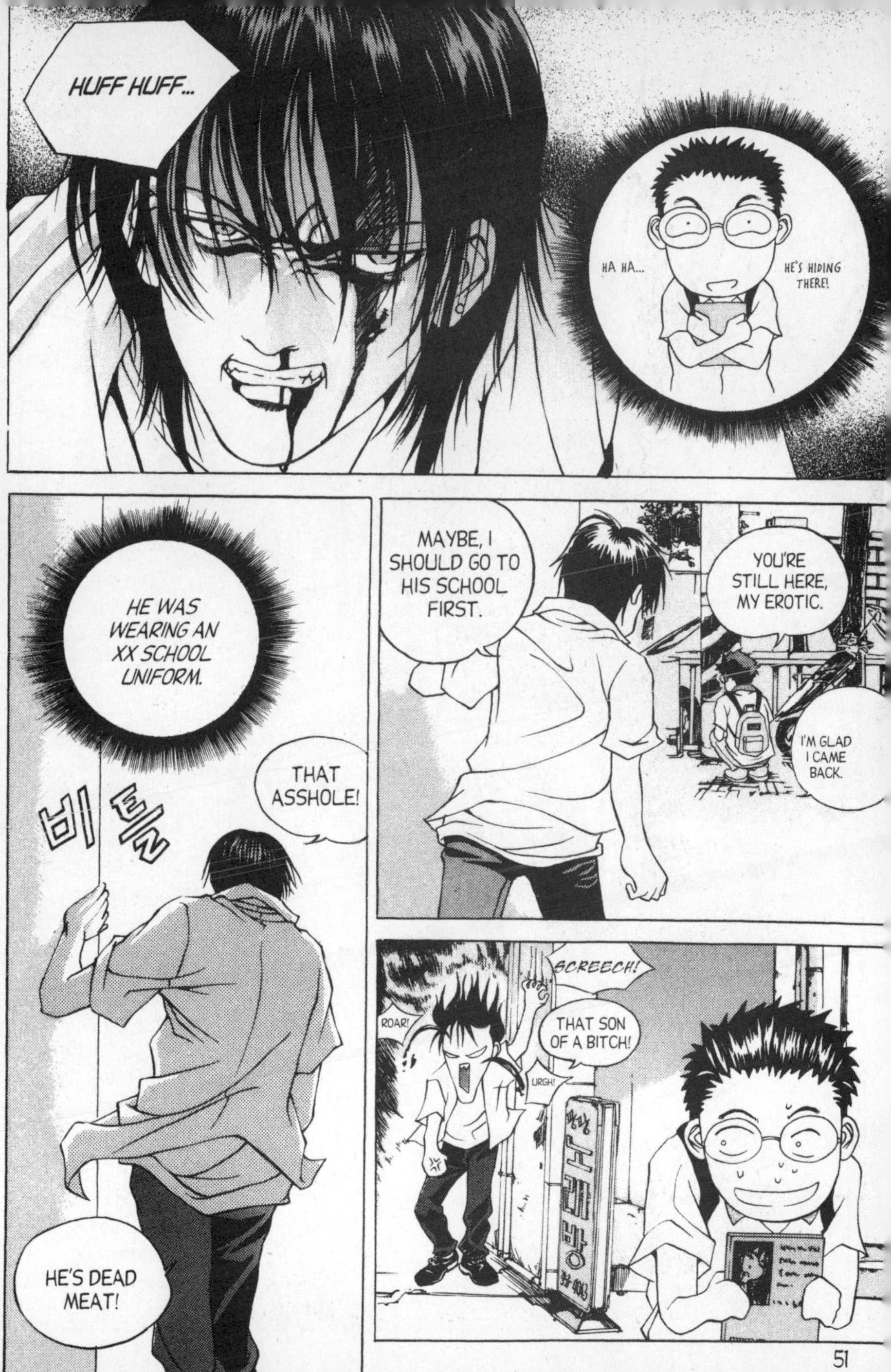
HUFF HUFF...
HA HA...
HE'S HIDING THERE!
HE WAS WEARING AN XX SCHOOL UNIFORM.
THAT ASSHOLE!
HE'S DEAD MEAT!
MAYBE, I SHOULD GO TO HIS SCHOOL FIRST.
YOU'RE STILL HERE, MY EROTIC.
I'M GLAD I CAME BACK.
SCREECH!
ROAR!
THAT SON OF A BITCH!
URGH!

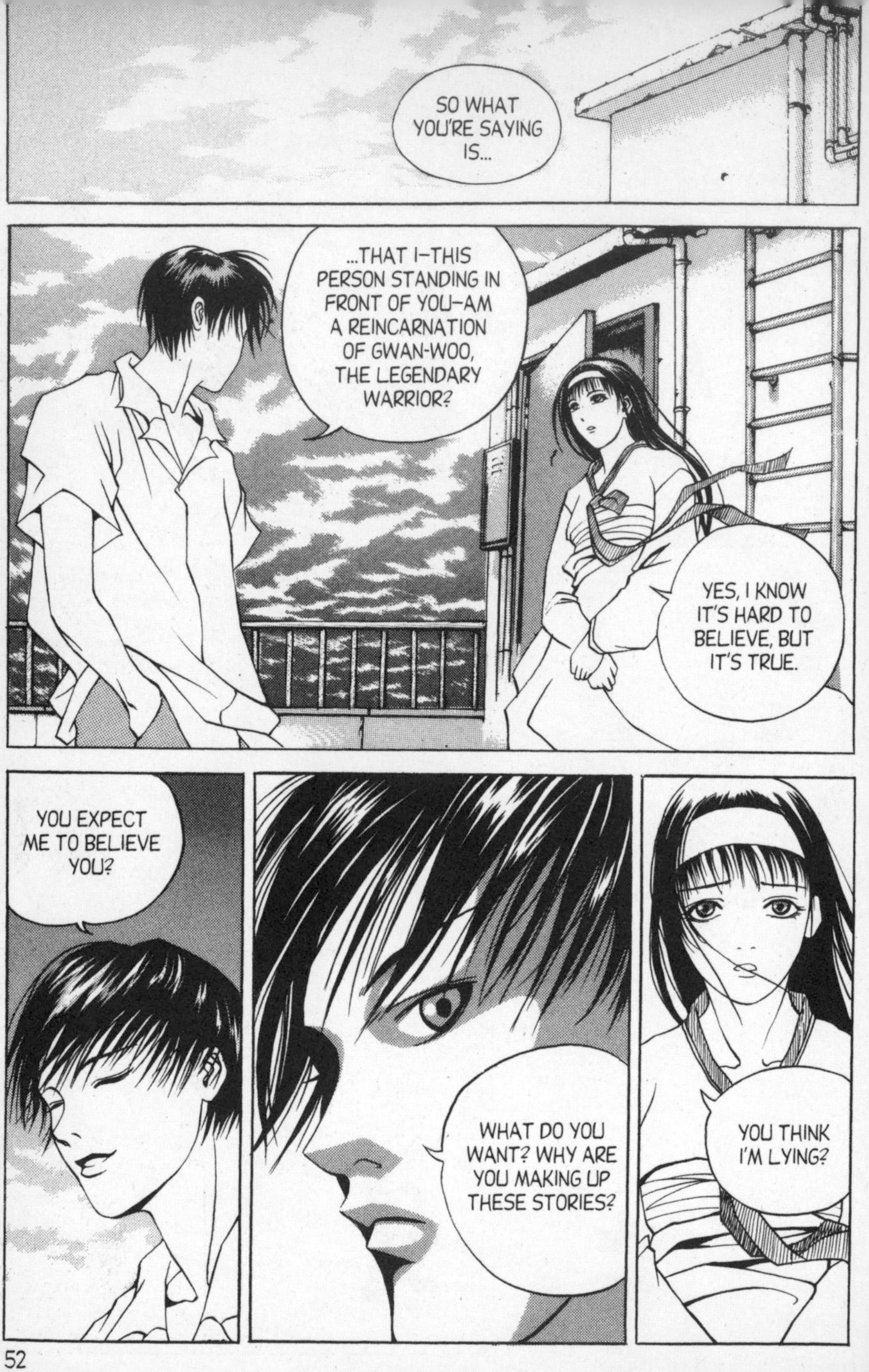
SO WHAT YOU'RE SAYING IS...
...THAT I—THIS PERSON STANDING IN FRONT OF YOU—AM A REINCARNATION OF GWAN-WOO, THE LEGENDARY WARRIOR?
YES, I KNOW IT'S HARD TO BELIEVE, BUT IT'S TRUE.
YOU EXPECT ME TO BELIEVE YOU?
WHAT DO YOU WANT? WHY ARE YOU MAKING UP THESE STORIES?
YOU THINK I'M LYING?

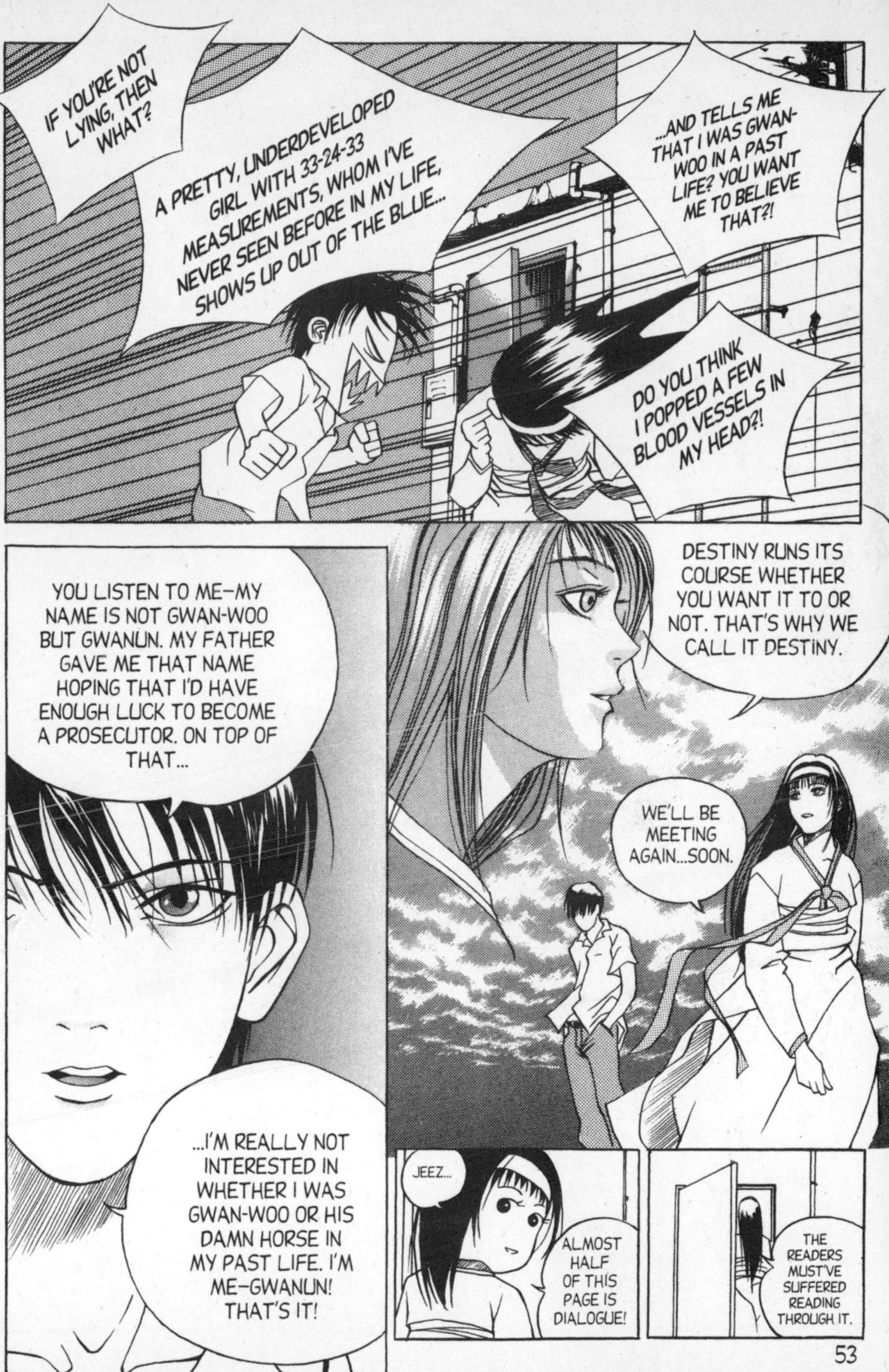
IF YOU'RE NOT LYING, THEN WHAT?
A PRETTY, UNDERDEVELOPED GIRL WITH 33-24-33 MEASUREMENTS, WHOM I'VE NEVER SEEN BEFORE IN MY LIFE, SHOWS UP OUT OF THE BLUE...
...AND TELLS ME THAT I WAS GWAN-WOO IN A PAST LIFE? YOU WANT ME TO BELIEVE THAT?!
DO YOU THINK I POPPED A FEW BLOOD VESSELS IN MY HEAD?!
YOU LISTEN TO ME—MY NAME IS NOT GWAN-WOO BUT GWANUN. MY FATHER GAVE ME THAT NAME HOPING THAT I'D HAVE ENOUGH LUCK TO BECOME A PROSECUTOR. ON TOP OF THAT...
...I'M REALLY NOT INTERESTED IN WHETHER I WAS GWAN-WOO OR HIS DAMN HORSE IN MY PAST LIFE. I'M ME—GWANUN! THAT'S IT!
DESTINY RUNS ITS COURSE WHETHER YOU WANT IT TO OR NOT. THAT'S WHY WE CALL IT DESTINY.
WE'LL BE MEETING AGAIN...SOON.
JEEZ...
ALMOST HALF OF THIS PAGE IS DIALOGUE!
THE READERS MUST'VE SUFFERED READING THROUGH IT.

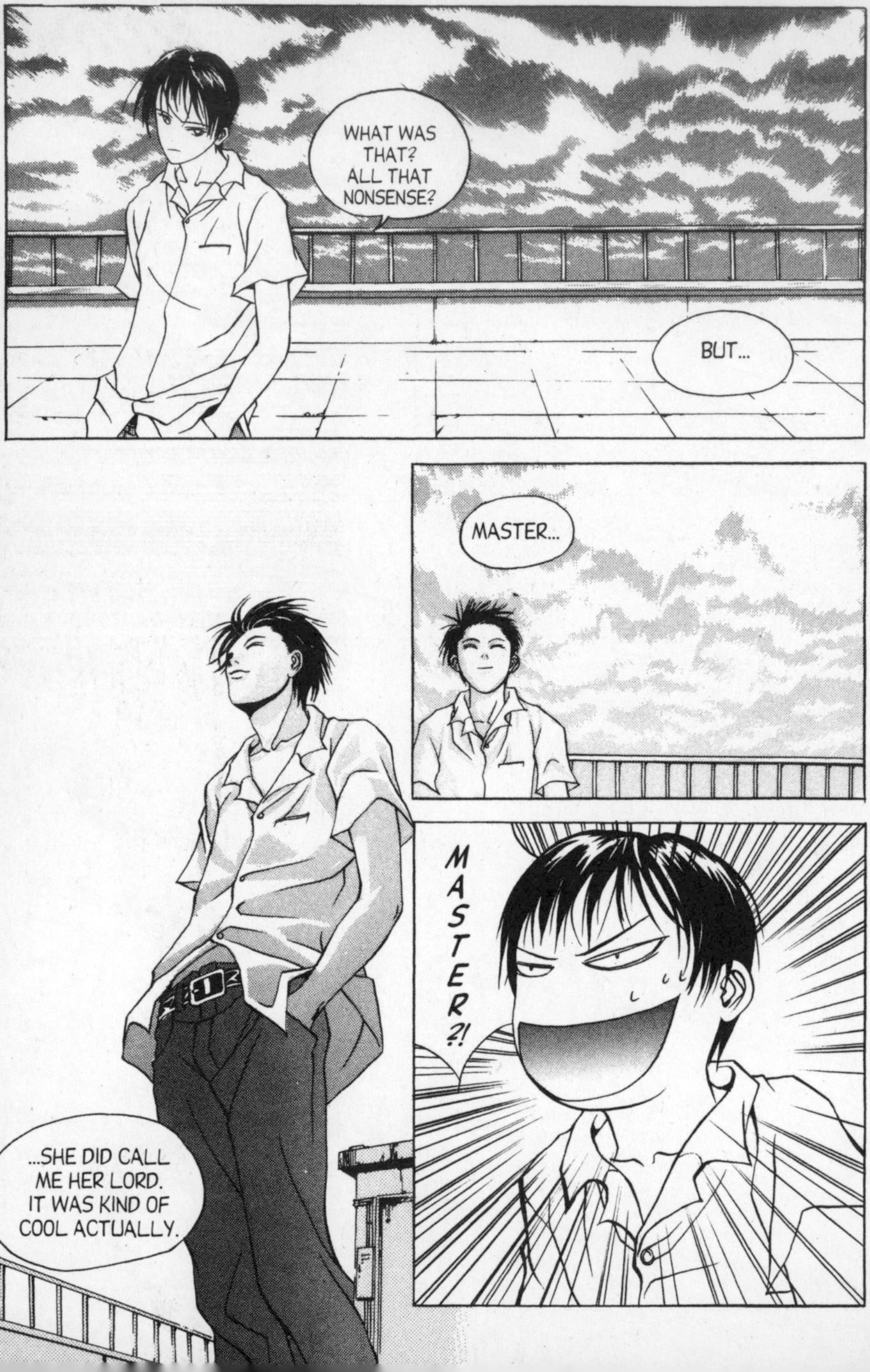
WHAT WAS THAT? ALL THAT NONSENSE?
BUT...
...SHE DID CALL ME HER LORD. IT WAS KIND OF COOL ACTUALLY.
MASTER...
MASTER?!

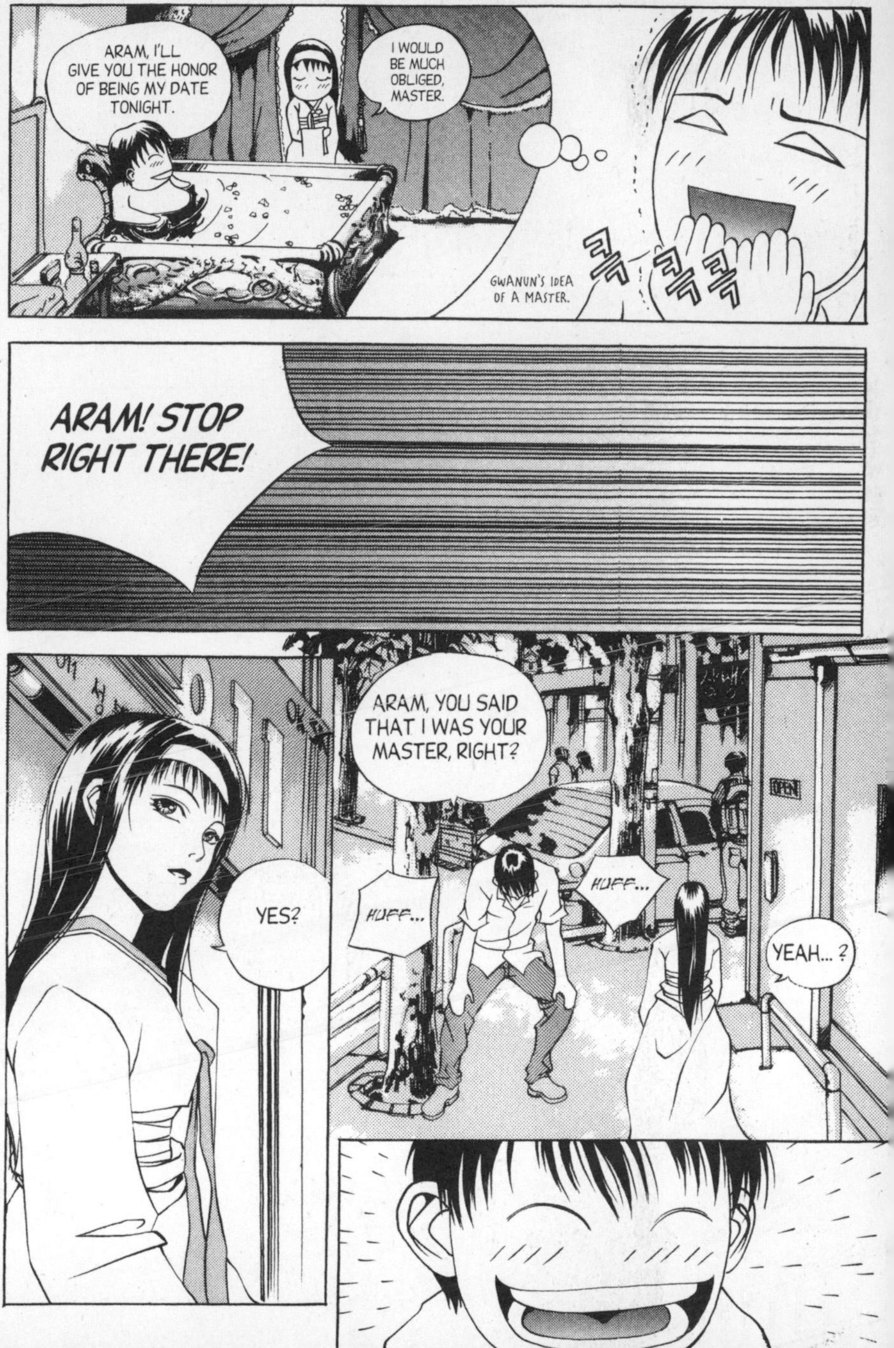
ARAM, I'LL GIVE YOU THE HONOR OF BEING MY DATE TONIGHT.
I WOULD BE MUCH OBLIGED, MASTER.
GWANUN'S IDEA OF A MASTER.
ARAM! STOP RIGHT THERE!
YES?
ARAM, YOU SAID THAT I WAS YOUR MASTER, RIGHT?
HUFF...
HUFF...
YEAH...?

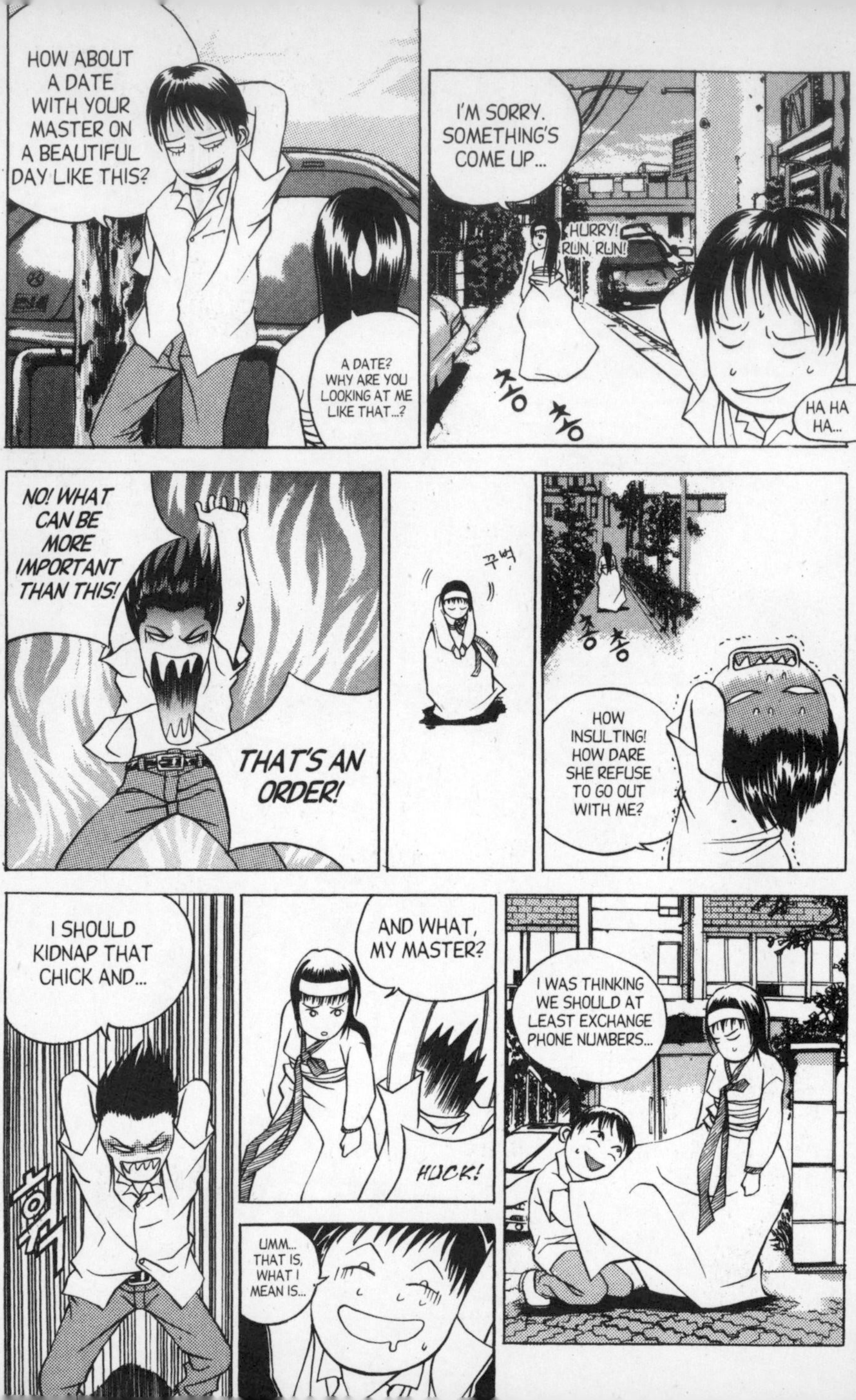
HOW ABOUT A DATE WITH YOUR MASTER ON A BEAUTIFUL DAY LIKE THIS?
A DATE? WHY ARE YOU LOOKING AT ME LIKE THAT...?
I'M SORRY. SOMETHING'S COME UP...
HURRY! RUN, RUN!
총 총
HA HA HA...
NO! WHAT CAN BE MORE IMPORTANT THAN THIS!
THAT'S AN ORDER!
꾸벅
총 총
HOW INSULTING! HOW DARE SHE REFUSE TO GO OUT WITH ME?
I SHOULD KIDNAP THAT CHICK AND...
AND WHAT, MY MASTER?
HUCK!
UMM... THAT IS, WHAT I MEAN IS...
I WAS THINKING WE SHOULD AT LEAST EXCHANGE PHONE NUMBERS...

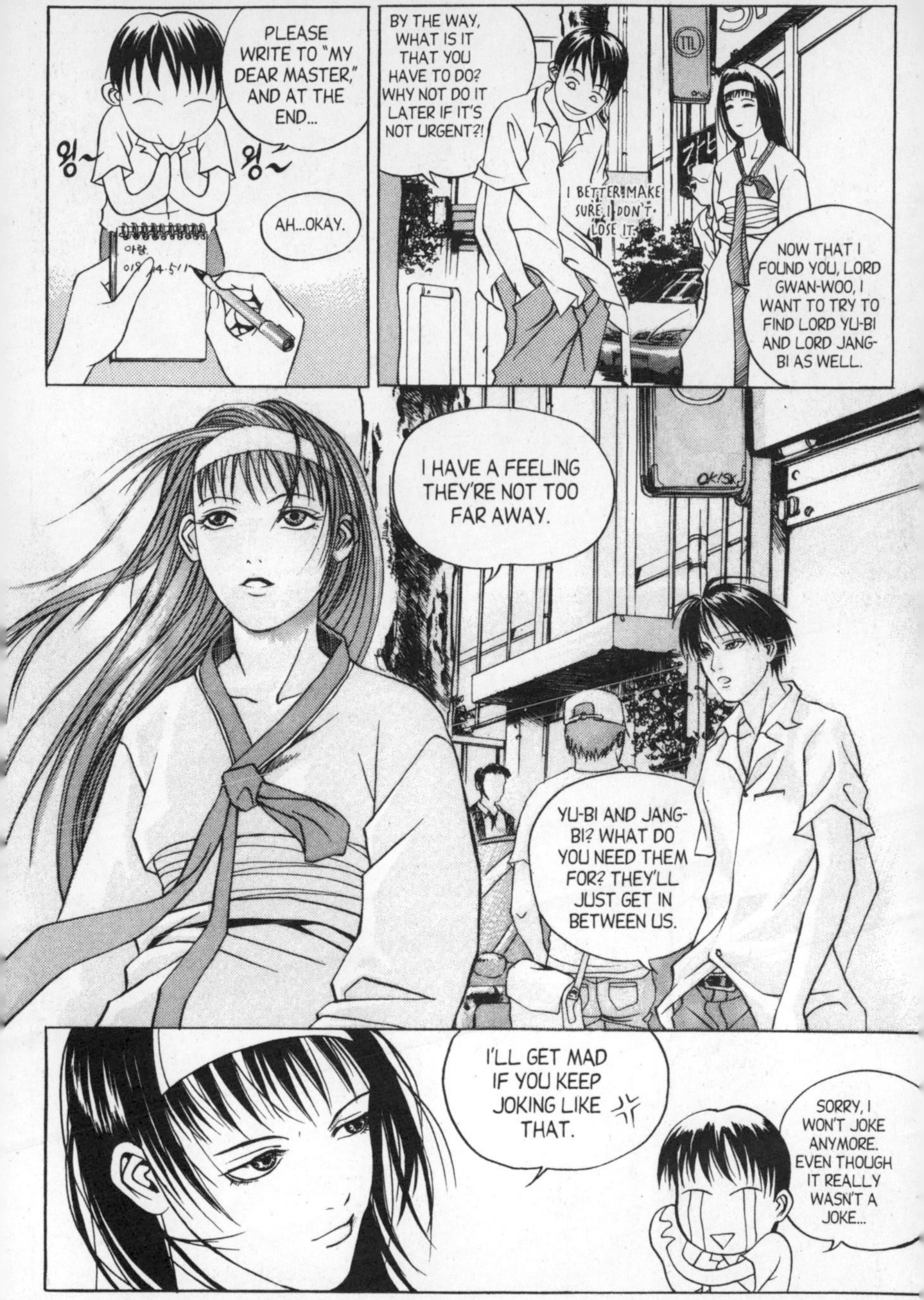
PLEASE WRITE TO "MY DEAR MASTER," AND AT THE END...
왕~
왕~
AH...OKAY.
BY THE WAY, WHAT IS IT THAT YOU HAVE TO DO? WHY NOT DO IT LATER IF IT'S NOT URGENT?!
I BETTER MAKE SURE I DON'T LOSE IT.
NOW THAT I FOUND YOU, LORD GWAN-WOO, I WANT TO TRY TO FIND LORD YU-BI AND LORD JANG-BI AS WELL.
I HAVE A FEELING THEY'RE NOT TOO FAR AWAY.
YU-BI AND JANG-BI? WHAT DO YOU NEED THEM FOR? THEY'LL JUST GET IN BETWEEN US.
I'LL GET MAD IF YOU KEEP JOKING LIKE THAT.
SORRY, I WON'T JOKE ANYMORE. EVEN THOUGH IT REALLY WASN'T A JOKE...

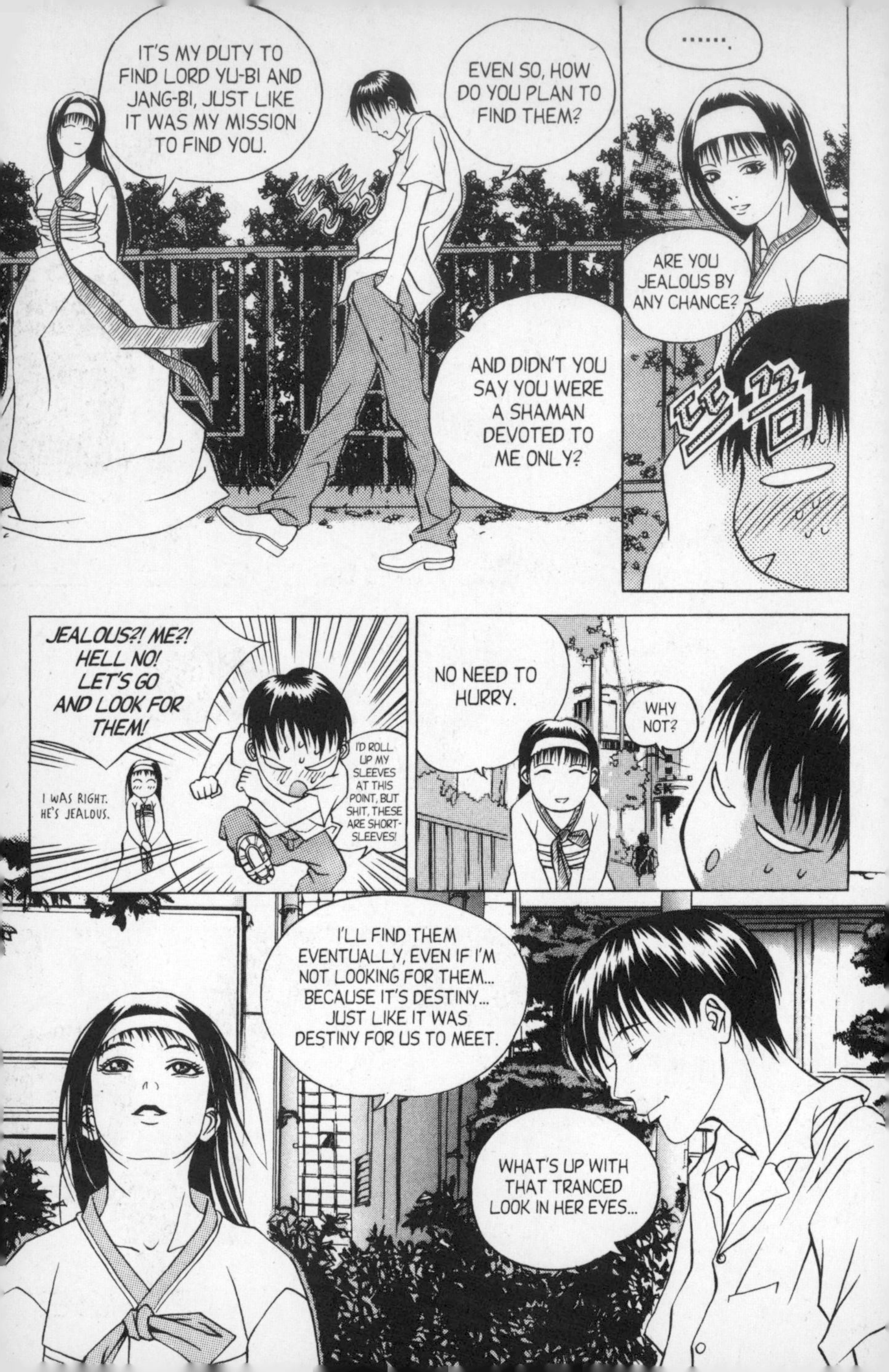
IT'S MY DUTY TO FIND LORD YU-BI AND JANG-BI, JUST LIKE IT WAS MY MISSION TO FIND YOU.
EVEN SO, HOW DO YOU PLAN TO FIND THEM?
AND DIDN'T YOU SAY YOU WERE A SHAMAN DEVOTED TO ME ONLY?
....
ARE YOU JEALOUS BY ANY CHANCE?
JEALOUS?! ME?! HELL NO! LET'S GO AND LOOK FOR THEM!
I'D ROLL UP MY SLEEVES AT THIS POINT, BUT SHIT, THESE ARE SHORT-SLEEVES!
I WAS RIGHT. HE'S JEALOUS.
NO NEED TO HURRY.
WHY NOT?
I'LL FIND THEM EVENTUALLY, EVEN IF I'M NOT LOOKING FOR THEM... BECAUSE IT'S DESTINY... JUST LIKE IT WAS DESTINY FOR US TO MEET.
WHAT'S UP WITH THAT TRANCED LOOK IN HER EYES...

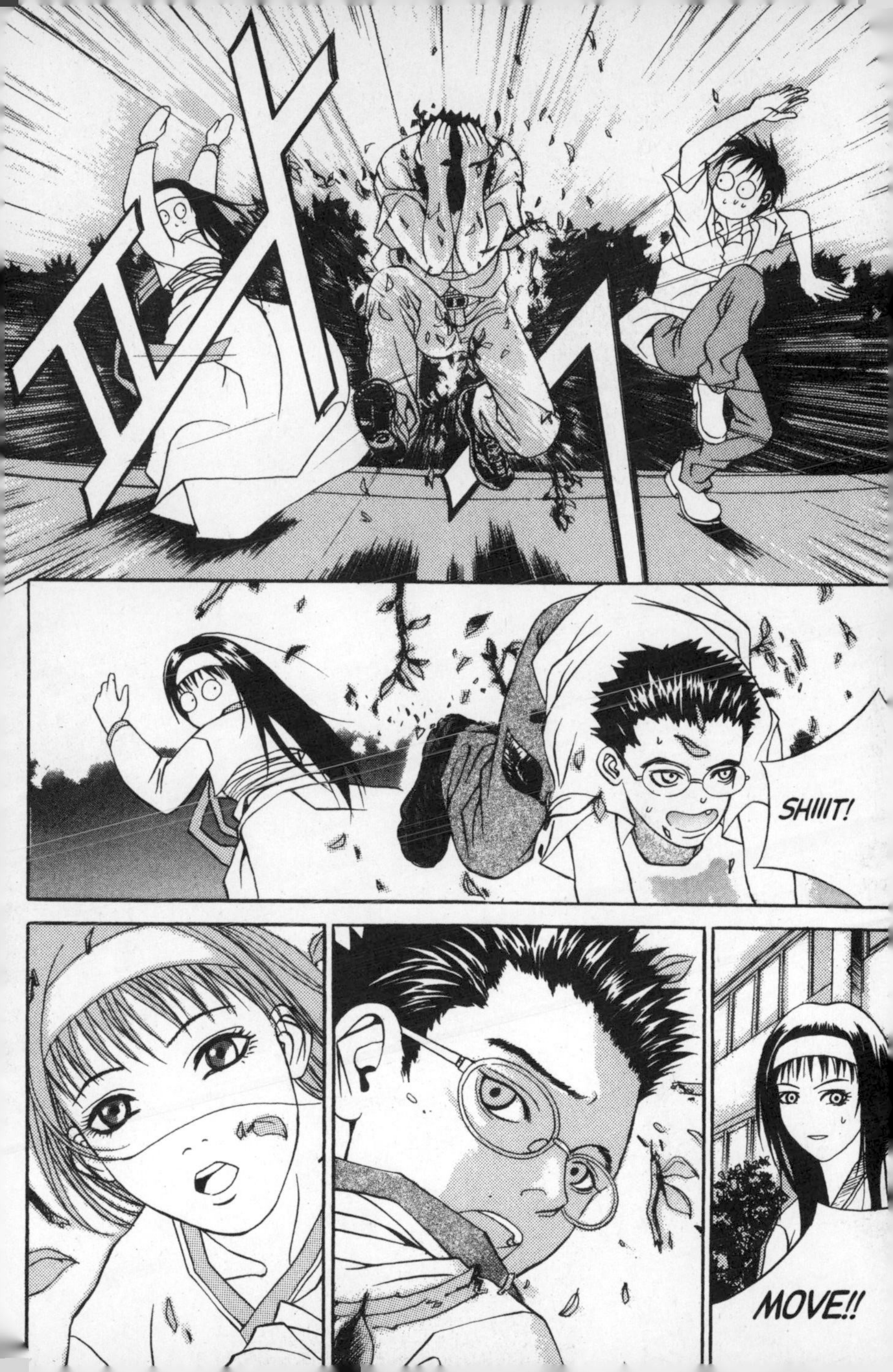
SHIIIT!
MOVE!!

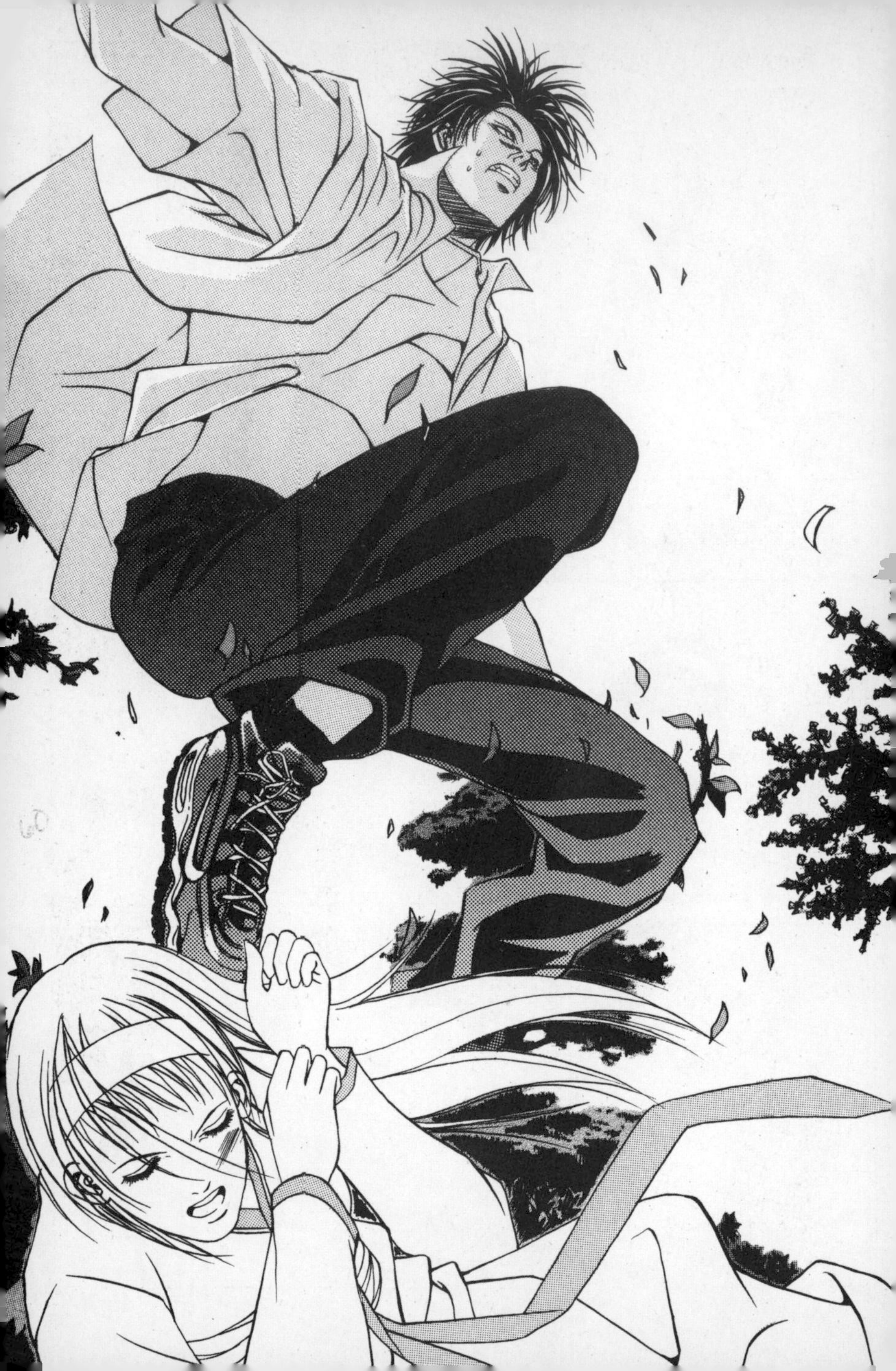

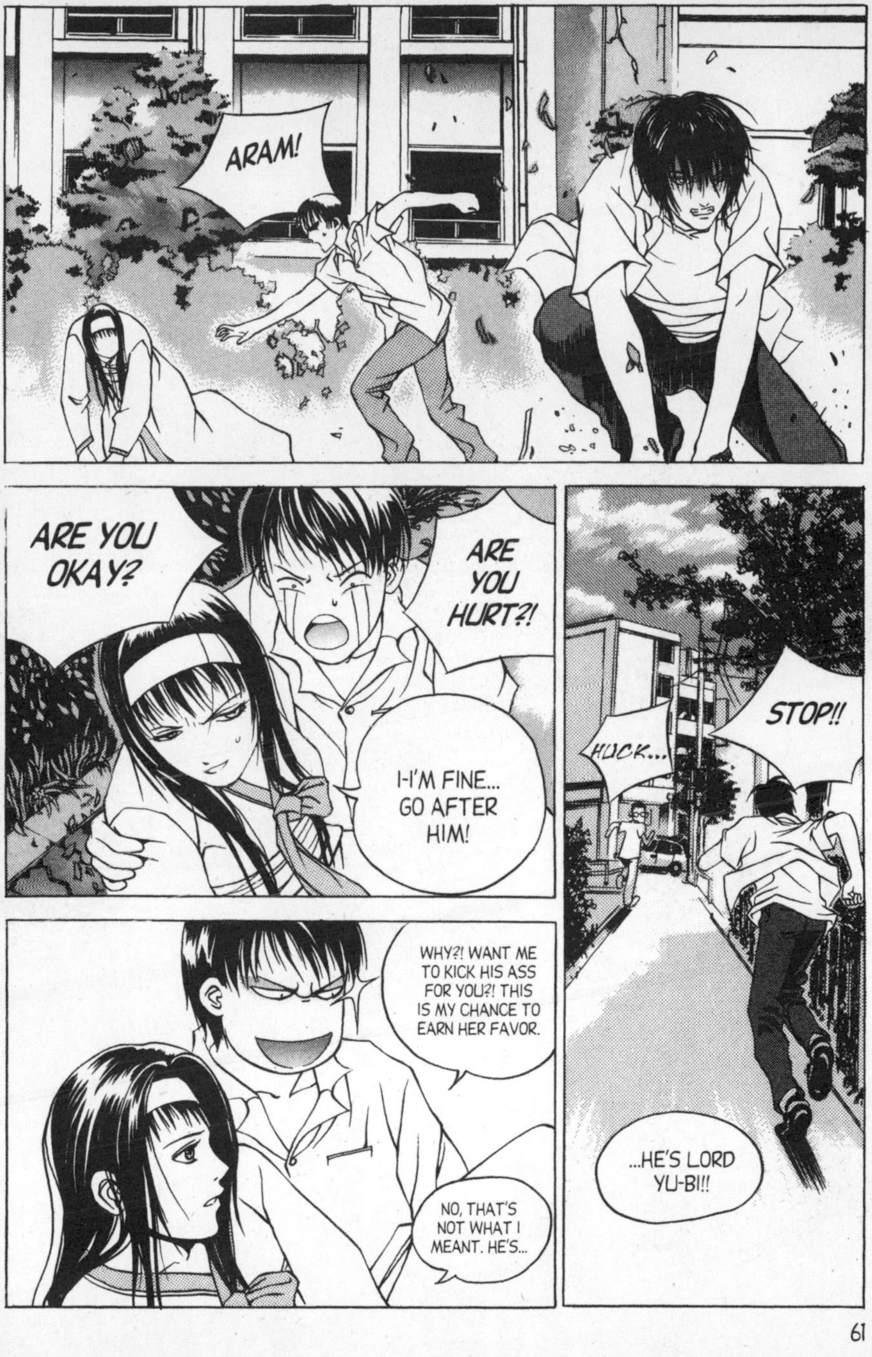
ARAM!
ARE YOU OKAY?
ARE YOU HURT?!
I-I'M FINE... GO AFTER HIM!
WHY?! WANT ME TO KICK HIS ASS FOR YOU?! THIS IS MY CHANCE TO EARN HER FAVOR.
NO, THAT'S NOT WHAT I MEANT. HE'S...
HUCK...
STOP!!
...HE'S LORD YU-BI!!

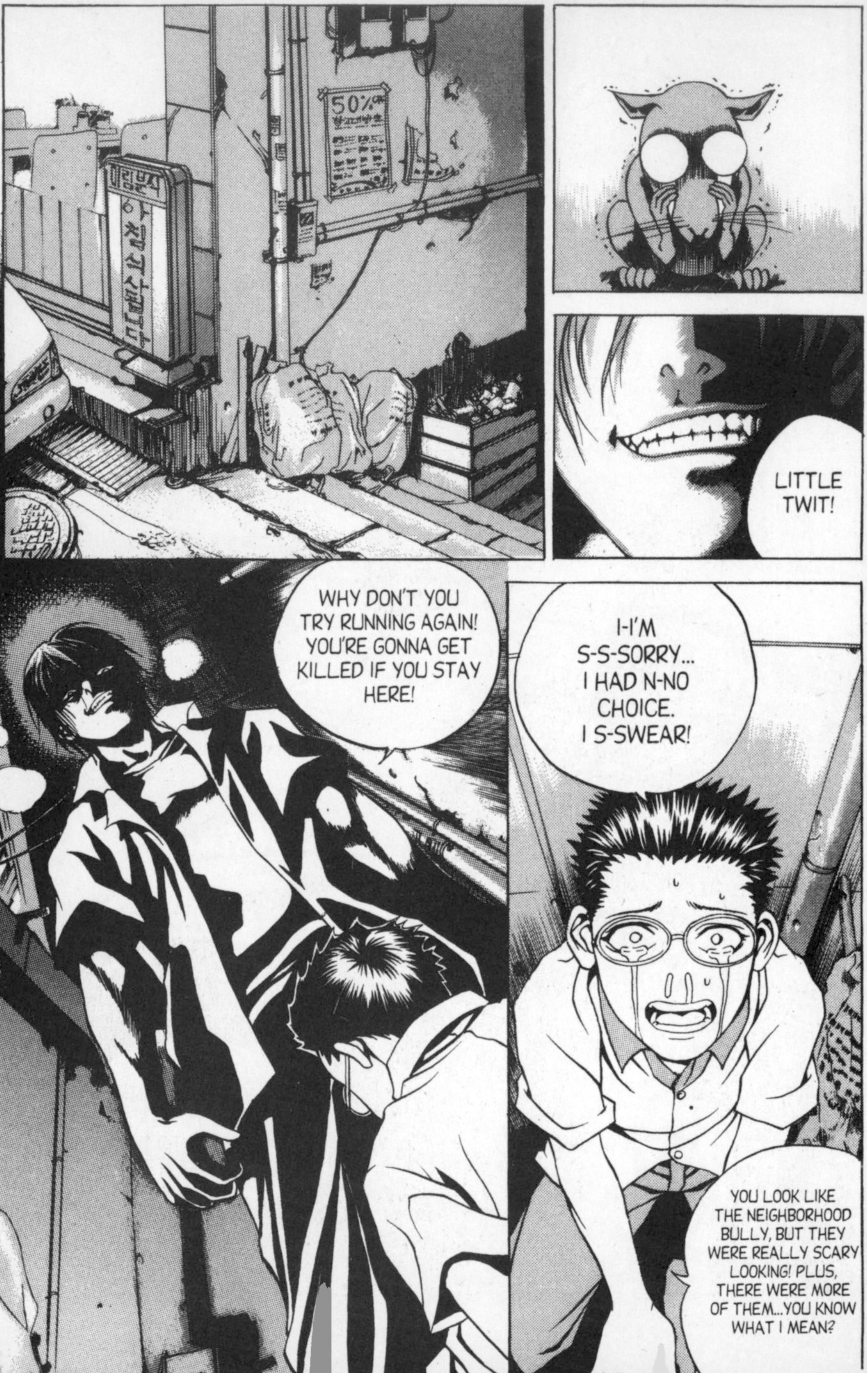
LITTLE TWIT!
WHY DON'T YOU TRY RUNNING AGAIN! YOU'RE GONNA GET KILLED IF YOU STAY HERE!
I-I'M S-S-SORRY... I HAD N-NO CHOICE. I S-SWEAR!
YOU LOOK LIKE THE NEIGHBORHOOD BULLY, BUT THEY WERE REALLY SCARY LOOKING! PLUS, THERE WERE MORE OF THEM...YOU KNOW WHAT I MEAN?

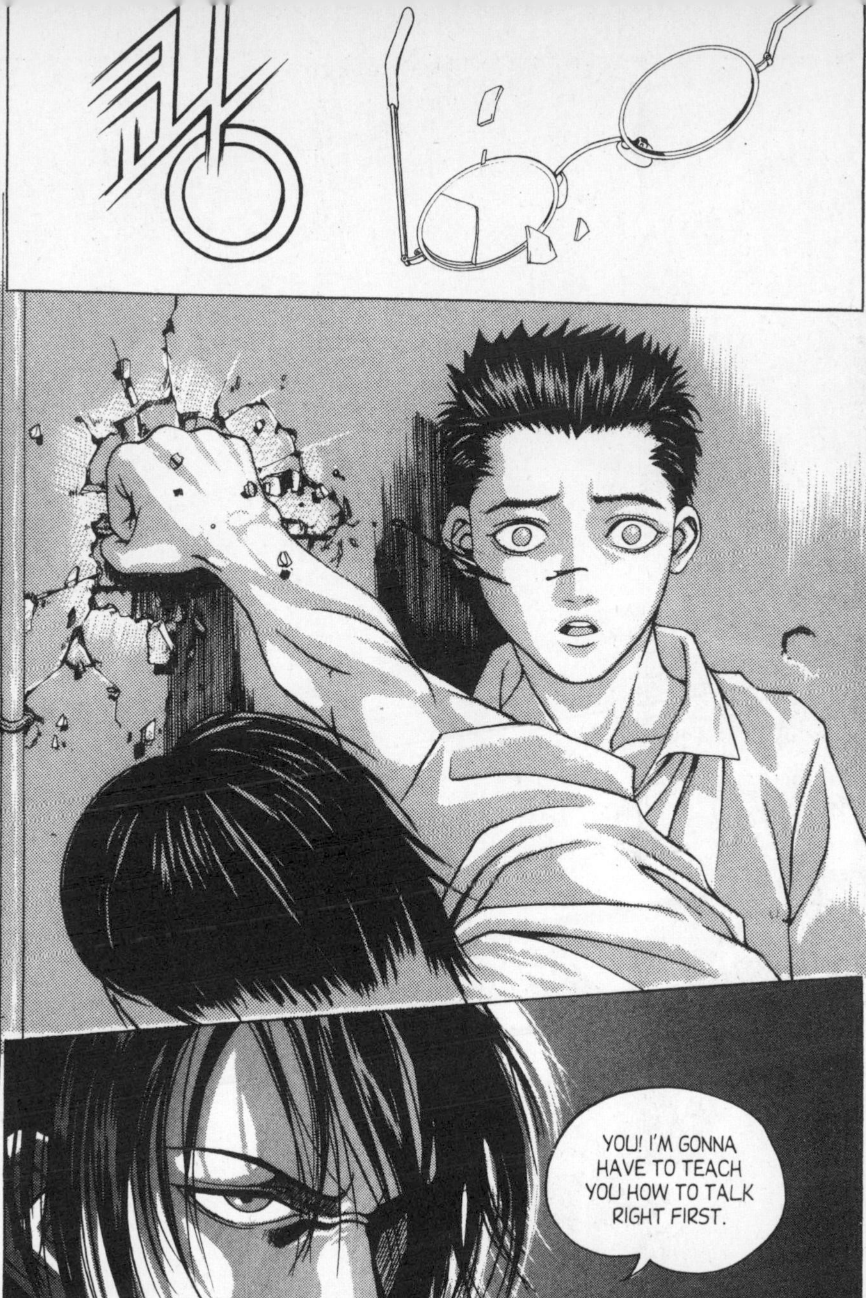
YOU! I'M GONNA HAVE TO TEACH YOU HOW TO TALK RIGHT FIRST.

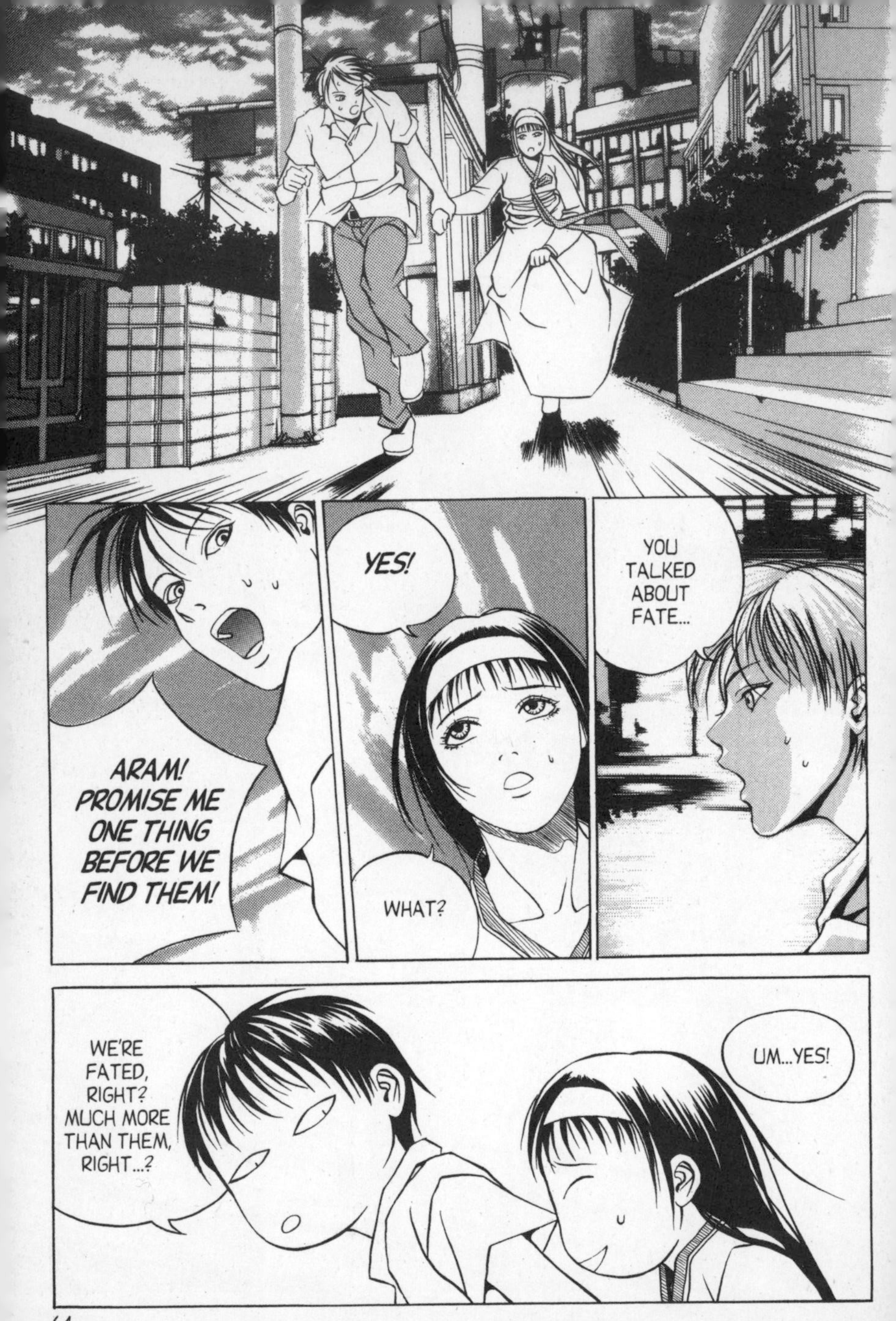
ARAM! PROMISE ME ONE THING BEFORE WE FIND THEM!
YES!
WHAT?
YOU TALKED ABOUT FATE...
WE'RE FATED, RIGHT? MUCH MORE THAN THEM, RIGHT...?
UM...YES!

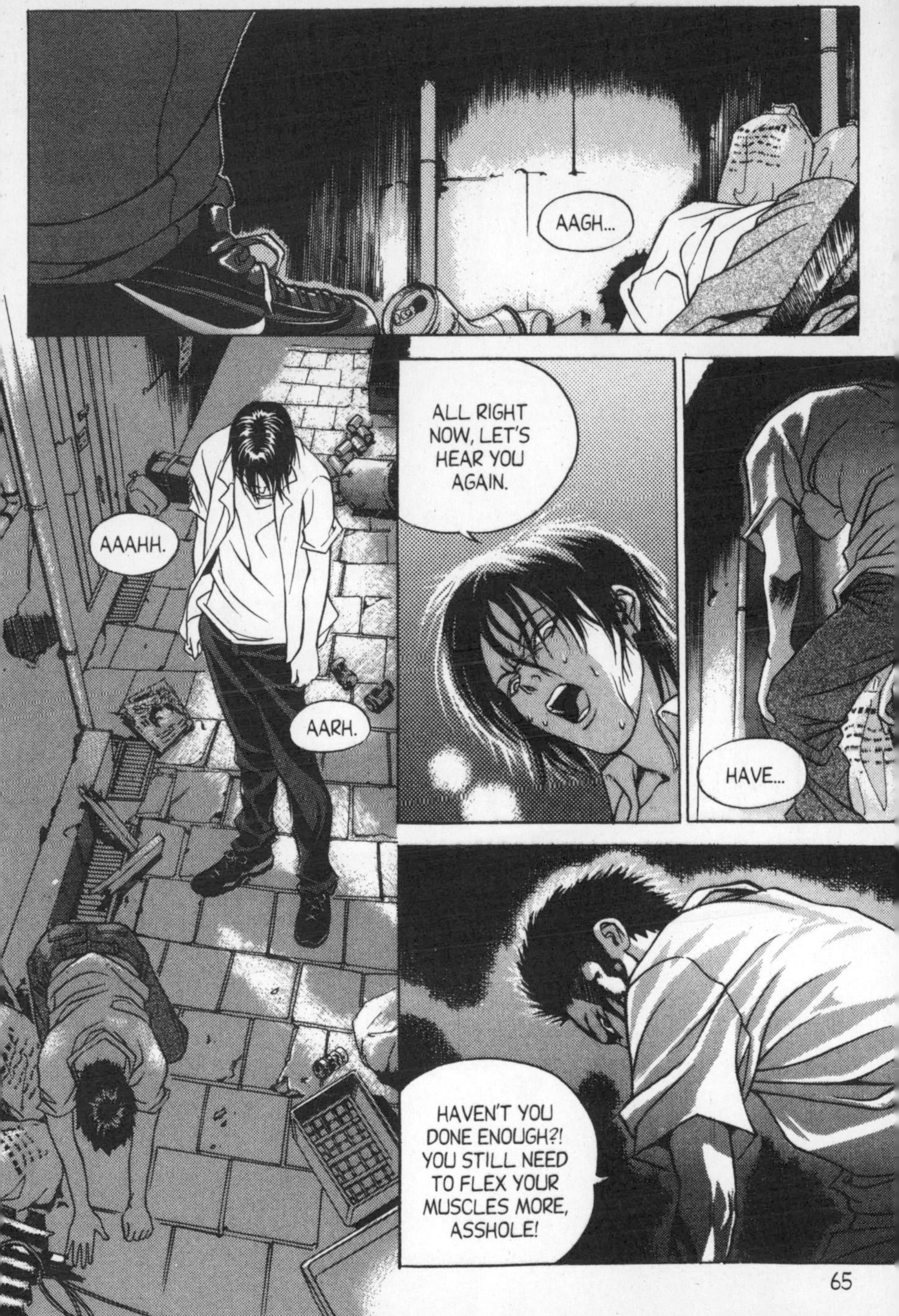
AAGH...
AAAHH.
AARH.
ALL RIGHT NOW, LET'S HEAR YOU AGAIN.
HAVE...
HAVEN'T YOU DONE ENOUGH?! YOU STILL NEED TO FLEX YOUR MUSCLES MORE, ASSHOLE!

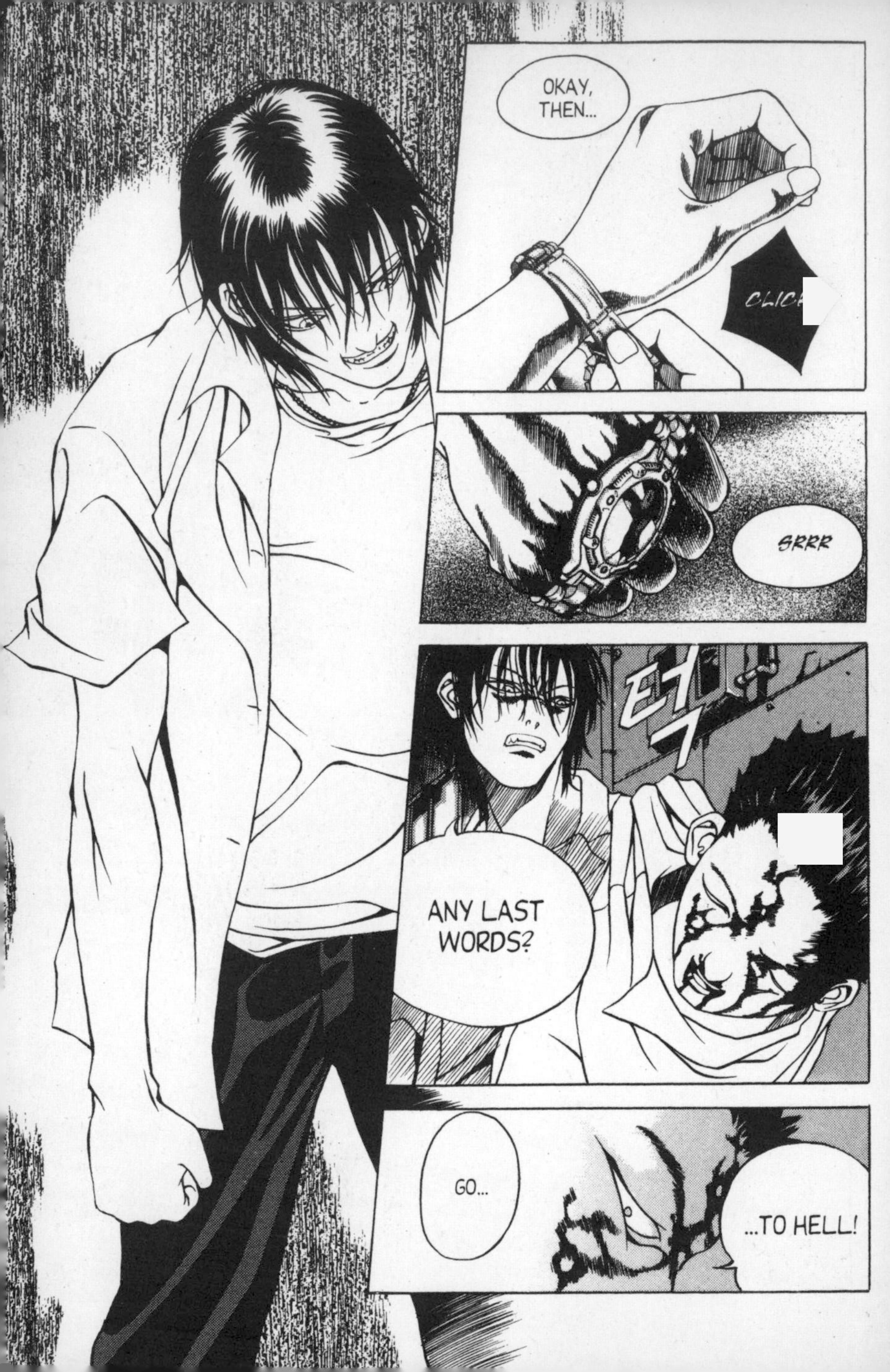
OKAY, THEN...
CLIC
SRRR
턱
ANY LAST WORDS?
GO...
...TO HELL!

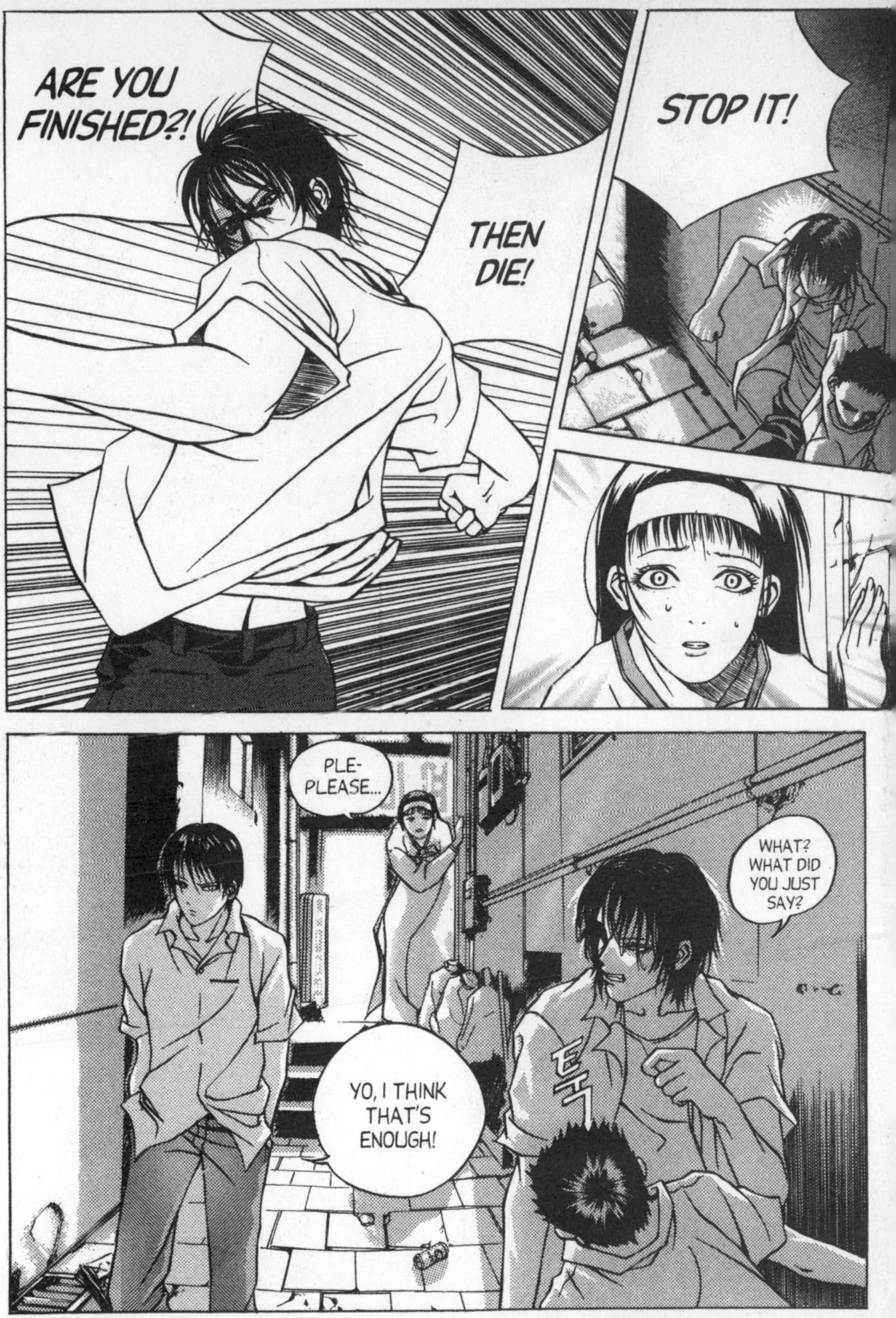
ARE YOU FINISHED?!
THEN DIE!
STOP IT!
PLE- PLEASE...
WHAT? WHAT DID YOU JUST SAY?
YO, I THINK THAT'S ENOUGH!

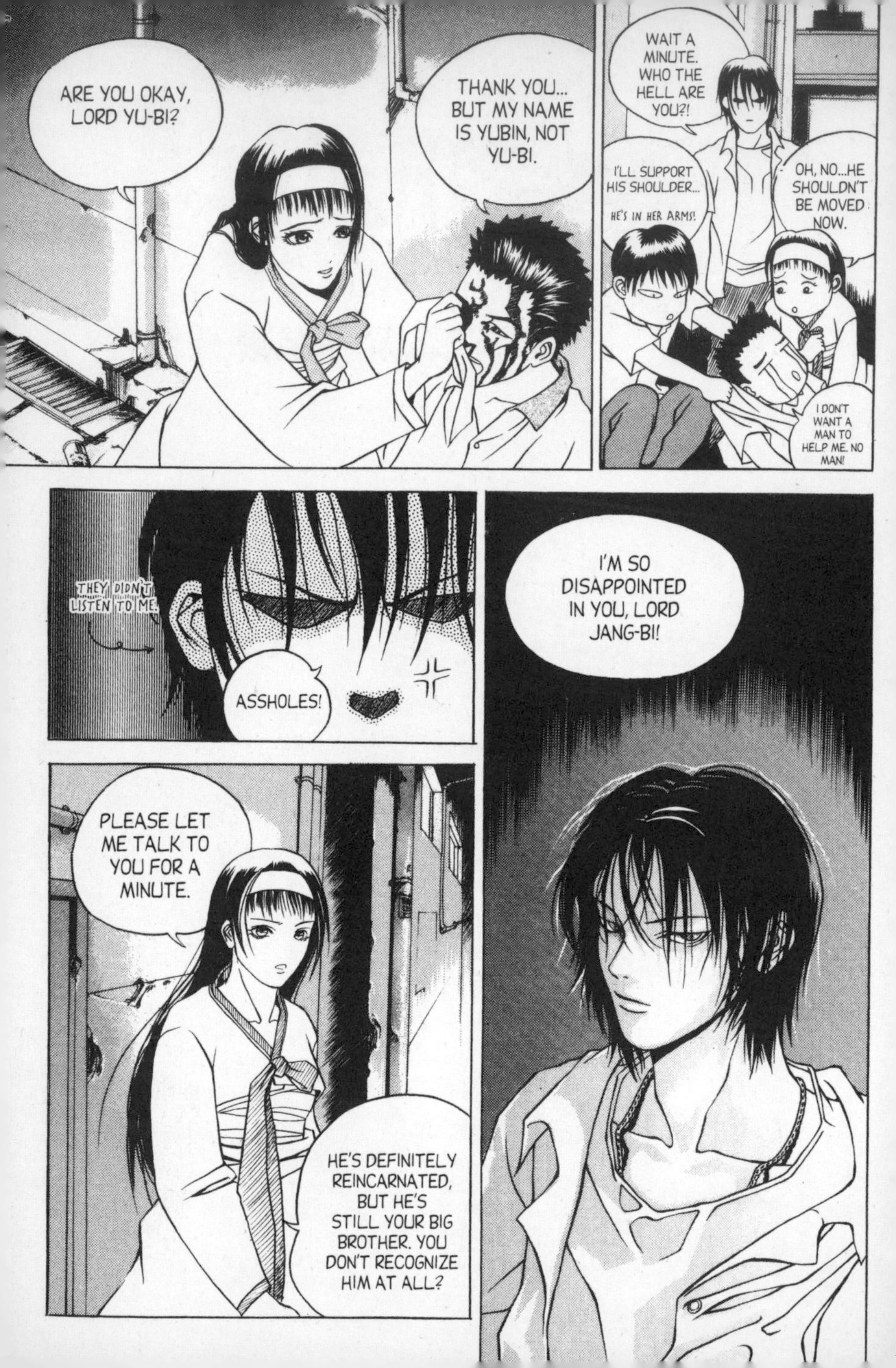
ARE YOU OKAY, LORD YU-BI?
THANK YOU... BUT MY NAME IS YUBIN, NOT YU-BI.
WAIT A MINUTE. WHO THE HELL ARE YOU?!
I'LL SUPPORT HIS SHOULDER...
HE'S IN HER ARMS!
OH, NO...HE SHOULDN'T BE MOVED NOW.
I DON'T WANT A MAN TO HELP ME. NO MAN!
THEY DIDN'T LISTEN TO ME.
ASSHOLES!
I'M SO DISAPPOINTED IN YOU, LORD JANG-BI!
PLEASE LET ME TALK TO YOU FOR A MINUTE.
HE'S DEFINITELY REINCARNATED, BUT HE'S STILL YOUR BIG BROTHER. YOU DON'T RECOGNIZE HIM AT ALL?

이터너티

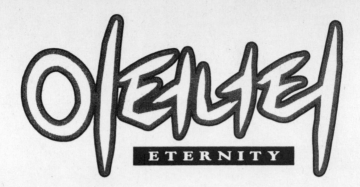

ETERNITY

#3 DESTINY

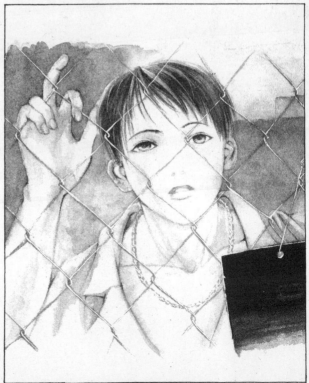

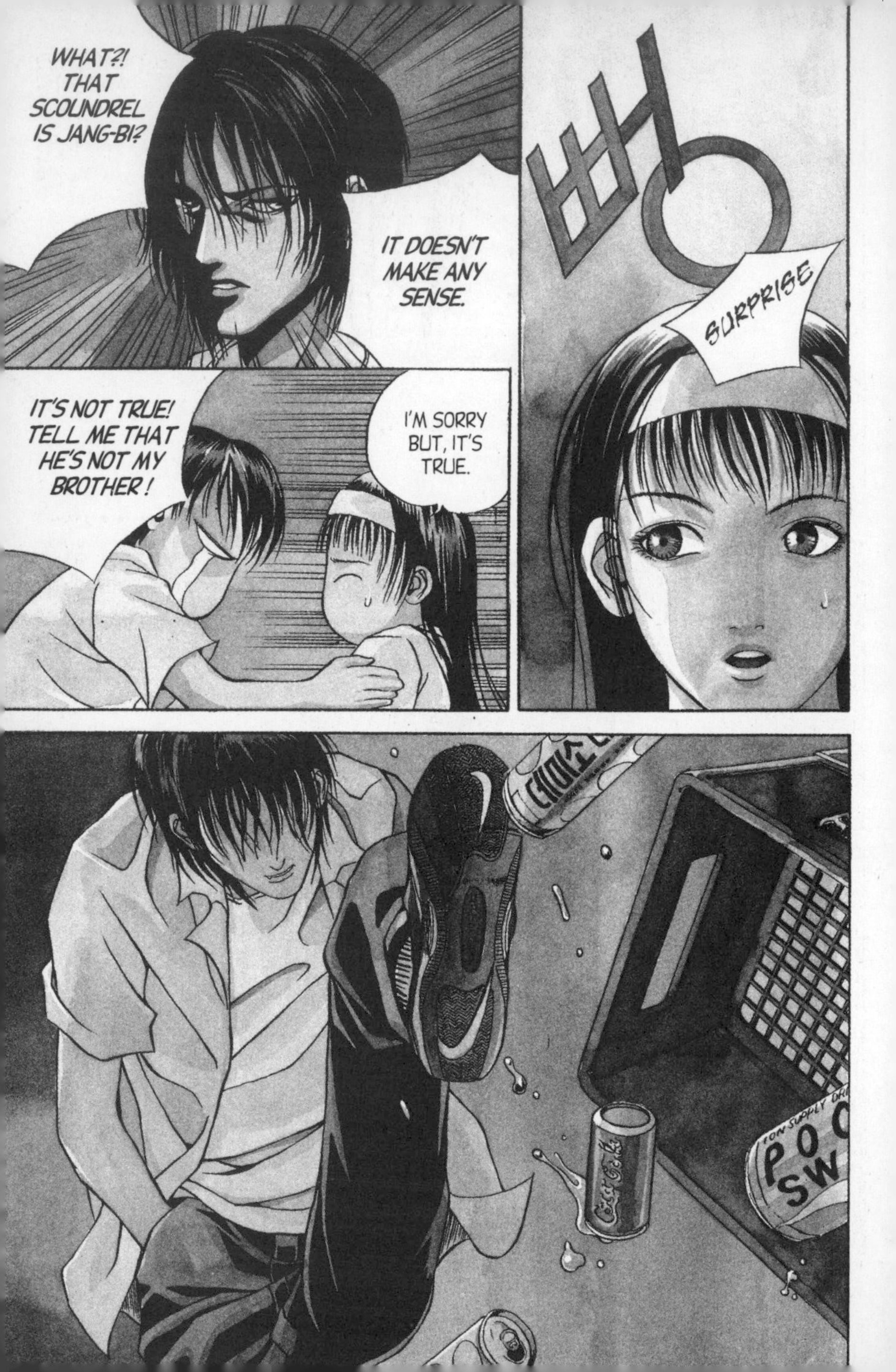
WHAT?! THAT SCOUNDREL IS JANG-BI?
IT DOESN'T MAKE ANY SENSE.
IT'S NOT TRUE! TELL ME THAT HE'S NOT MY BROTHER!
I'M SORRY BUT, IT'S TRUE.
SURPRISE

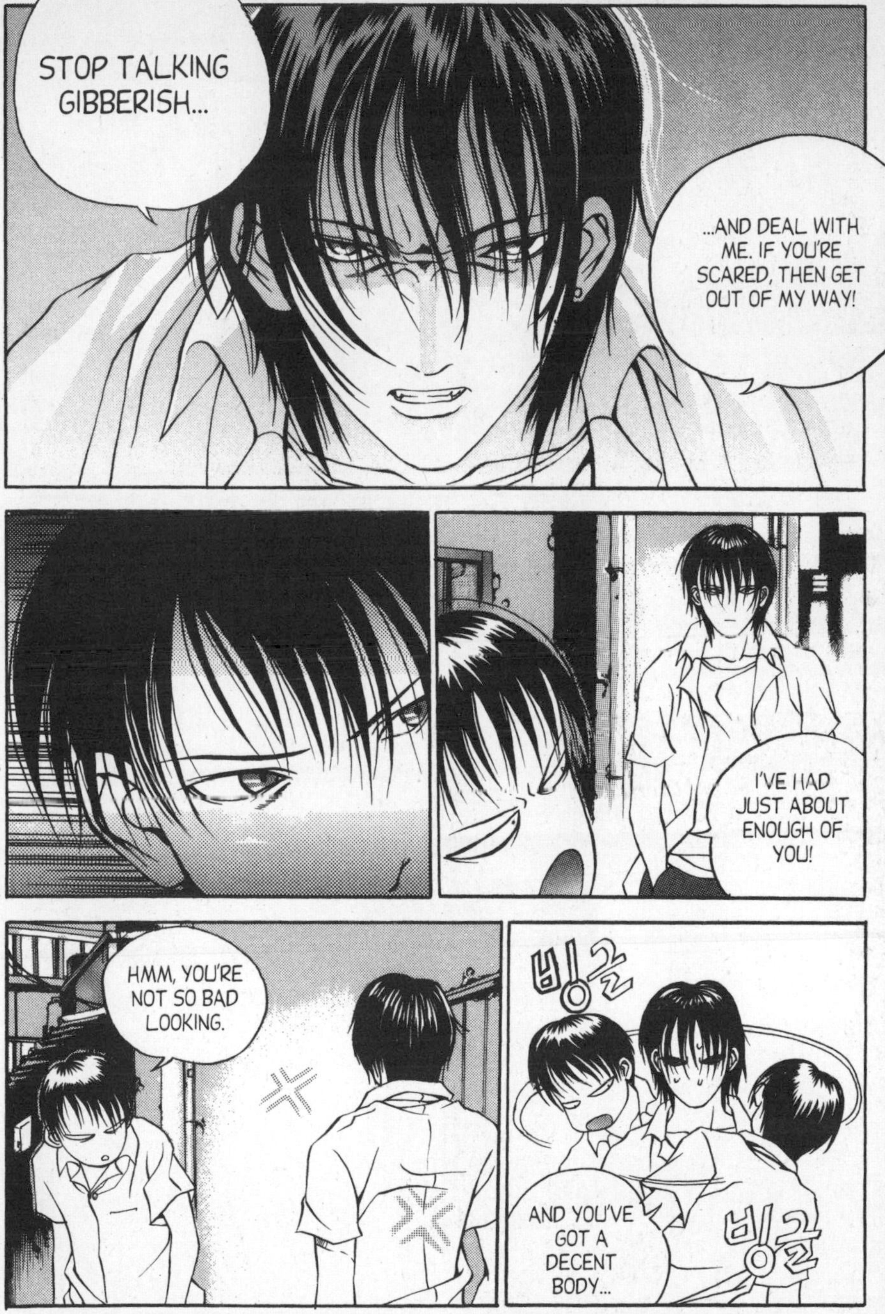
STOP TALKING GIBBERISH...
...AND DEAL WITH ME. IF YOU'RE SCARED, THEN GET OUT OF MY WAY!
I'VE HAD JUST ABOUT ENOUGH OF YOU!
HMM, YOU'RE NOT SO BAD LOOKING.
빙글
AND YOU'VE GOT A DECENT BODY...
빙글

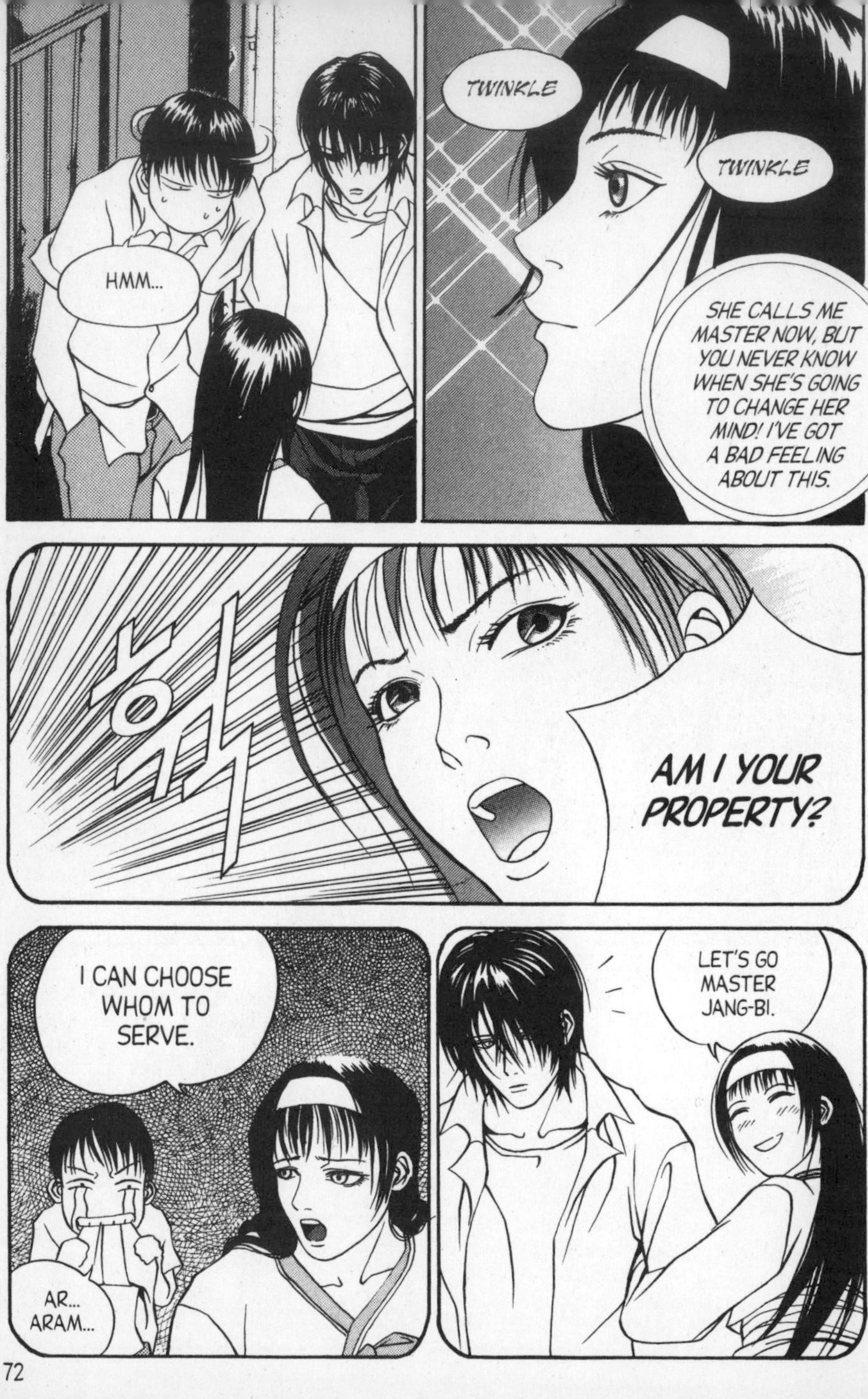
HMM...
TWINKLE
TWINKLE
SHE CALLS ME MASTER NOW, BUT YOU NEVER KNOW WHEN SHE'S GOING TO CHANGE HER MIND! I'VE GOT A BAD FEELING ABOUT THIS.
AM I YOUR PROPERTY?
I CAN CHOOSE WHOM TO SERVE.
AR... ARAM...
LET'S GO MASTER JANG-BI.

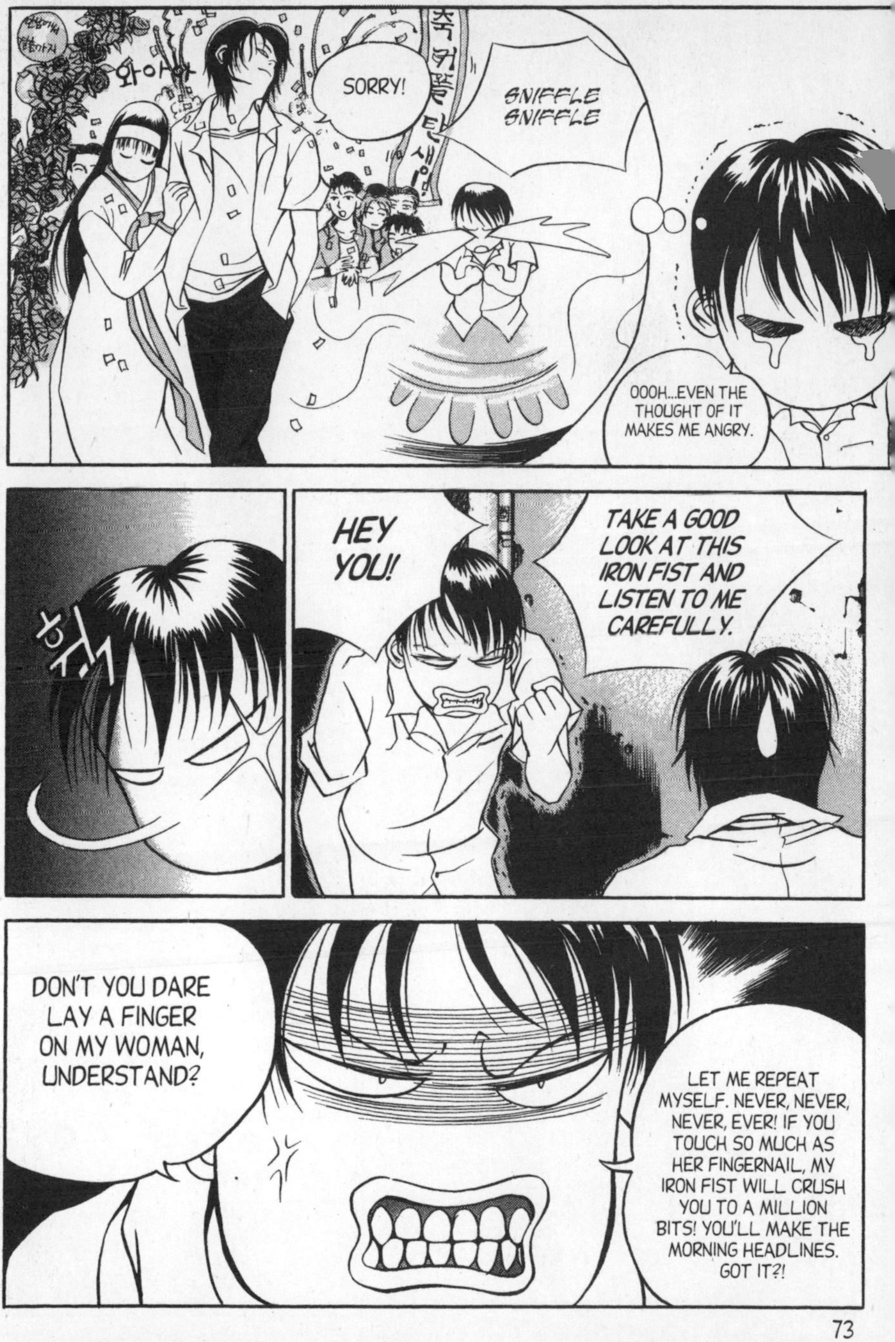
와아아
축커플탄생!
SORRY!
SNIFFLE SNIFFLE
OOOH...EVEN THE THOUGHT OF IT MAKES ME ANGRY.
HEY YOU!
TAKE A GOOD LOOK AT THIS IRON FIST AND LISTEN TO ME CAREFULLY.
DON'T YOU DARE LAY A FINGER ON MY WOMAN, UNDERSTAND?
LET ME REPEAT MYSELF. NEVER, NEVER, NEVER, EVER! IF YOU TOUCH SO MUCH AS HER FINGERNAIL, MY IRON FIST WILL CRUSH YOU TO A MILLION BITS! YOU'LL MAKE THE MORNING HEADLINES. GOT IT?!

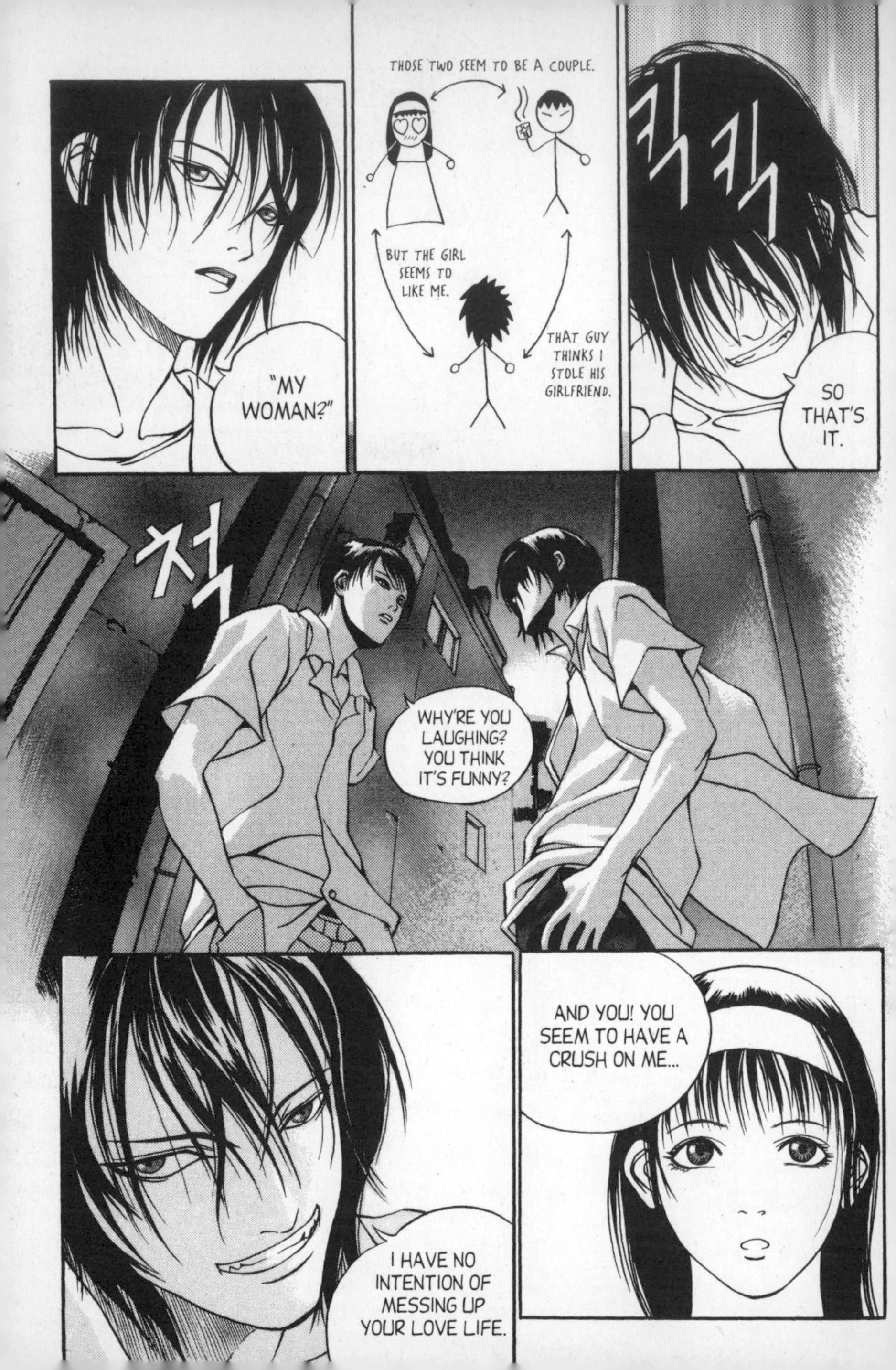
"MY WOMAN?"
THOSE TWO SEEM TO BE A COUPLE.
BUT THE GIRL SEEMS TO LIKE ME.
THAT GUY THINKS I STOLE HIS GIRLFRIEND.
SO THAT'S IT.
척
WHY'RE YOU LAUGHING? YOU THINK IT'S FUNNY?
I HAVE NO INTENTION OF MESSING UP YOUR LOVE LIFE.
AND YOU! YOU SEEM TO HAVE A CRUSH ON ME...

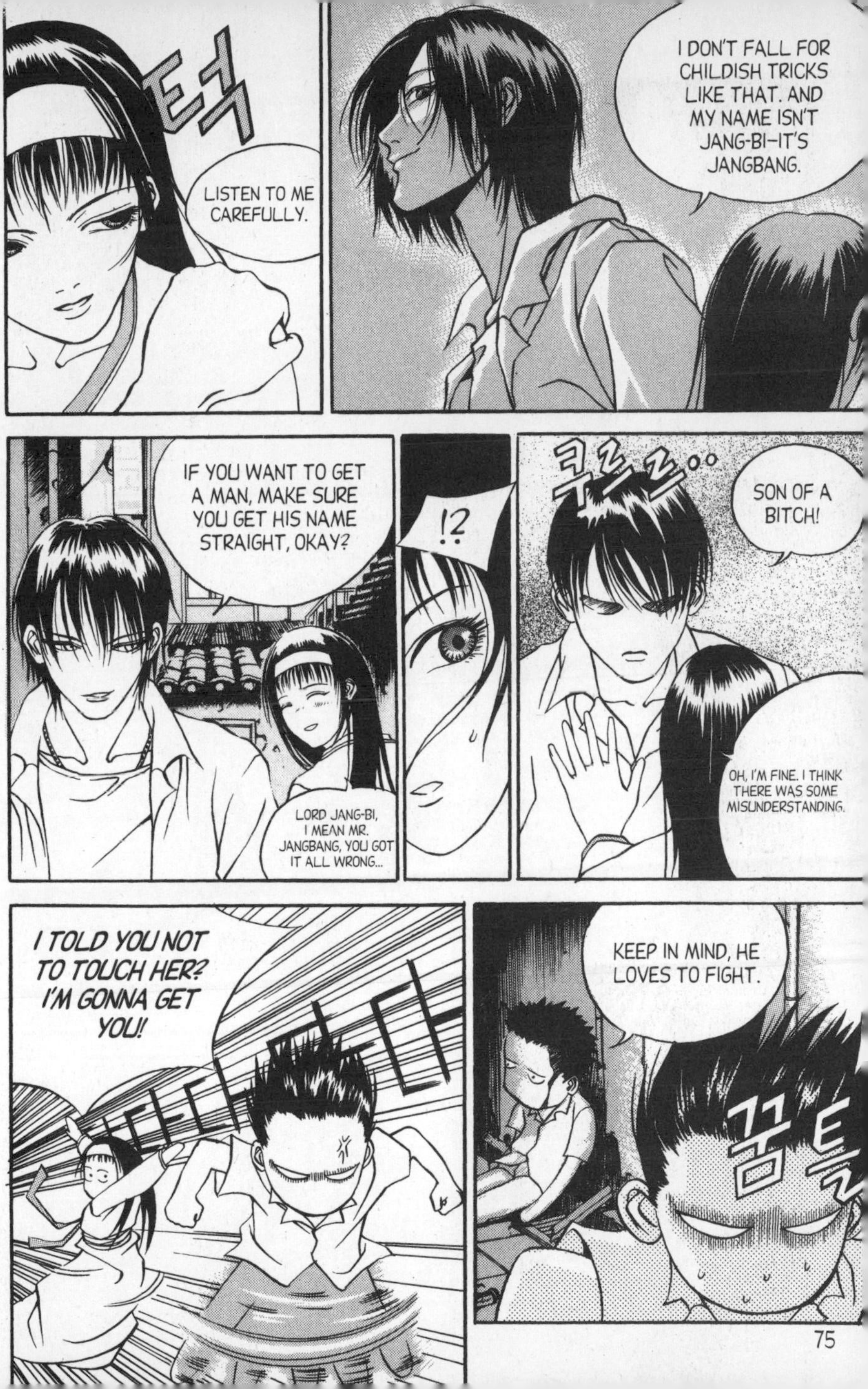
턱
LISTEN TO ME CAREFULLY.
I DON'T FALL FOR CHILDISH TRICKS LIKE THAT. AND MY NAME ISN'T JANG-BI—IT'S JANGBANG.
IF YOU WANT TO GET A MAN, MAKE SURE YOU GET HIS NAME STRAIGHT, OKAY?
LORD JANG-BI, I MEAN MR. JANGBANG, YOU GOT IT ALL WRONG...
!?
SON OF A BITCH!
OH, I'M FINE. I THINK THERE WAS SOME MISUNDERSTANDING.
I TOLD YOU NOT TO TOUCH HER? I'M GONNA GET YOU!
KEEP IN MIND, HE LOVES TO FIGHT.

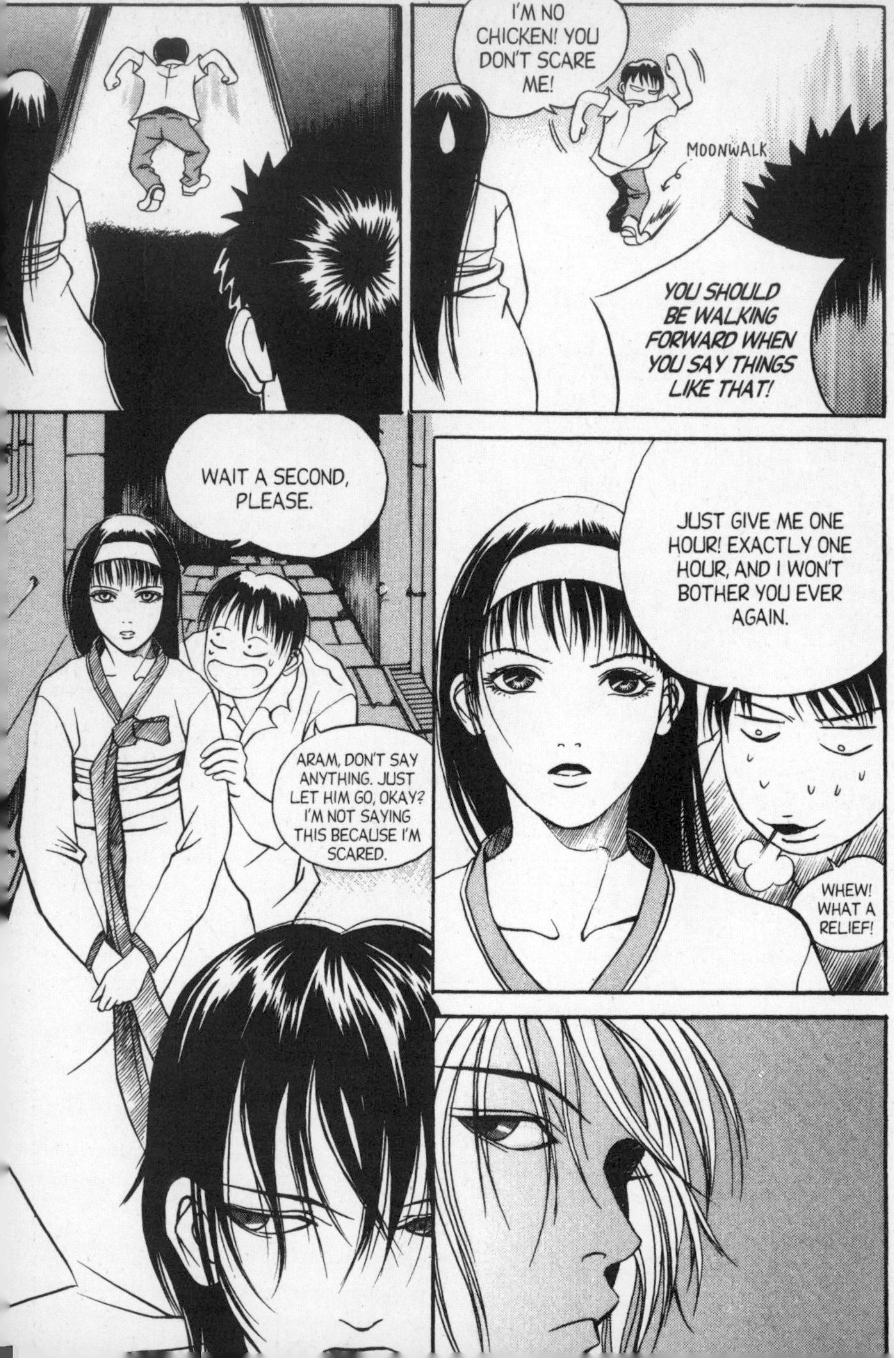
I'M NO CHICKEN! YOU DON'T SCARE ME!
MOONWALK
YOU SHOULD BE WALKING FORWARD WHEN YOU SAY THINGS LIKE THAT!
WAIT A SECOND, PLEASE.
ARAM, DON'T SAY ANYTHING. JUST LET HIM GO, OKAY? I'M NOT SAYING THIS BECAUSE I'M SCARED.
JUST GIVE ME ONE HOUR! EXACTLY ONE HOUR, AND I WON'T BOTHER YOU EVER AGAIN.
WHEW! WHAT A RELIEF!

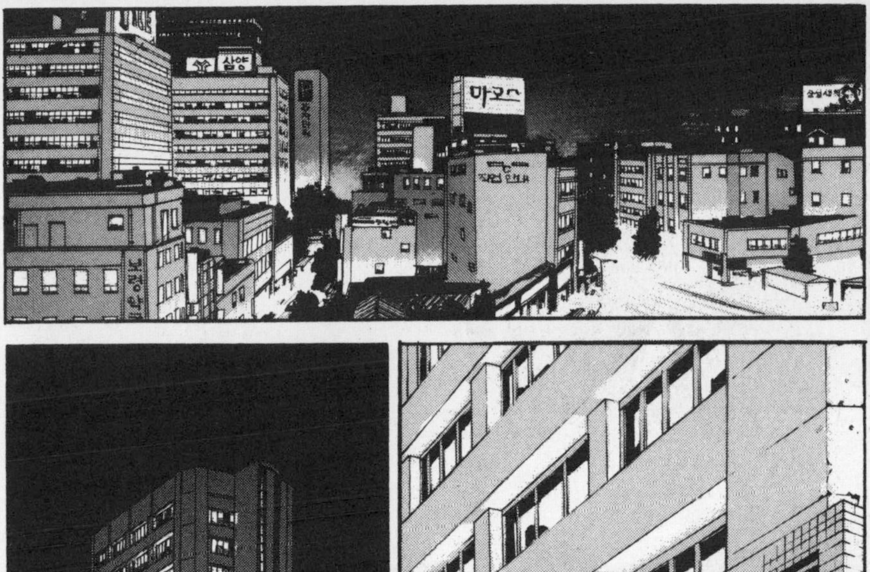
FLOTEX
WHERE ARE WE? WHY'D YOU BRING US HERE?

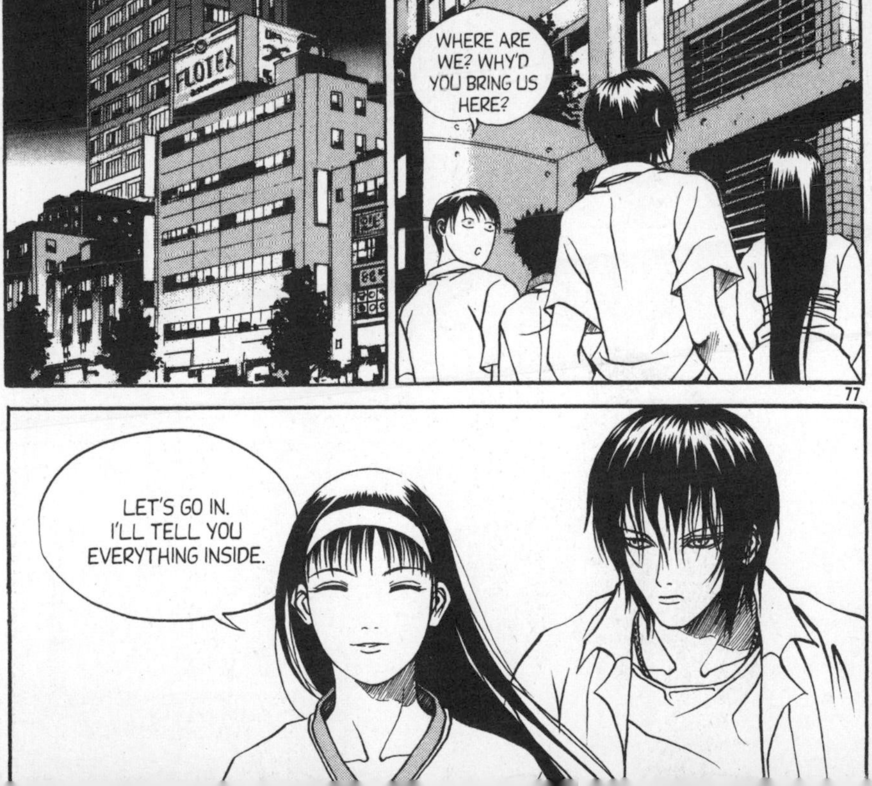
LET'S GO IN. I'LL TELL YOU EVERYTHING INSIDE.

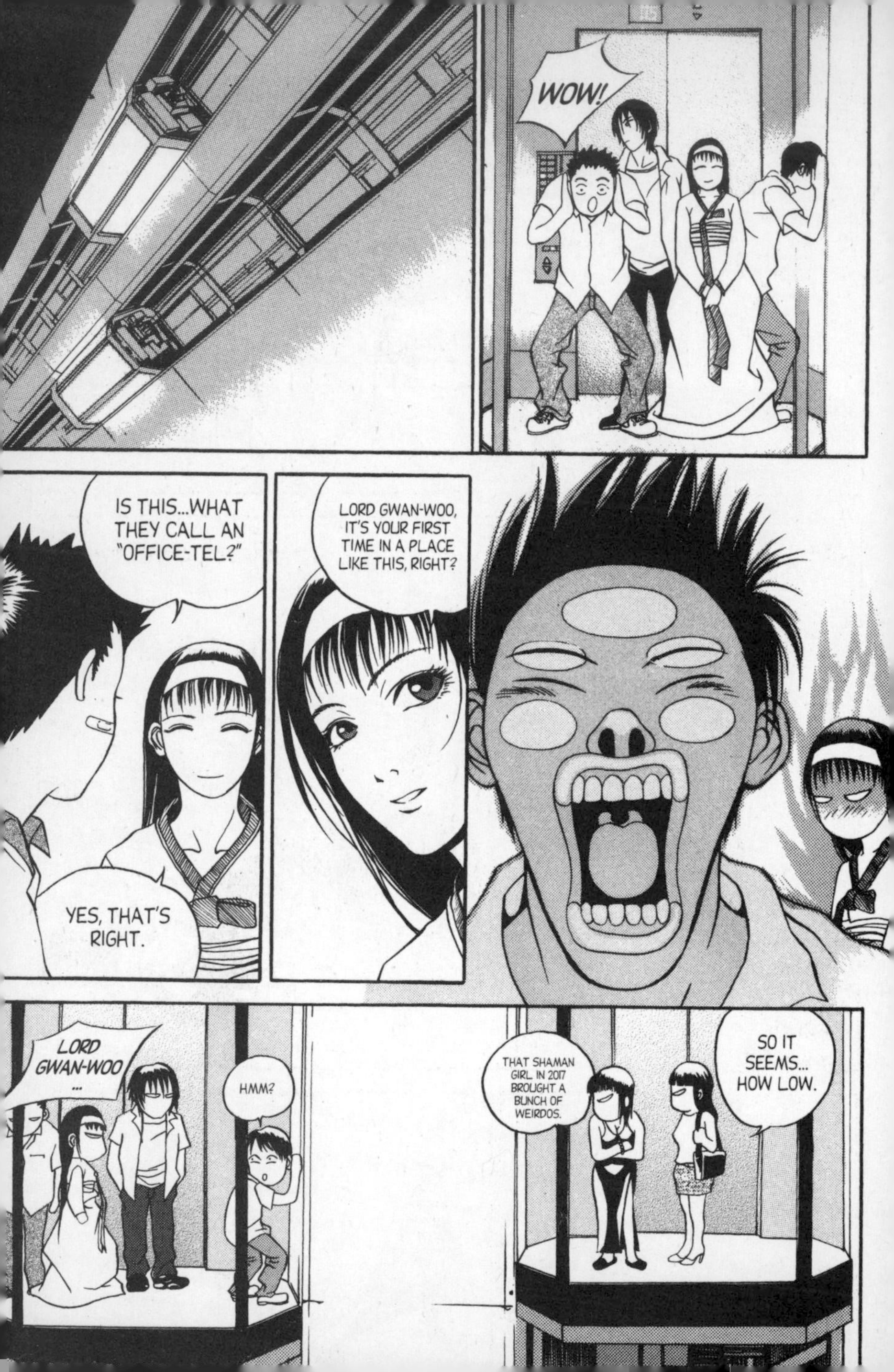
WOW!
IS THIS...WHAT THEY CALL AN "OFFICE-TEL?"
YES, THAT'S RIGHT.
LORD GWAN-WOO, IT'S YOUR FIRST TIME IN A PLACE LIKE THIS, RIGHT?
LORD GWAN-WOO ...
HMM?
THAT SHAMAN GIRL IN 2017 BROUGHT A BUNCH OF WEIRDOS.
SO IT SEEMS... HOW LOW.

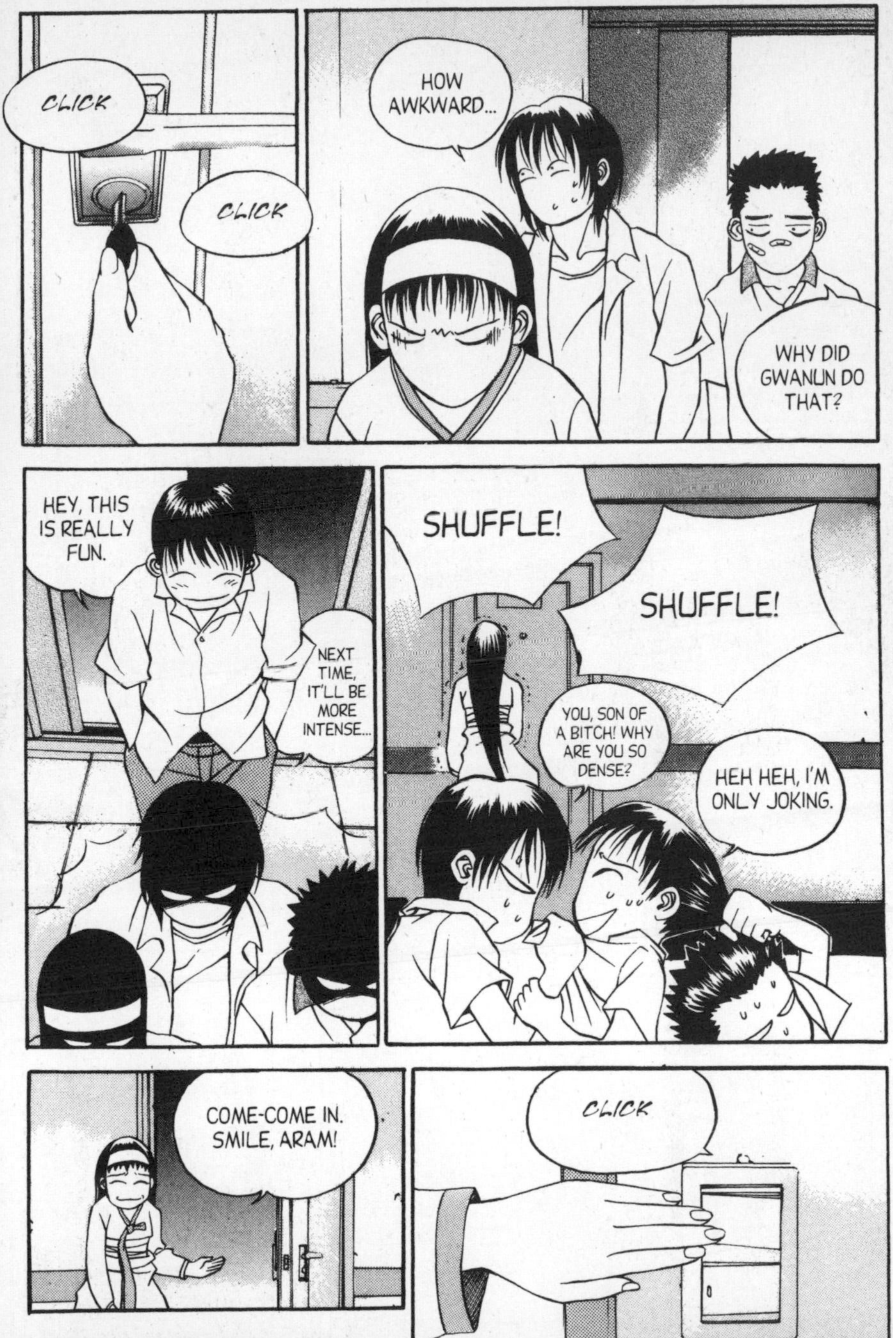
CLICK
CLICK
HOW AWKWARD...
WHY DID GWANUN DO THAT?
HEY, THIS IS REALLY FUN.
NEXT TIME, IT'LL BE MORE INTENSE...
SHUFFLE!
SHUFFLE!
YOU, SON OF A BITCH! WHY ARE YOU SO DENSE?
HEH HEH, I'M ONLY JOKING.
COME-COME IN. SMILE, ARAM!
CLICK

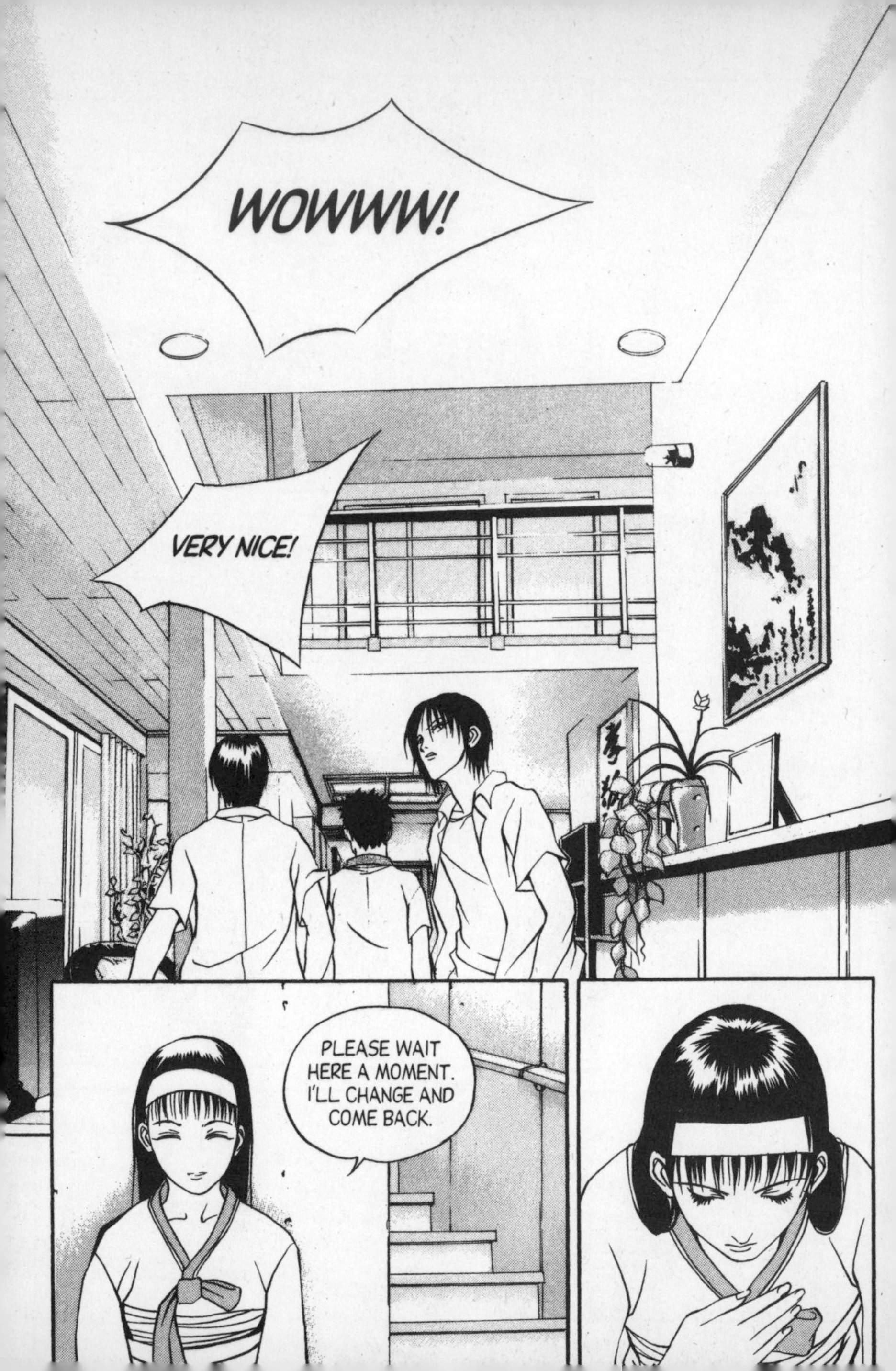
WOWWW!
VERY NICE!
PLEASE WAIT HERE A MOMENT. I'LL CHANGE AND COME BACK.

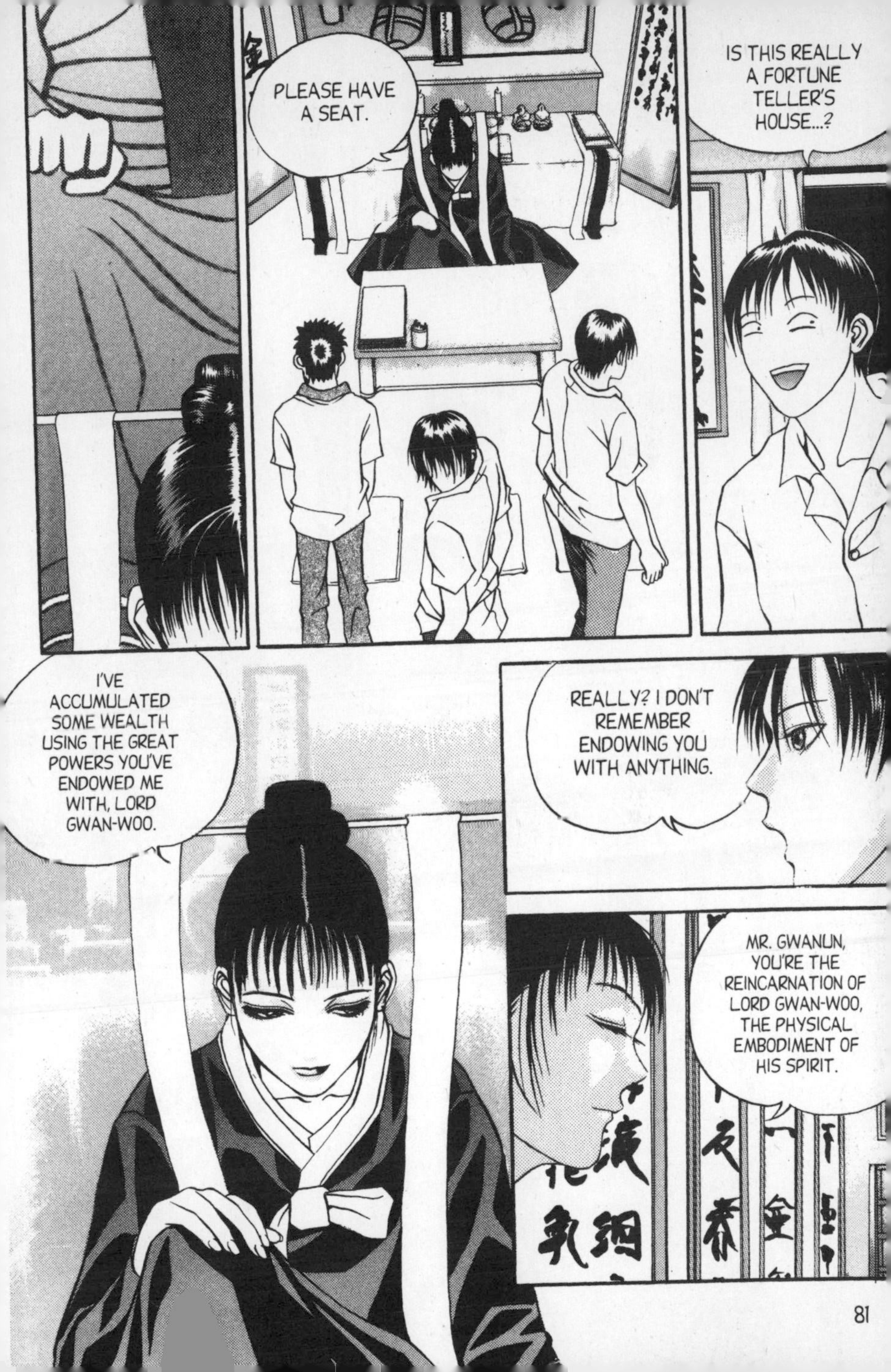
PLEASE HAVE A SEAT.
IS THIS REALLY A FORTUNE TELLER'S HOUSE...?
I'VE ACCUMULATED SOME WEALTH USING THE GREAT POWERS YOU'VE ENDOWED ME WITH, LORD GWAN-WOO.
REALLY? I DON'T REMEMBER ENDOWING YOU WITH ANYTHING.
MR. GWANUN, YOU'RE THE REINCARNATION OF LORD GWAN-WOO, THE PHYSICAL EMBODIMENT OF HIS SPIRIT.

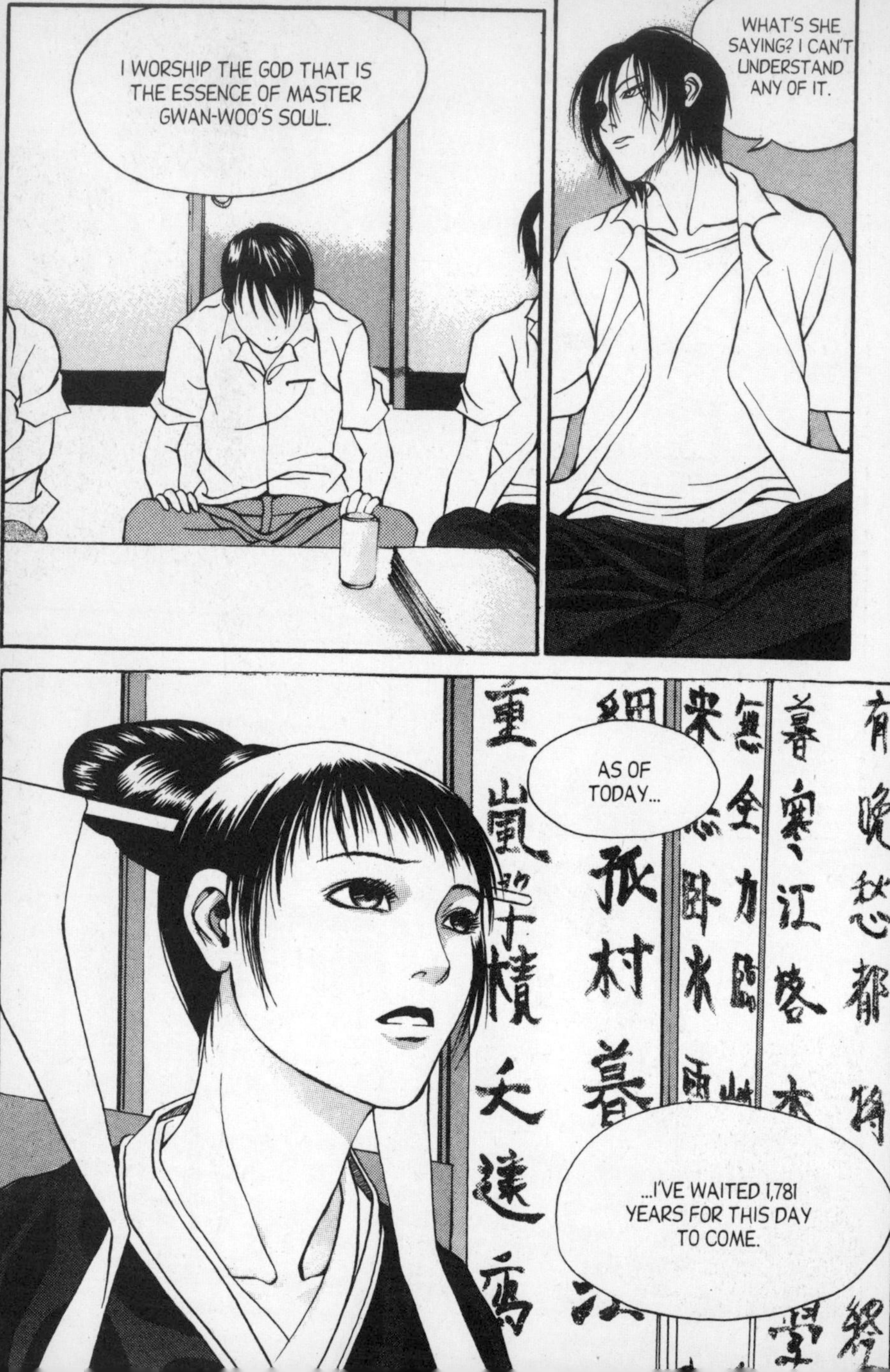
I WORSHIP THE GOD THAT IS THE ESSENCE OF MASTER GWAN-WOO'S SOUL.
WHAT'S SHE SAYING? I CAN'T UNDERSTAND ANY OF IT.
AS OF TODAY...
...I'VE WAITED 1,781 YEARS FOR THIS DAY TO COME.

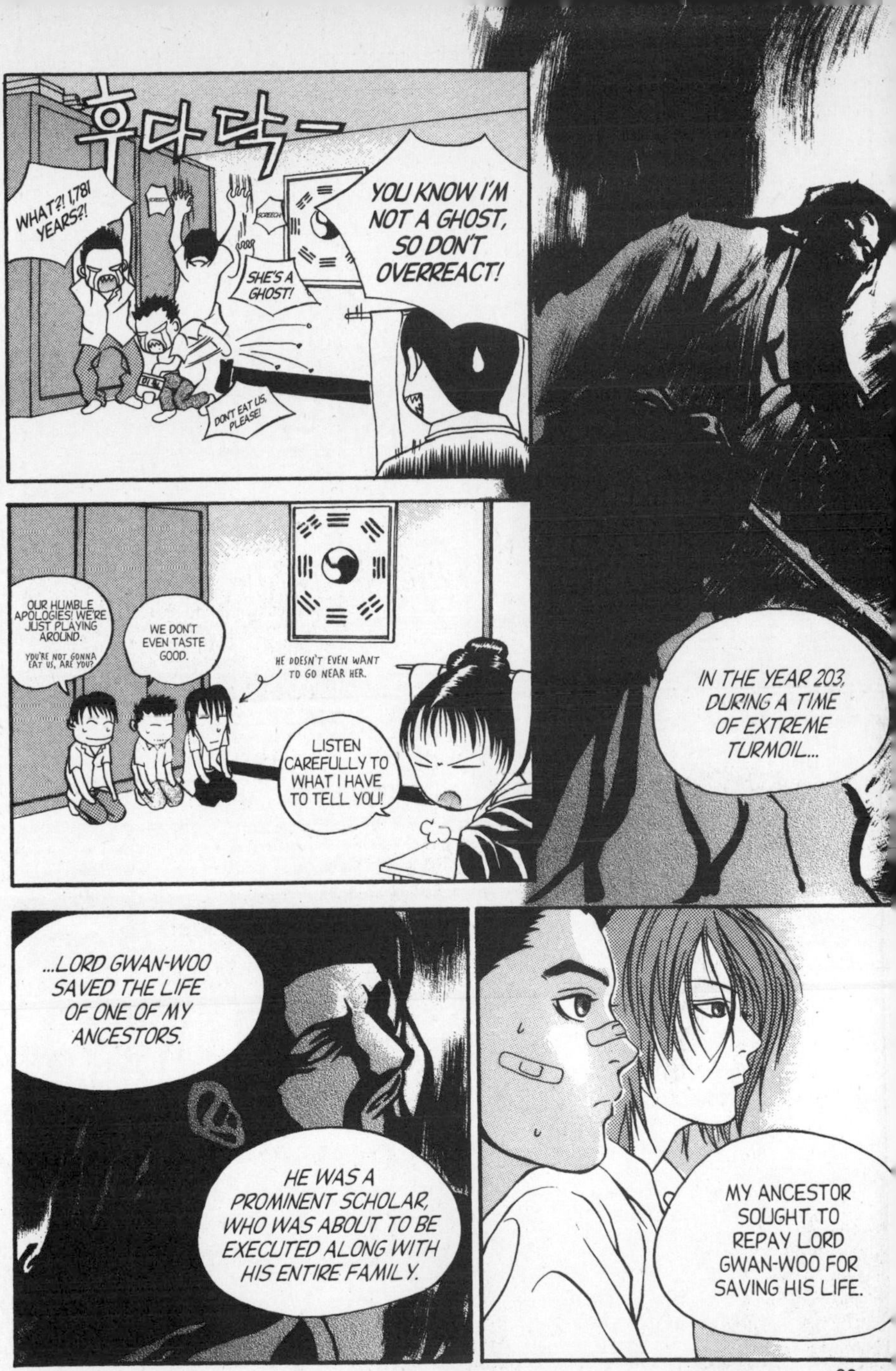

후다닥—
WHAT?! 1,781 YEARS?!
SCREECH
SCREECH
SHE'S A GHOST!
DON'T EAT US, PLEASE!
YOU KNOW I'M NOT A GHOST, SO DON'T OVERREACT!
OUR HUMBLE APOLOGIES! WE'RE JUST PLAYING AROUND.
YOU'RE NOT GONNA EAT US, ARE YOU?
WE DON'T EVEN TASTE GOOD.
HE DOESN'T EVEN WANT TO GO NEAR HER.
LISTEN CAREFULLY TO WHAT I HAVE TO TELL YOU!
IN THE YEAR 203, DURING A TIME OF EXTREME TURMOIL...
...LORD GWAN-WOO SAVED THE LIFE OF ONE OF MY ANCESTORS.
HE WAS A PROMINENT SCHOLAR, WHO WAS ABOUT TO BE EXECUTED ALONG WITH HIS ENTIRE FAMILY.
MY ANCESTOR SOUGHT TO REPAY LORD GWAN-WOO FOR SAVING HIS LIFE.

BUT ACCORDING TO THE SPIRIT WORLD, THERE WAS NO WAY TO SERVE LORD GWAN-WOO DURING HIS LIFETIME.

A SON MAY CONTINUE THE FAMILY LINE, BUT A DAUGHTER MUST BE RAISED AS A SHAMAN...

...SO SHE CAN SERVE LORD GWAN-WOO IN HIS REINCARNATED FORM.

HOW...?

IT'S BECAUSE ONLY A SHAMAN CAN RECOGNIZE LORD GWAN-WOO'S REINCARNATED FORM.

WITH MUCH REGRET, MY ANCESTOR LEFT INSTRUCTIONS FOR FUTURE GENERATIONS.

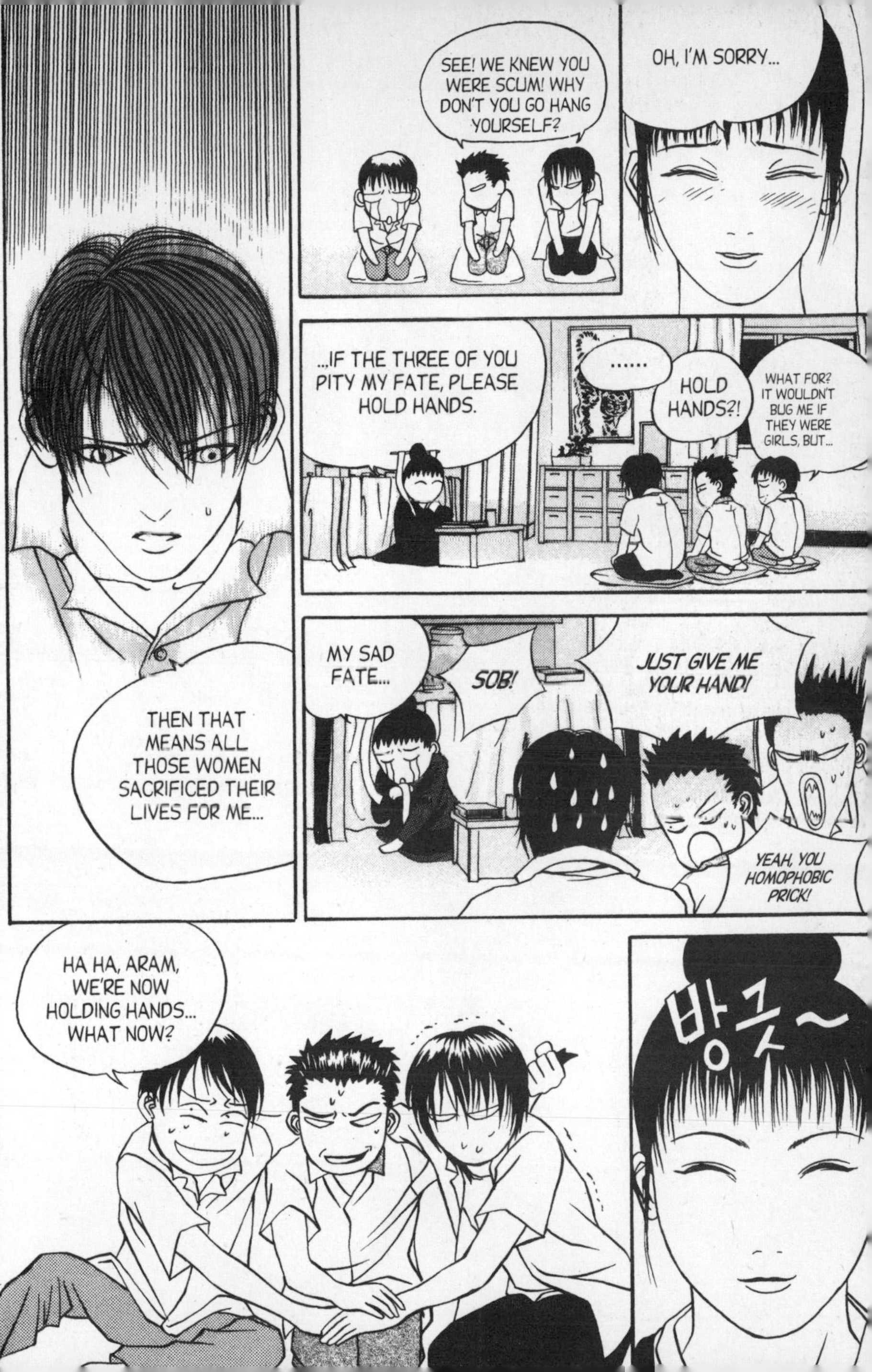
THEN THAT MEANS ALL THOSE WOMEN SACRIFICED THEIR LIVES FOR ME...
SEE! WE KNEW YOU WERE SCUM! WHY DON'T YOU GO HANG YOURSELF?
OH, I'M SORRY...
...IF THE THREE OF YOU PITY MY FATE, PLEASE HOLD HANDS.
......
HOLD HANDS?!
WHAT FOR? IT WOULDN'T BUG ME IF THEY WERE GIRLS, BUT...
MY SAD FATE...
SOB!
JUST GIVE ME YOUR HAND!
YEAH, YOU HOMOPHOBIC PRICK!
HA HA, ARAM, WE'RE NOW HOLDING HANDS... WHAT NOW?
방긋~

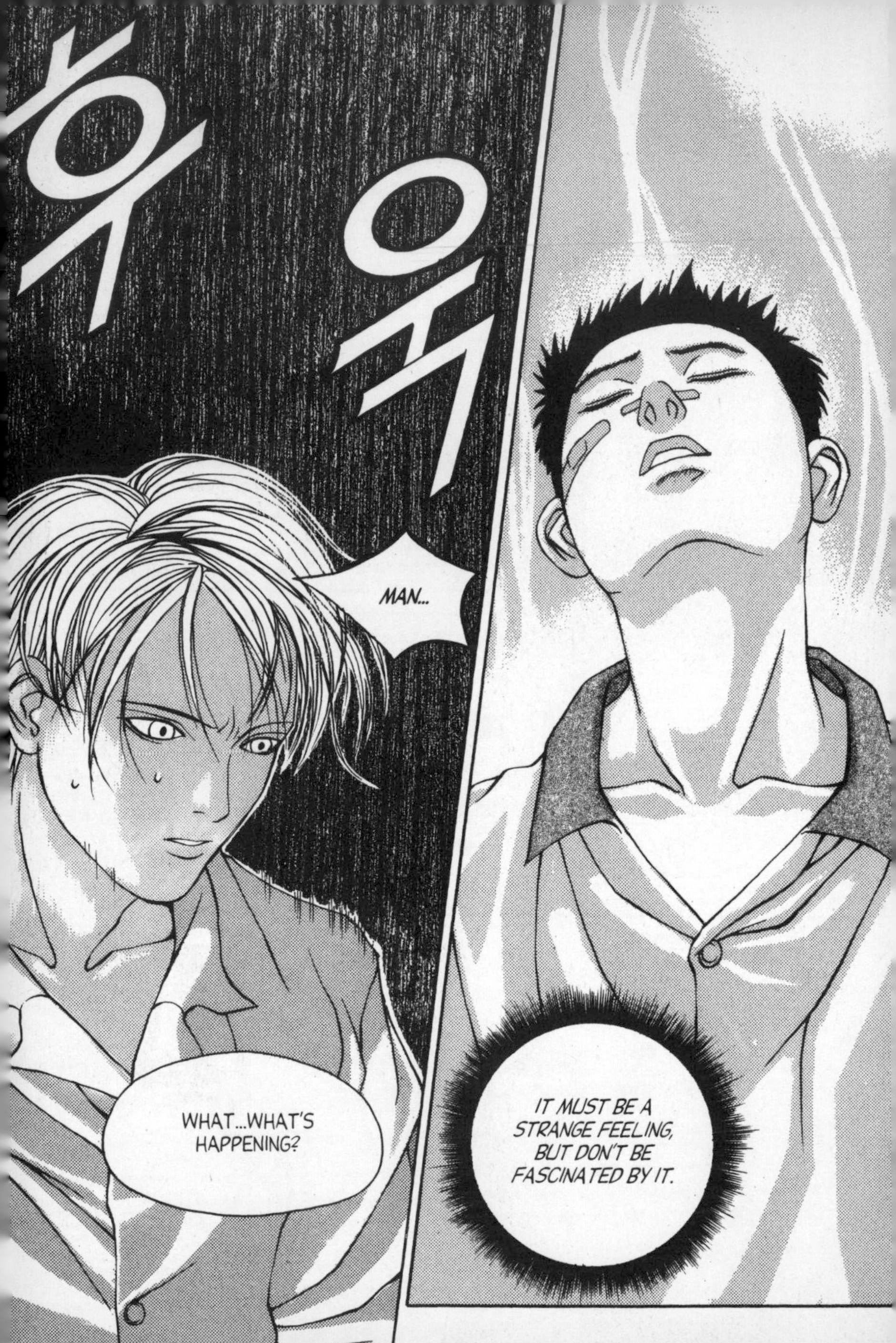
MAN...
WHAT...WHAT'S HAPPENING?
IT MUST BE A STRANGE FEELING, BUT DON'T BE FASCINATED BY IT.

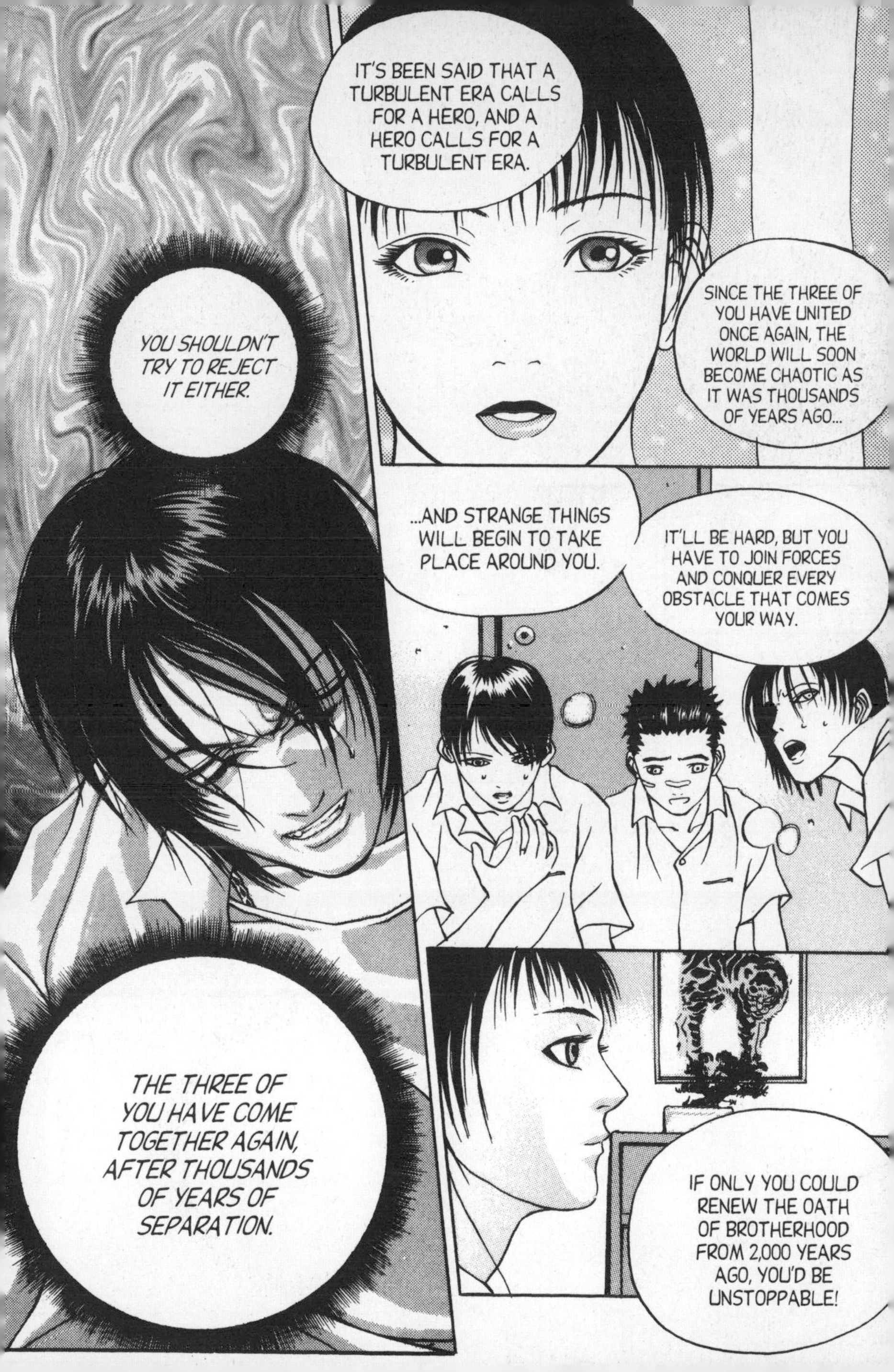
YOU SHOULDN'T TRY TO REJECT IT EITHER.
THE THREE OF YOU HAVE COME TOGETHER AGAIN, AFTER THOUSANDS OF YEARS OF SEPARATION.
IT'S BEEN SAID THAT A TURBULENT ERA CALLS FOR A HERO, AND A HERO CALLS FOR A TURBULENT ERA.
SINCE THE THREE OF YOU HAVE UNITED ONCE AGAIN, THE WORLD WILL SOON BECOME CHAOTIC AS IT WAS THOUSANDS OF YEARS AGO...
...AND STRANGE THINGS WILL BEGIN TO TAKE PLACE AROUND YOU.
IT'LL BE HARD, BUT YOU HAVE TO JOIN FORCES AND CONQUER EVERY OBSTACLE THAT COMES YOUR WAY.
IF ONLY YOU COULD RENEW THE OATH OF BROTHERHOOD FROM 2,000 YEARS AGO, YOU'D BE UNSTOPPABLE!

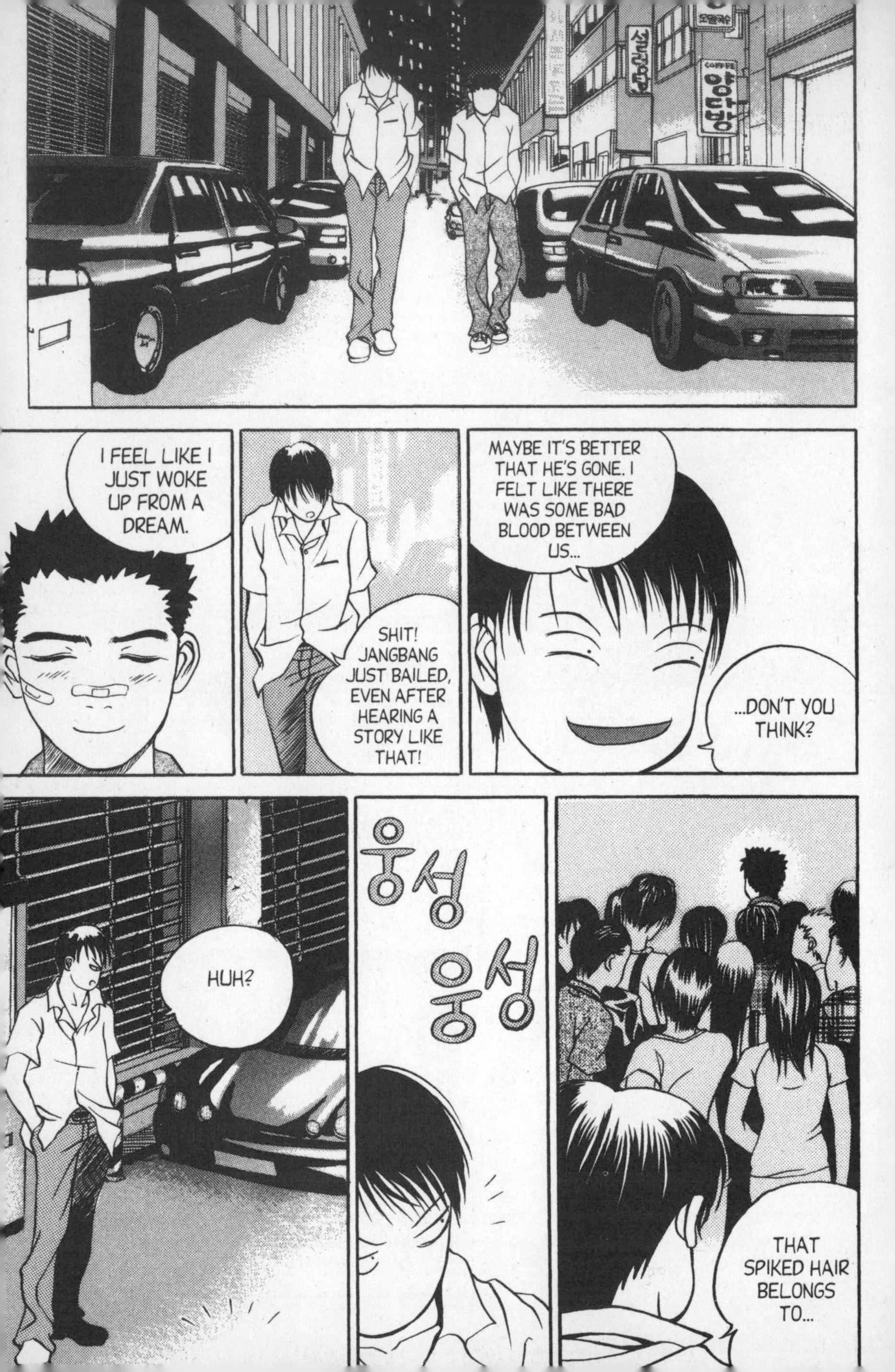
COFFEE
양다방
I FEEL LIKE I JUST WOKE UP FROM A DREAM.
SHIT! JANGBANG JUST BAILED, EVEN AFTER HEARING A STORY LIKE THAT!
MAYBE IT'S BETTER THAT HE'S GONE. I FELT LIKE THERE WAS SOME BAD BLOOD BETWEEN US...
...DON'T YOU THINK?
HUH?
웅성 웅성
THAT SPIKED HAIR BELONGS TO...

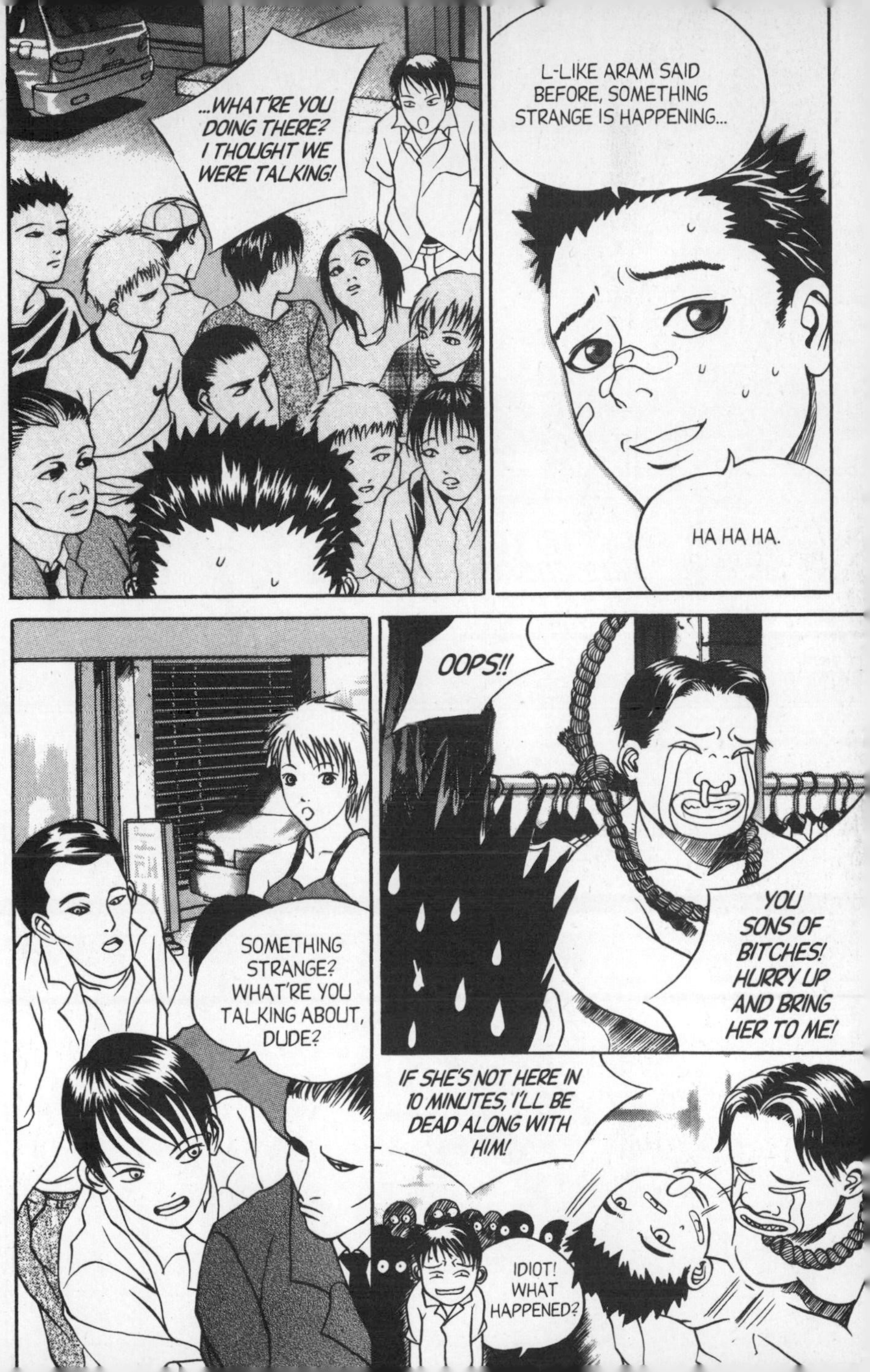
...WHAT'RE YOU DOING THERE? I THOUGHT WE WERE TALKING!
L-LIKE ARAM SAID BEFORE, SOMETHING STRANGE IS HAPPENING...
HA HA HA.
SOMETHING STRANGE? WHAT'RE YOU TALKING ABOUT, DUDE?
OOPS!!
YOU SONS OF BITCHES! HURRY UP AND BRING HER TO ME!
IF SHE'S NOT HERE IN 10 MINUTES, I'LL BE DEAD ALONG WITH HIM!
IDIOT! WHAT HAPPENED?

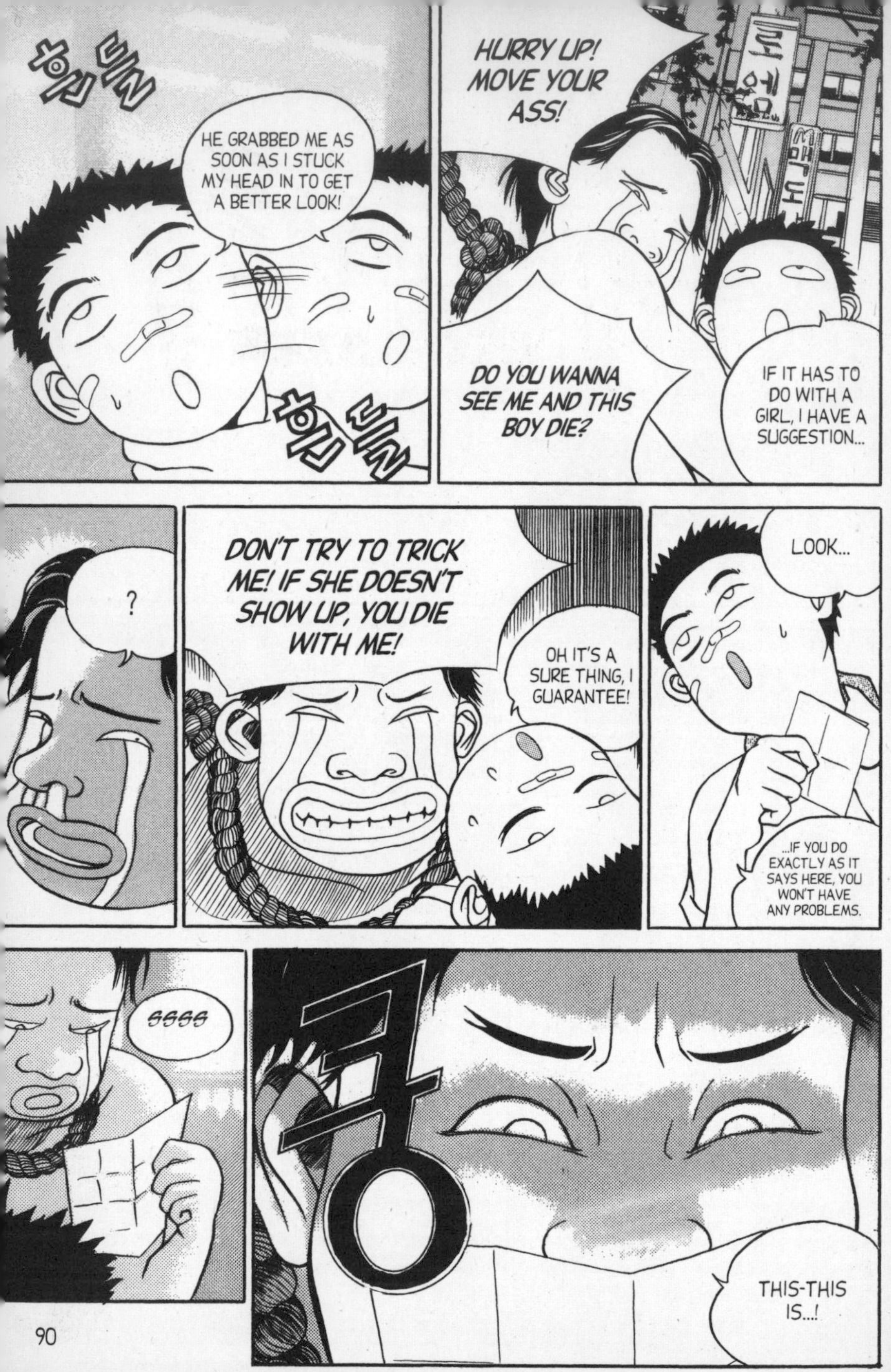
HE GRABBED ME AS SOON AS I STUCK MY HEAD IN TO GET A BETTER LOOK!
HURRY UP! MOVE YOUR ASS!
DO YOU WANNA SEE ME AND THIS BOY DIE?
IF IT HAS TO DO WITH A GIRL, I HAVE A SUGGESTION...
?
DON'T TRY TO TRICK ME! IF SHE DOESN'T SHOW UP, YOU DIE WITH ME!
OH IT'S A SURE THING, I GUARANTEE!
LOOK...
...IF YOU DO EXACTLY AS IT SAYS HERE, YOU WON'T HAVE ANY PROBLEMS.
SSSS
THIS-THIS IS...!

이터니티

ETERNITY

#4 A NEMESIS APPEARS

ETERNITY

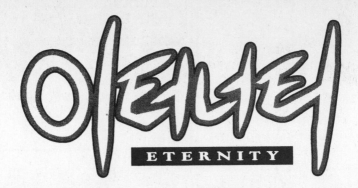

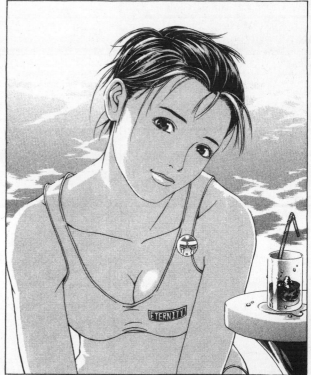

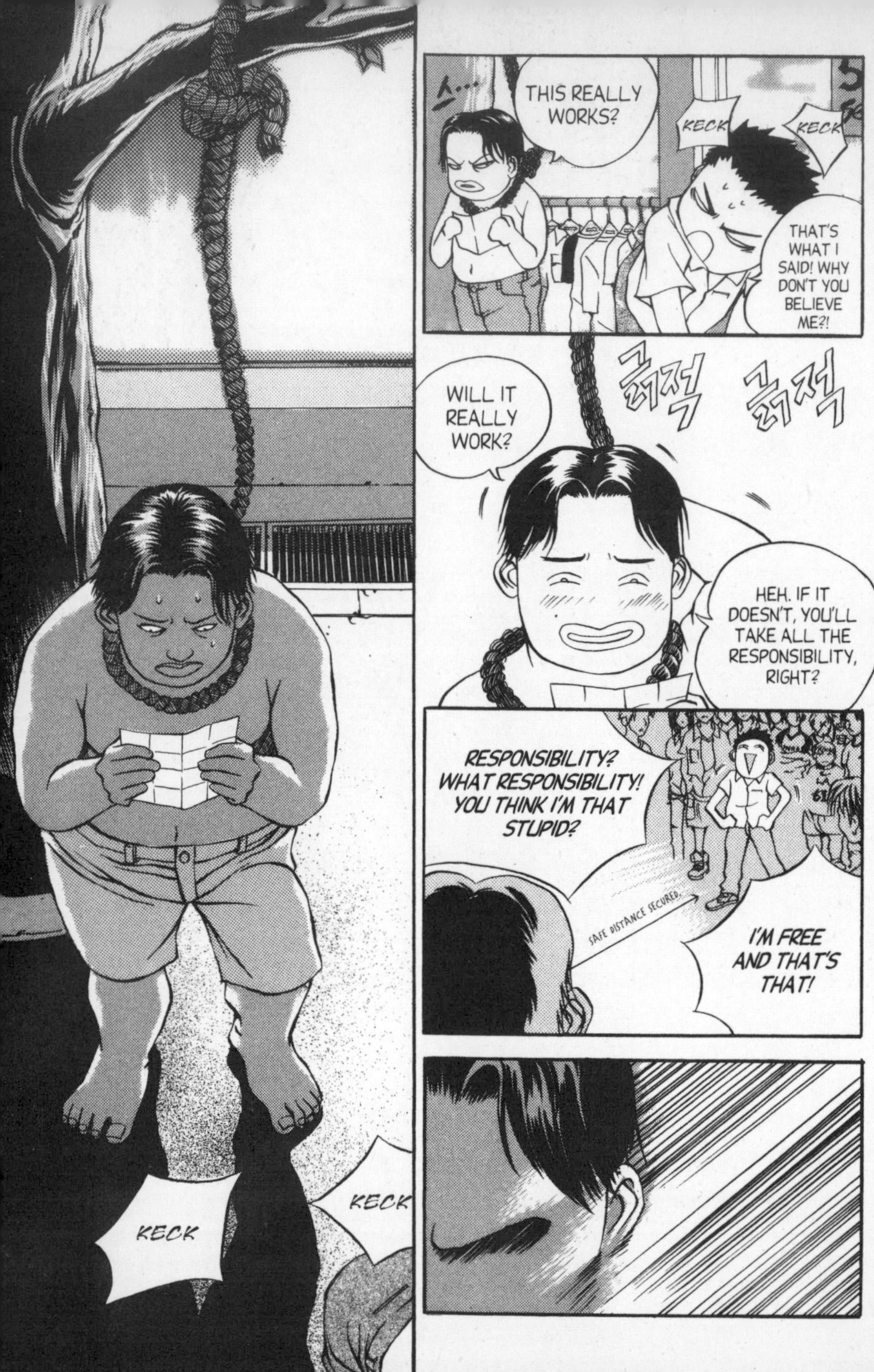
KECK
KECK
스...
THIS REALLY WORKS?
KECK
KECK
THAT'S WHAT I SAID! WHY DON'T YOU BELIEVE ME?!
WILL IT REALLY WORK?
긁적
긁적
HEH. IF IT DOESN'T, YOU'LL TAKE ALL THE RESPONSIBILITY, RIGHT?
RESPONSIBILITY? WHAT RESPONSIBILITY! YOU THINK I'M THAT STUPID?
SAFE DISTANCE SECURED.
I'M FREE AND THAT'S THAT!

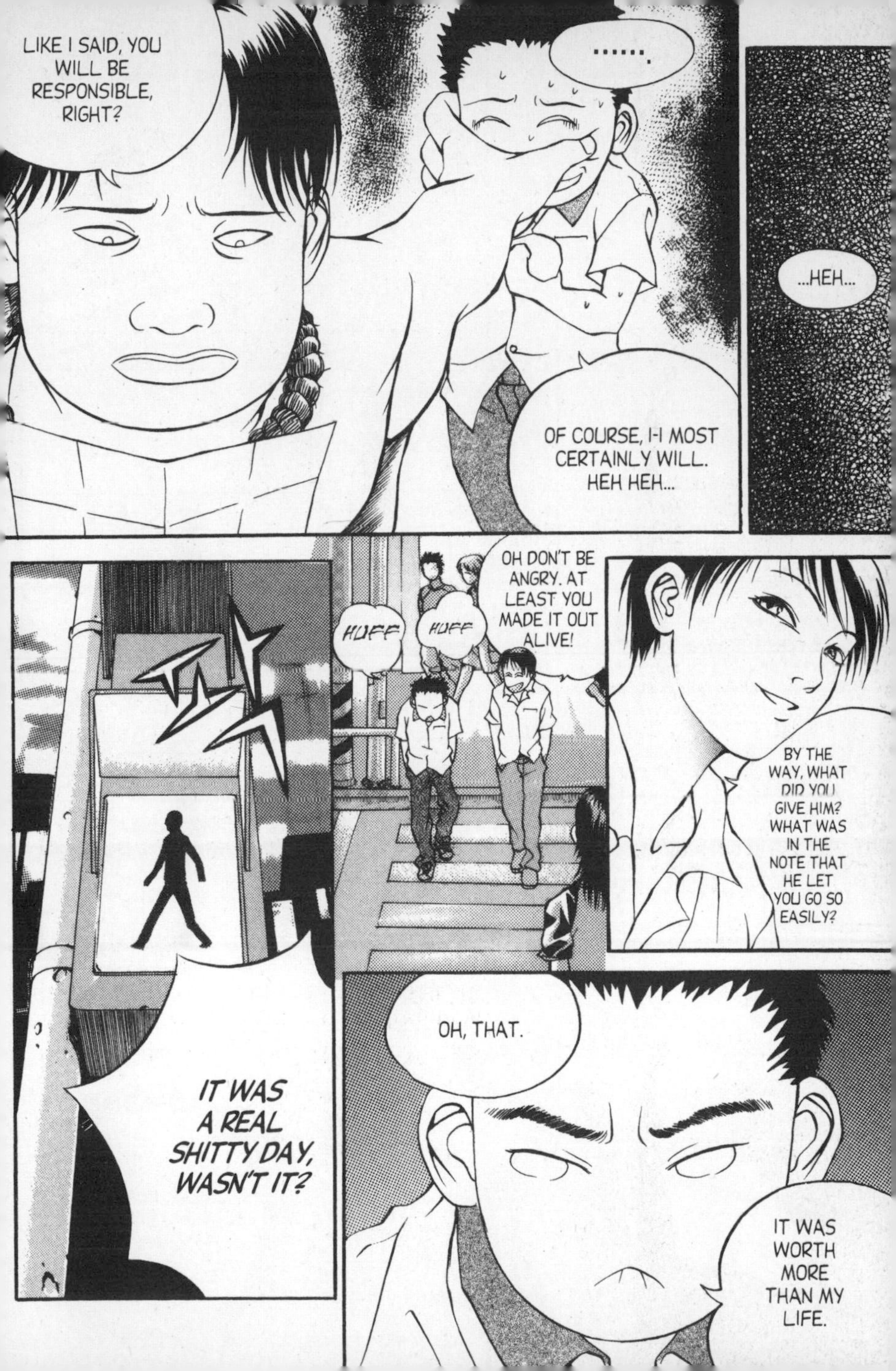
LIKE I SAID, YOU WILL BE RESPONSIBLE, RIGHT?
......
OF COURSE, I-I MOST CERTAINLY WILL. HEH HEH...
...HEH...
IT WAS A REAL SHITTY DAY, WASN'T IT?
HUFF
HUFF
OH DON'T BE ANGRY. AT LEAST YOU MADE IT OUT ALIVE!
BY THE WAY, WHAT DID YOU GIVE HIM? WHAT WAS IN THE NOTE THAT HE LET YOU GO SO EASILY?
OH, THAT.
IT WAS WORTH MORE THAN MY LIFE.

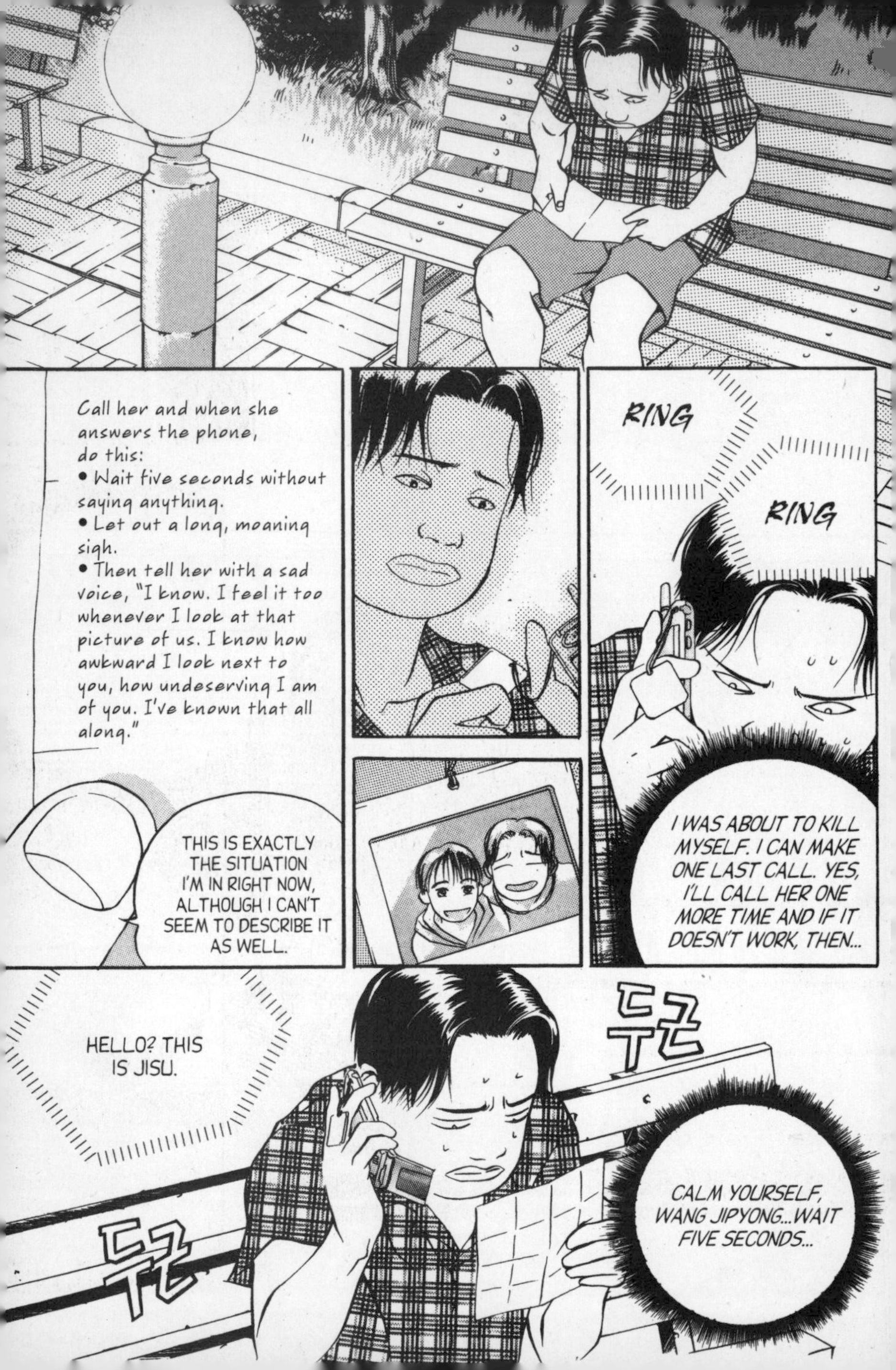
Call her and when she answers the phone, do this:
• Wait five seconds without saying anything.
• Let out a long, moaning sigh.
• Then tell her with a sad voice, "I know. I feel it too whenever I look at that picture of us. I know how awkward I look next to you, how undeserving I am of you. I've known that all along."
THIS IS EXACTLY THE SITUATION I'M IN RIGHT NOW, ALTHOUGH I CAN'T SEEM TO DESCRIBE IT AS WELL.
RING
RING
I WAS ABOUT TO KILL MYSELF. I CAN MAKE ONE LAST CALL. YES, I'LL CALL HER ONE MORE TIME AND IF IT DOESN'T WORK, THEN...
HELLO? THIS IS JISU.
CALM YOURSELF, WANG JIPYONG...WAIT FIVE SECONDS...

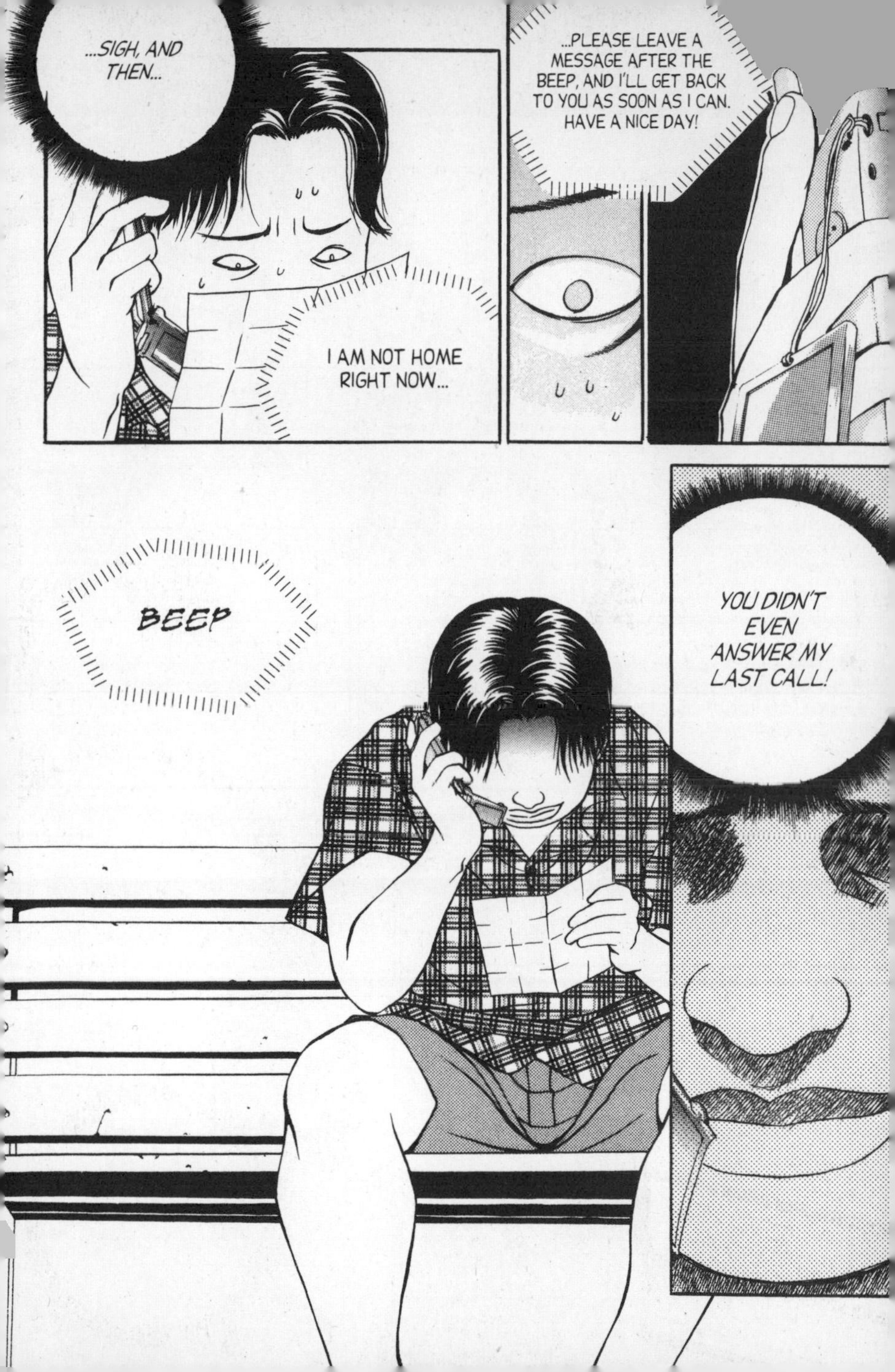
...SIGH, AND THEN...
I AM NOT HOME RIGHT NOW...
...PLEASE LEAVE A MESSAGE AFTER THE BEEP, AND I'LL GET BACK TO YOU AS SOON AS I CAN. HAVE A NICE DAY!
BEEP
YOU DIDN'T EVEN ANSWER MY LAST CALL!

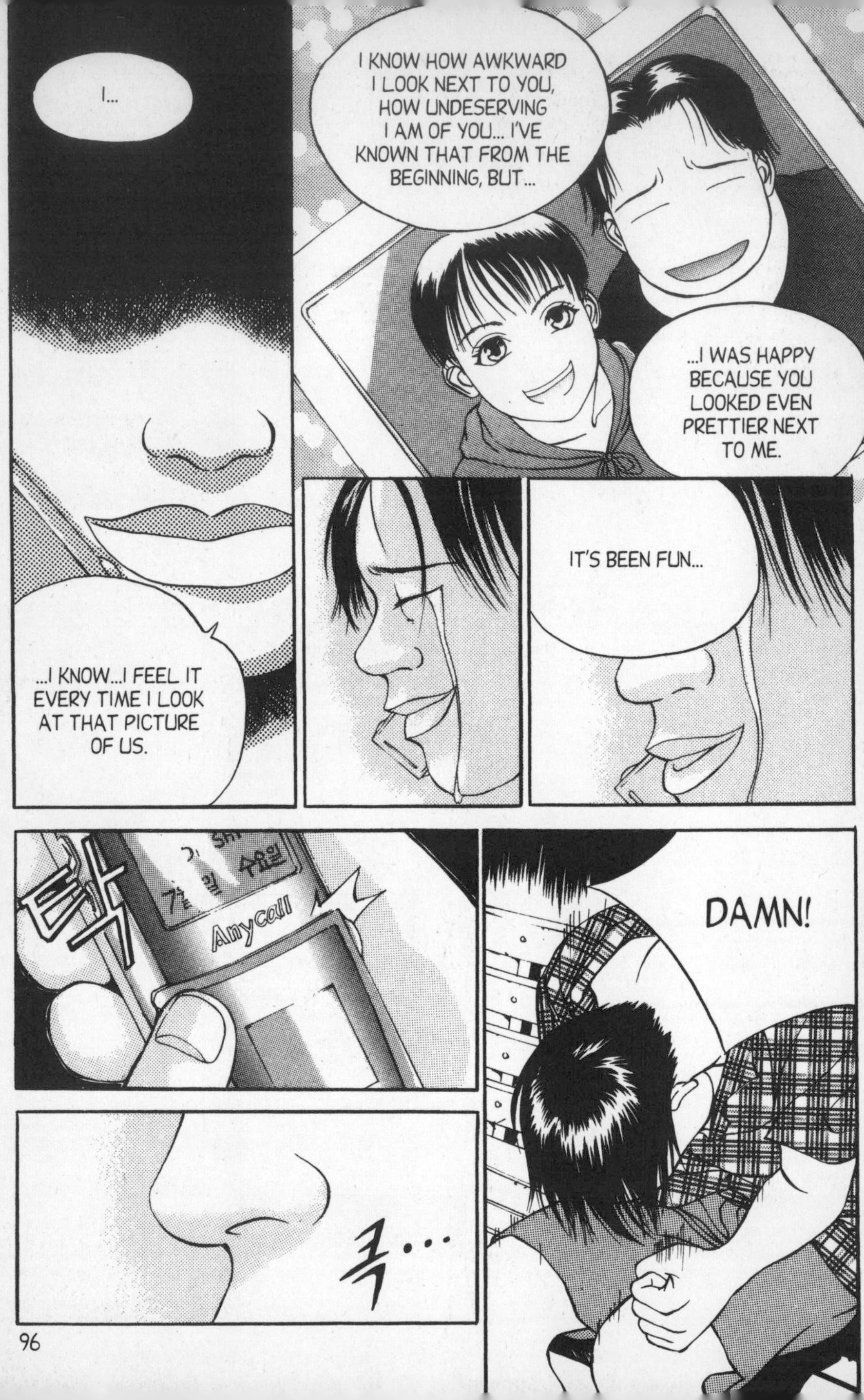
I...
...I KNOW...I FEEL IT EVERY TIME I LOOK AT THAT PICTURE OF US.
I KNOW HOW AWKWARD I LOOK NEXT TO YOU, HOW UNDESERVING I AM OF YOU... I'VE KNOWN THAT FROM THE BEGINNING, BUT...
...I WAS HAPPY BECAUSE YOU LOOKED EVEN PRETTIER NEXT TO ME.
IT'S BEEN FUN...
탁
Anycall
크...
DAMN!

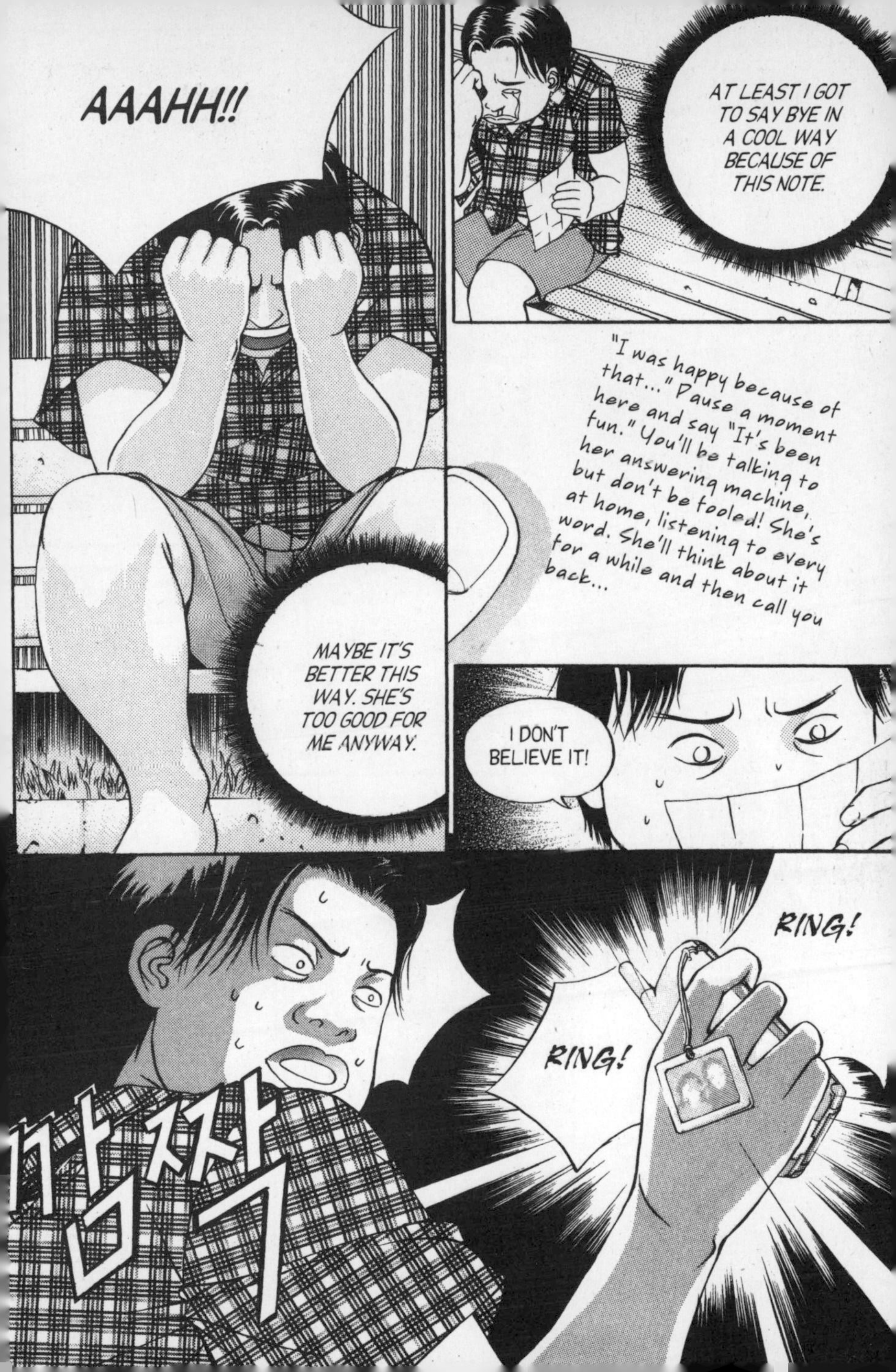
AAAHH!!
MAYBE IT'S BETTER THIS WAY. SHE'S TOO GOOD FOR ME ANYWAY.
AT LEAST I GOT TO SAY BYE IN A COOL WAY BECAUSE OF THIS NOTE.
"I was happy because of that..." Pause a moment here and say "It's been fun." You'll be talking to her answering machine, but don't be fooled! She's at home, listening to every word. She'll think about it for a while and then call you back...
I DON'T BELIEVE IT!
RING!
RING!

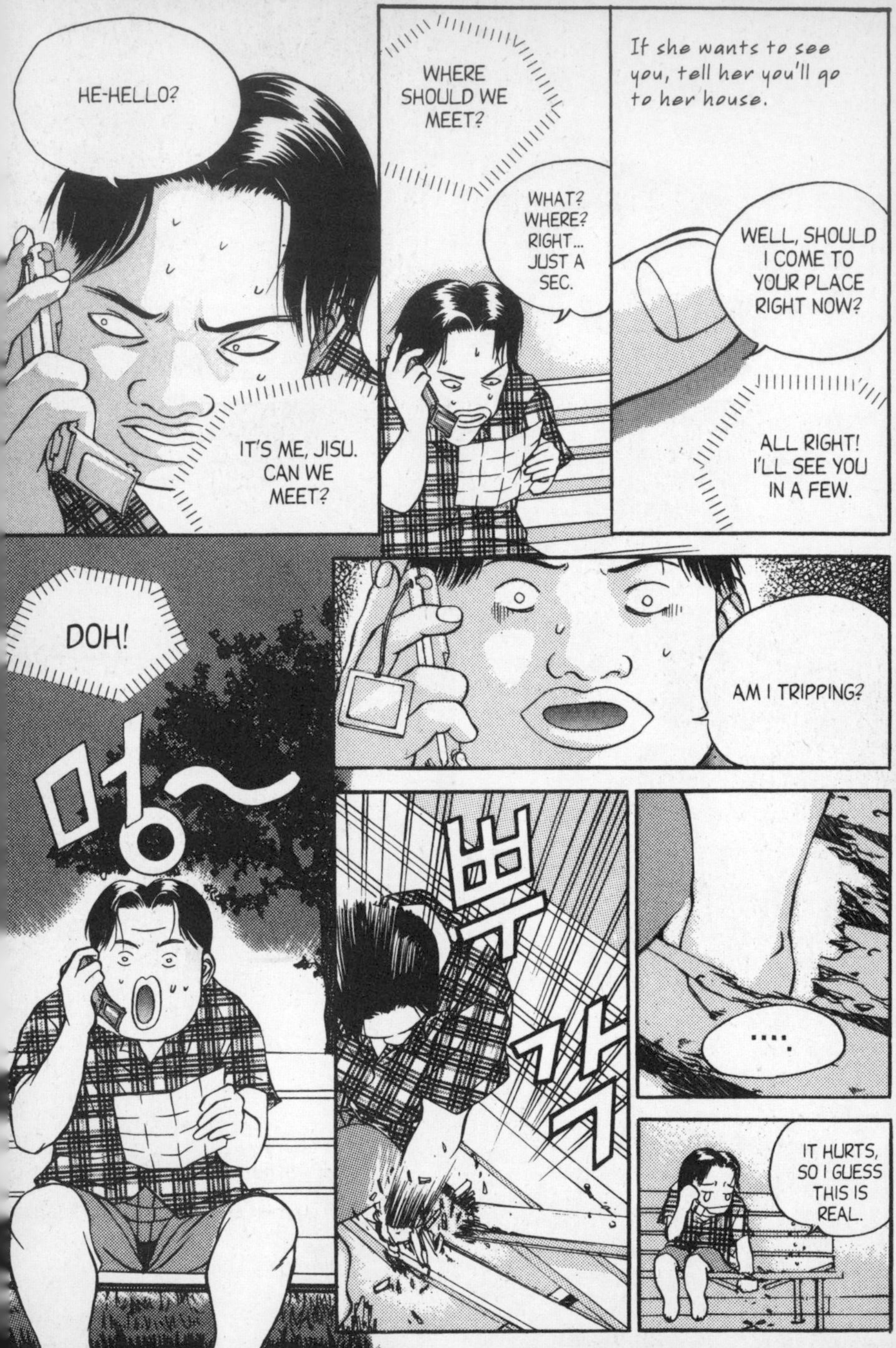
HE-HELLO?
IT'S ME, JISU. CAN WE MEET?
WHERE SHOULD WE MEET?
WHAT? WHERE? RIGHT... JUST A SEC.
If she wants to see you, tell her you'll go to her house.
WELL, SHOULD I COME TO YOUR PLACE RIGHT NOW?
ALL RIGHT! I'LL SEE YOU IN A FEW.
DOH!
멍~
AM I TRIPPING?
....
IT HURTS, SO I GUESS THIS IS REAL.

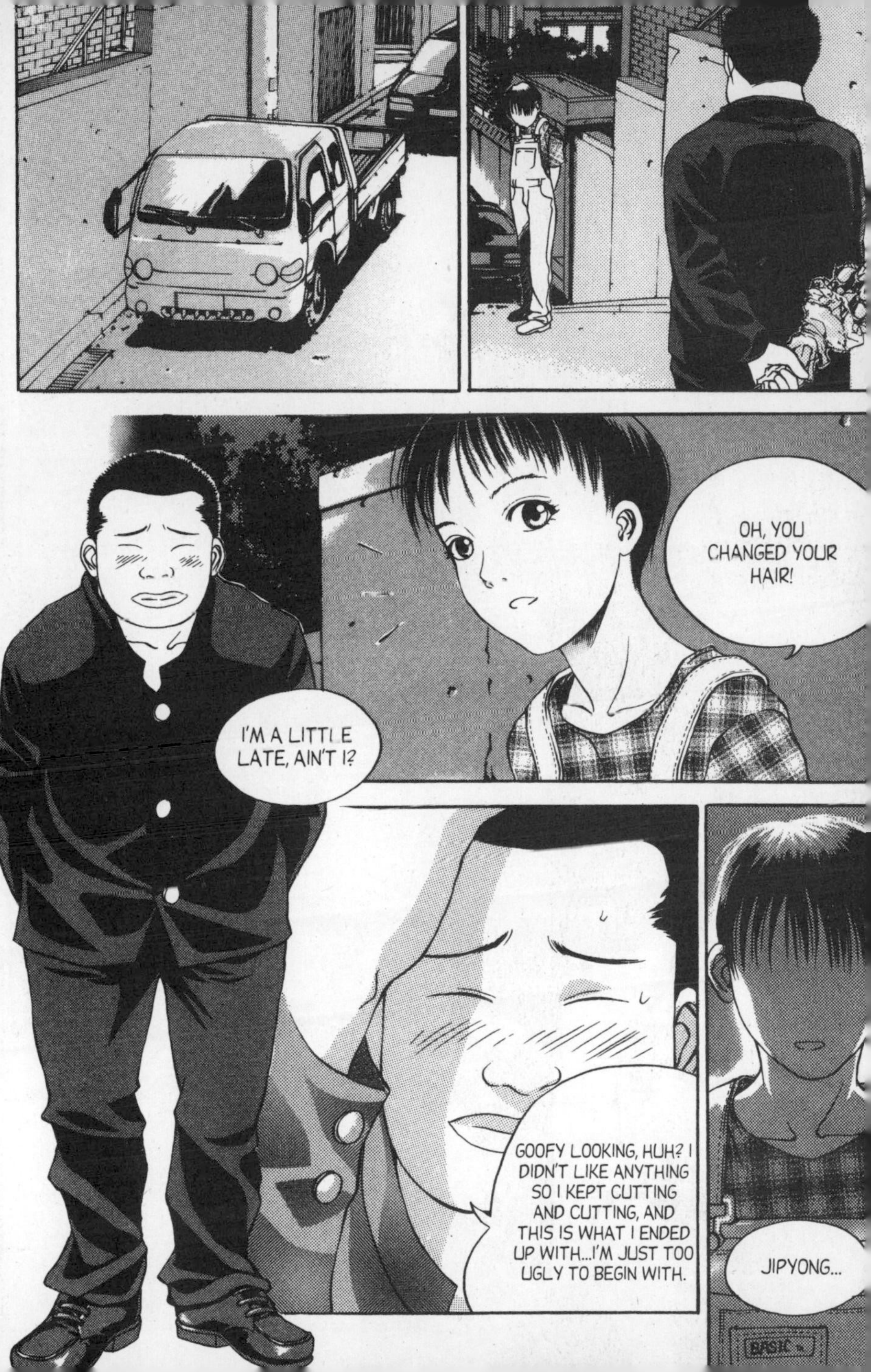
I'M A LITTLE LATE, AIN'T I?
OH, YOU CHANGED YOUR HAIR!
GOOFY LOOKING, HUH? I DIDN'T LIKE ANYTHING SO I KEPT CUTTING AND CUTTING, AND THIS IS WHAT I ENDED UP WITH...I'M JUST TOO UGLY TO BEGIN WITH.
JIPYONG...

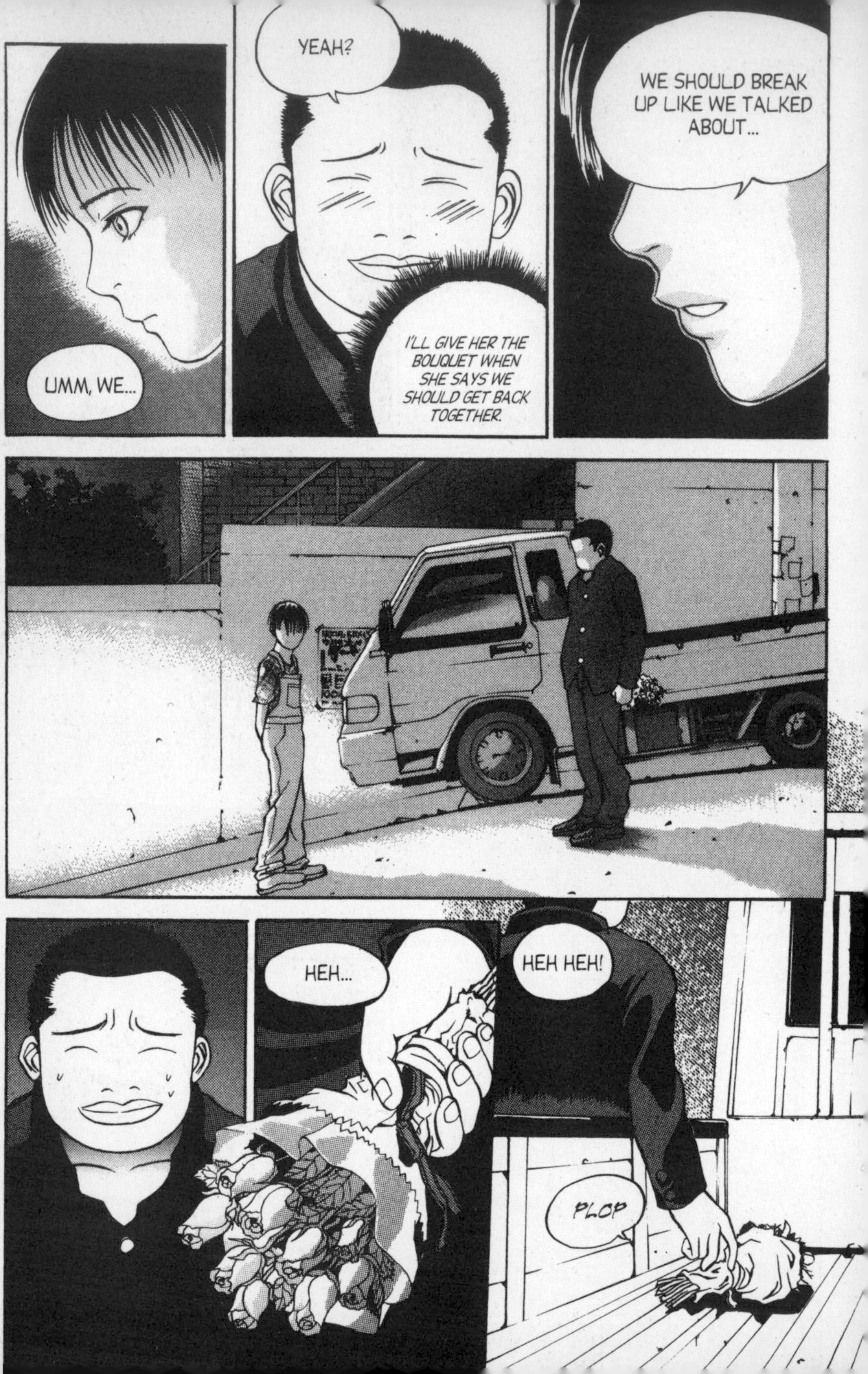
UMM, WE...
YEAH?
I'LL GIVE HER THE BOUQUET WHEN SHE SAYS WE SHOULD GET BACK TOGETHER.
WE SHOULD BREAK UP LIKE WE TALKED ABOUT...
HEH...
HEH HEH!
PLOP

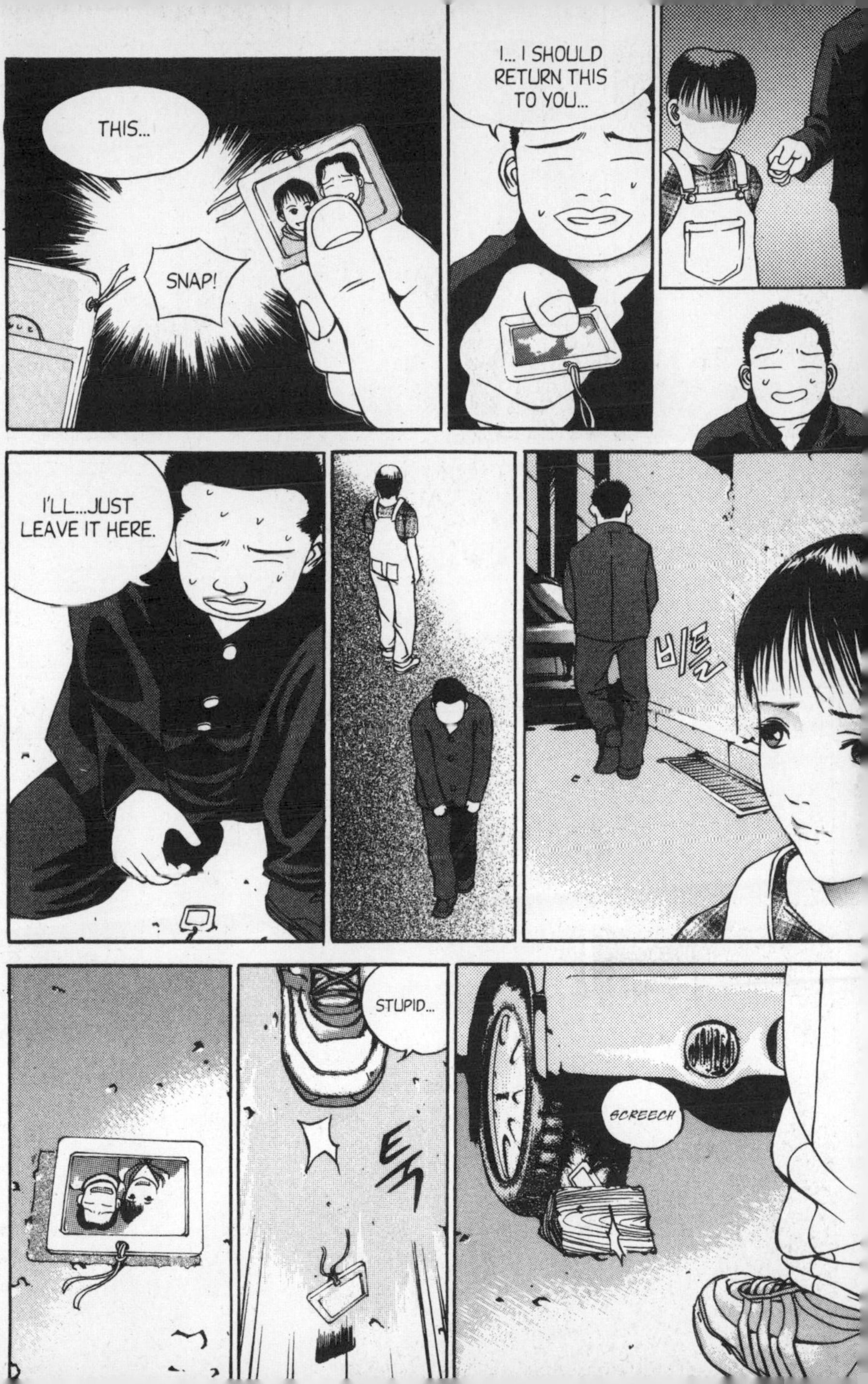
THIS...
SNAP!
I... I SHOULD RETURN THIS TO YOU...
I'LL...JUST LEAVE IT HERE.
비틀
STUPID...
툭
SCREECH

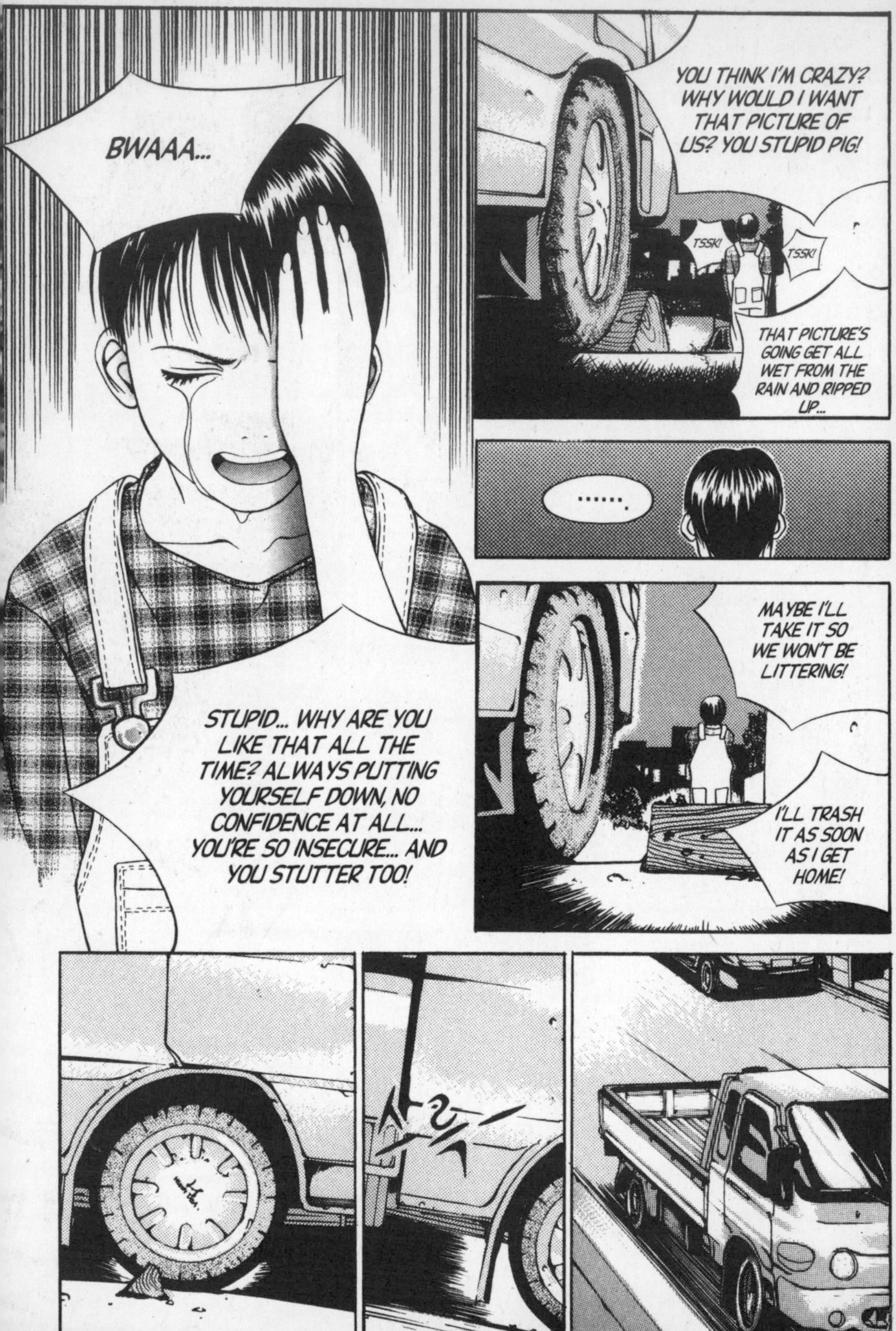
BWAAA...
STUPID... WHY ARE YOU LIKE THAT ALL THE TIME? ALWAYS PUTTING YOURSELF DOWN, NO CONFIDENCE AT ALL... YOU'RE SO INSECURE... AND YOU STUTTER TOO!
YOU THINK I'M CRAZY? WHY WOULD I WANT THAT PICTURE OF US? YOU STUPID PIG!
TSSK!
TSSK!
THAT PICTURE'S GOING GET ALL WET FROM THE RAIN AND RIPPED UP...
......
MAYBE I'LL TAKE IT SO WE WON'T BE LITTERING!
I'LL TRASH IT AS SOON AS I GET HOME!

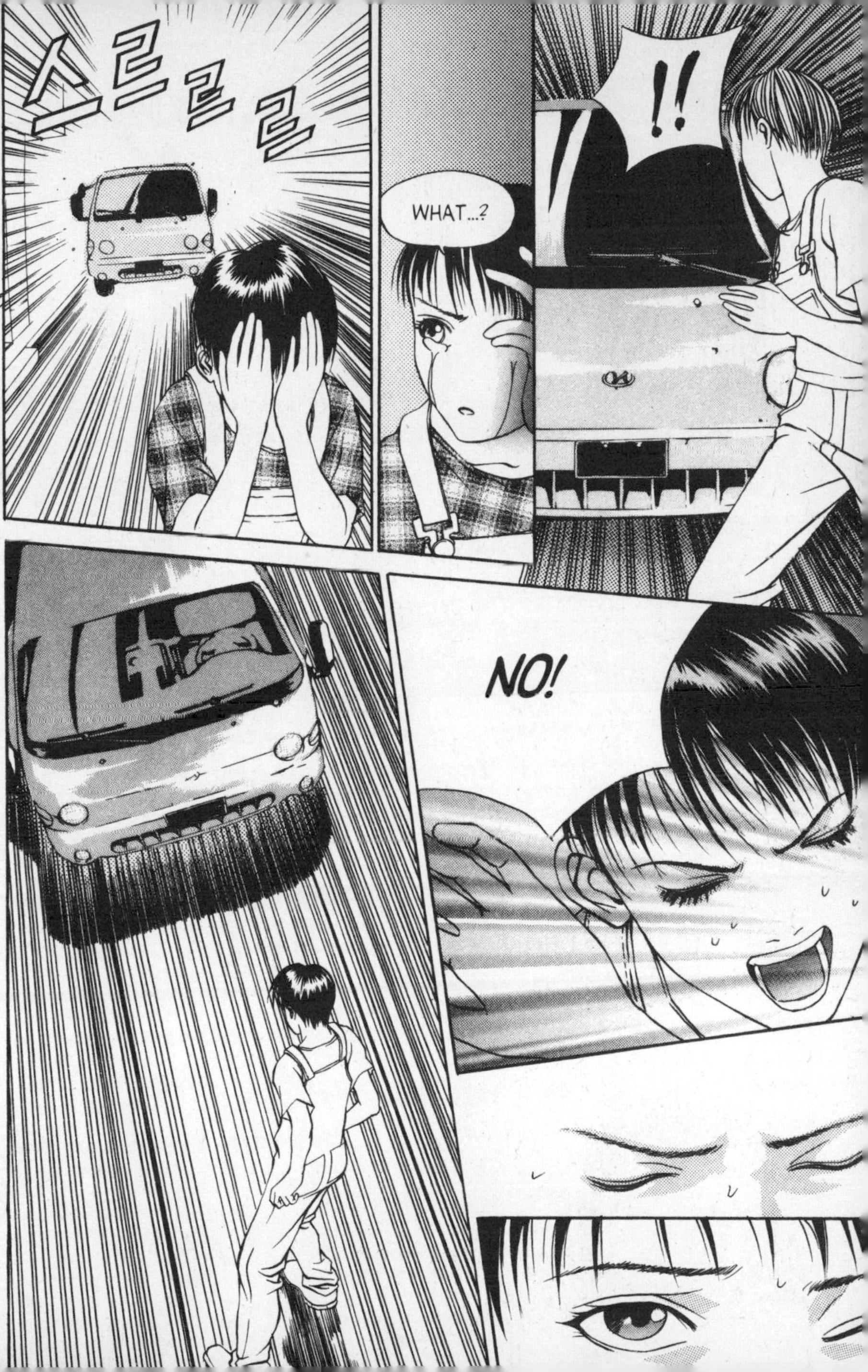
스르르르
WHAT...?
!!
NO!

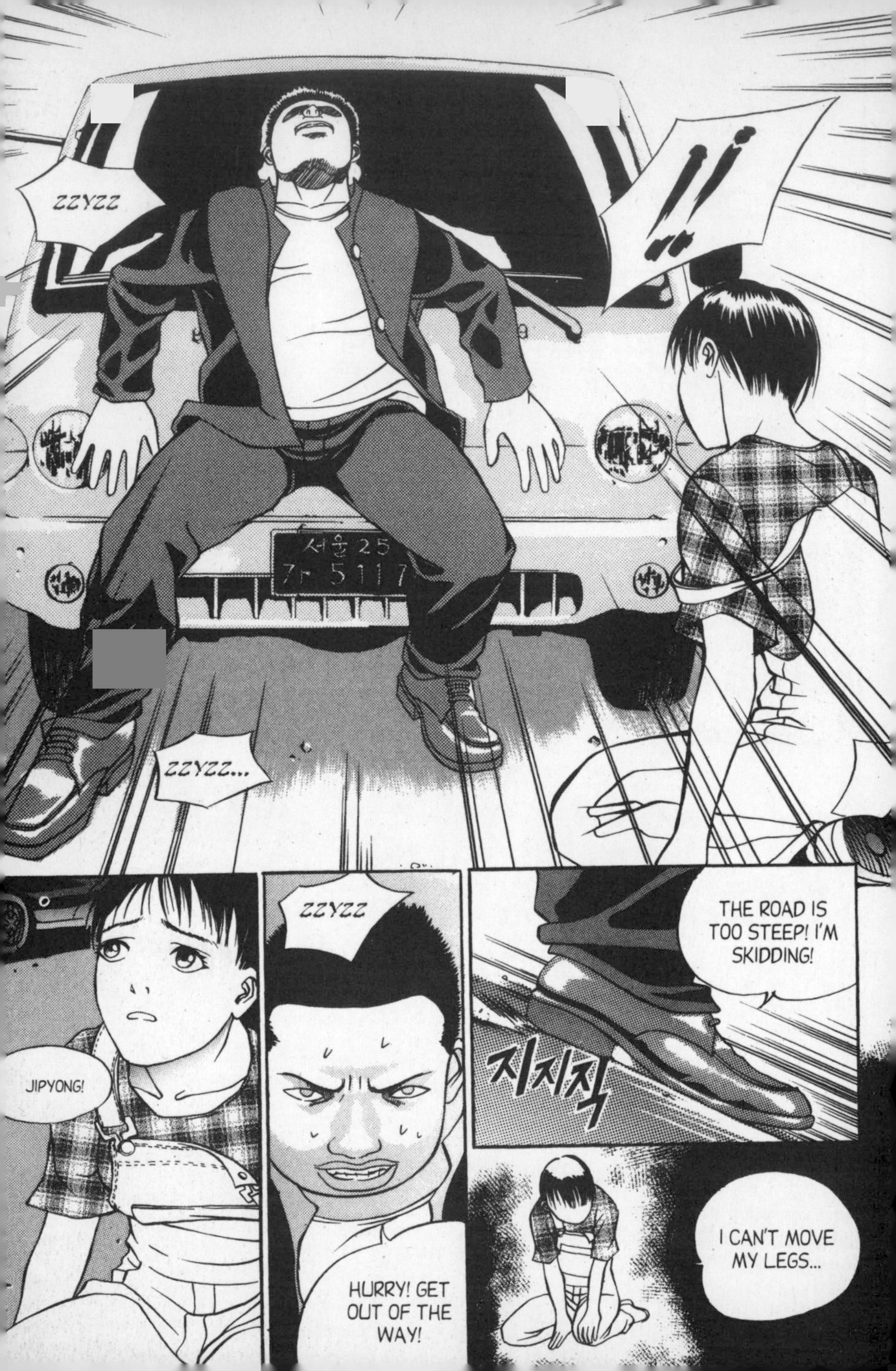
ZZYZZ
!!
ZZYZZ...
JIPYONG!
ZZYZZ
HURRY! GET OUT OF THE WAY!
THE ROAD IS TOO STEEP! I'M SKIDDING!
지지직
I CAN'T MOVE MY LEGS...

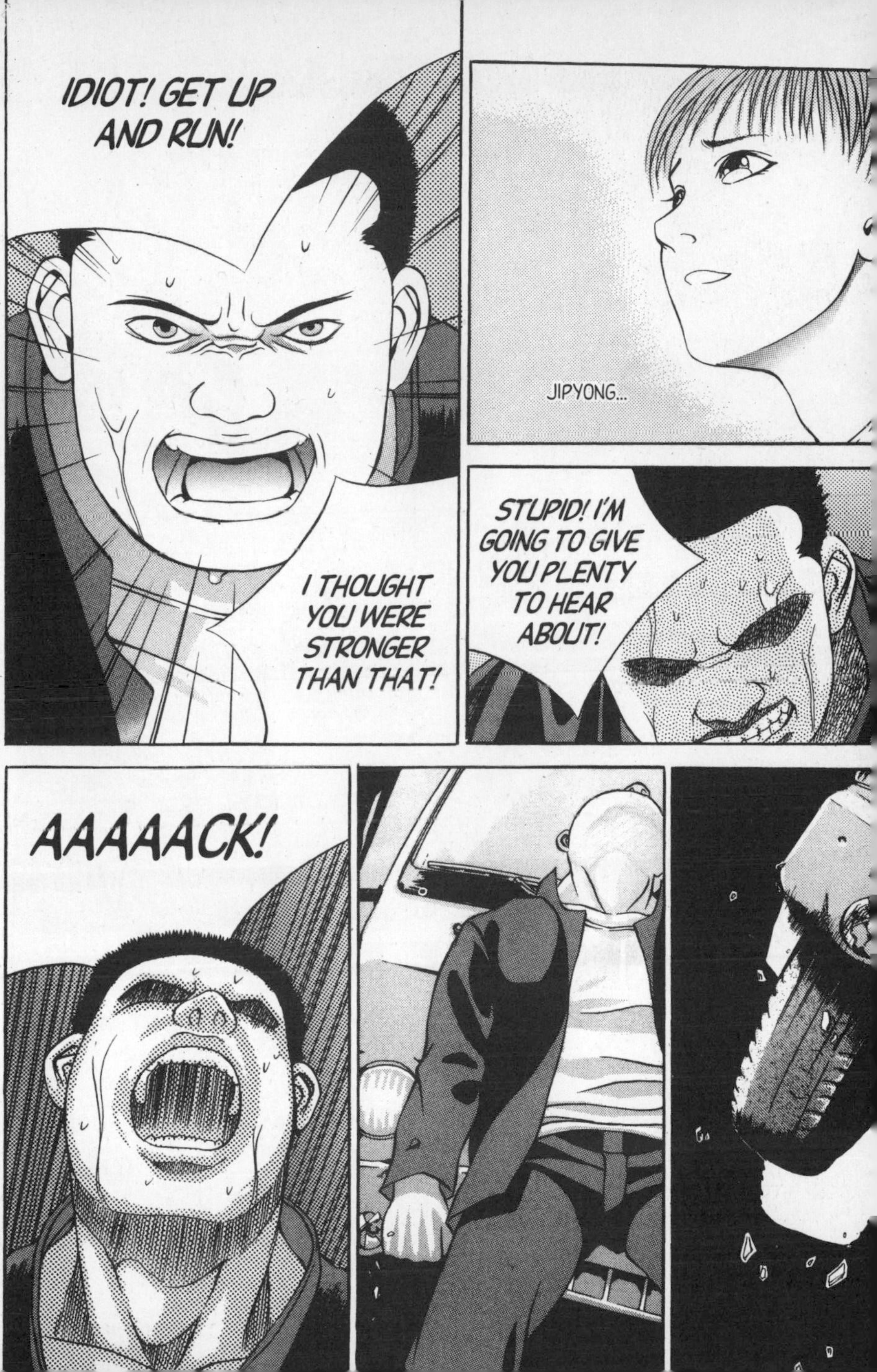
IDIOT! GET UP AND RUN!
I THOUGHT YOU WERE STRONGER THAN THAT!
JIPYONG...
STUPID! I'M GOING TO GIVE YOU PLENTY TO HEAR ABOUT!
AAAAACK!

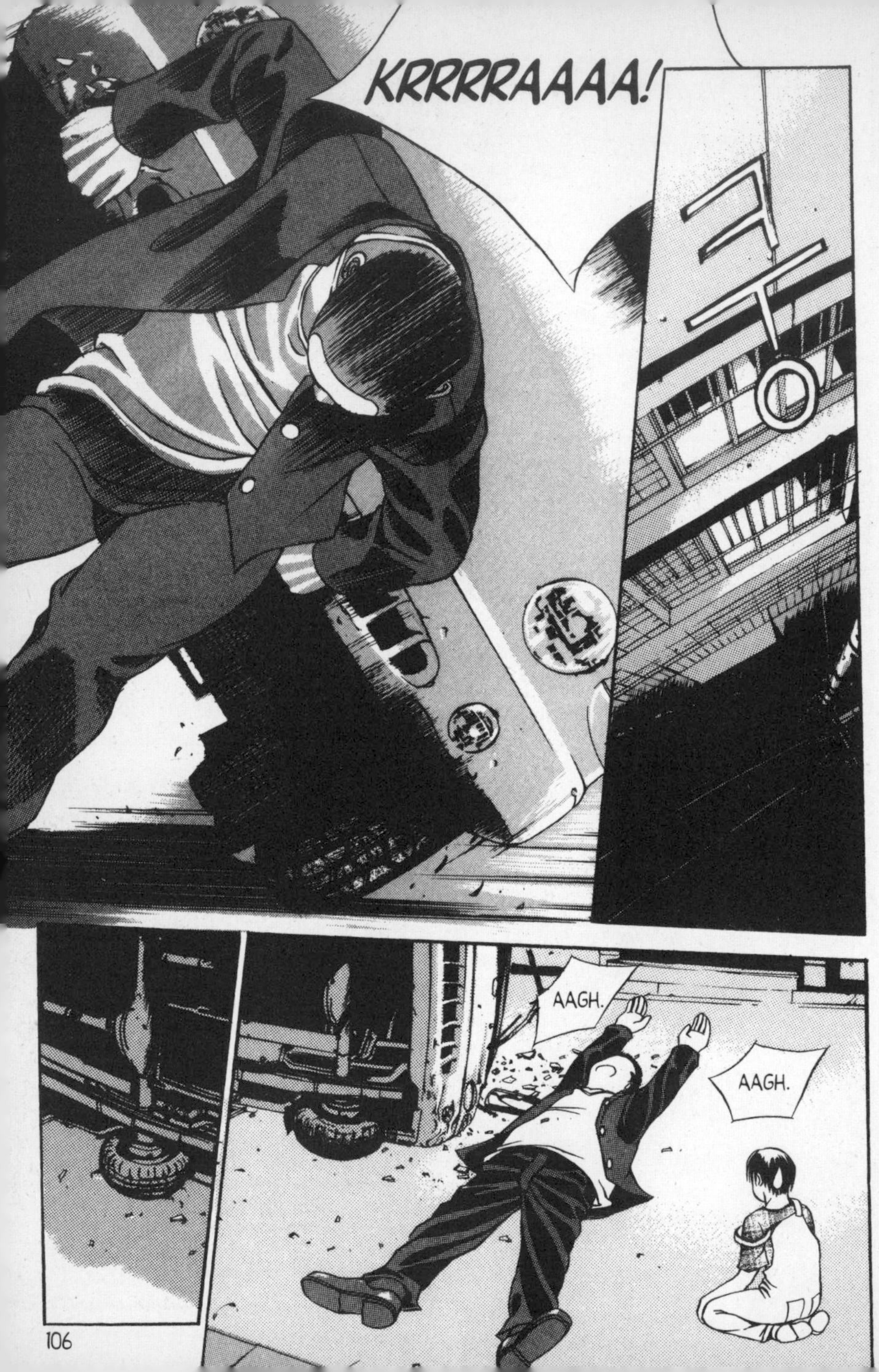
KRRRRAAAA!
AAGH.
AAGH.

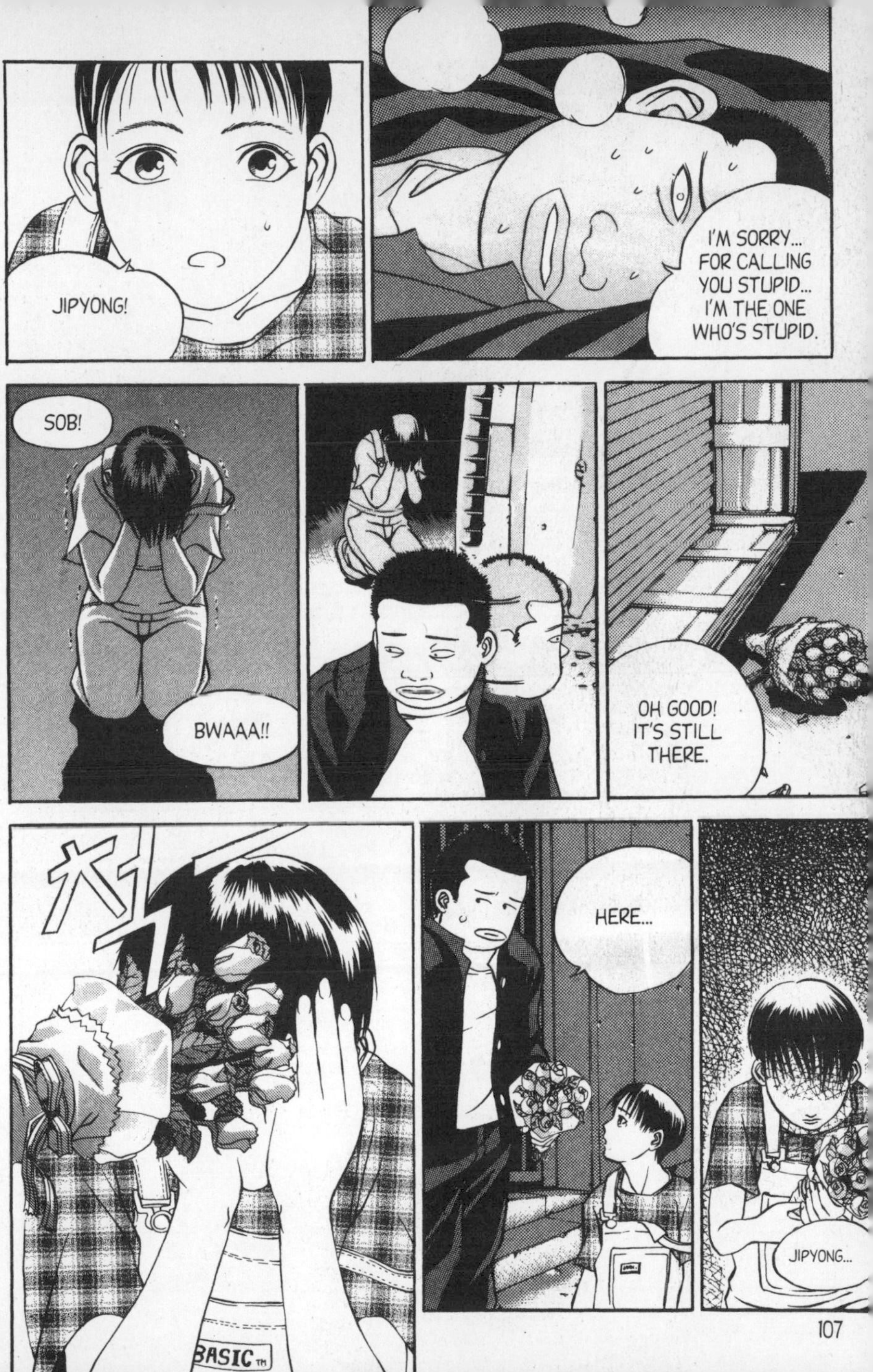
JIPYONG!
I'M SORRY... FOR CALLING YOU STUPID... I'M THE ONE WHO'S STUPID.
SOB!
BWAAA!!
OH GOOD! IT'S STILL THERE.
HERE...
JIPYONG...
BASIC TM

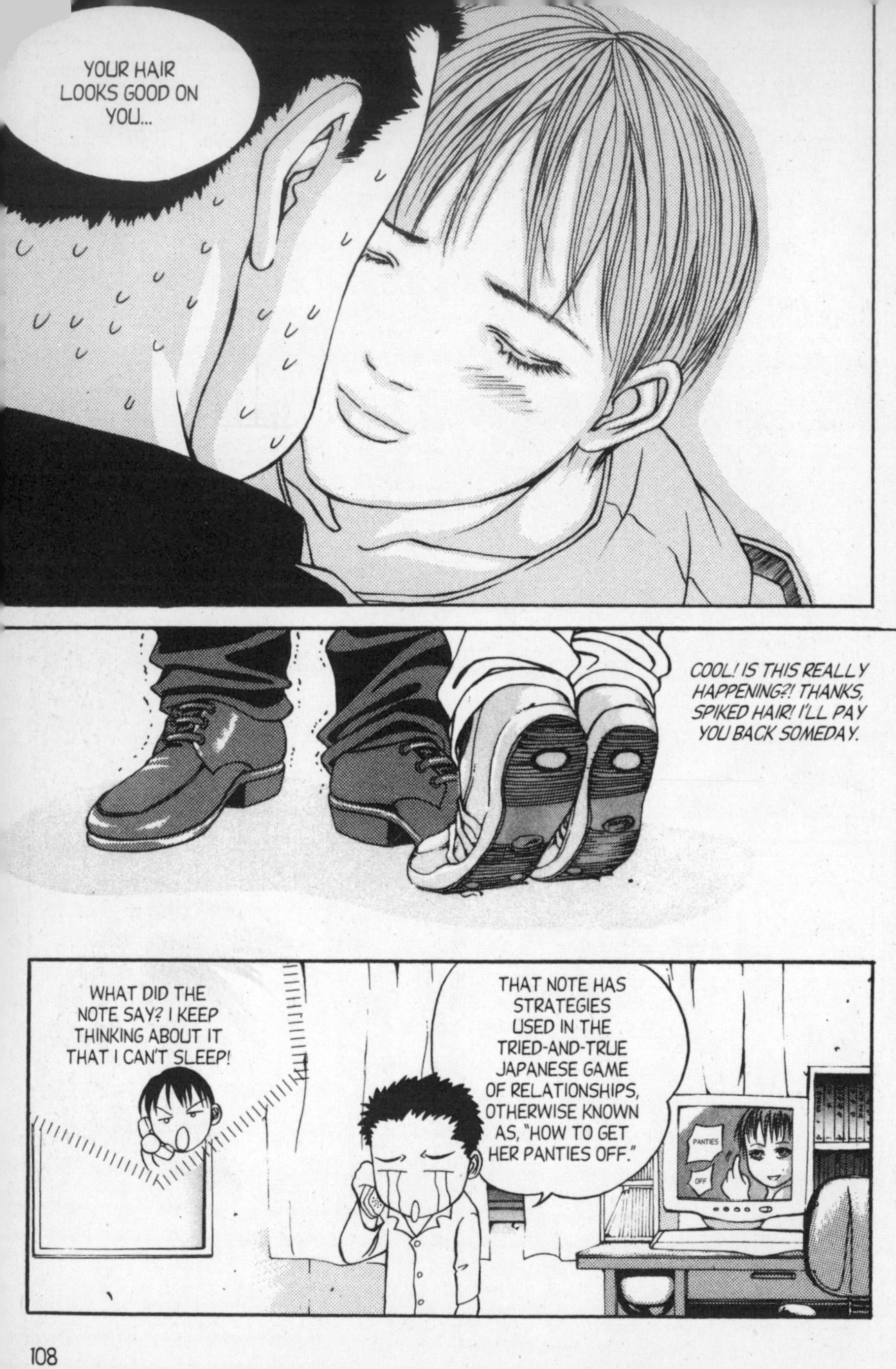
YOUR HAIR LOOKS GOOD ON YOU...
COOL! IS THIS REALLY HAPPENING?! THANKS, SPIKED HAIR! I'LL PAY YOU BACK SOMEDAY.
WHAT DID THE NOTE SAY? I KEEP THINKING ABOUT IT THAT I CAN'T SLEEP!
THAT NOTE HAS STRATEGIES USED IN THE TRIED-AND-TRUE JAPANESE GAME OF RELATIONSHIPS, OTHERWISE KNOWN AS, "HOW TO GET HER PANTIES OFF."
PANTIES
OFF

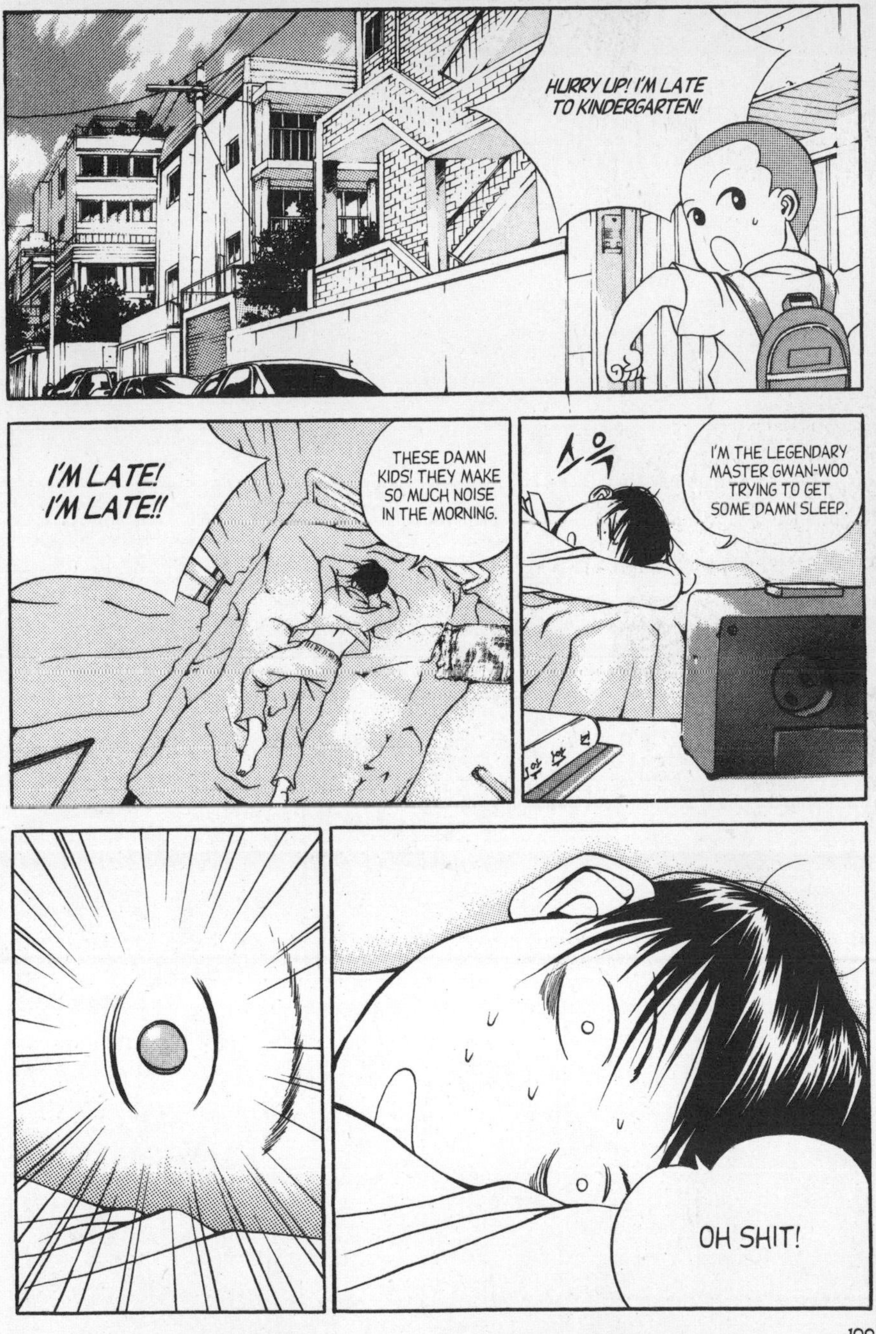
HURRY UP! I'M LATE TO KINDERGARTEN!
I'M LATE! I'M LATE!!
THESE DAMN KIDS! THEY MAKE SO MUCH NOISE IN THE MORNING.
스윽
I'M THE LEGENDARY MASTER GWAN-WOO TRYING TO GET SOME DAMN SLEEP.
OH SHIT!

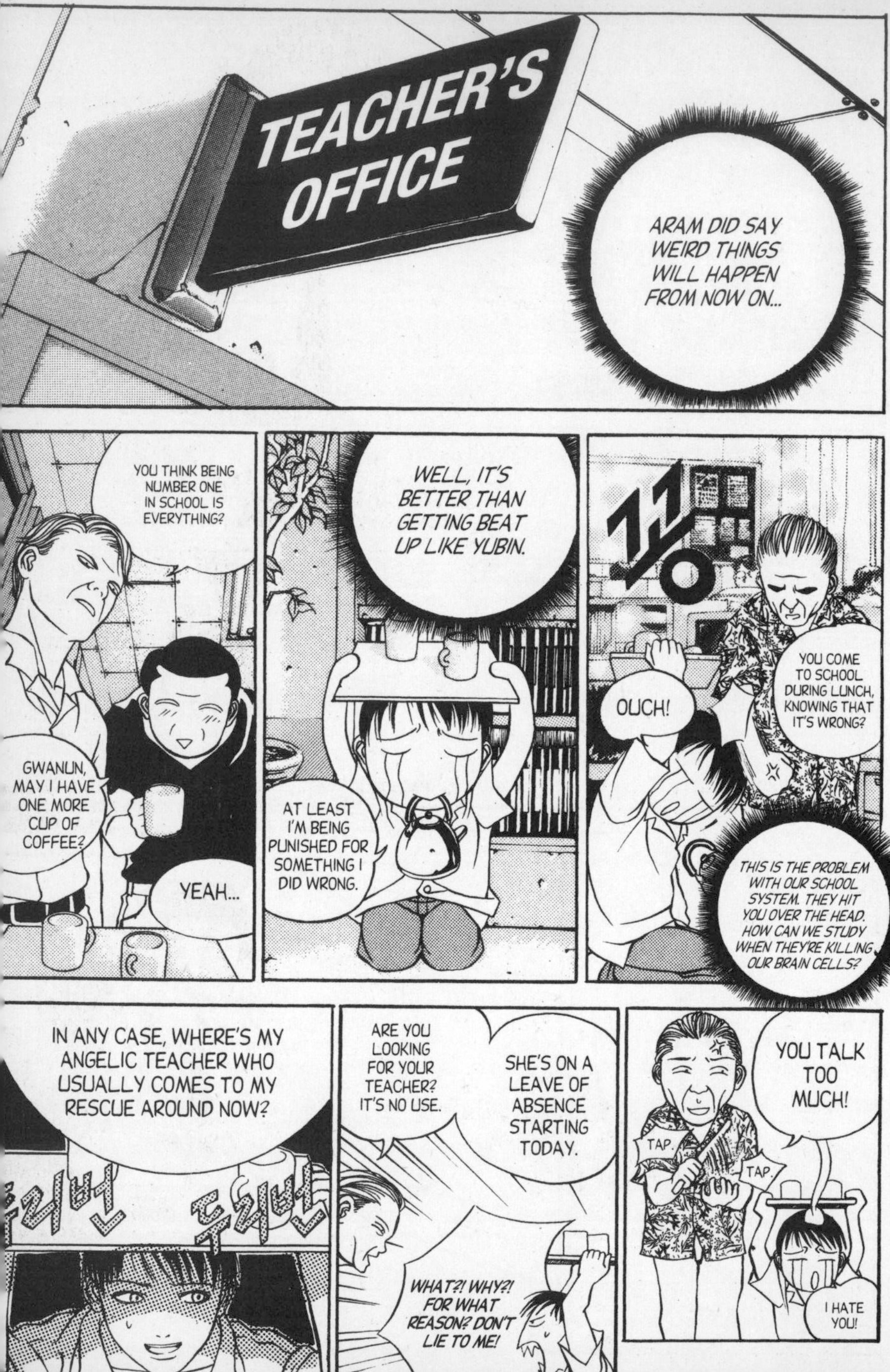

TEACHER'S OFFICE
ARAM DID SAY WEIRD THINGS WILL HAPPEN FROM NOW ON...
YOU THINK BEING NUMBER ONE IN SCHOOL IS EVERYTHING?
GWANUN, MAY I HAVE ONE MORE CUP OF COFFEE?
YEAH...
WELL, IT'S BETTER THAN GETTING BEAT UP LIKE YUBIN.
AT LEAST I'M BEING PUNISHED FOR SOMETHING I DID WRONG.
OUCH!
YOU COME TO SCHOOL DURING LUNCH, KNOWING THAT IT'S WRONG?
THIS IS THE PROBLEM WITH OUR SCHOOL SYSTEM. THEY HIT YOU OVER THE HEAD. HOW CAN WE STUDY WHEN THEY'RE KILLING OUR BRAIN CELLS?
IN ANY CASE, WHERE'S MY ANGELIC TEACHER WHO USUALLY COMES TO MY RESCUE AROUND NOW?
ARE YOU LOOKING FOR YOUR TEACHER? IT'S NO USE.
SHE'S ON A LEAVE OF ABSENCE STARTING TODAY.
WHAT?! WHY?! FOR WHAT REASON? DON'T LIE TO ME!
YOU TALK TOO MUCH!
TAP.
TAP.
I HATE YOU!

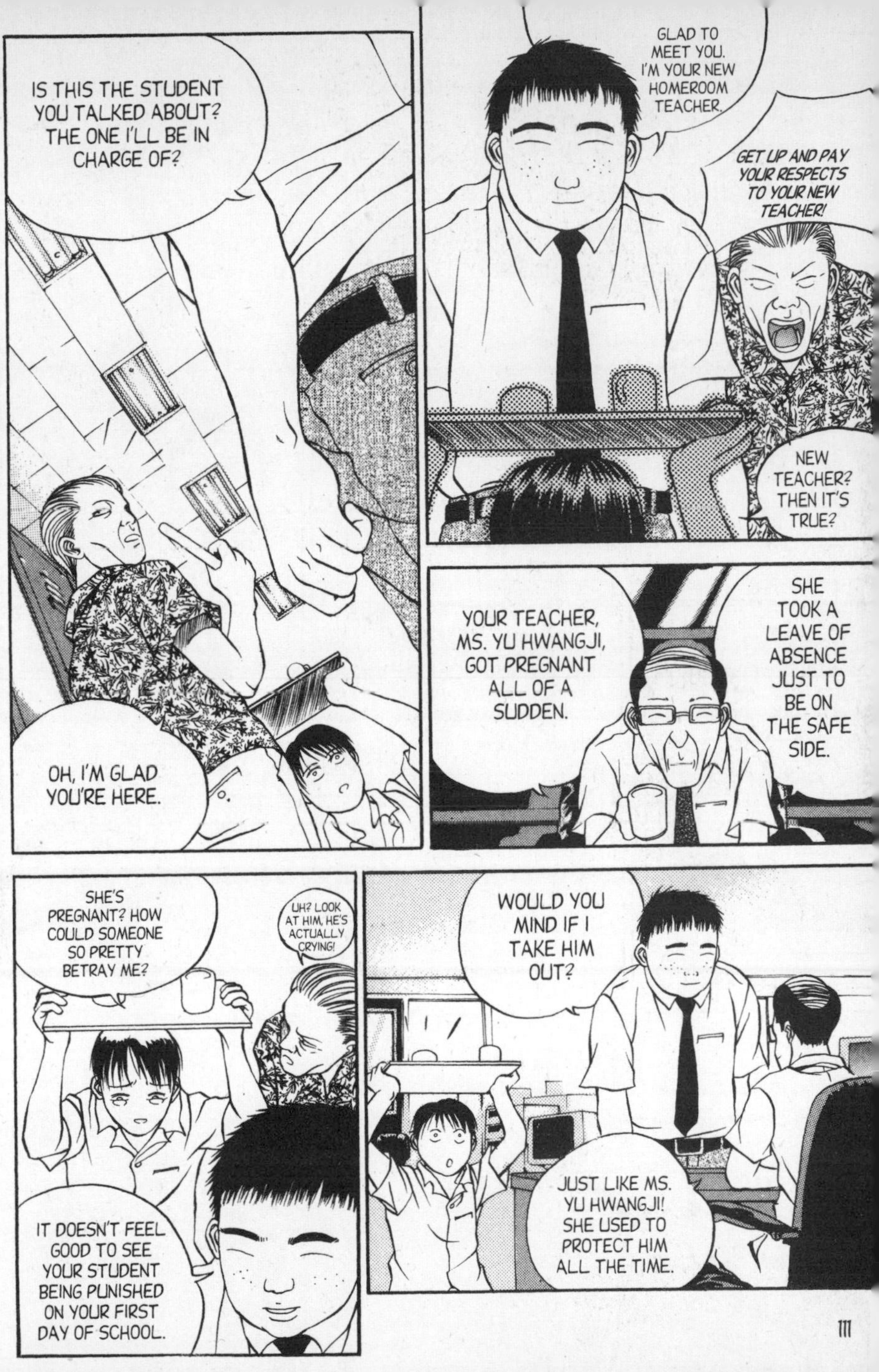
IS THIS THE STUDENT YOU TALKED ABOUT? THE ONE I'LL BE IN CHARGE OF?
OH, I'M GLAD YOU'RE HERE.
GLAD TO MEET YOU. I'M YOUR NEW HOMEROOM TEACHER.
GET UP AND PAY YOUR RESPECTS TO YOUR NEW TEACHER!
NEW TEACHER? THEN IT'S TRUE?
YOUR TEACHER, MS. YU HWANGJI, GOT PREGNANT ALL OF A SUDDEN.
SHE TOOK A LEAVE OF ABSENCE JUST TO BE ON THE SAFE SIDE.
SHE'S PREGNANT? HOW COULD SOMEONE SO PRETTY BETRAY ME?
UH? LOOK AT HIM, HE'S ACTUALLY CRYING!
IT DOESN'T FEEL GOOD TO SEE YOUR STUDENT BEING PUNISHED ON YOUR FIRST DAY OF SCHOOL.
WOULD YOU MIND IF I TAKE HIM OUT?
JUST LIKE MS. YU HWANGJI! SHE USED TO PROTECT HIM ALL THE TIME.

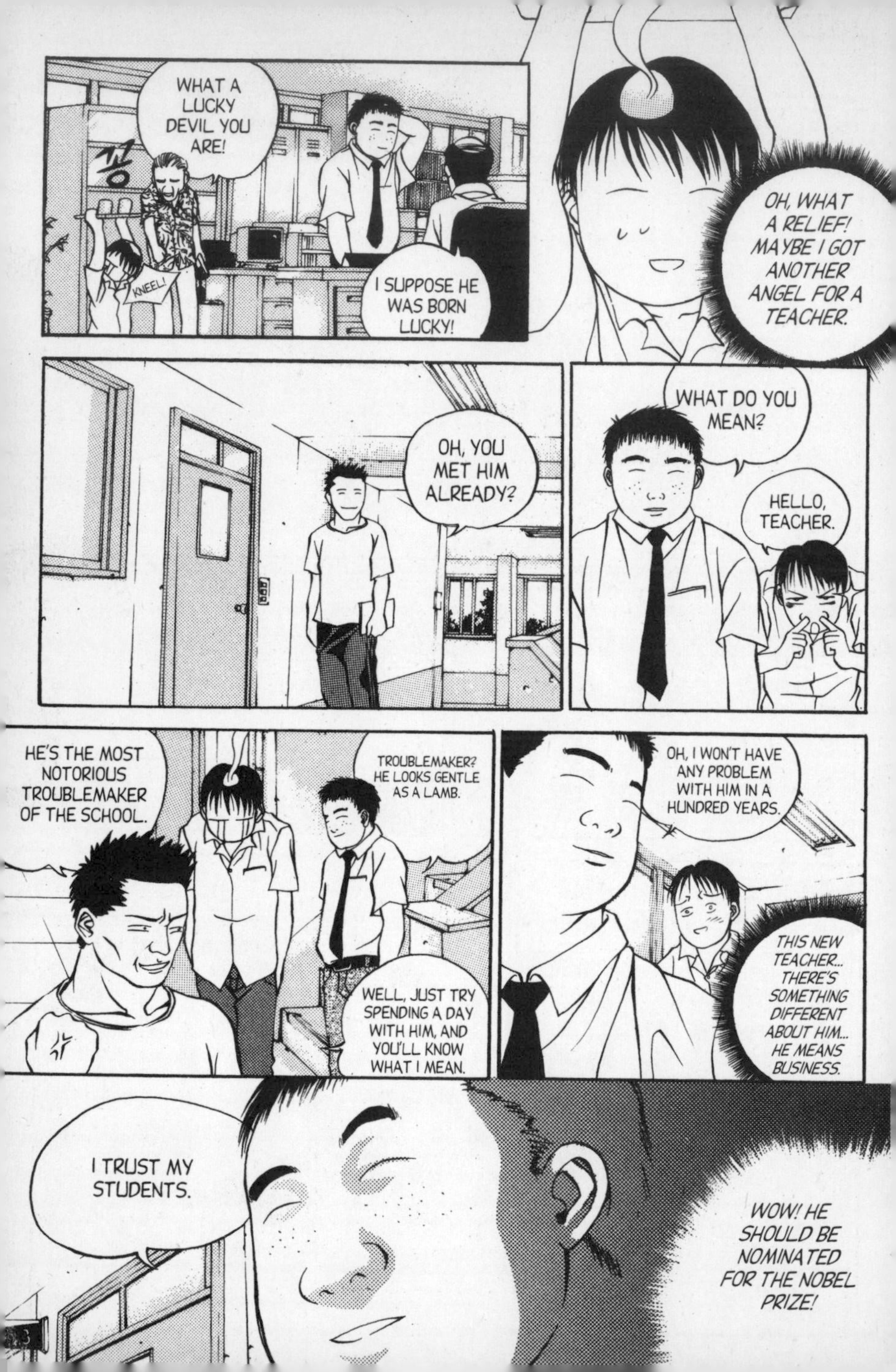
WHAT A LUCKY DEVIL YOU ARE!
찡
KNEEL!
I SUPPOSE HE WAS BORN LUCKY!
OH, WHAT A RELIEF! MAYBE I GOT ANOTHER ANGEL FOR A TEACHER.
OH, YOU MET HIM ALREADY?
WHAT DO YOU MEAN?
HELLO, TEACHER.
HE'S THE MOST NOTORIOUS TROUBLEMAKER OF THE SCHOOL.
TROUBLEMAKER? HE LOOKS GENTLE AS A LAMB.
WELL, JUST TRY SPENDING A DAY WITH HIM, AND YOU'LL KNOW WHAT I MEAN.
OH, I WON'T HAVE ANY PROBLEM WITH HIM IN A HUNDRED YEARS.
THIS NEW TEACHER... THERE'S SOMETHING DIFFERENT ABOUT HIM... HE MEANS BUSINESS.
I TRUST MY STUDENTS.
WOW! HE SHOULD BE NOMINATED FOR THE NOBEL PRIZE!

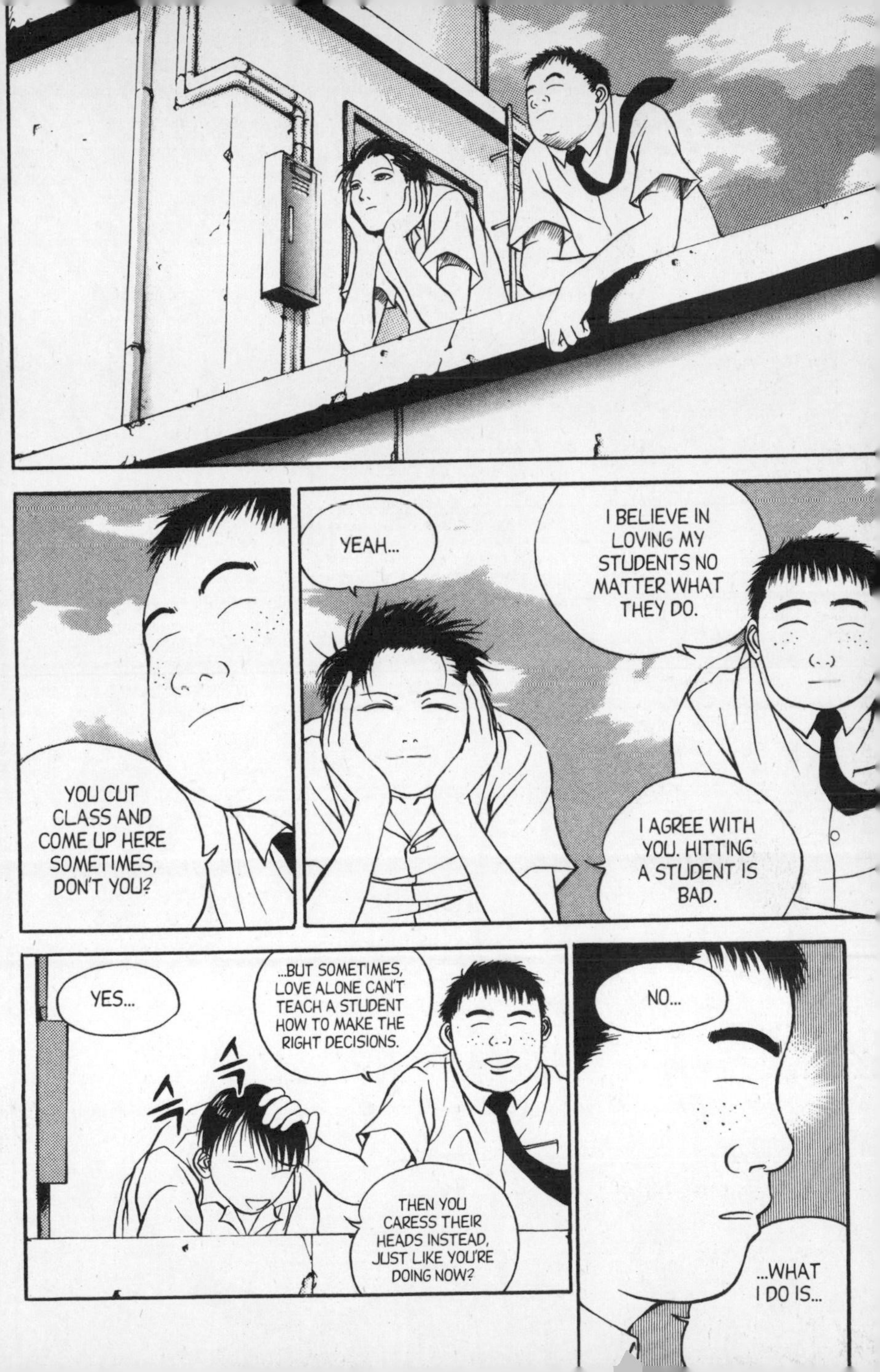
YOU CUT CLASS AND COME UP HERE SOMETIMES, DON'T YOU?
YEAH...
I BELIEVE IN LOVING MY STUDENTS NO MATTER WHAT THEY DO.
I AGREE WITH YOU. HITTING A STUDENT IS BAD.
YES...
...BUT SOMETIMES, LOVE ALONE CAN'T TEACH A STUDENT HOW TO MAKE THE RIGHT DECISIONS.
THEN YOU CARESS THEIR HEADS INSTEAD, JUST LIKE YOU'RE DOING NOW?
NO...
...WHAT I DO IS...

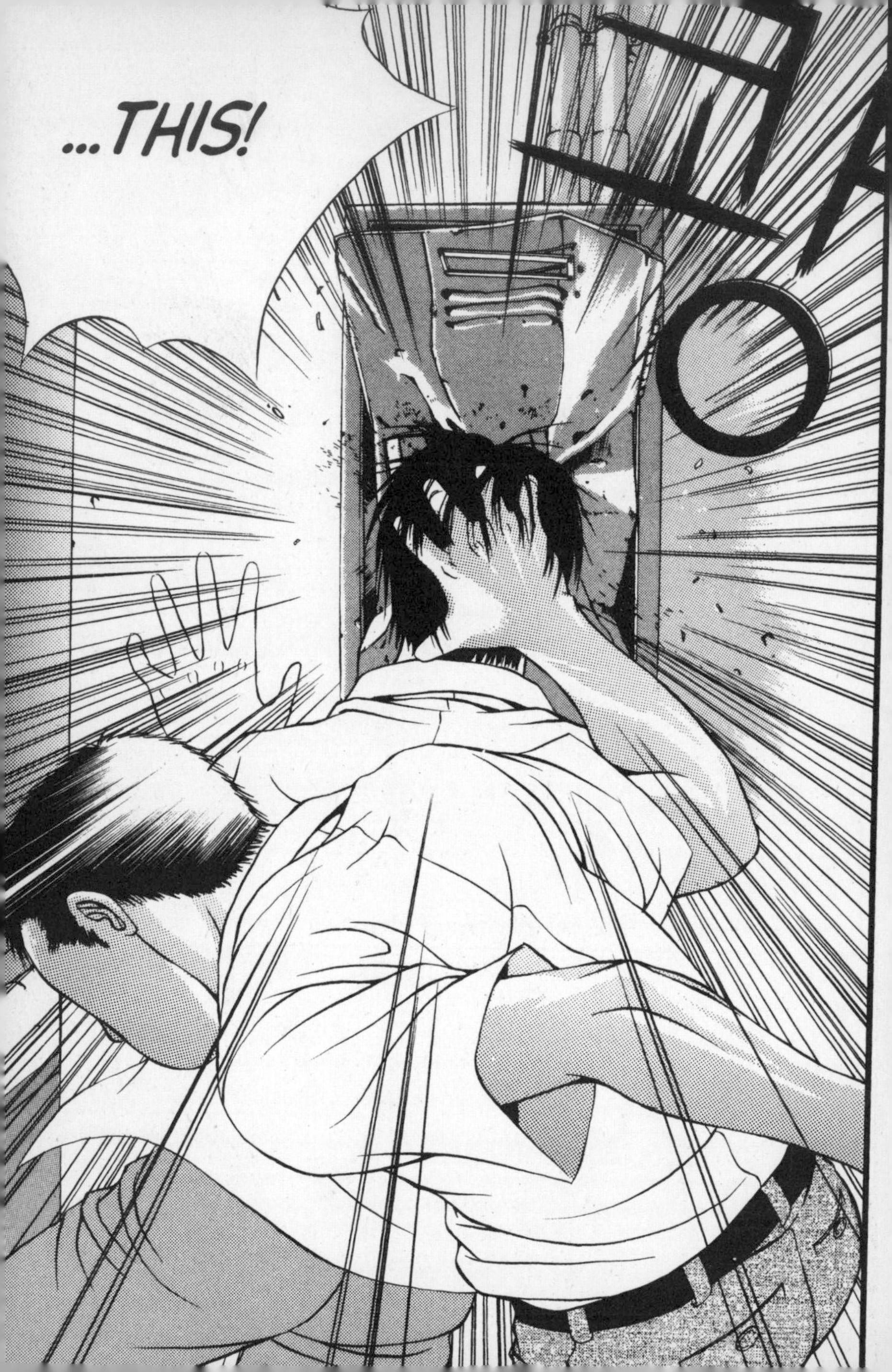
...THIS!

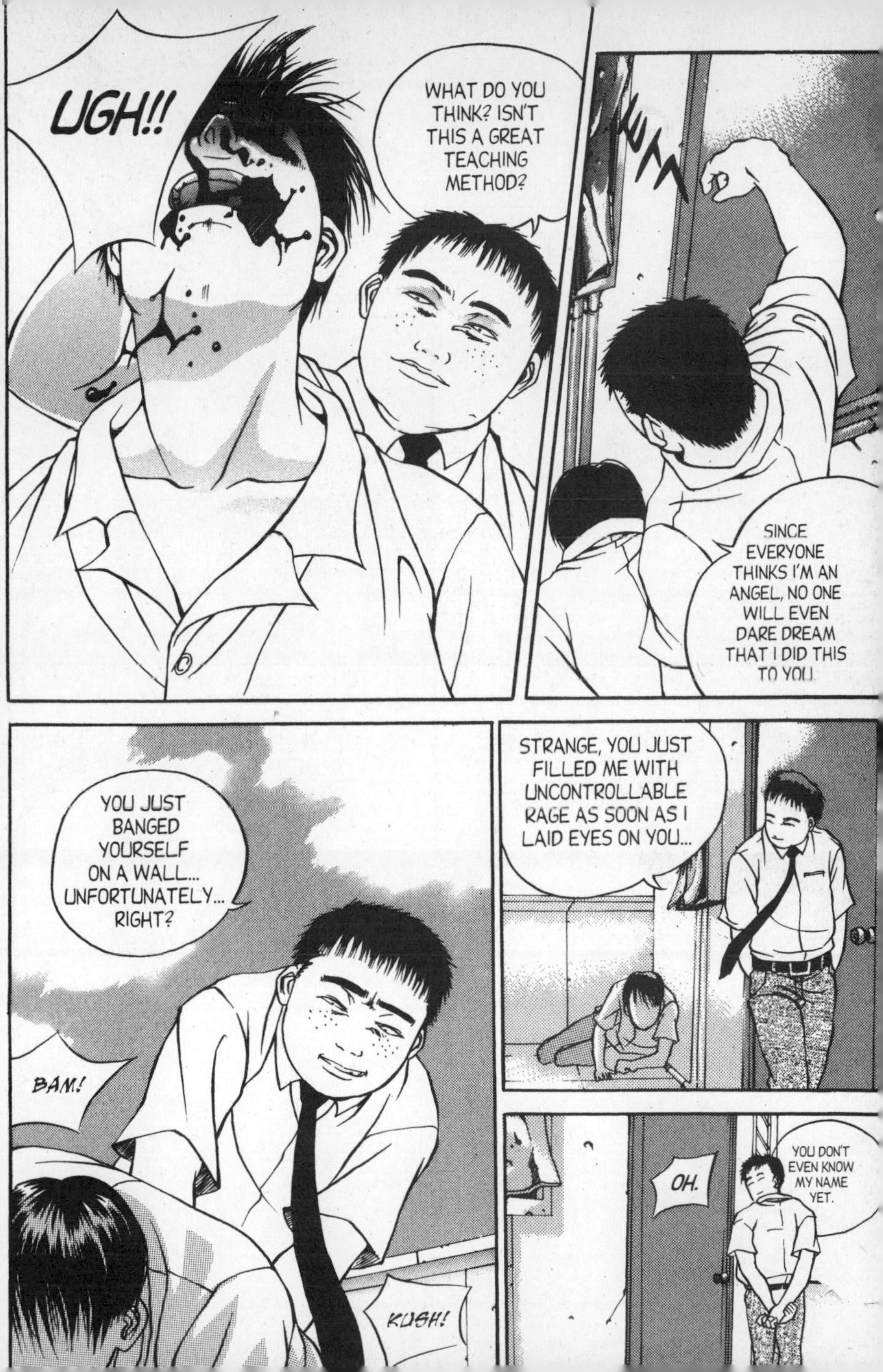
UGH!!
WHAT DO YOU THINK? ISN'T THIS A GREAT TEACHING METHOD?
SINCE EVERYONE THINKS I'M AN ANGEL, NO ONE WILL EVEN DARE DREAM THAT I DID THIS TO YOU.
YOU JUST BANGED YOURSELF ON A WALL... UNFORTUNATELY... RIGHT?
BAM!
KUSH!
STRANGE, YOU JUST FILLED ME WITH UNCONTROLLABLE RAGE AS SOON AS I LAID EYES ON YOU...
OH.
YOU DON'T EVEN KNOW MY NAME YET.

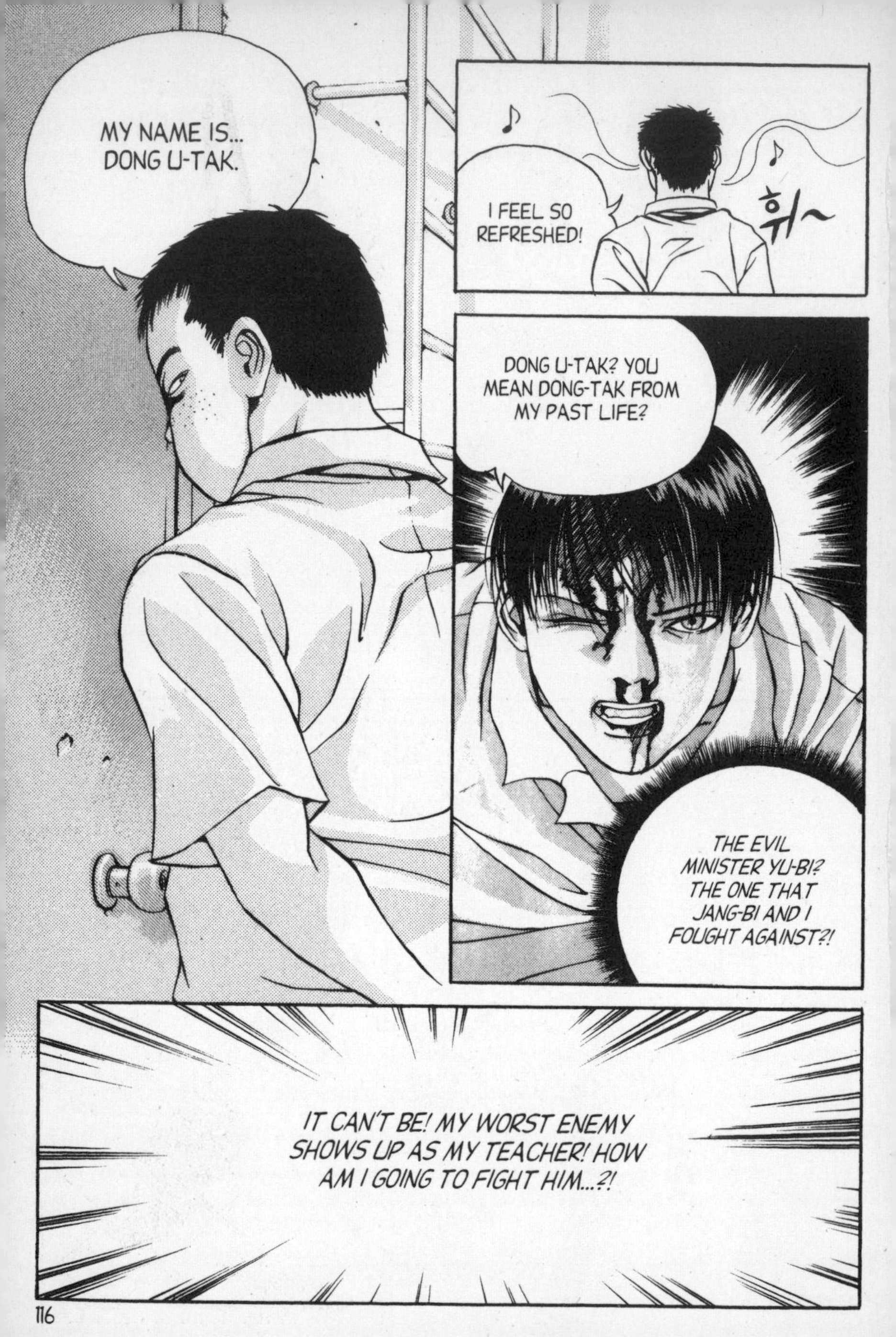
MY NAME IS... DONG U-TAK.
I FEEL SO REFRESHED!
휘~
DONG U-TAK? YOU MEAN DONG-TAK FROM MY PAST LIFE?
THE EVIL MINISTER YU-BI? THE ONE THAT JANG-BI AND I FOUGHT AGAINST?!
IT CAN'T BE! MY WORST ENEMY SHOWS UP AS MY TEACHER! HOW AM I GOING TO FIGHT HIM...?!

이터니티
ETERNITY

#5 DONG-TAK VS. GWAN-WOO

ION SUPPLY DRINK
LOTTE

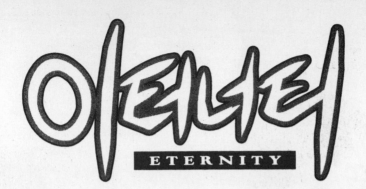

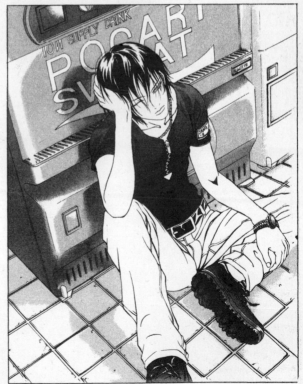

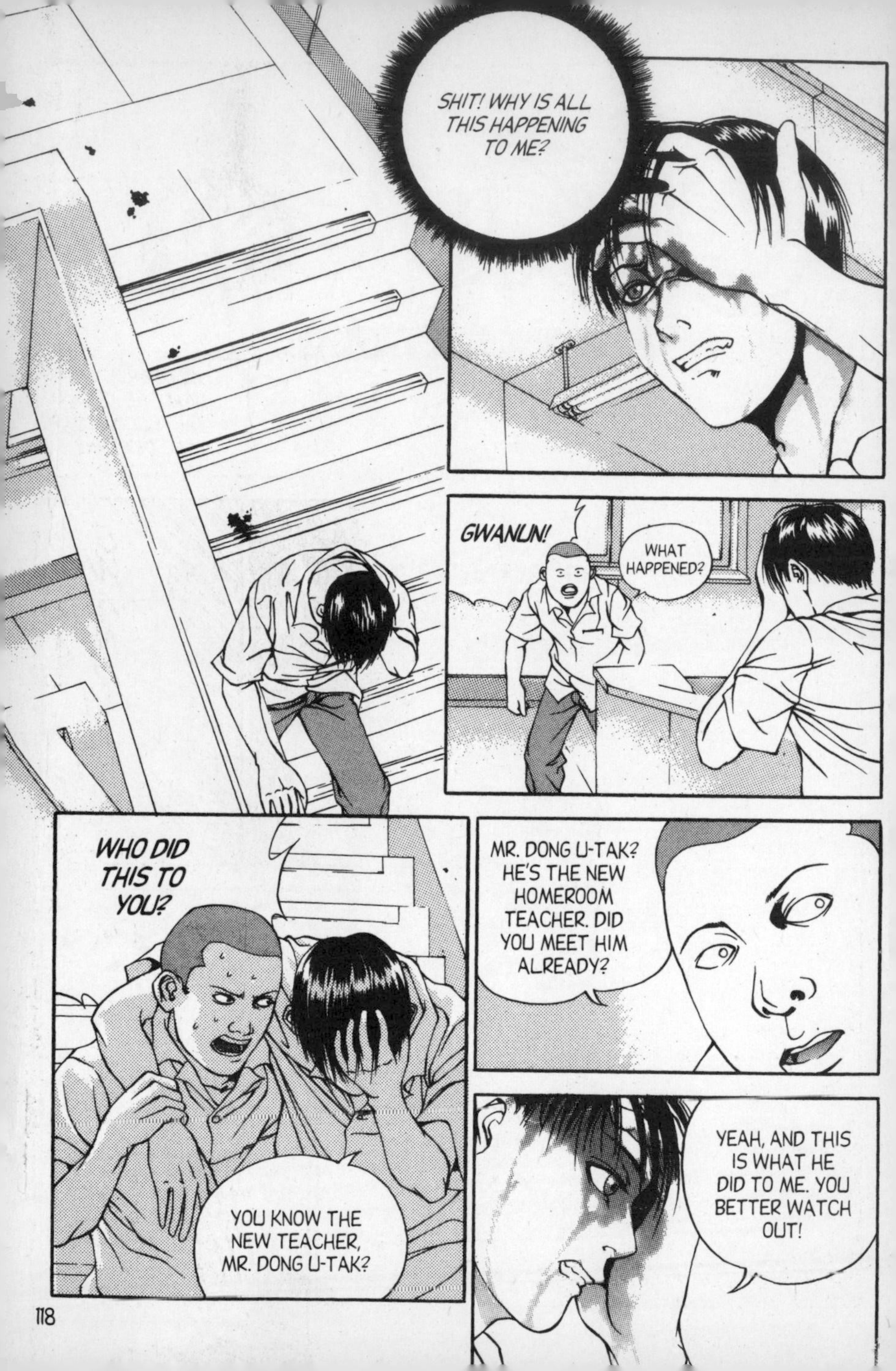
SHIT! WHY IS ALL THIS HAPPENING TO ME?
GWANUN!
WHAT HAPPENED?
WHO DID THIS TO YOU?
YOU KNOW THE NEW TEACHER, MR. DONG U-TAK?
MR. DONG U-TAK? HE'S THE NEW HOMEROOM TEACHER. DID YOU MEET HIM ALREADY?
YEAH, AND THIS IS WHAT HE DID TO ME. YOU BETTER WATCH OUT!

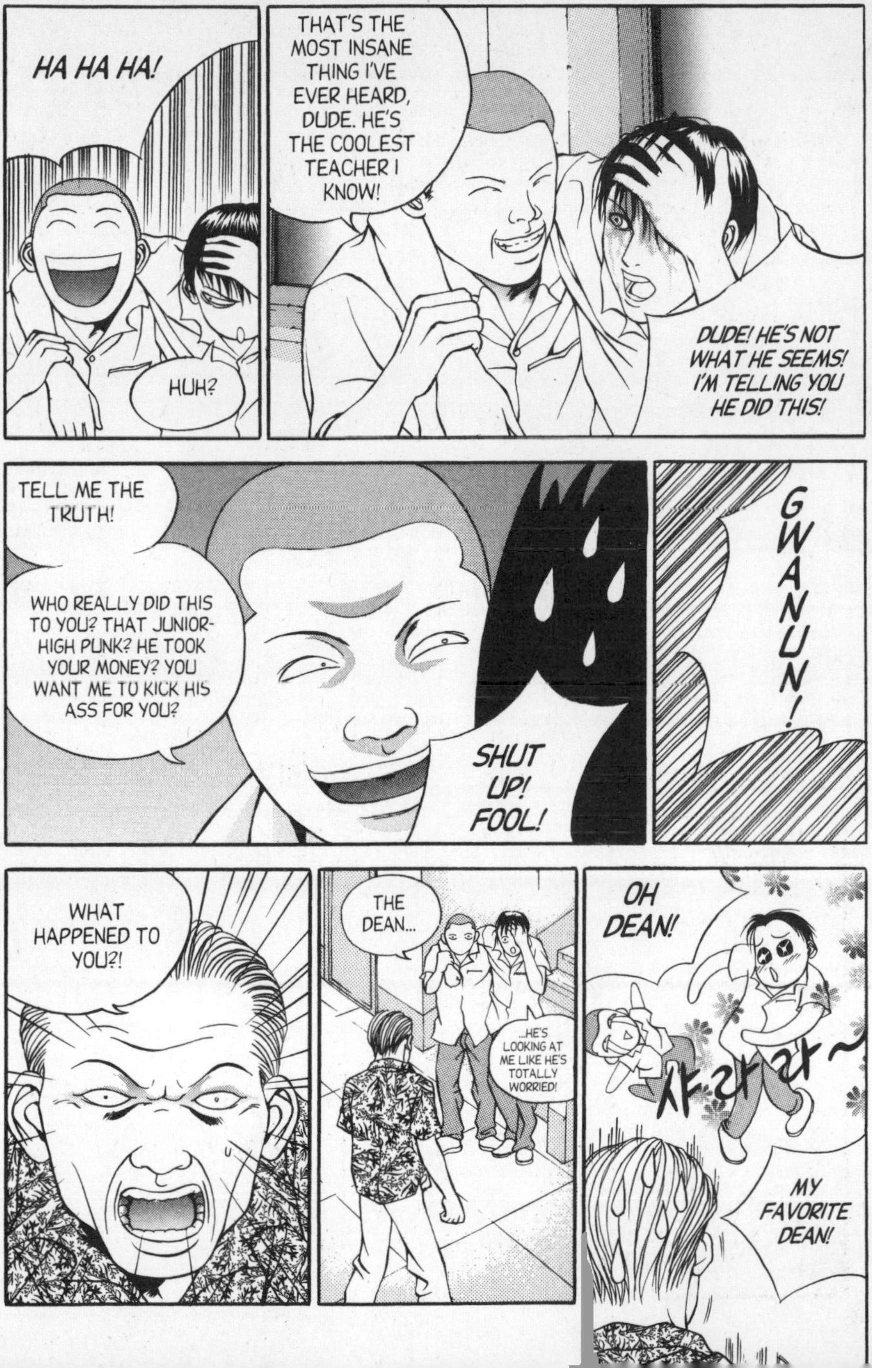
HA HA HA!
HUH?
THAT'S THE MOST INSANE THING I'VE EVER HEARD, DUDE. HE'S THE COOLEST TEACHER I KNOW!
DUDE! HE'S NOT WHAT HE SEEMS! I'M TELLING YOU HE DID THIS!
TELL ME THE TRUTH!
WHO REALLY DID THIS TO YOU? THAT JUNIOR-HIGH PUNK? HE TOOK YOUR MONEY? YOU WANT ME TO KICK HIS ASS FOR YOU?
SHUT UP! FOOL!
GWANUN!
WHAT HAPPENED TO YOU?!
THE DEAN...
...HE'S LOOKING AT ME LIKE HE'S TOTALLY WORRIED!
OH DEAN!
사각각~
MY FAVORITE DEAN!

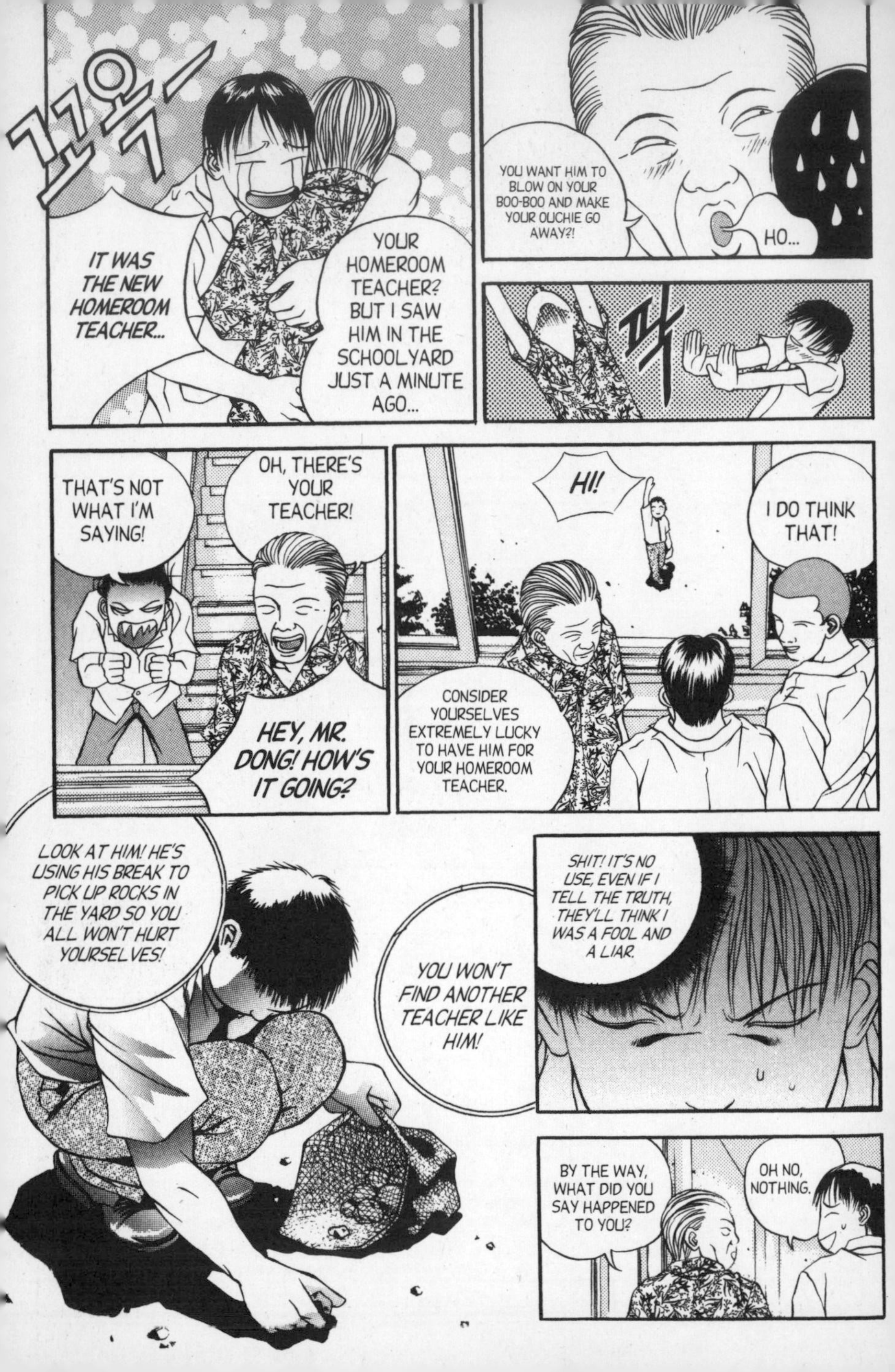
IT WAS THE NEW HOMEROOM TEACHER...
YOUR HOMEROOM TEACHER? BUT I SAW HIM IN THE SCHOOLYARD JUST A MINUTE AGO...
YOU WANT HIM TO BLOW ON YOUR BOO-BOO AND MAKE YOUR OUCHIE GO AWAY?!
HO...
퍽
THAT'S NOT WHAT I'M SAYING!
OH, THERE'S YOUR TEACHER!
HEY, MR. DONG! HOW'S IT GOING?
HI!
I DO THINK THAT!
CONSIDER YOURSELVES EXTREMELY LUCKY TO HAVE HIM FOR YOUR HOMEROOM TEACHER.
LOOK AT HIM! HE'S USING HIS BREAK TO PICK UP ROCKS IN THE YARD SO YOU ALL WON'T HURT YOURSELVES!
YOU WON'T FIND ANOTHER TEACHER LIKE HIM!
SHIT! IT'S NO USE, EVEN IF I TELL THE TRUTH, THEY'LL THINK I WAS A FOOL AND A LIAR.
BY THE WAY, WHAT DID YOU SAY HAPPENED TO YOU?
OH NO, NOTHING.

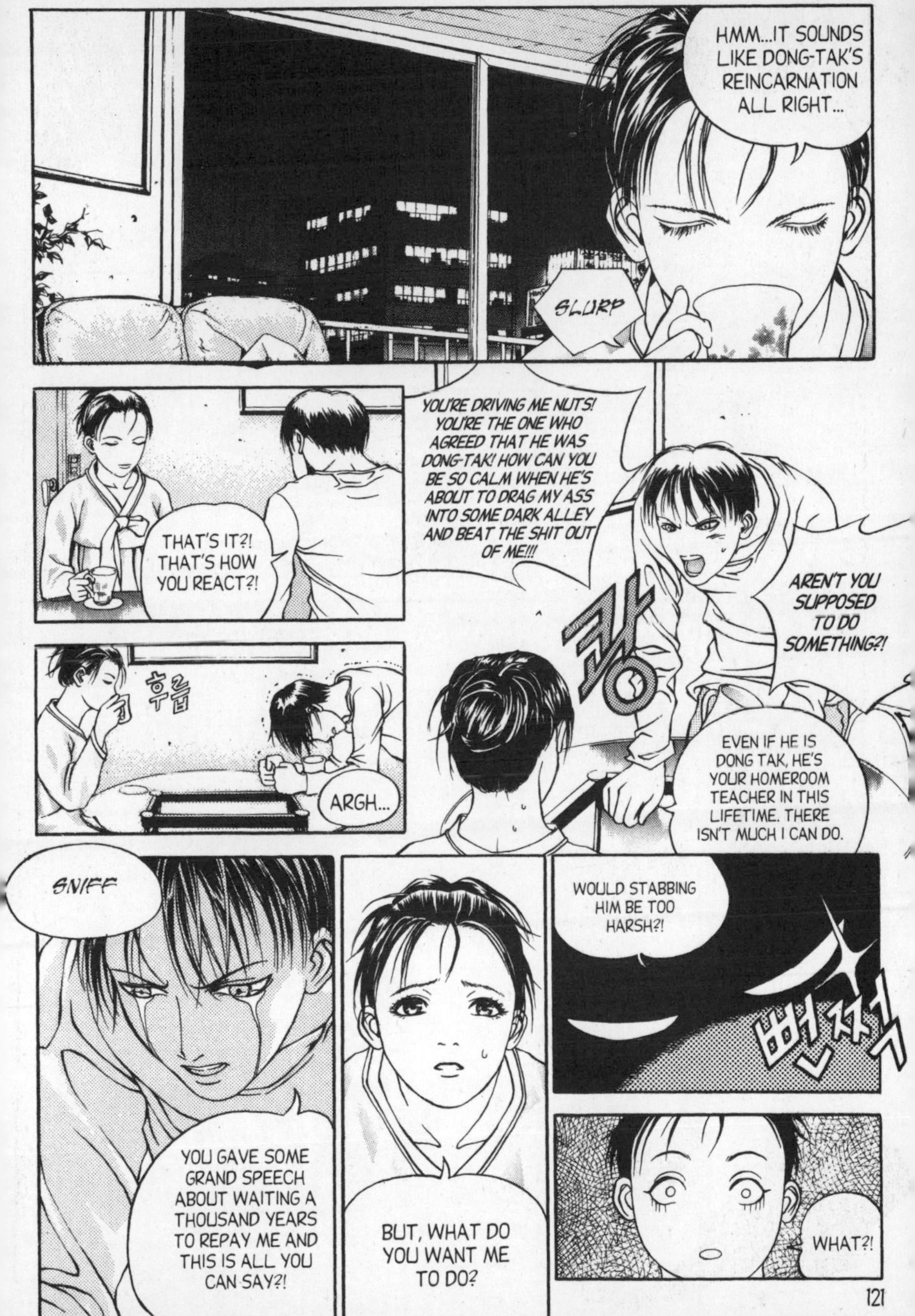

SLURP
HMM...IT SOUNDS LIKE DONG-TAK'S REINCARNATION ALL RIGHT...
THAT'S IT?! THAT'S HOW YOU REACT?!
후릅
ARGH...
YOU'RE DRIVING ME NUTS! YOU'RE THE ONE WHO AGREED THAT HE WAS DONG-TAK! HOW CAN YOU BE SO CALM WHEN HE'S ABOUT TO DRAG MY ASS INTO SOME DARK ALLEY AND BEAT THE SHIT OUT OF ME!!!
쾅
AREN'T YOU SUPPOSED TO DO SOMETHING?!
EVEN IF HE IS DONG TAK, HE'S YOUR HOMEROOM TEACHER IN THIS LIFETIME. THERE ISN'T MUCH I CAN DO.
SNIFF
YOU GAVE SOME GRAND SPEECH ABOUT WAITING A THOUSAND YEARS TO REPAY ME AND THIS IS ALL YOU CAN SAY?!
BUT, WHAT DO YOU WANT ME TO DO?
WOULD STABBING HIM BE TOO HARSH?!
번쩍
WHAT?!

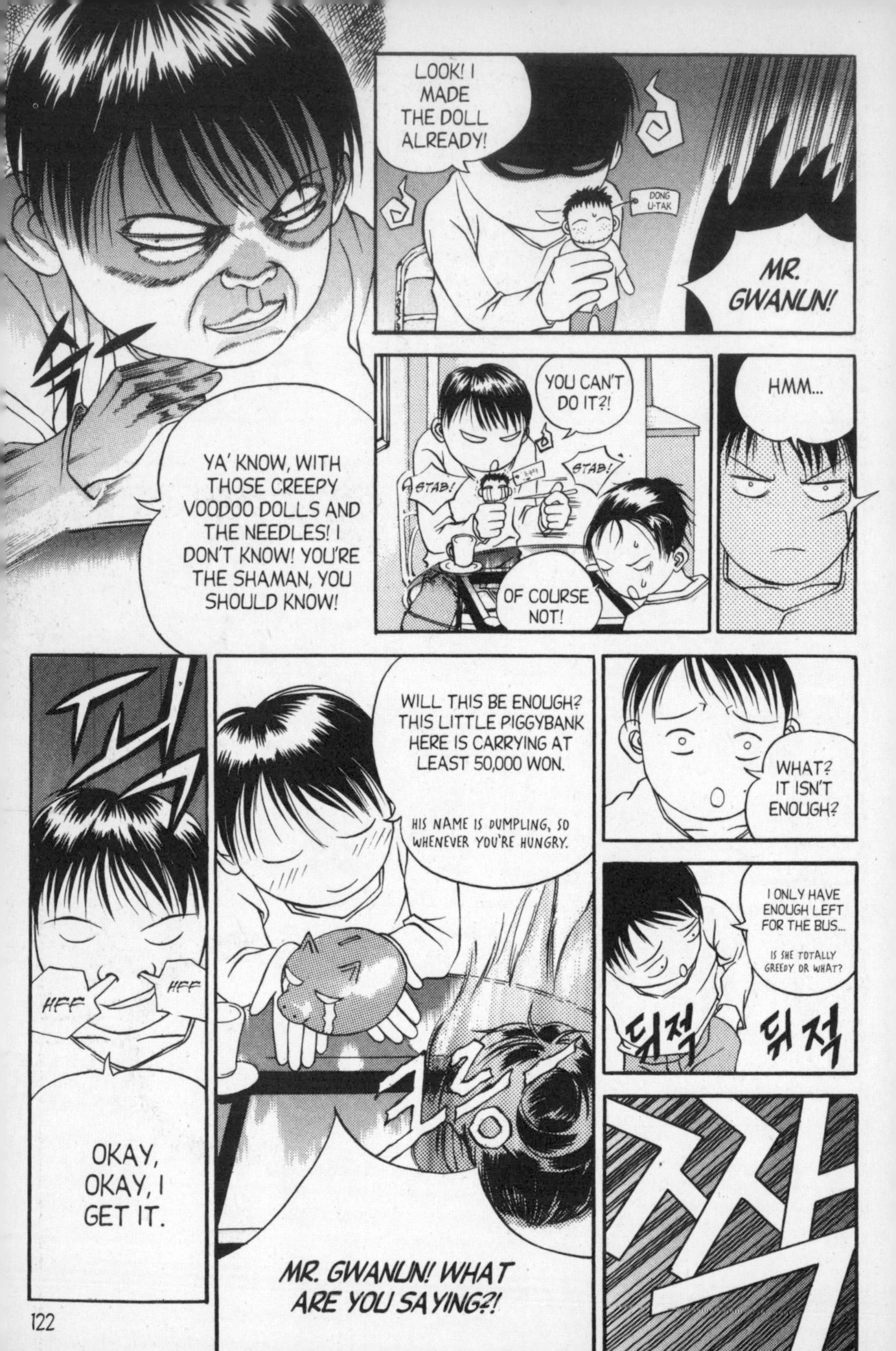
YA' KNOW, WITH THOSE CREEPY VOODOO DOLLS AND THE NEEDLES! I DON'T KNOW! YOU'RE THE SHAMAN, YOU SHOULD KNOW!
LOOK! I MADE THE DOLL ALREADY!
DONG U-TAK
MR. GWANUN!
YOU CAN'T DO IT?!
STAB!
STAB!
OF COURSE NOT!
HMM...
OKAY, OKAY, I GET IT.
HFF
HFF
WILL THIS BE ENOUGH? THIS LITTLE PIGGYBANK HERE IS CARRYING AT LEAST 50,000 WON.
HIS NAME IS DUMPLING, SO WHENEVER YOU'RE HUNGRY.
MR. GWANUN! WHAT ARE YOU SAYING?!
WHAT? IT ISN'T ENOUGH?
I ONLY HAVE ENOUGH LEFT FOR THE BUS...
IS SHE TOTALLY GREEDY OR WHAT?
뒤적 뒤적

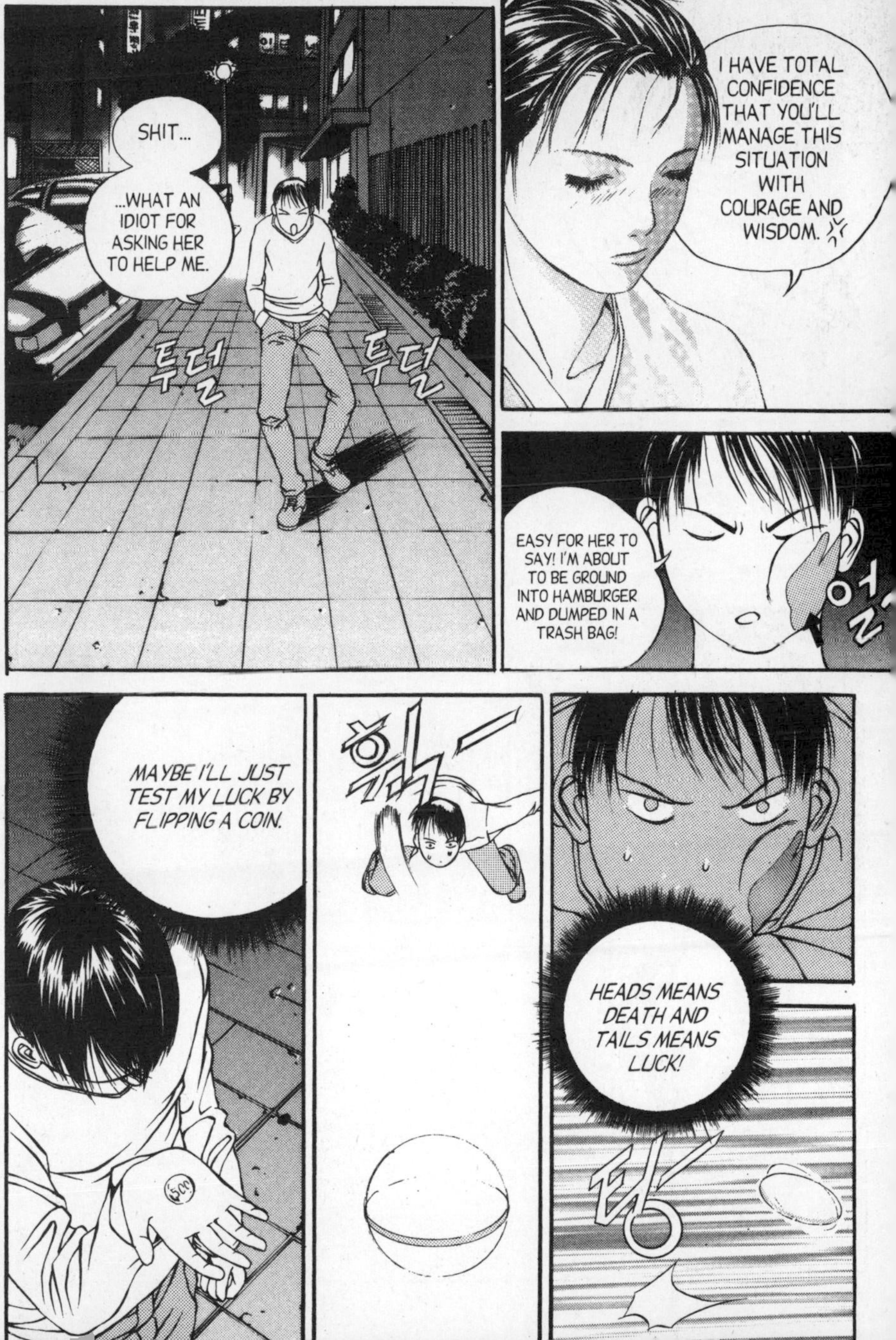
SHIT...
...WHAT AN IDIOT FOR ASKING HER TO HELP ME.
투덜
투덜
I HAVE TOTAL CONFIDENCE THAT YOU'LL MANAGE THIS SITUATION WITH COURAGE AND WISDOM.
EASY FOR HER TO SAY! I'M ABOUT TO BE GROUND INTO HAMBURGER AND DUMPED IN A TRASH BAG!
MAYBE I'LL JUST TEST MY LUCK BY FLIPPING A COIN.
HEADS MEANS DEATH AND TAILS MEANS LUCK!

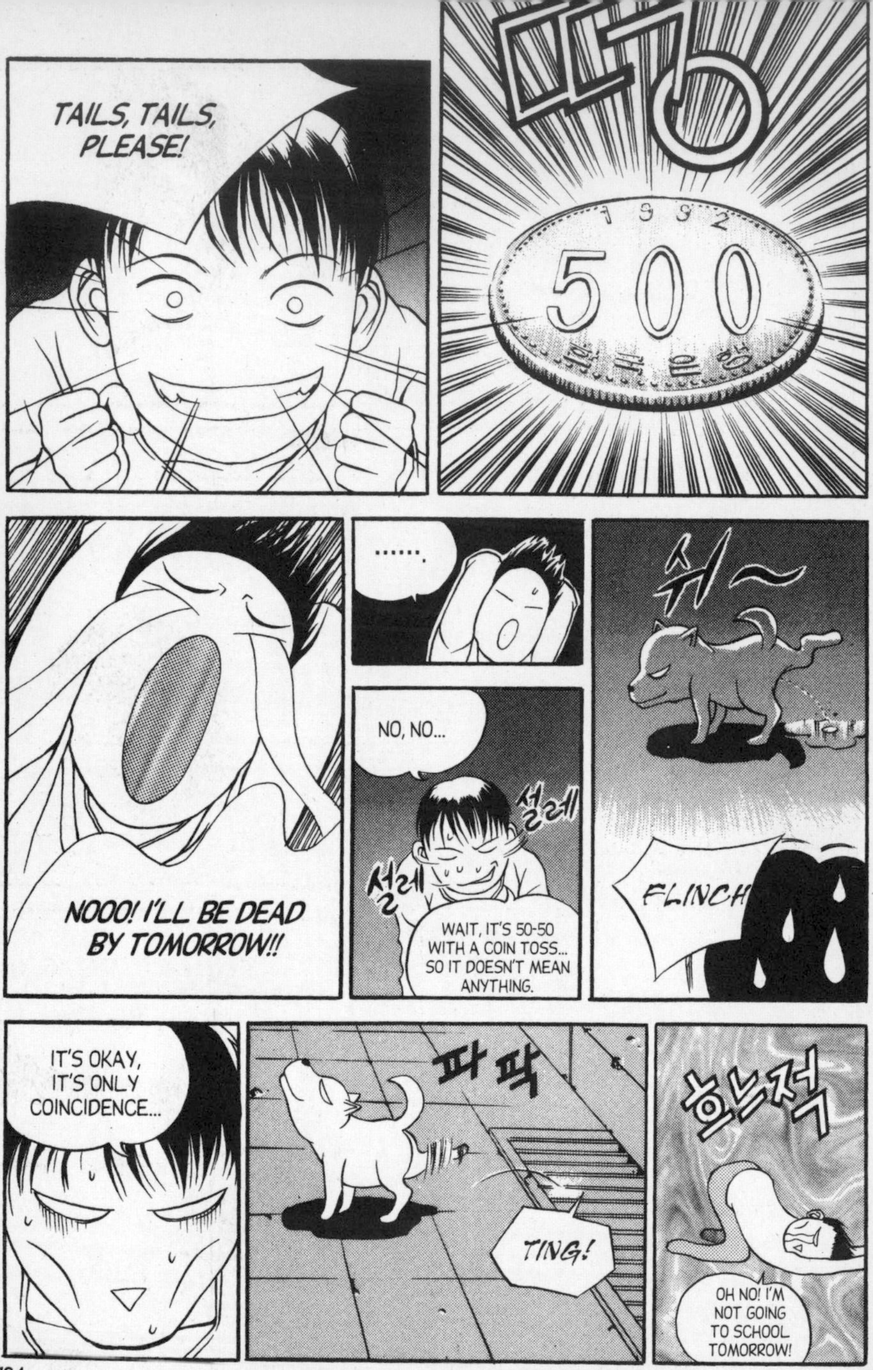
TAILS, TAILS, PLEASE!
1992
500
NOOO! I'LL BE DEAD BY TOMORROW!!
....
NO, NO...
설레
설레
WAIT, IT'S 50-50 WITH A COIN TOSS... SO IT DOESN'T MEAN ANYTHING.
쉬~
FLINCH
IT'S OKAY, IT'S ONLY COINCIDENCE...
파팍
TING!
흐느적
OH NO! I'M NOT GOING TO SCHOOL TOMORROW!

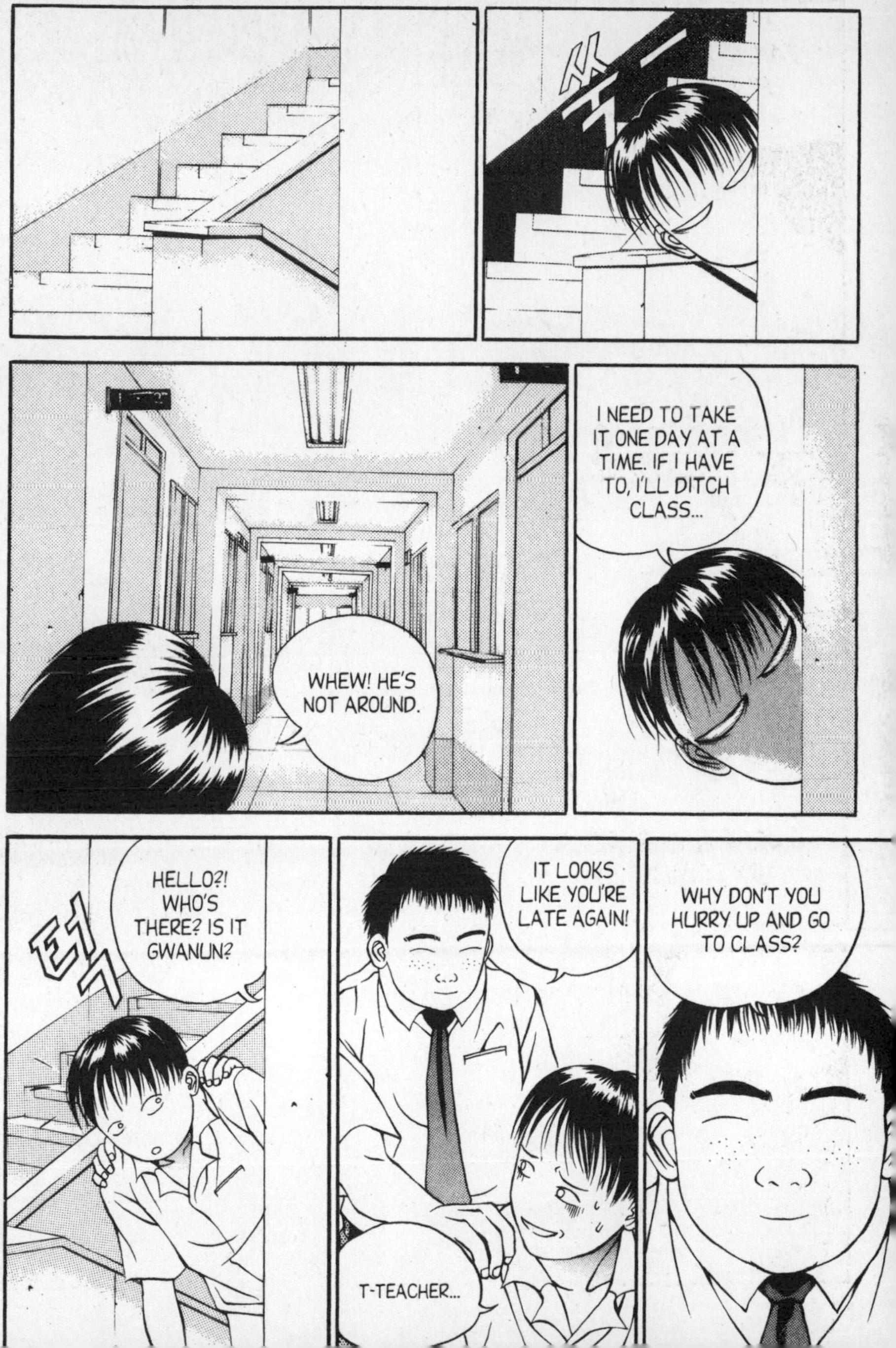
WHEW! HE'S NOT AROUND.
I NEED TO TAKE IT ONE DAY AT A TIME. IF I HAVE TO, I'LL DITCH CLASS...
HELLO?! WHO'S THERE? IS IT GWANUN?
IT LOOKS LIKE YOU'RE LATE AGAIN!
T-TEACHER...
WHY DON'T YOU HURRY UP AND GO TO CLASS?

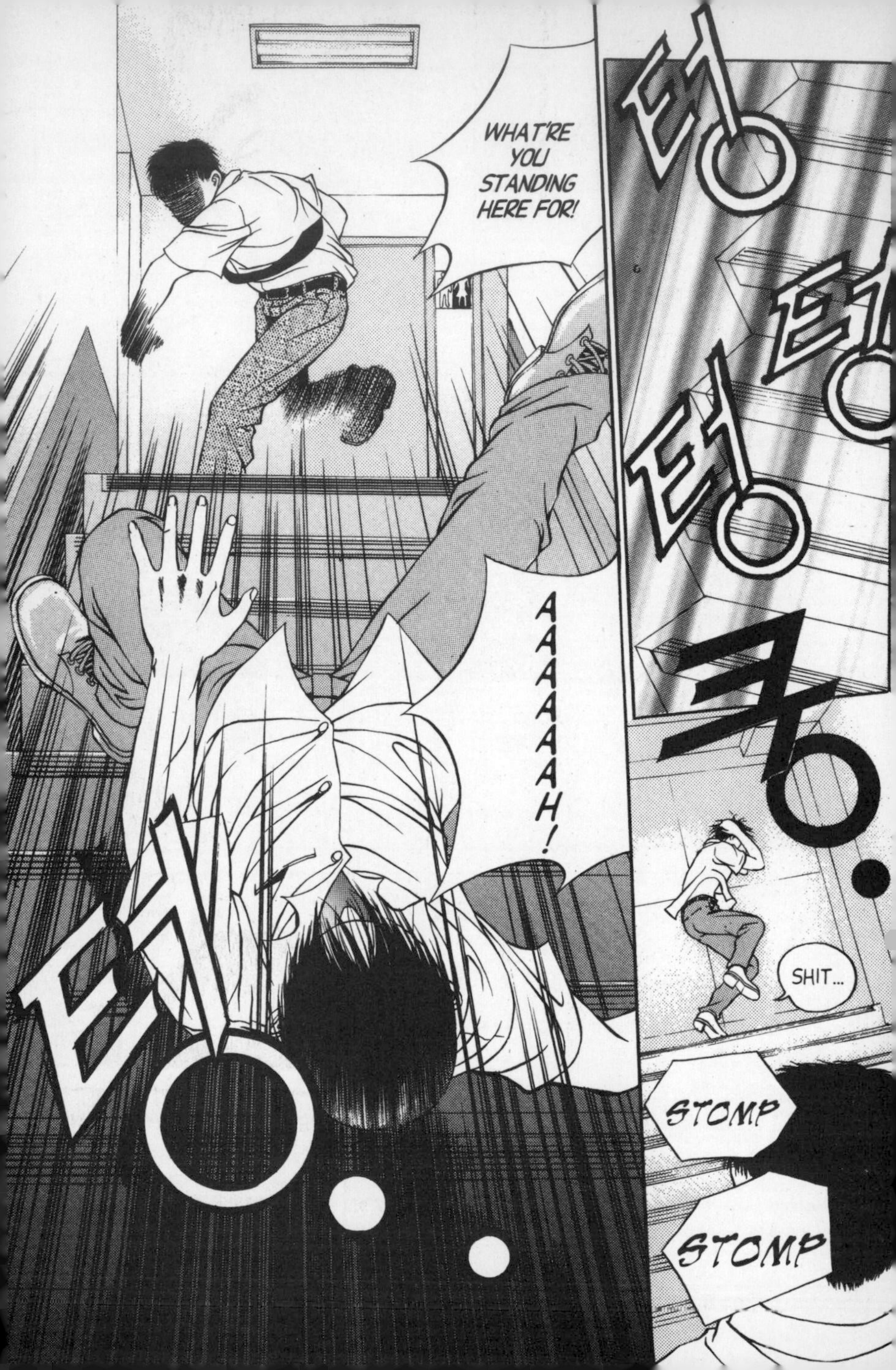
WHAT'RE YOU STANDING HERE FOR!
AAAAAAAH!
텅...
텅
텅
텅
SHIT...
STOMP
STOMP

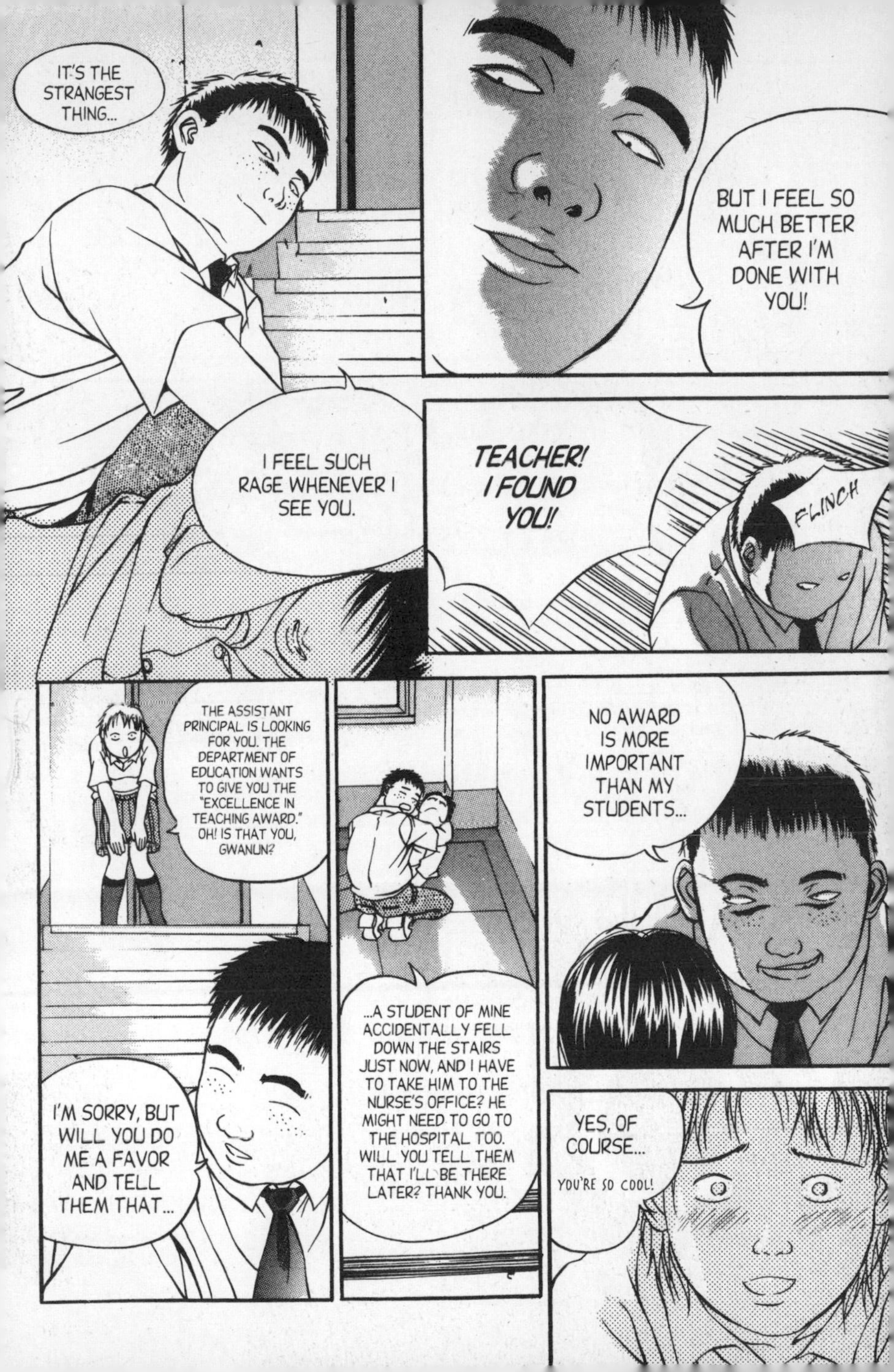
IT'S THE STRANGEST THING...
BUT I FEEL SO MUCH BETTER AFTER I'M DONE WITH YOU!
I FEEL SUCH RAGE WHENEVER I SEE YOU.
TEACHER! I FOUND YOU!
FLINCH
THE ASSISTANT PRINCIPAL IS LOOKING FOR YOU. THE DEPARTMENT OF EDUCATION WANTS TO GIVE YOU THE "EXCELLENCE IN TEACHING AWARD." OH! IS THAT YOU, GWANUN?
NO AWARD IS MORE IMPORTANT THAN MY STUDENTS...
I'M SORRY, BUT WILL YOU DO ME A FAVOR AND TELL THEM THAT...
...A STUDENT OF MINE ACCIDENTALLY FELL DOWN THE STAIRS JUST NOW, AND I HAVE TO TAKE HIM TO THE NURSE'S OFFICE? HE MIGHT NEED TO GO TO THE HOSPITAL TOO. WILL YOU TELL THEM THAT I'LL BE THERE LATER? THANK YOU.
YES, OF COURSE...
YOU'RE SO COOL!

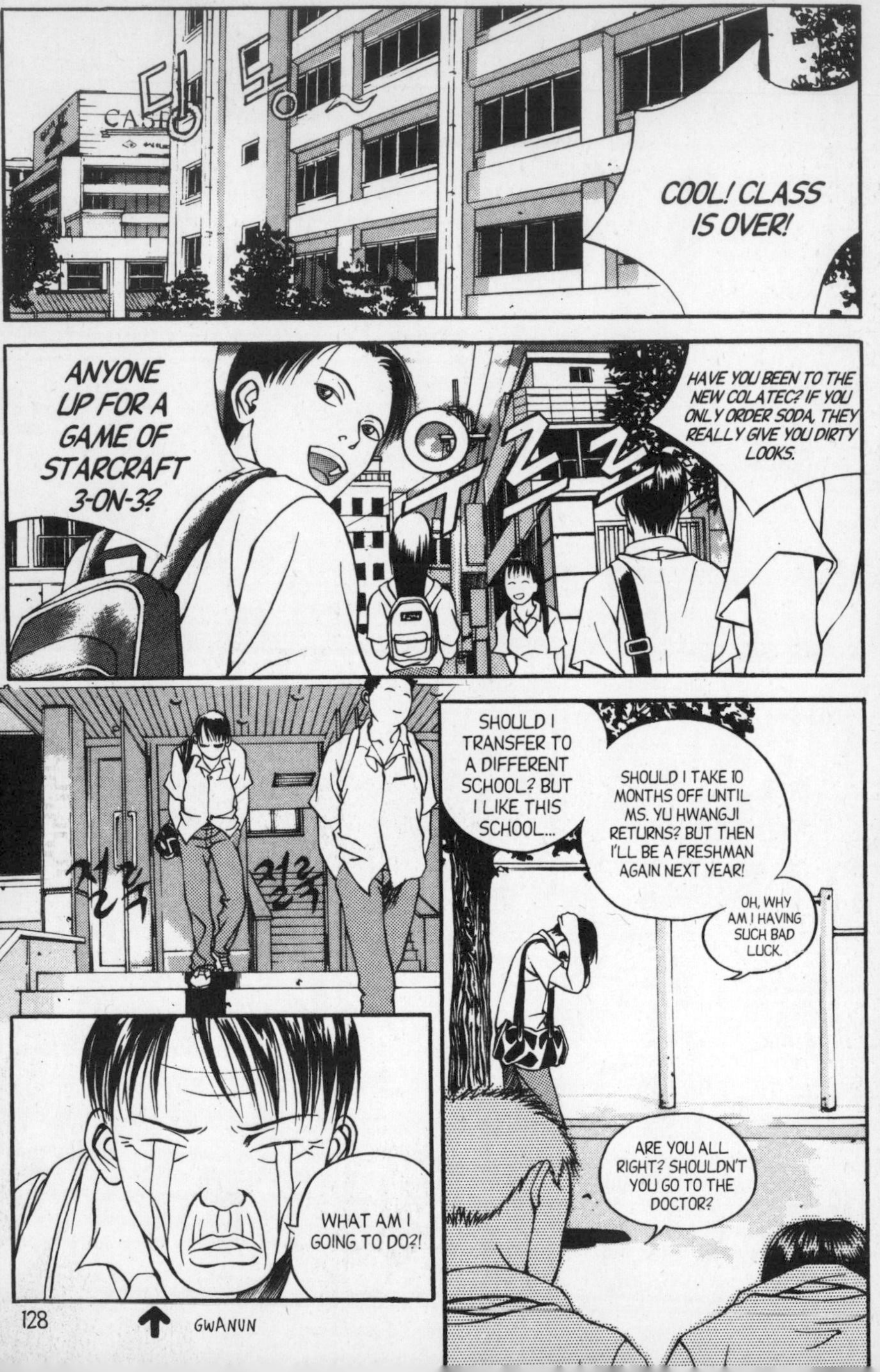
COOL! CLASS IS OVER!
ANYONE UP FOR A GAME OF STARCRAFT 3-ON-3?
HAVE YOU BEEN TO THE NEW COLATEC? IF YOU ONLY ORDER SODA, THEY REALLY GIVE YOU DIRTY LOOKS.
WHAT AM I GOING TO DO?!
GWANUN
SHOULD I TRANSFER TO A DIFFERENT SCHOOL? BUT I LIKE THIS SCHOOL...
SHOULD I TAKE 10 MONTHS OFF UNTIL MS. YU HWANGJI RETURNS? BUT THEN I'LL BE A FRESHMAN AGAIN NEXT YEAR!
OH, WHY AM I HAVING SUCH BAD LUCK.
ARE YOU ALL RIGHT? SHOULDN'T YOU GO TO THE DOCTOR?

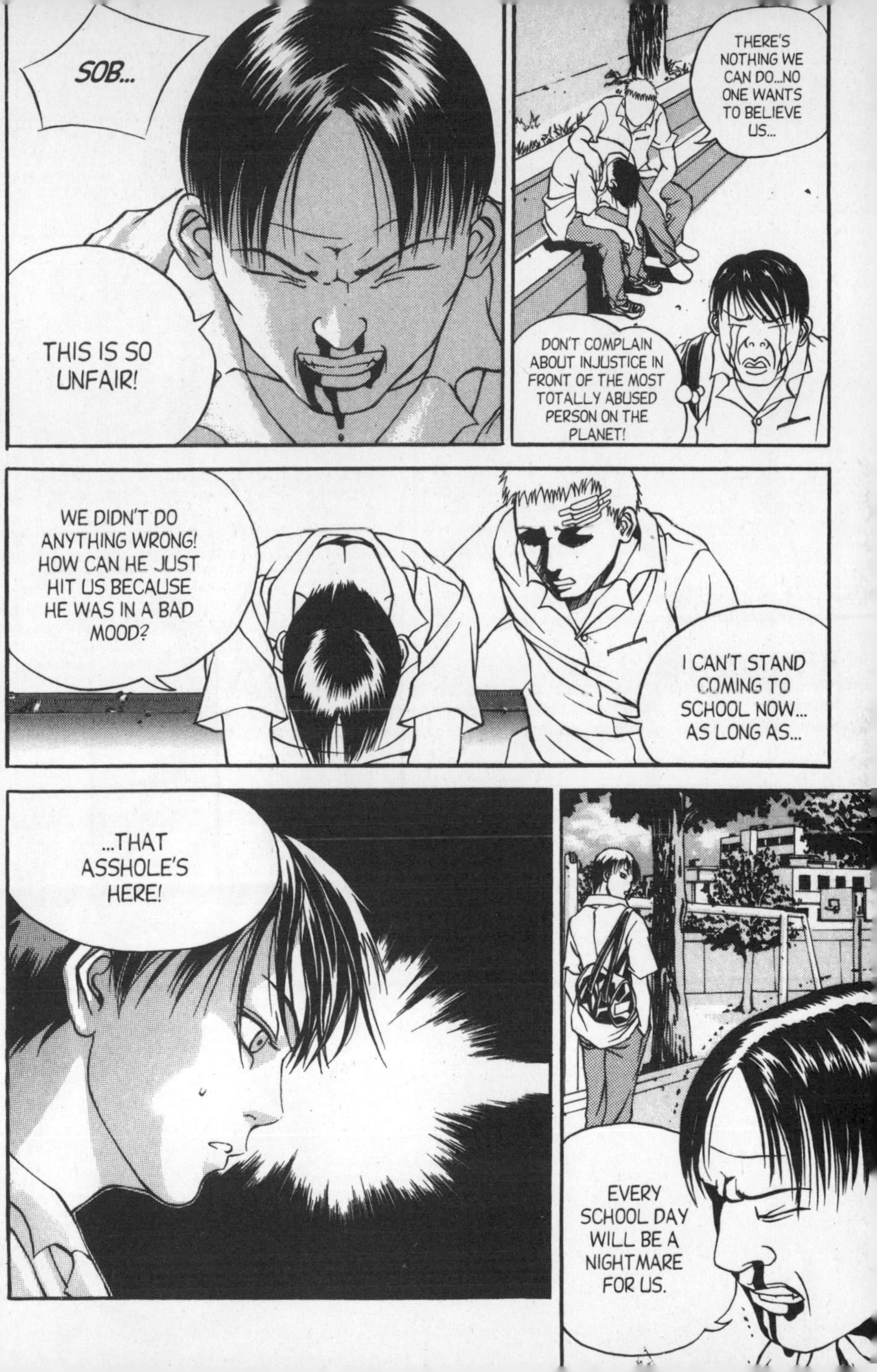
SOB...
THIS IS SO UNFAIR!
THERE'S NOTHING WE CAN DO...NO ONE WANTS TO BELIEVE US...
DON'T COMPLAIN ABOUT INJUSTICE IN FRONT OF THE MOST TOTALLY ABUSED PERSON ON THE PLANET!
WE DIDN'T DO ANYTHING WRONG! HOW CAN HE JUST HIT US BECAUSE HE WAS IN A BAD MOOD?
I CAN'T STAND COMING TO SCHOOL NOW... AS LONG AS...
...THAT ASSHOLE'S HERE!
EVERY SCHOOL DAY WILL BE A NIGHTMARE FOR US.

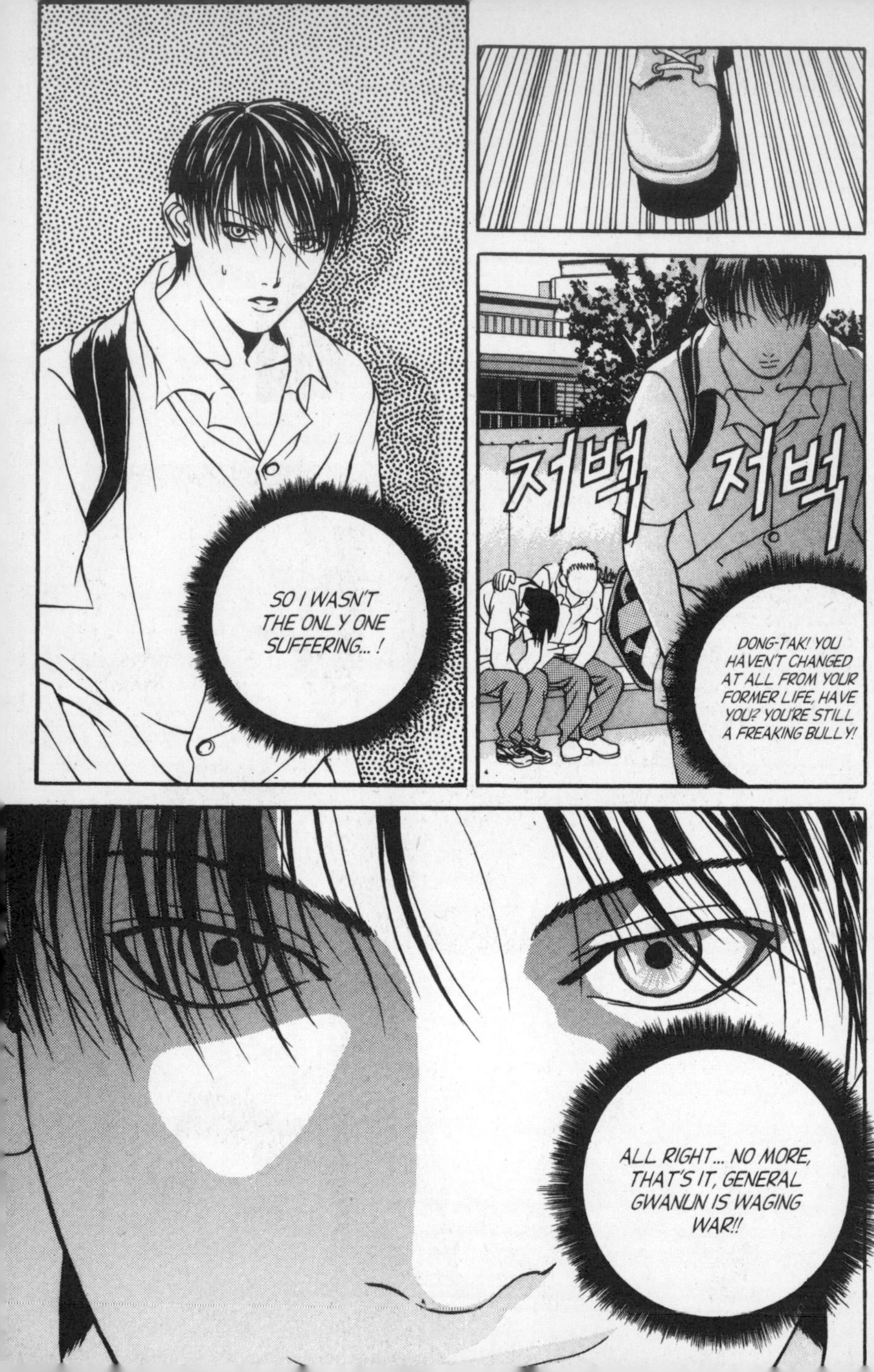
SO I WASN'T THE ONLY ONE SUFFERING... !
저벅 저벅
DONG-TAK! YOU HAVEN'T CHANGED AT ALL FROM YOUR FORMER LIFE, HAVE YOU? YOU'RE STILL A FREAKING BULLY!
ALL RIGHT... NO MORE, THAT'S IT, GENERAL GWANUN IS WAGING WAR!!

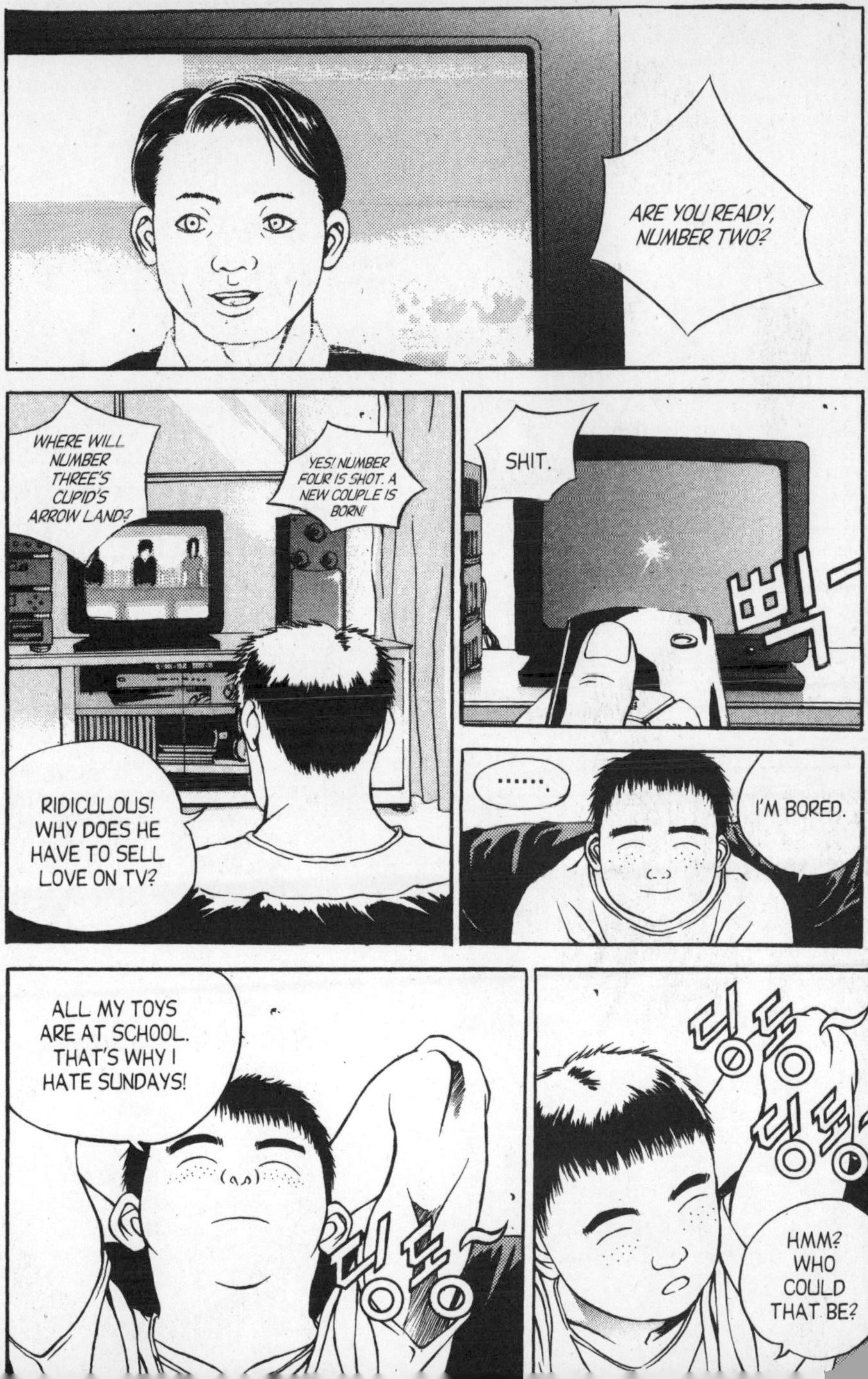

ARE YOU READY, NUMBER TWO?
WHERE WILL NUMBER THREE'S CUPID'S ARROW LAND?
YES! NUMBER FOUR IS SHOT. A NEW COUPLE IS BORN!
RIDICULOUS! WHY DOES HE HAVE TO SELL LOVE ON TV?
SHIT.
....
I'M BORED.
ALL MY TOYS ARE AT SCHOOL. THAT'S WHY I HATE SUNDAYS!
딩동~
딩동~
딩동~
HMM? WHO COULD THAT BE?

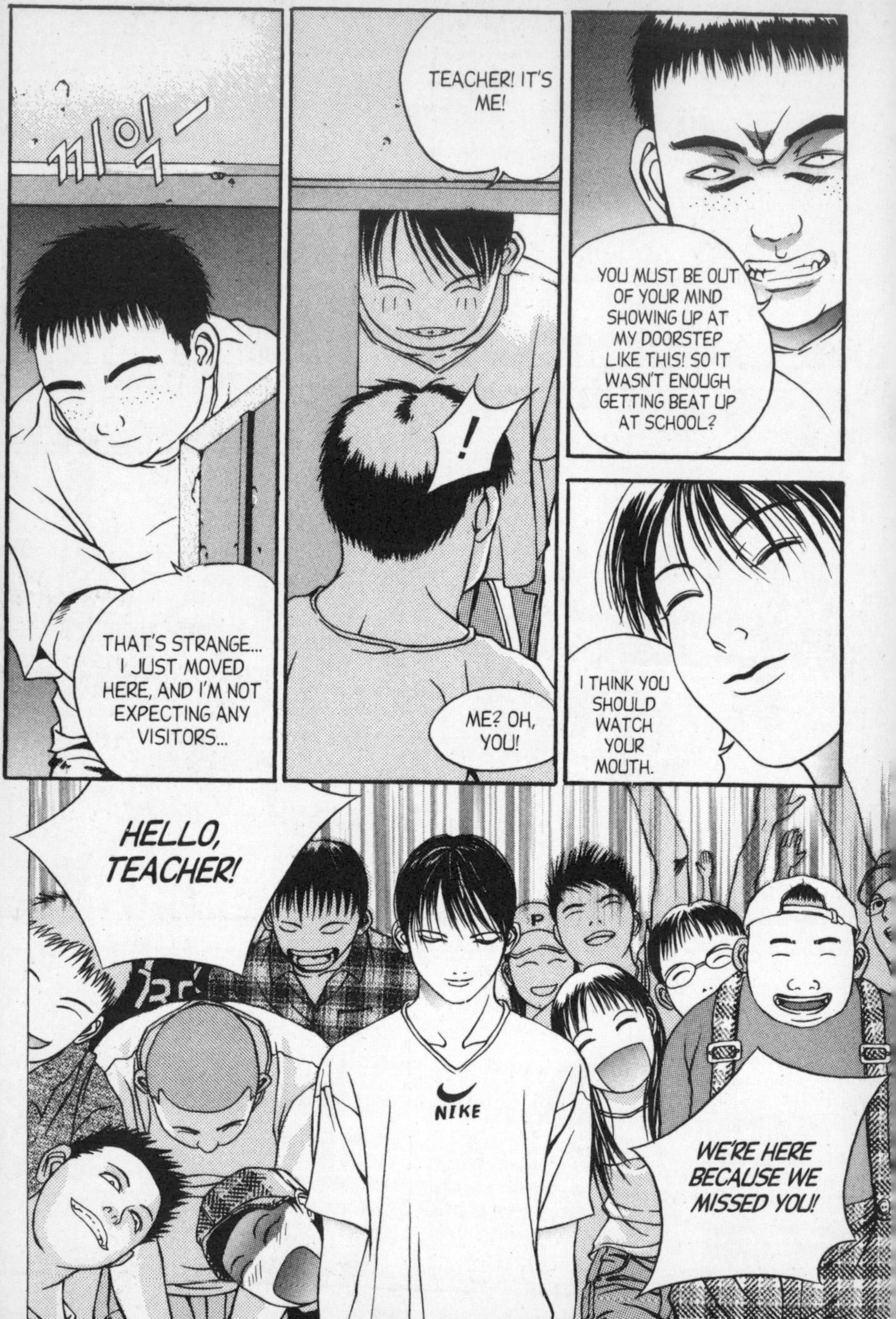
THAT'S STRANGE... I JUST MOVED HERE, AND I'M NOT EXPECTING ANY VISITORS...
TEACHER! IT'S ME!
!
ME? OH, YOU!
YOU MUST BE OUT OF YOUR MIND SHOWING UP AT MY DOORSTEP LIKE THIS! SO IT WASN'T ENOUGH GETTING BEAT UP AT SCHOOL?
I THINK YOU SHOULD WATCH YOUR MOUTH.
HELLO, TEACHER!
NIKE
WE'RE HERE BECAUSE WE MISSED YOU!

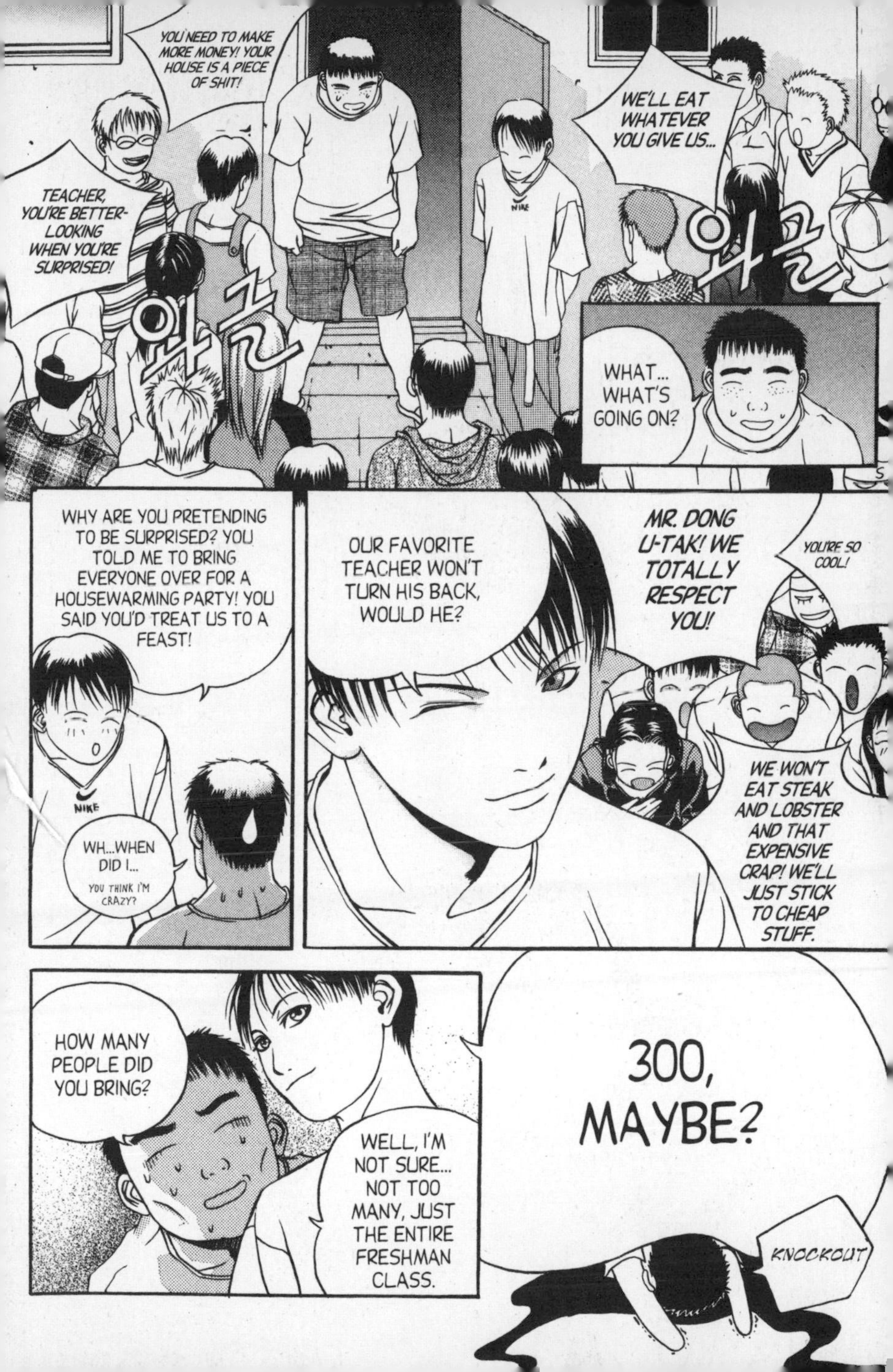
YOU NEED TO MAKE MORE MONEY! YOUR HOUSE IS A PIECE OF SHIT!
TEACHER, YOU'RE BETTER-LOOKING WHEN YOU'RE SURPRISED!
와글
WE'LL EAT WHATEVER YOU GIVE US...
와글
WHAT... WHAT'S GOING ON?
WHY ARE YOU PRETENDING TO BE SURPRISED? YOU TOLD ME TO BRING EVERYONE OVER FOR A HOUSEWARMING PARTY! YOU SAID YOU'D TREAT US TO A FEAST!
NIKE
WH...WHEN DID I...
YOU THINK I'M CRAZY?
OUR FAVORITE TEACHER WON'T TURN HIS BACK, WOULD HE?
MR. DONG U-TAK! WE TOTALLY RESPECT YOU!
YOU'RE SO COOL!
WE WON'T EAT STEAK AND LOBSTER AND THAT EXPENSIVE CRAP! WE'LL JUST STICK TO CHEAP STUFF.
HOW MANY PEOPLE DID YOU BRING?
WELL, I'M NOT SURE... NOT TOO MANY, JUST THE ENTIRE FRESHMAN CLASS.
300, MAYBE?
KNOCKOUT

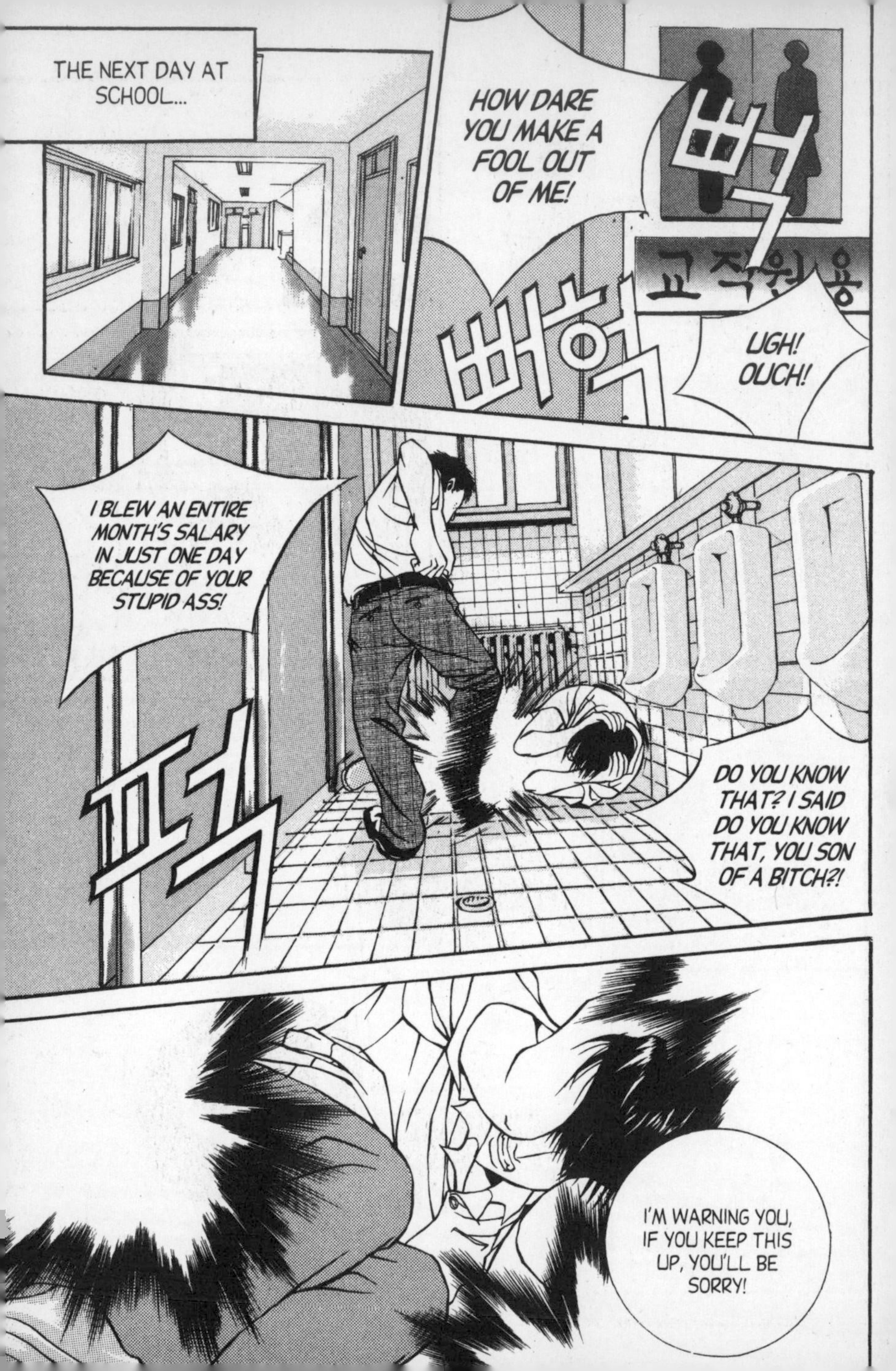
THE NEXT DAY AT SCHOOL...
HOW DARE YOU MAKE A FOOL OUT OF ME!
빡
교직원용
UGH! OUCH!
I BLEW AN ENTIRE MONTH'S SALARY IN JUST ONE DAY BECAUSE OF YOUR STUPID ASS!
퍽
DO YOU KNOW THAT? I SAID DO YOU KNOW THAT, YOU SON OF A BITCH?!
I'M WARNING YOU, IF YOU KEEP THIS UP, YOU'LL BE SORRY!

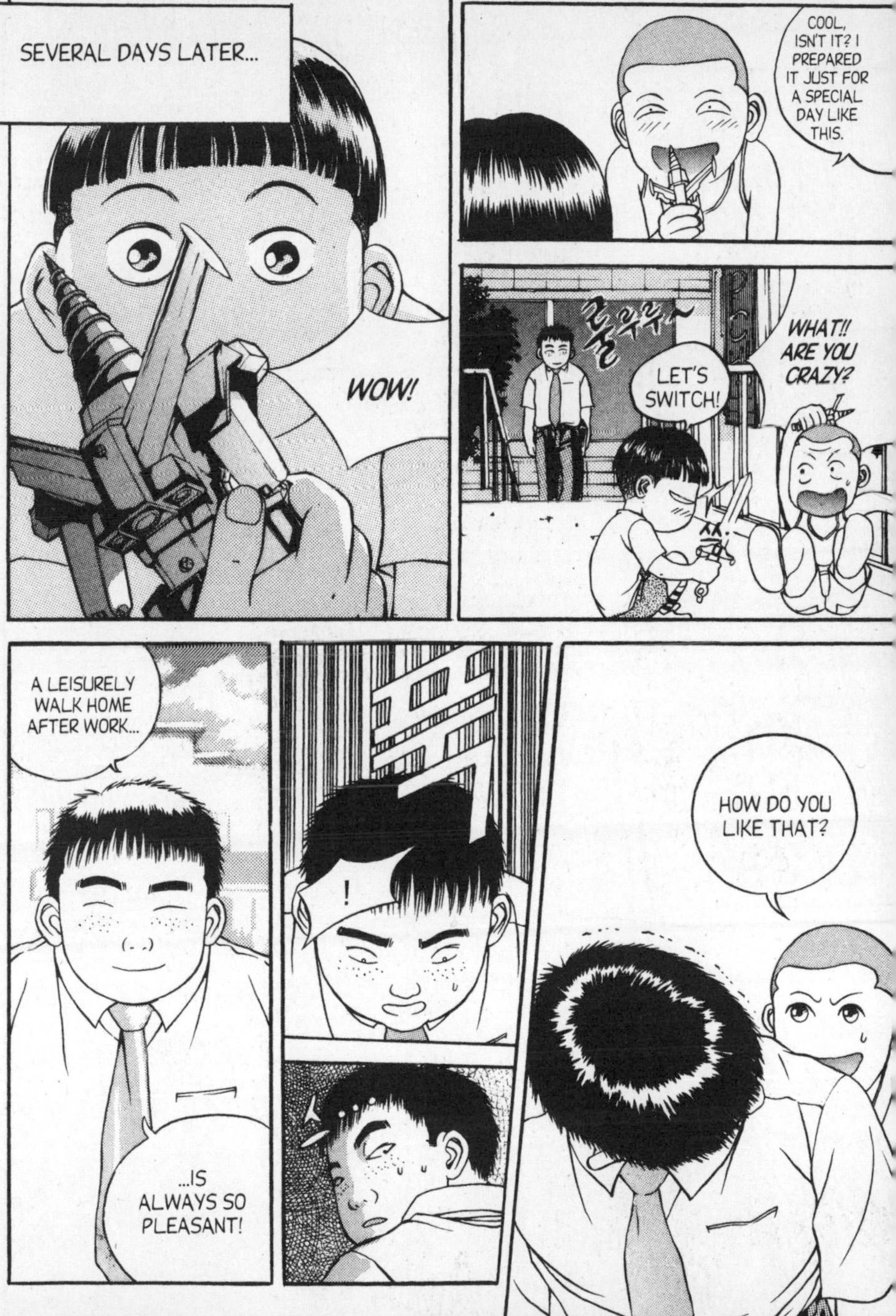
SEVERAL DAYS LATER...
WOW!
COOL, ISN'T IT? I PREPARED IT JUST FOR A SPECIAL DAY LIKE THIS.
LET'S SWITCH!
WHAT!! ARE YOU CRAZY?
A LEISURELY WALK HOME AFTER WORK...
...IS ALWAYS SO PLEASANT!
!
HOW DO YOU LIKE THAT?

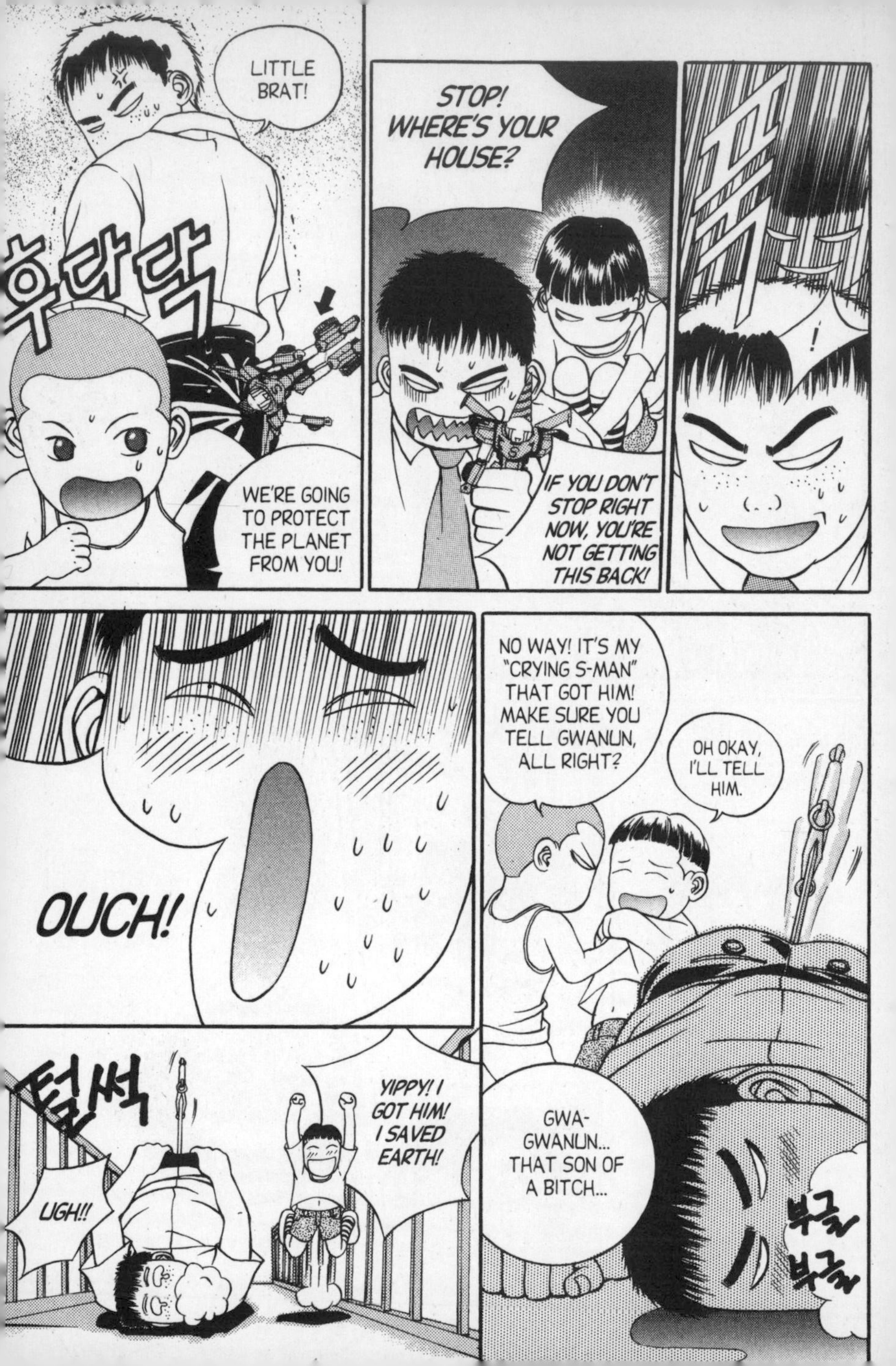
LITTLE BRAT!
후다닥
WE'RE GOING TO PROTECT THE PLANET FROM YOU!
STOP! WHERE'S YOUR HOUSE?
IF YOU DON'T STOP RIGHT NOW, YOU'RE NOT GETTING THIS BACK!
!
OUCH!
털썩
UGH!!
YIPPY! I GOT HIM! I SAVED EARTH!
NO WAY! IT'S MY "CRYING S-MAN" THAT GOT HIM! MAKE SURE YOU TELL GWANUN, ALL RIGHT?
OH OKAY, I'LL TELL HIM.
GWA- GWANUN... THAT SON OF A BITCH...
부글
부글

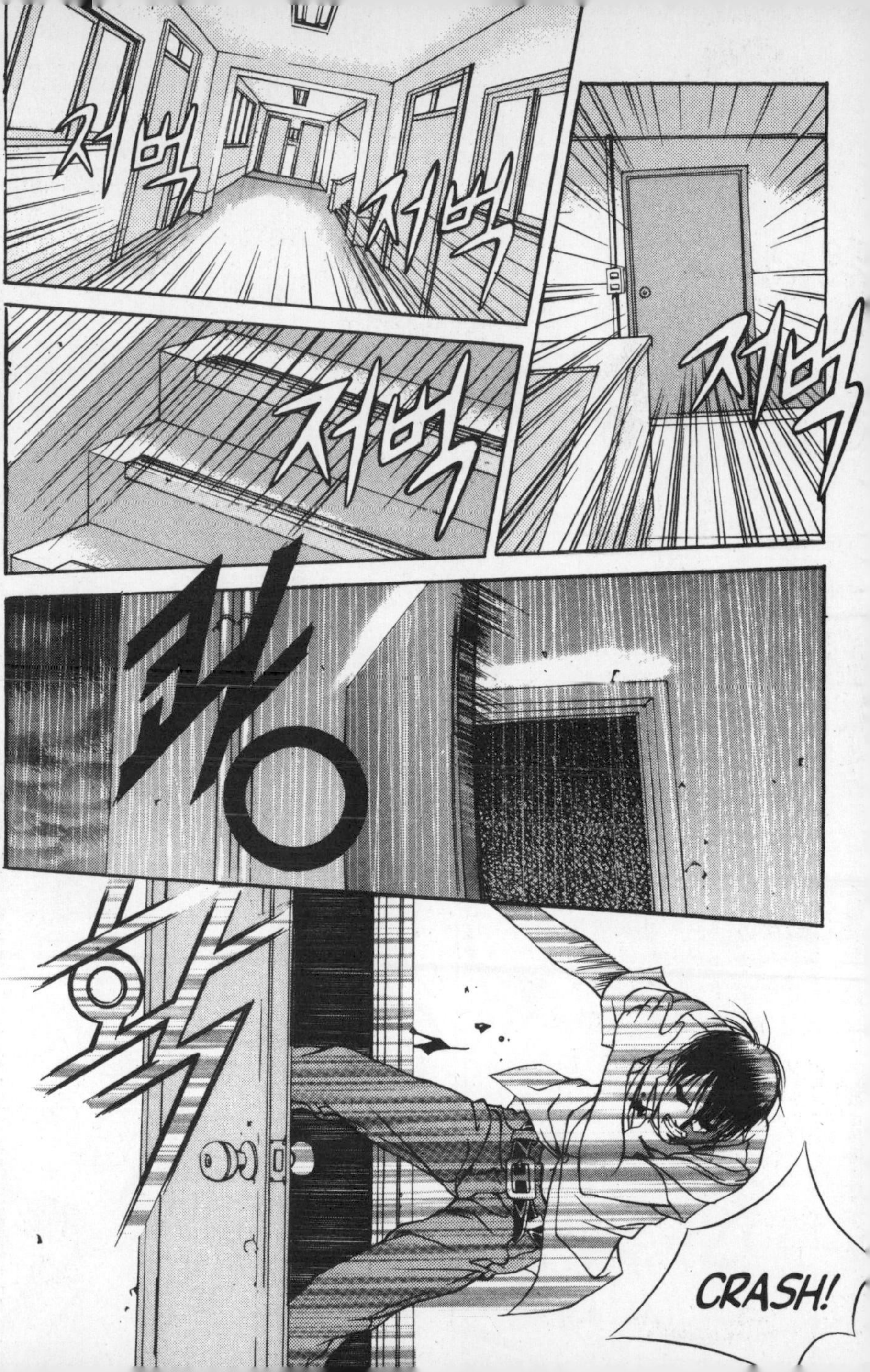

저벅
저벅
저벅
저벅
쾅
CRASH!

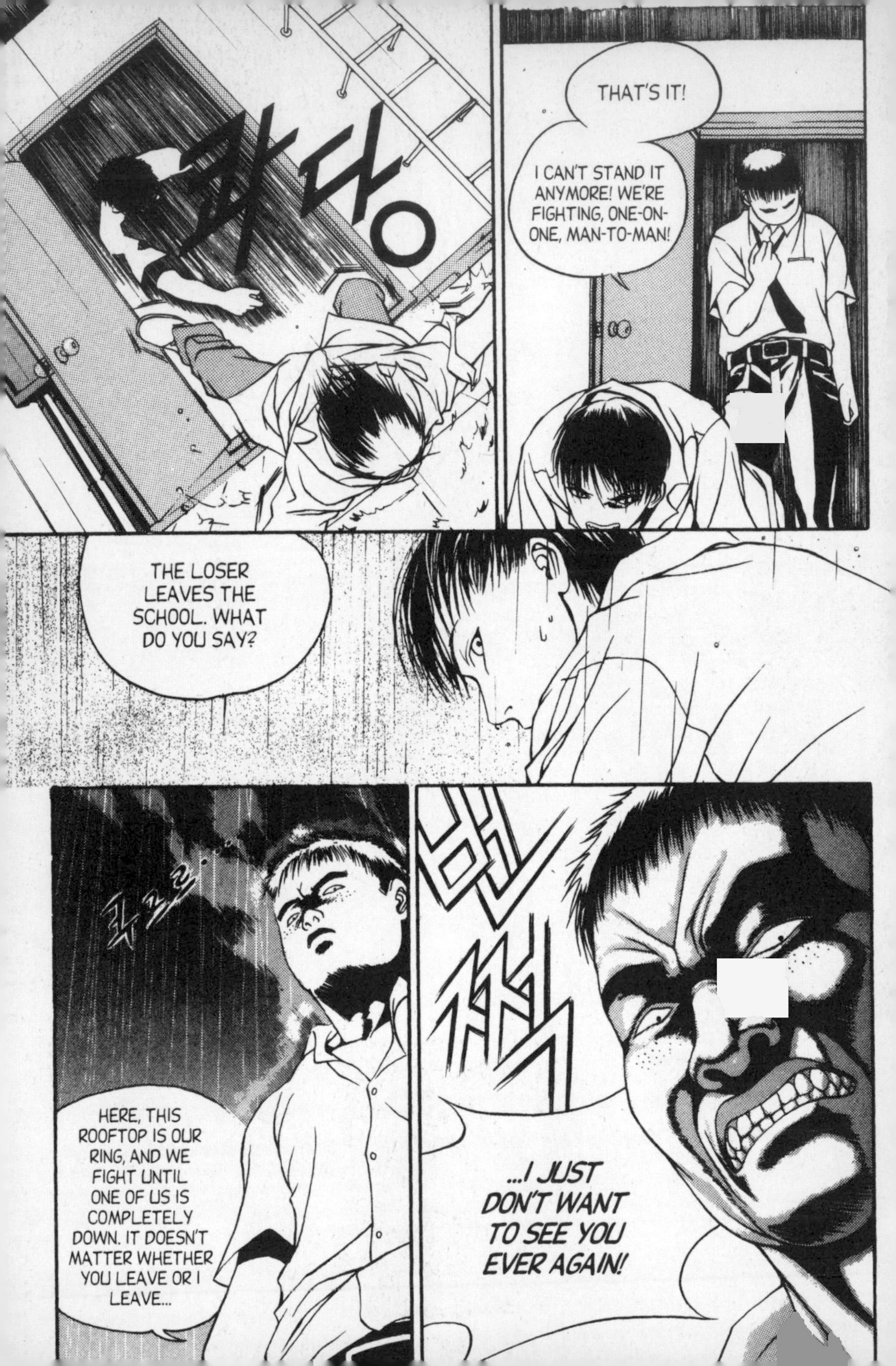
THAT'S IT!
I CAN'T STAND IT ANYMORE! WE'RE FIGHTING, ONE-ON-ONE, MAN-TO-MAN!
THE LOSER LEAVES THE SCHOOL. WHAT DO YOU SAY?
HERE, THIS ROOFTOP IS OUR RING, AND WE FIGHT UNTIL ONE OF US IS COMPLETELY DOWN. IT DOESN'T MATTER WHETHER YOU LEAVE OR I LEAVE...
...I JUST DON'T WANT TO SEE YOU EVER AGAIN!

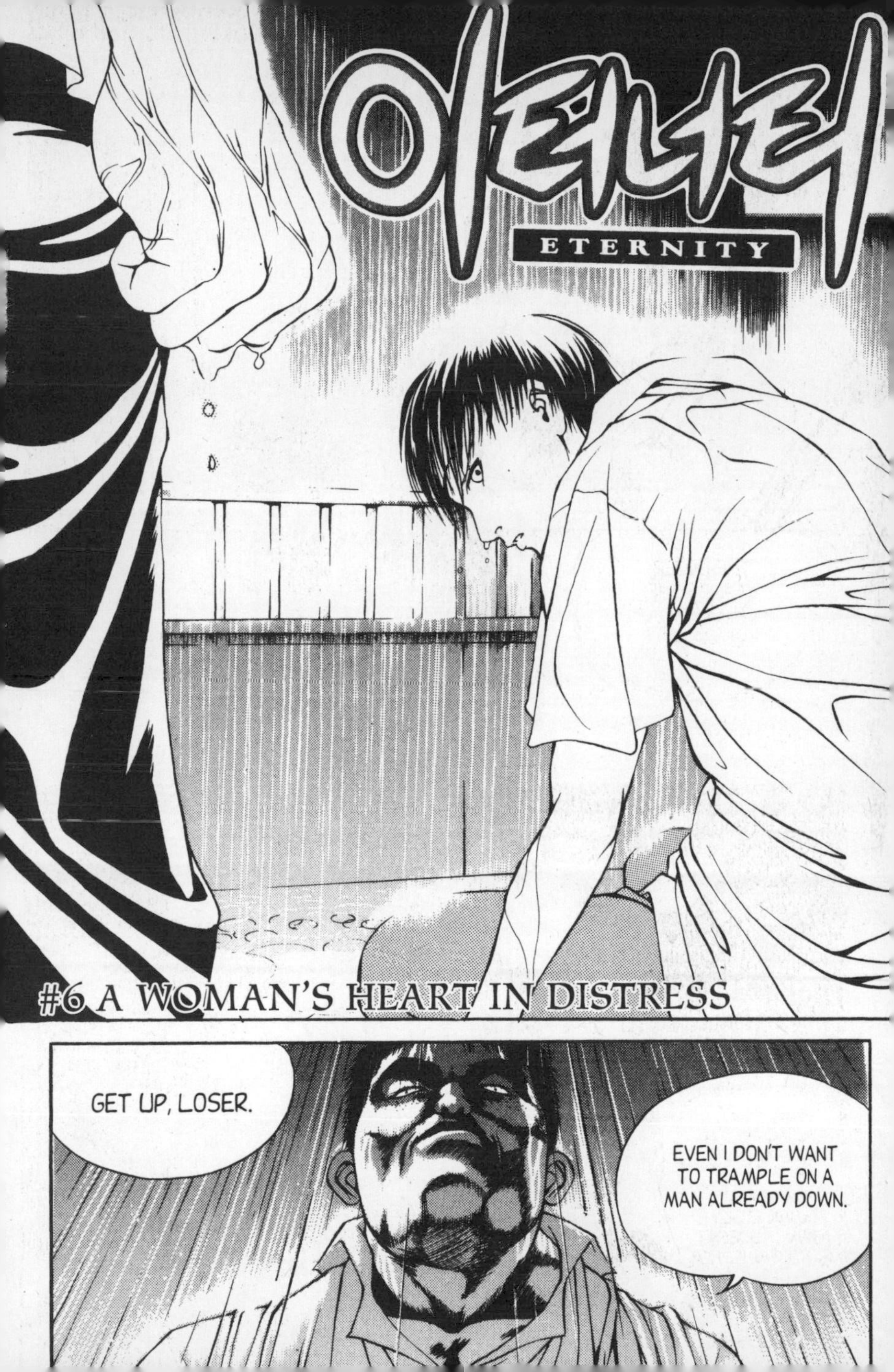
이터니티
ETERNITY
#6 A WOMAN'S HEART IN DISTRESS
GET UP, LOSER.
EVEN I DON'T WANT TO TRAMPLE ON A MAN ALREADY DOWN.

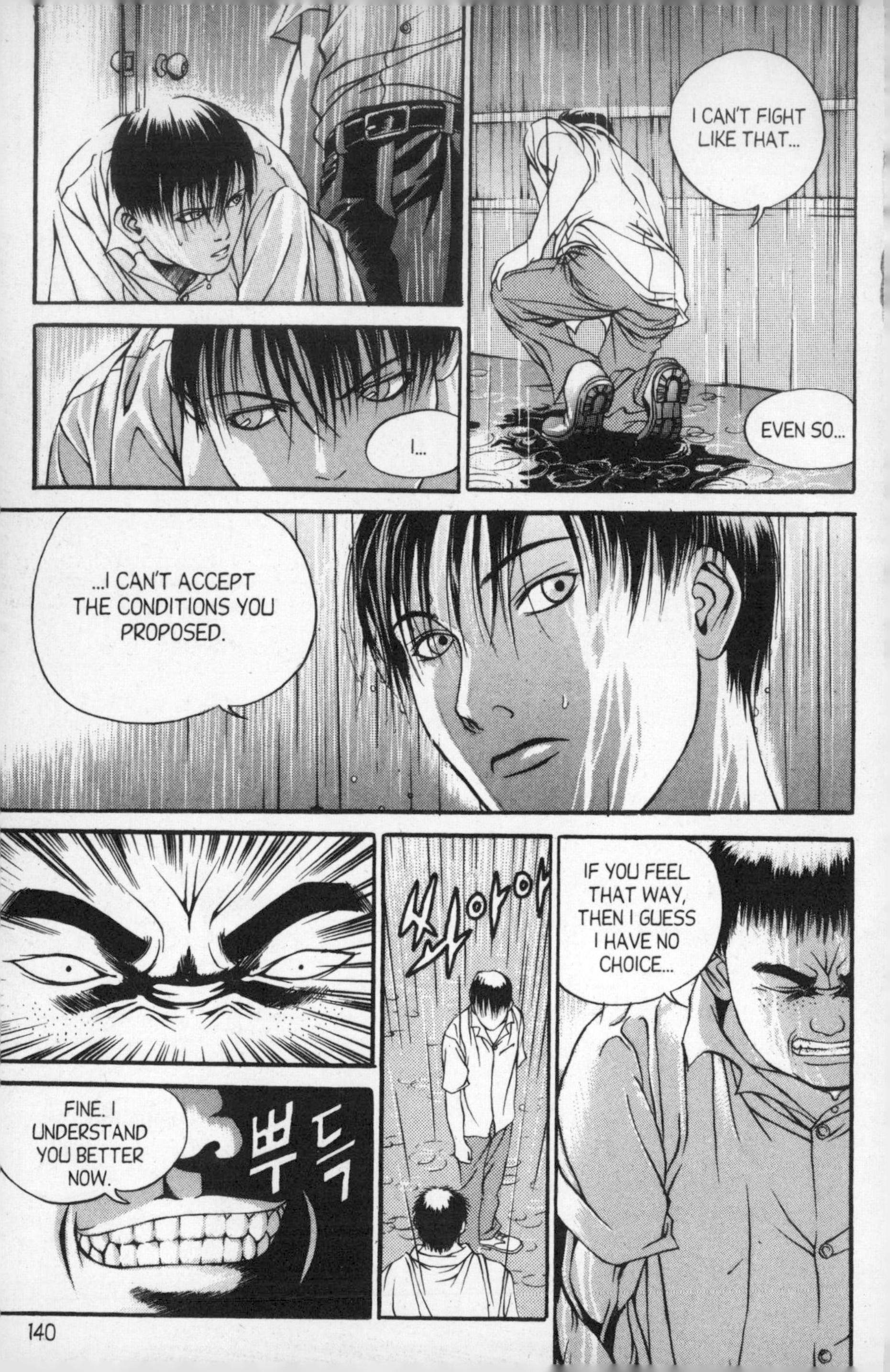
I...
I CAN'T FIGHT LIKE THAT...
EVEN SO...
...I CAN'T ACCEPT THE CONDITIONS YOU PROPOSED.
FINE. I UNDERSTAND YOU BETTER NOW.
뿌득
쏴아아
IF YOU FEEL THAT WAY, THEN I GUESS I HAVE NO CHOICE...

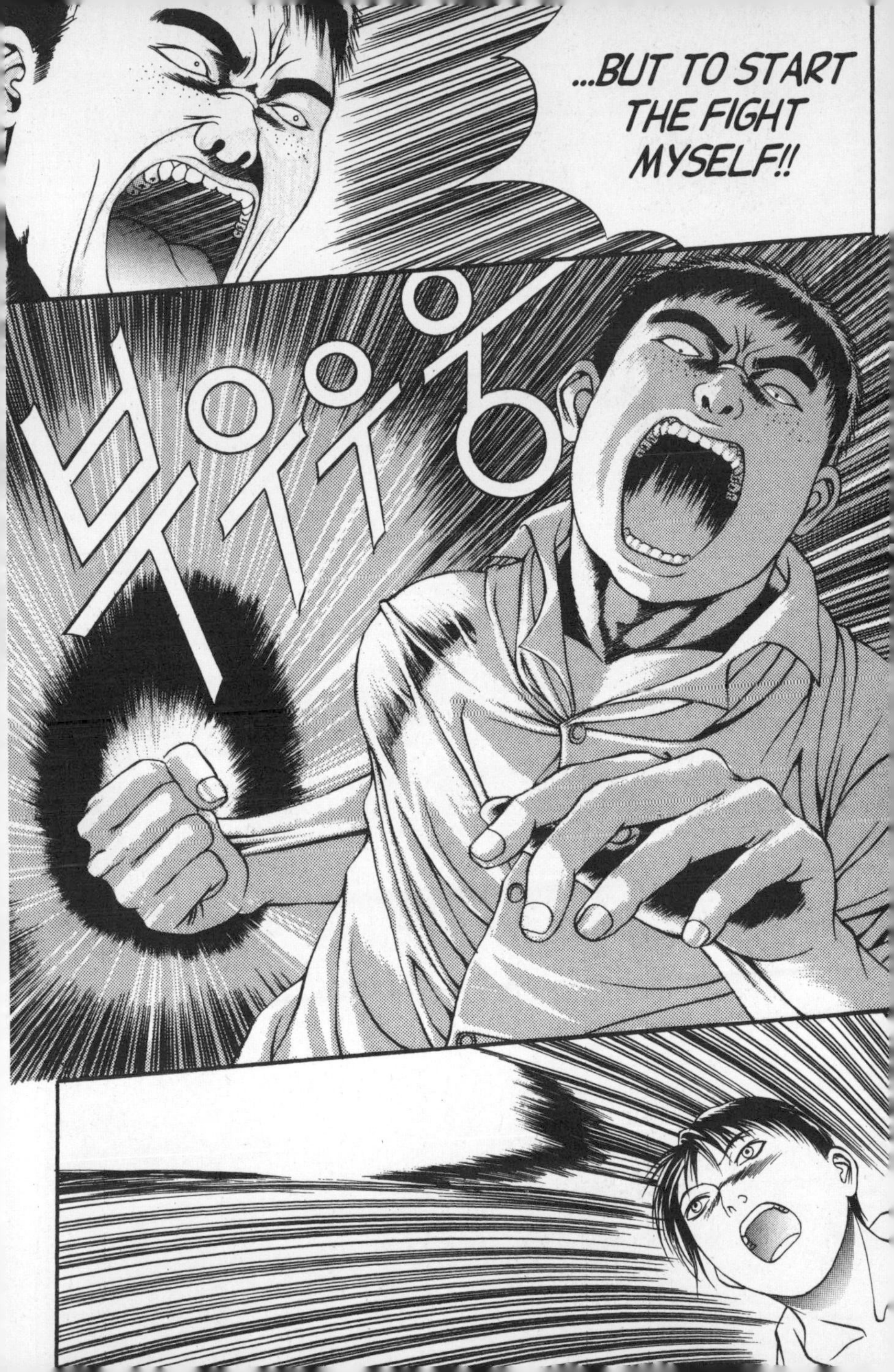
...BUT TO START THE FIGHT MYSELF!!
부우우웅

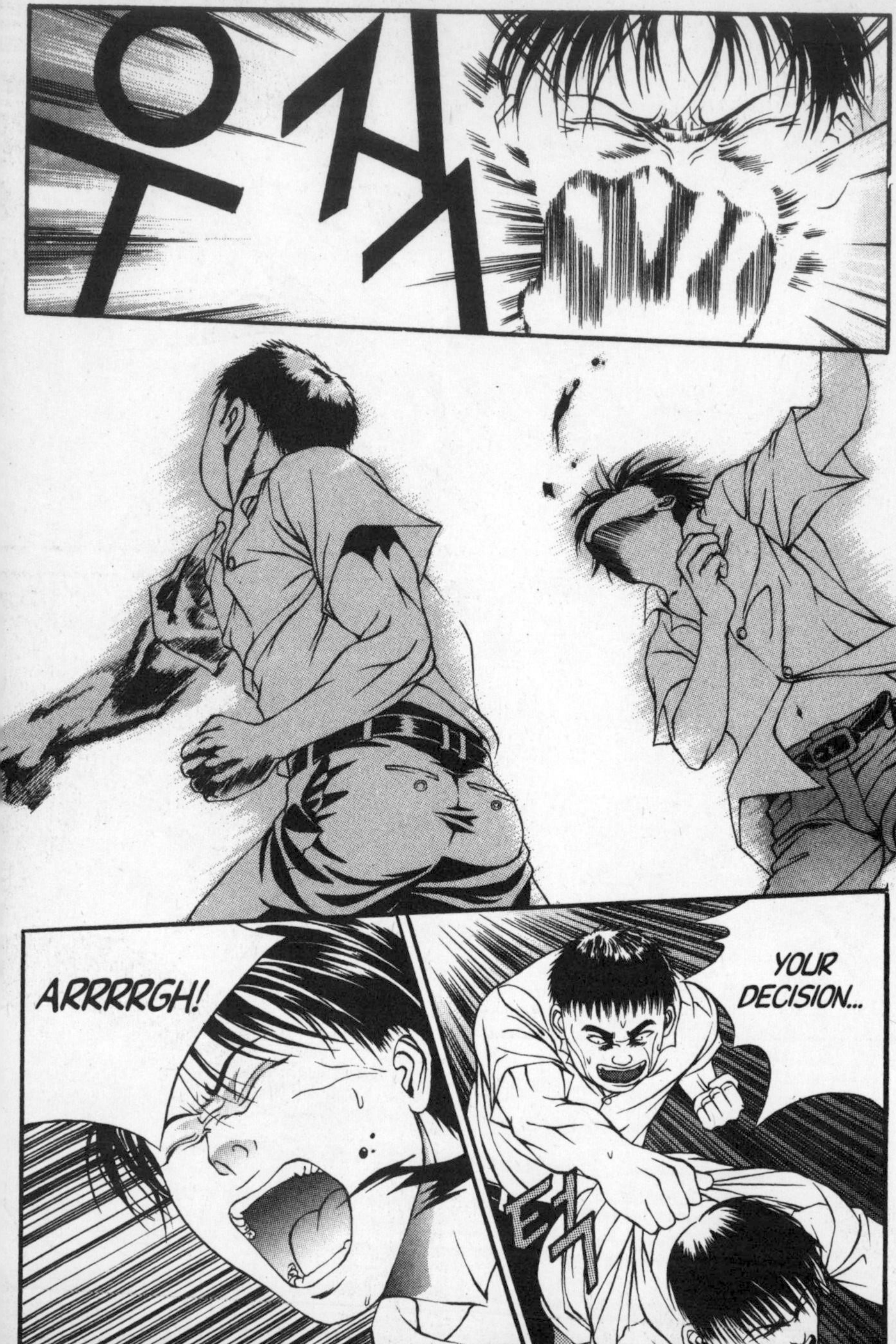
ARRRRGH!
YOUR DECISION...

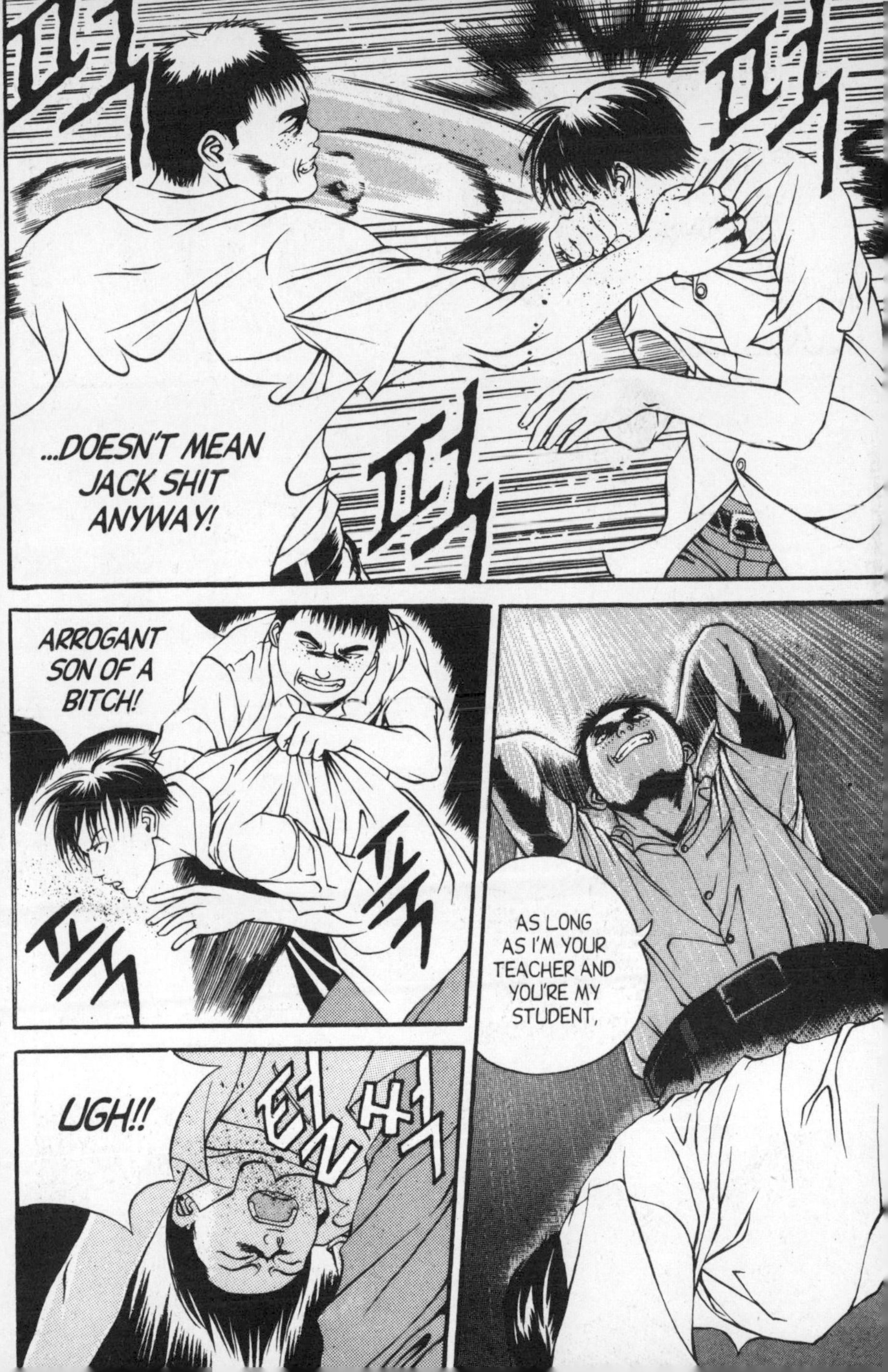
...DOESN'T MEAN JACK SHIT ANYWAY!
ARROGANT SON OF A BITCH!
AS LONG AS I'M YOUR TEACHER AND YOU'RE MY STUDENT,
UGH!!

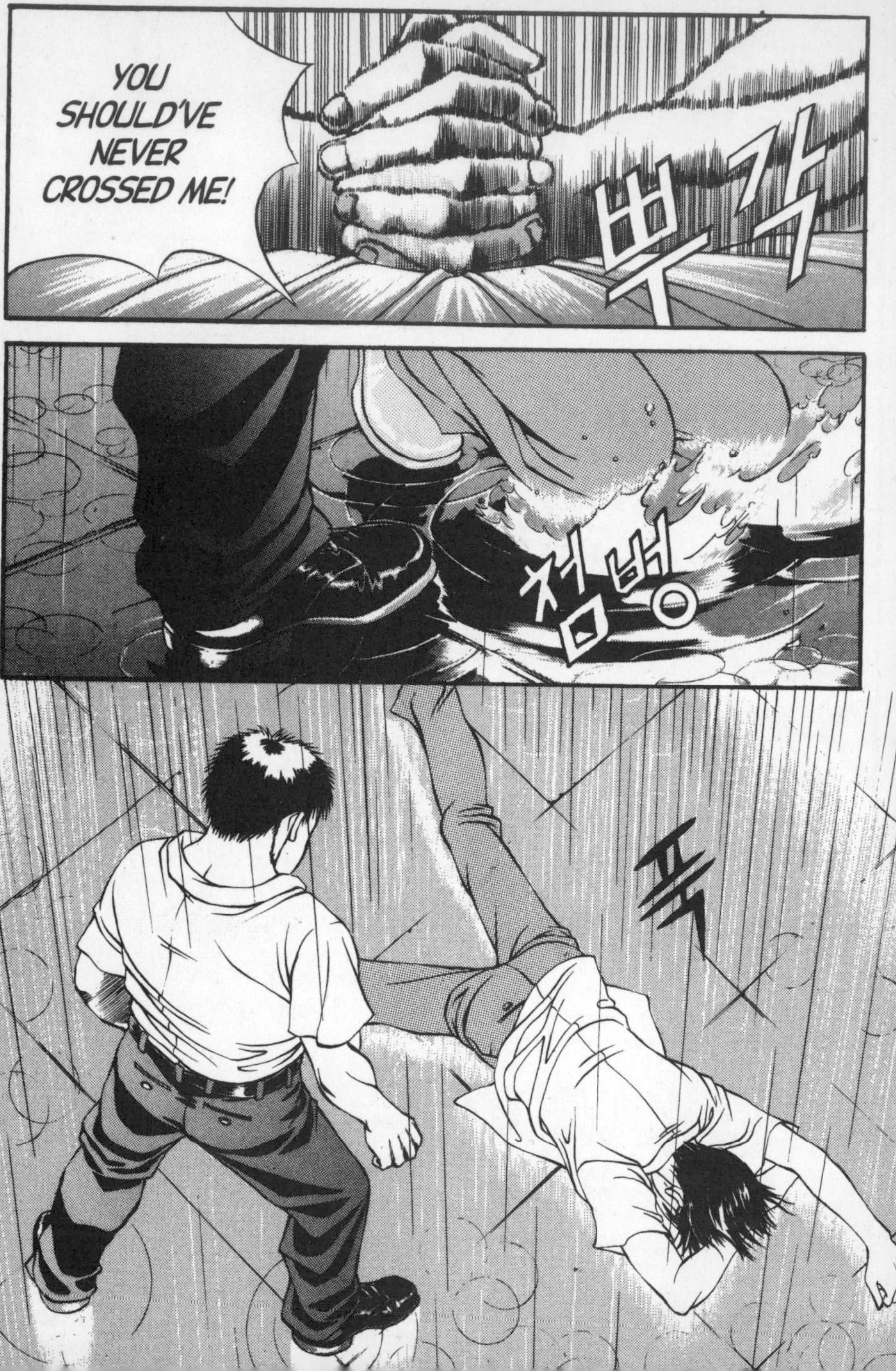
YOU SHOULD'VE NEVER CROSSED ME!
뿌각
첨벙
푹

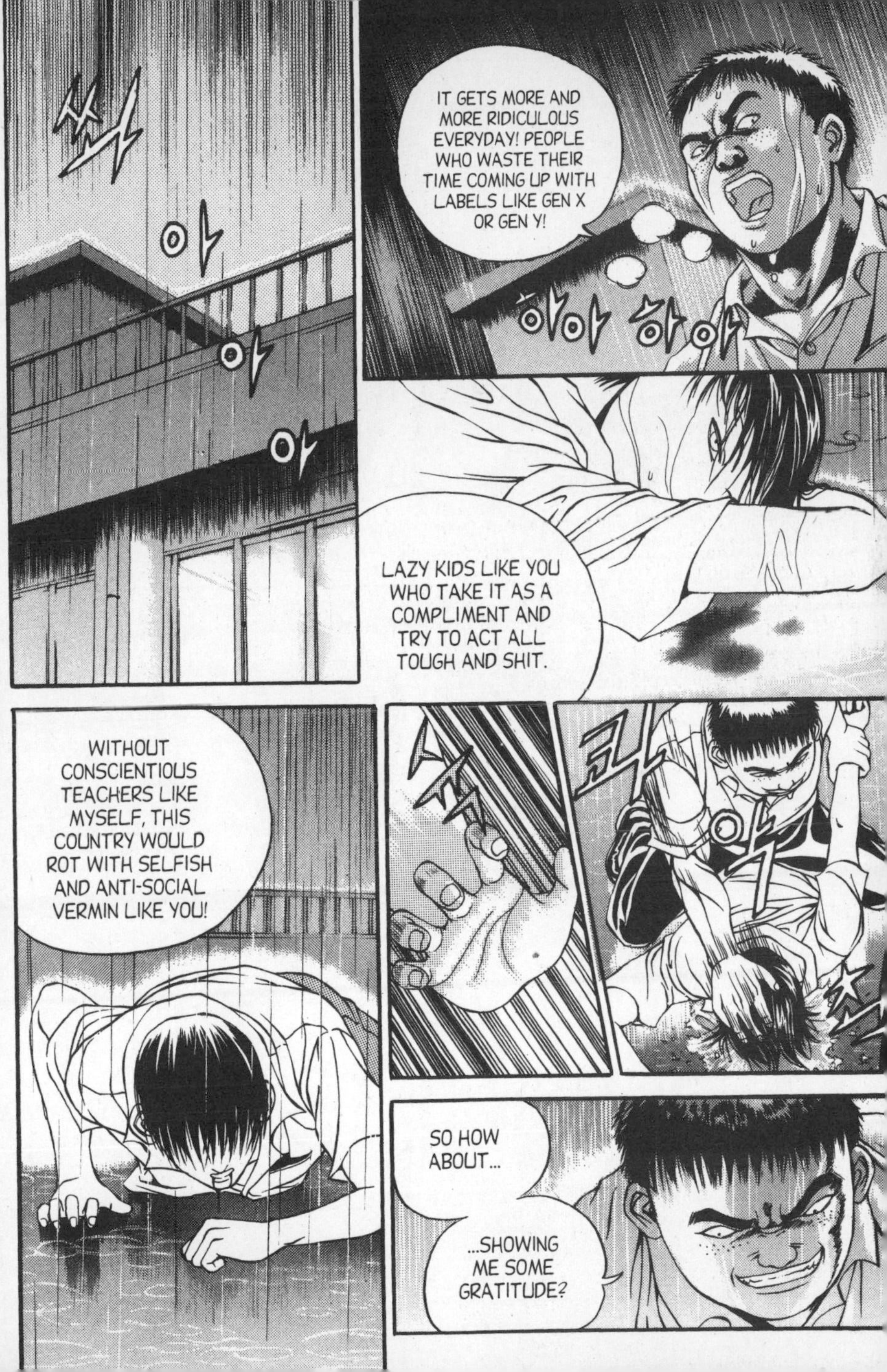
아
아
아
IT GETS MORE AND MORE RIDICULOUS EVERYDAY! PEOPLE WHO WASTE THEIR TIME COMING UP WITH LABELS LIKE GEN X OR GEN Y!
하아 하아
LAZY KIDS LIKE YOU WHO TAKE IT AS A COMPLIMENT AND TRY TO ACT ALL TOUGH AND SHIT.
WITHOUT CONSCIENTIOUS TEACHERS LIKE MYSELF, THIS COUNTRY WOULD ROT WITH SELFISH AND ANTI-SOCIAL VERMIN LIKE YOU!
SO HOW ABOUT...
...SHOWING ME SOME GRATITUDE?

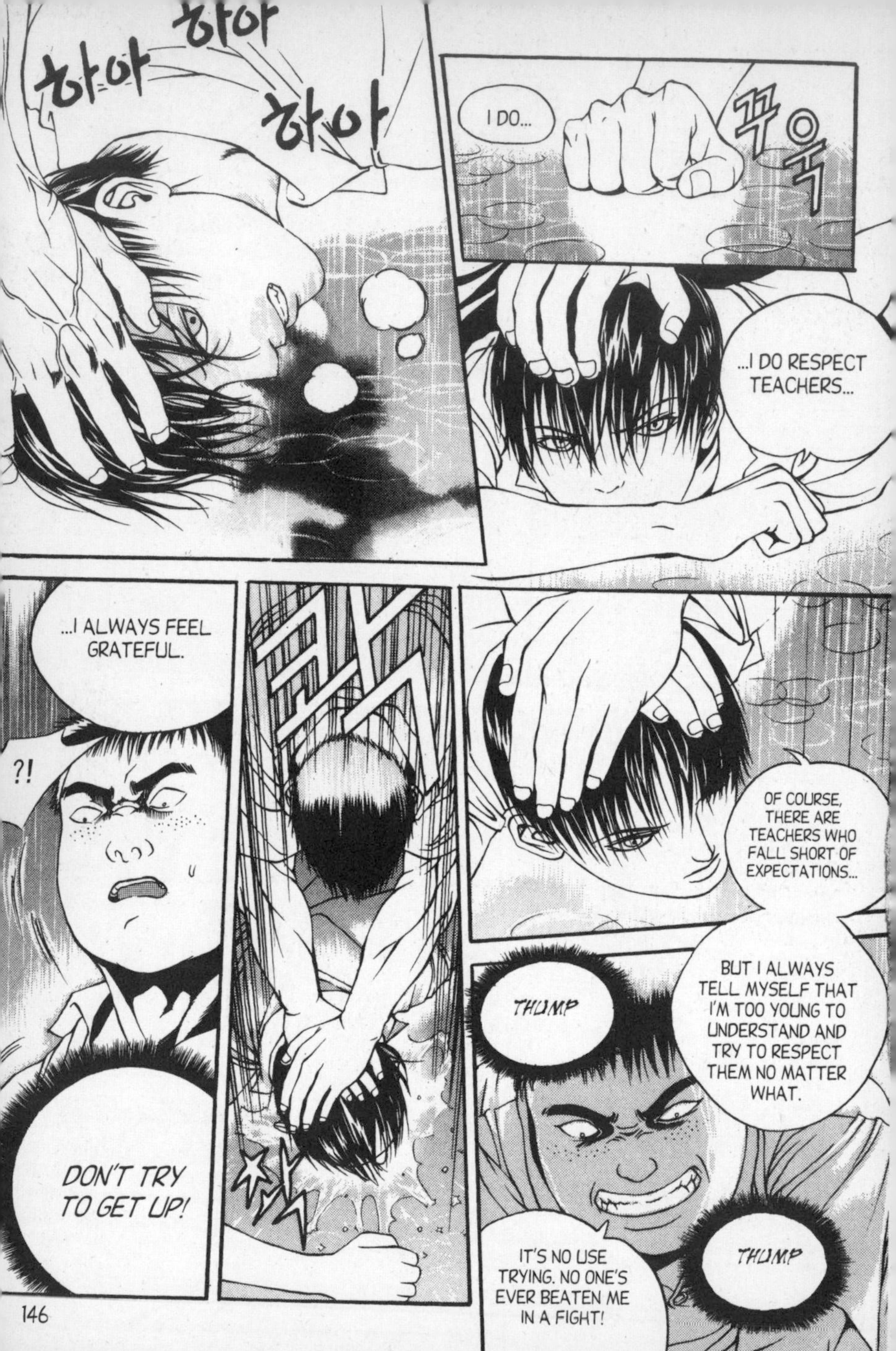
하아
하아
하아
I DO...
...I DO RESPECT TEACHERS...
...I ALWAYS FEEL GRATEFUL.
?!
DON'T TRY TO GET UP!
OF COURSE, THERE ARE TEACHERS WHO FALL SHORT OF EXPECTATIONS...
THUMP
BUT I ALWAYS TELL MYSELF THAT I'M TOO YOUNG TO UNDERSTAND AND TRY TO RESPECT THEM NO MATTER WHAT.
IT'S NO USE TRYING. NO ONE'S EVER BEATEN ME IN A FIGHT!
THUMP

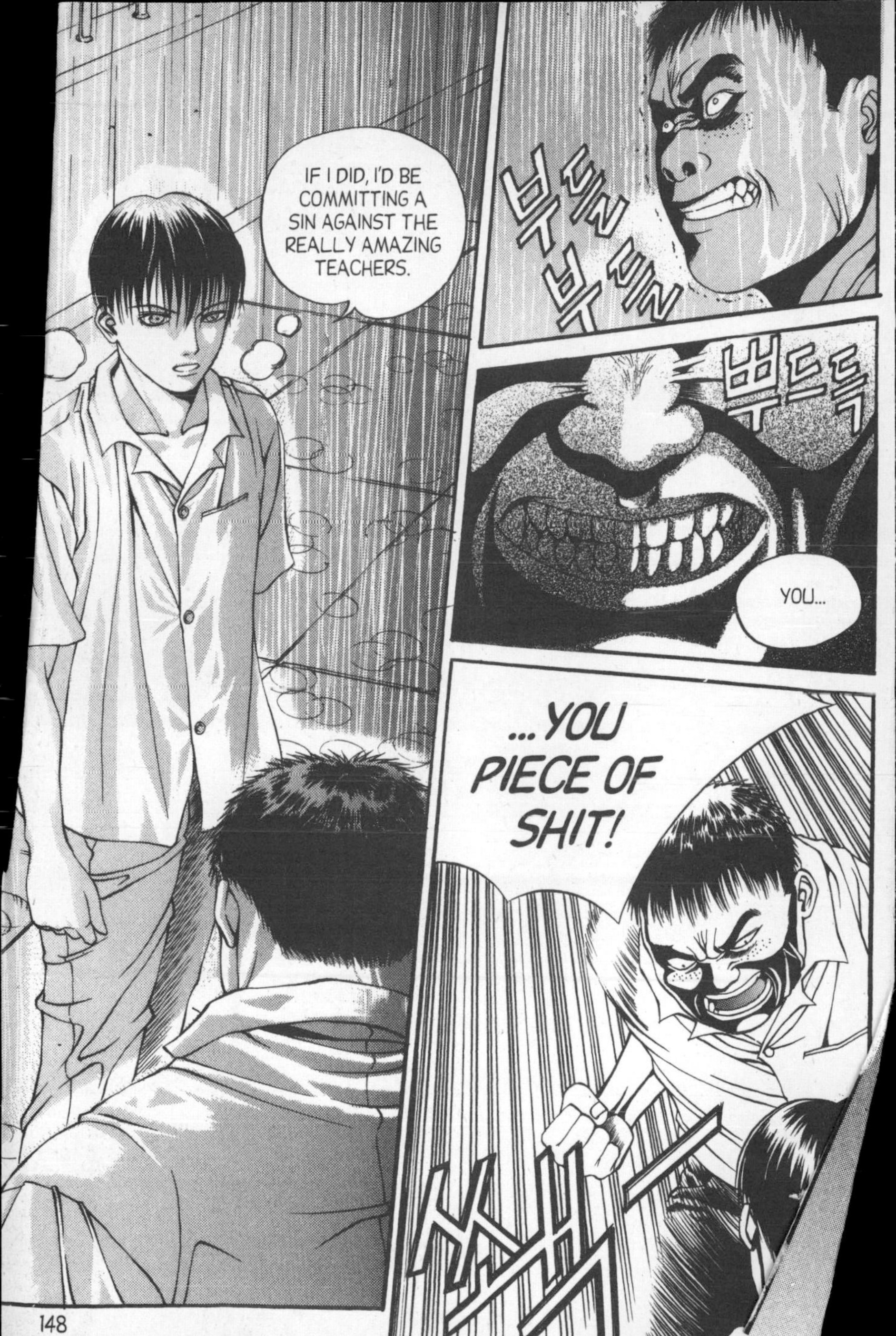
IF I DID, I'D BE COMMITTING A SIN AGAINST THE REALLY AMAZING TEACHERS.
뿌드득
YOU...
...YOU PIECE OF SHIT!

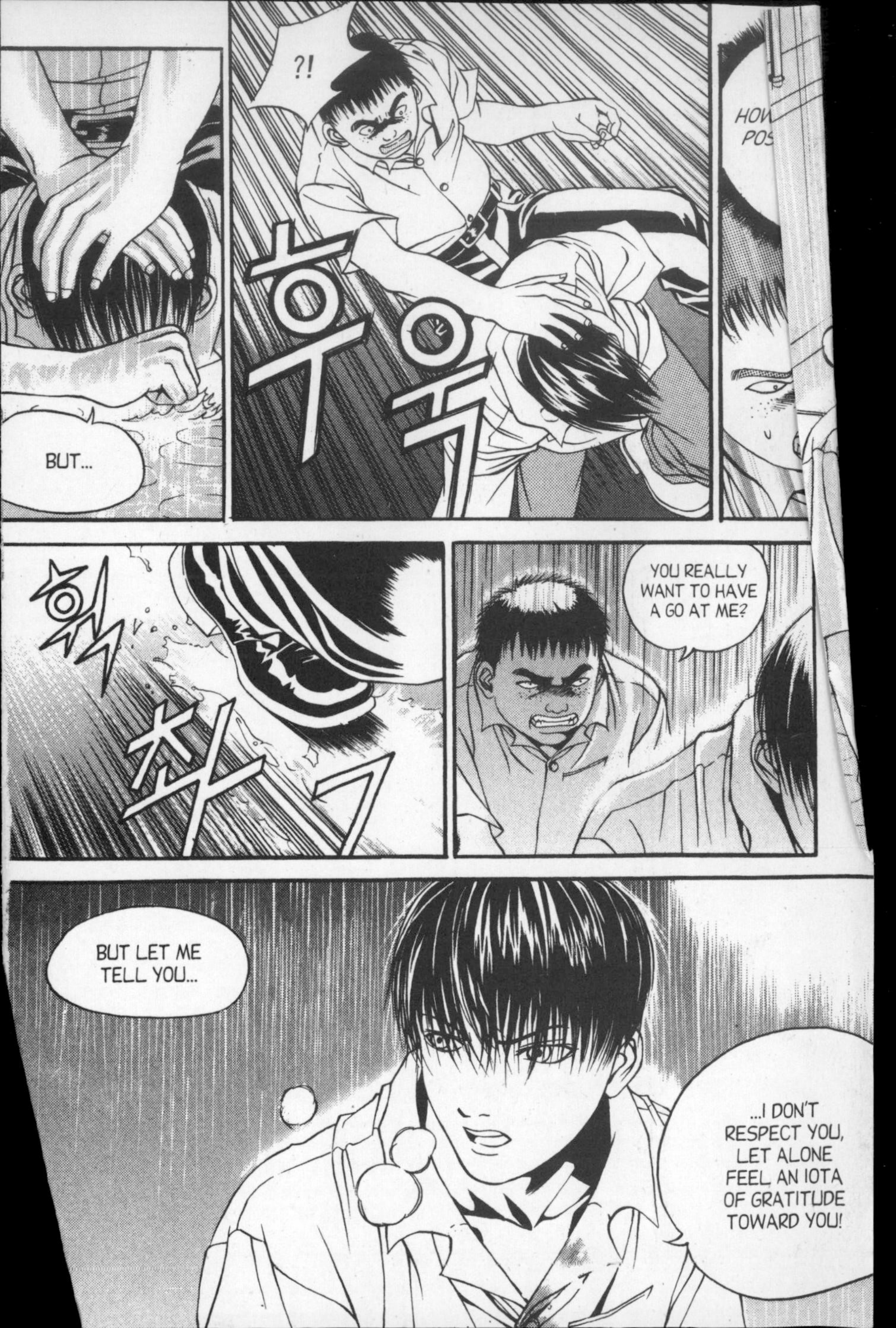
BUT...
?!
HOW
POS
YOU REALLY WANT TO HAVE A GO AT ME?
BUT LET ME TELL YOU...
...I DON'T RESPECT YOU, LET ALONE FEEL AN IOTA OF GRATITUDE TOWARD YOU!

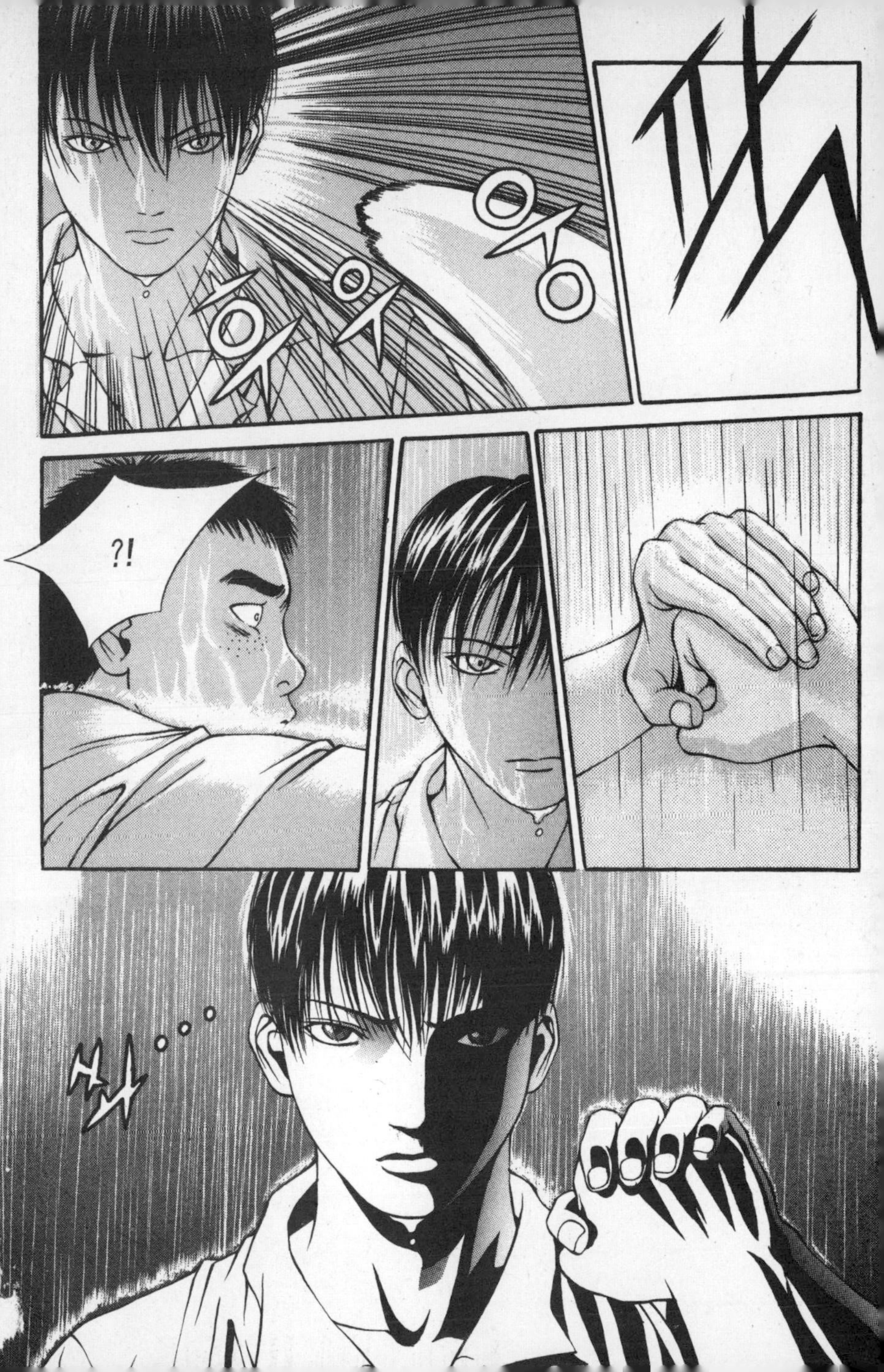
?!

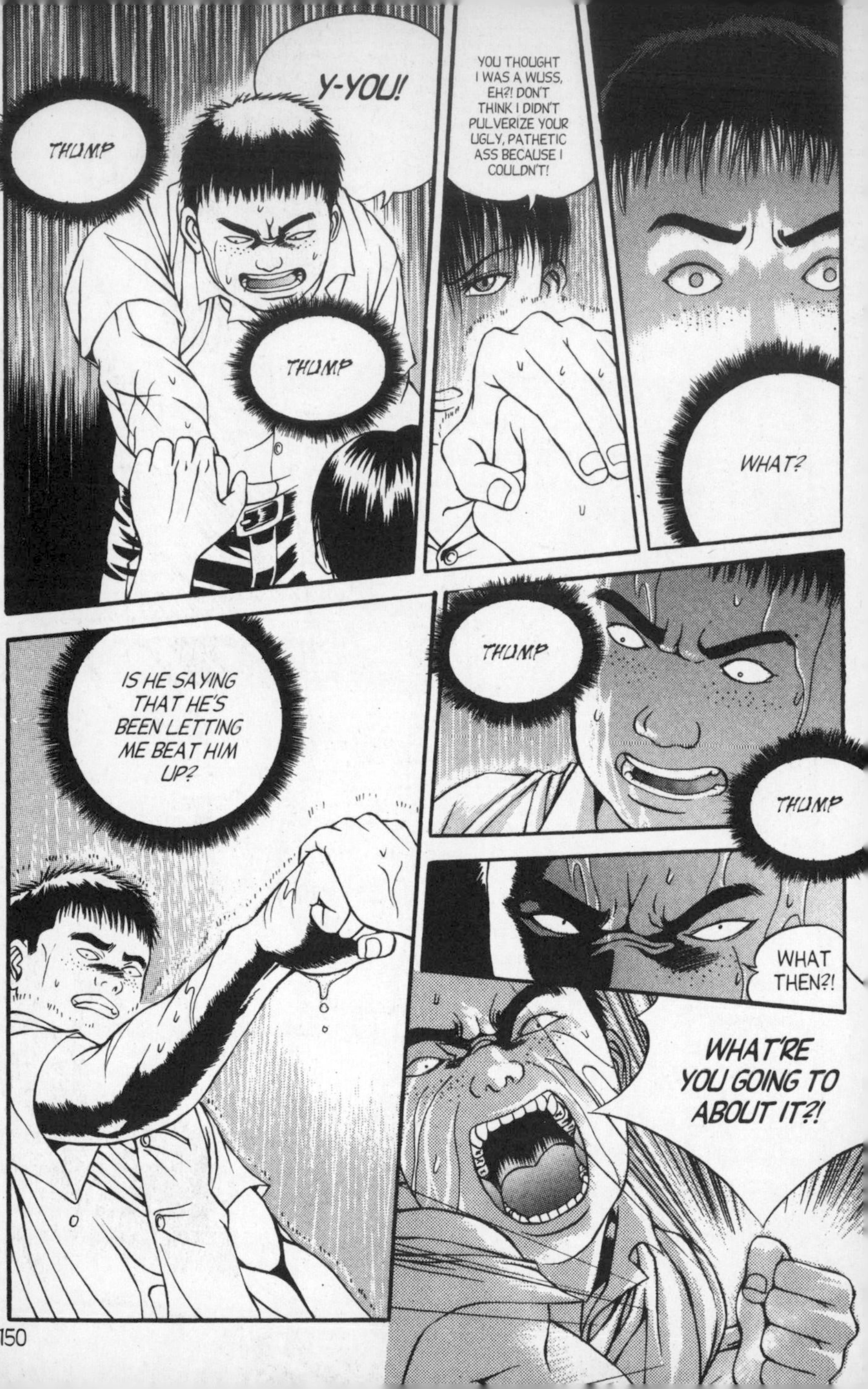
THUMP
Y-YOU!
THUMP
YOU THOUGHT I WAS A WUSS, EH?! DON'T THINK I DIDN'T PULVERIZE YOUR UGLY, PATHETIC ASS BECAUSE I COULDN'T!
WHAT?
IS HE SAYING THAT HE'S BEEN LETTING ME BEAT HIM UP?
THUMP
THUMP
WHAT THEN?!
WHAT'RE YOU GOING TO ABOUT IT?!

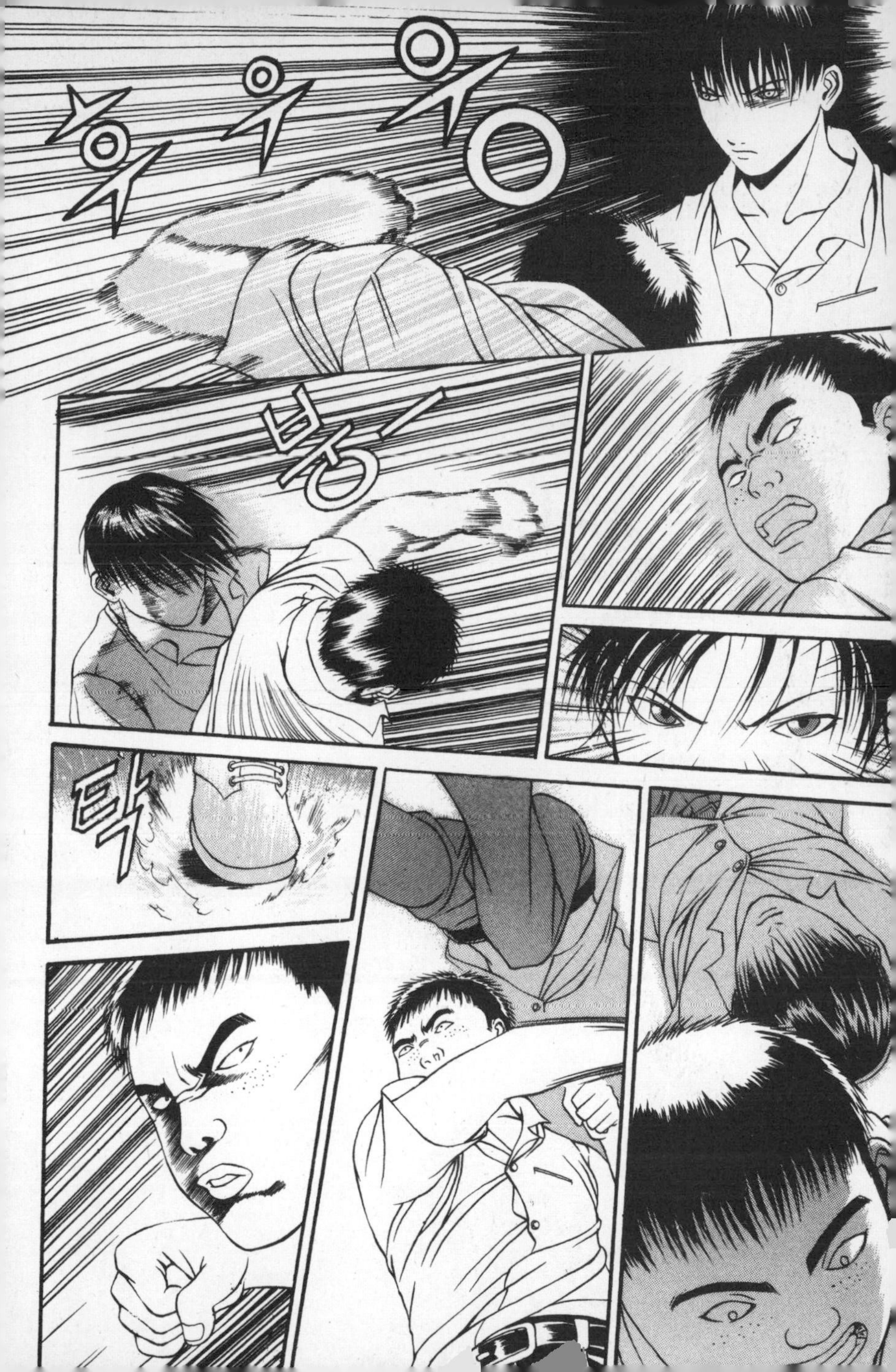
붕—
탁

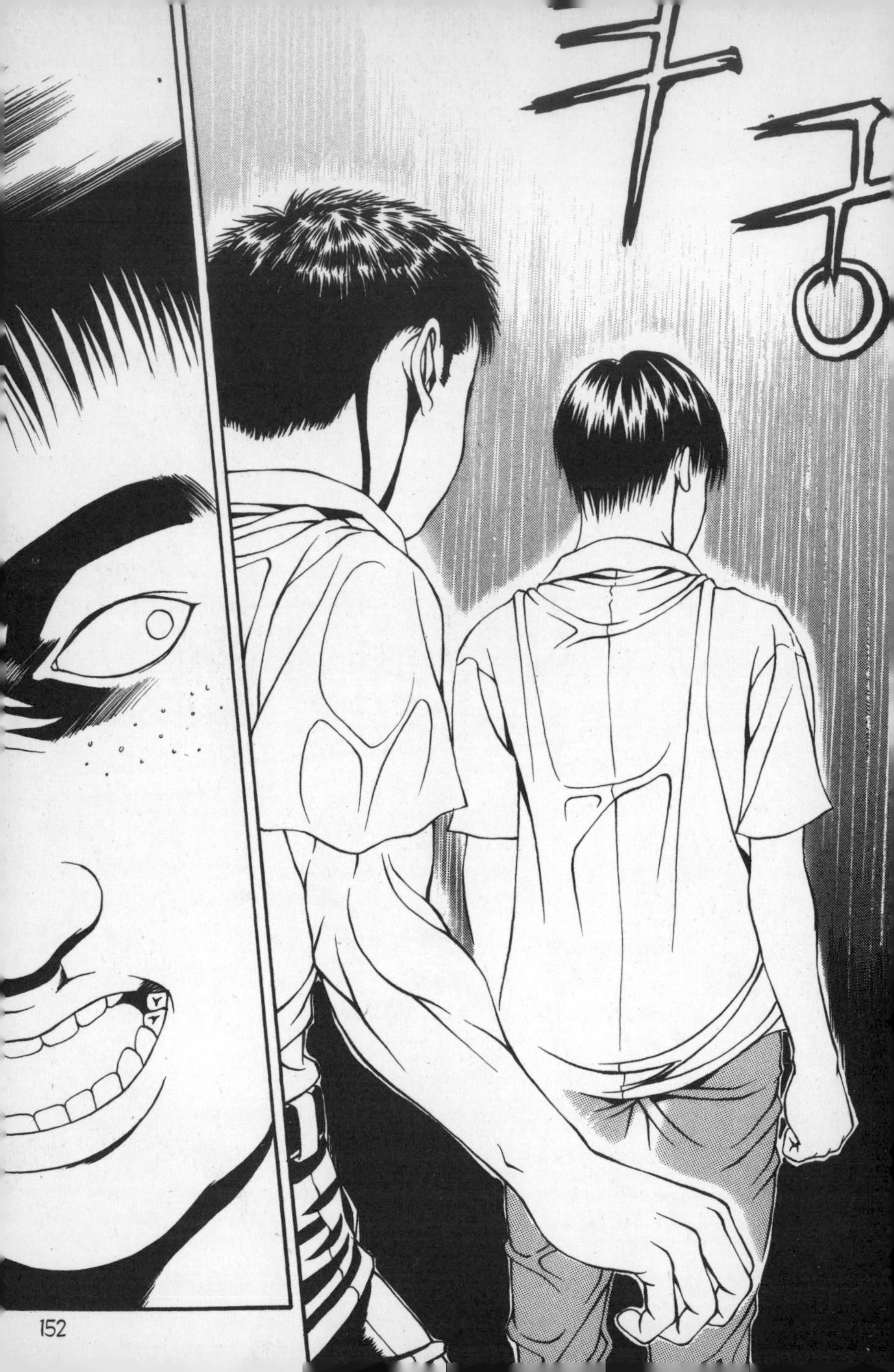

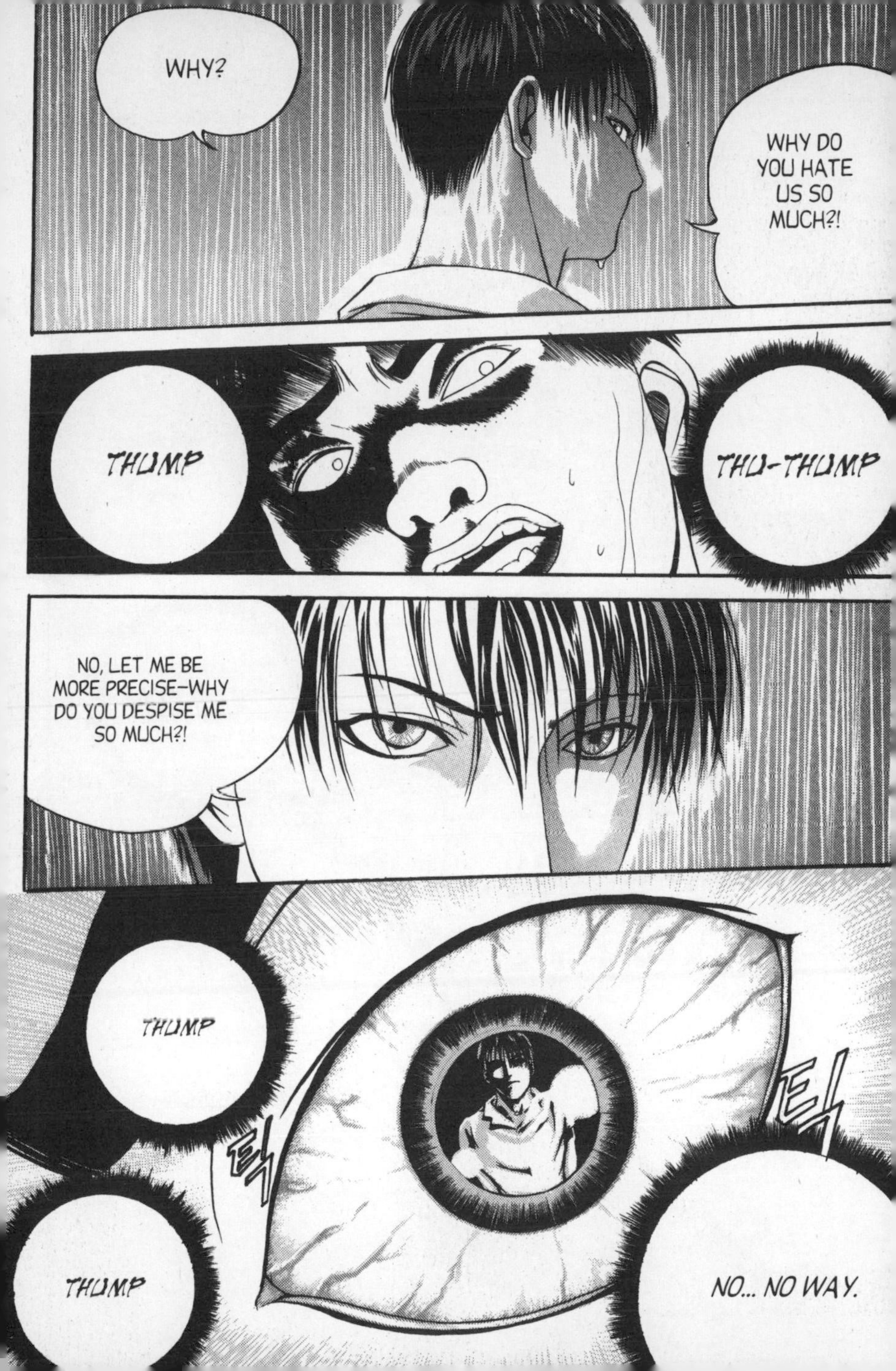
WHY?
WHY DO YOU HATE US SO MUCH?!
THUMP
THU-THUMP
NO, LET ME BE MORE PRECISE—WHY DO YOU DESPISE ME SO MUCH?!
THUMP
THUMP
NO... NO WAY.

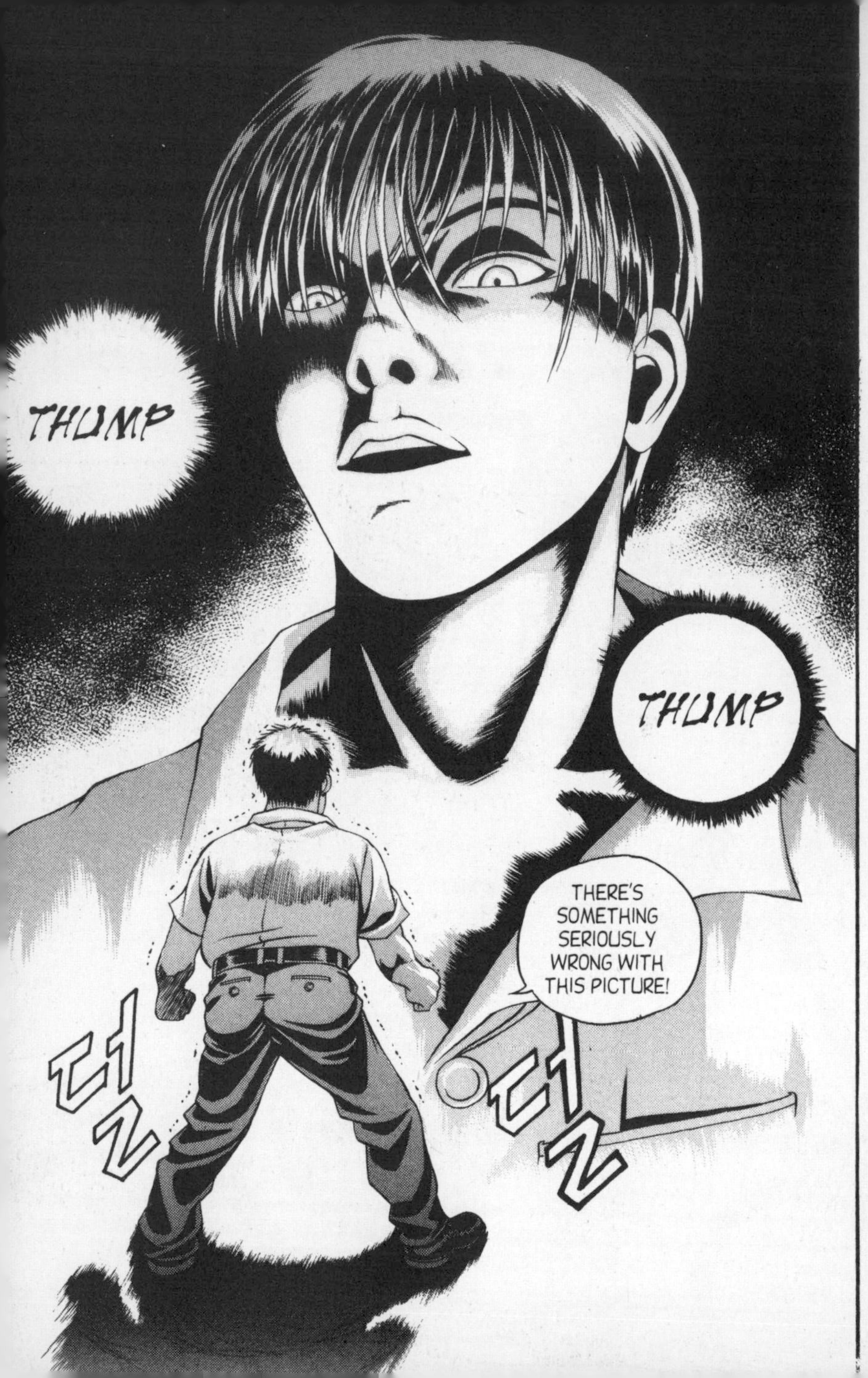
THUMP
THUMP
THERE'S SOMETHING SERIOUSLY WRONG WITH THIS PICTURE!

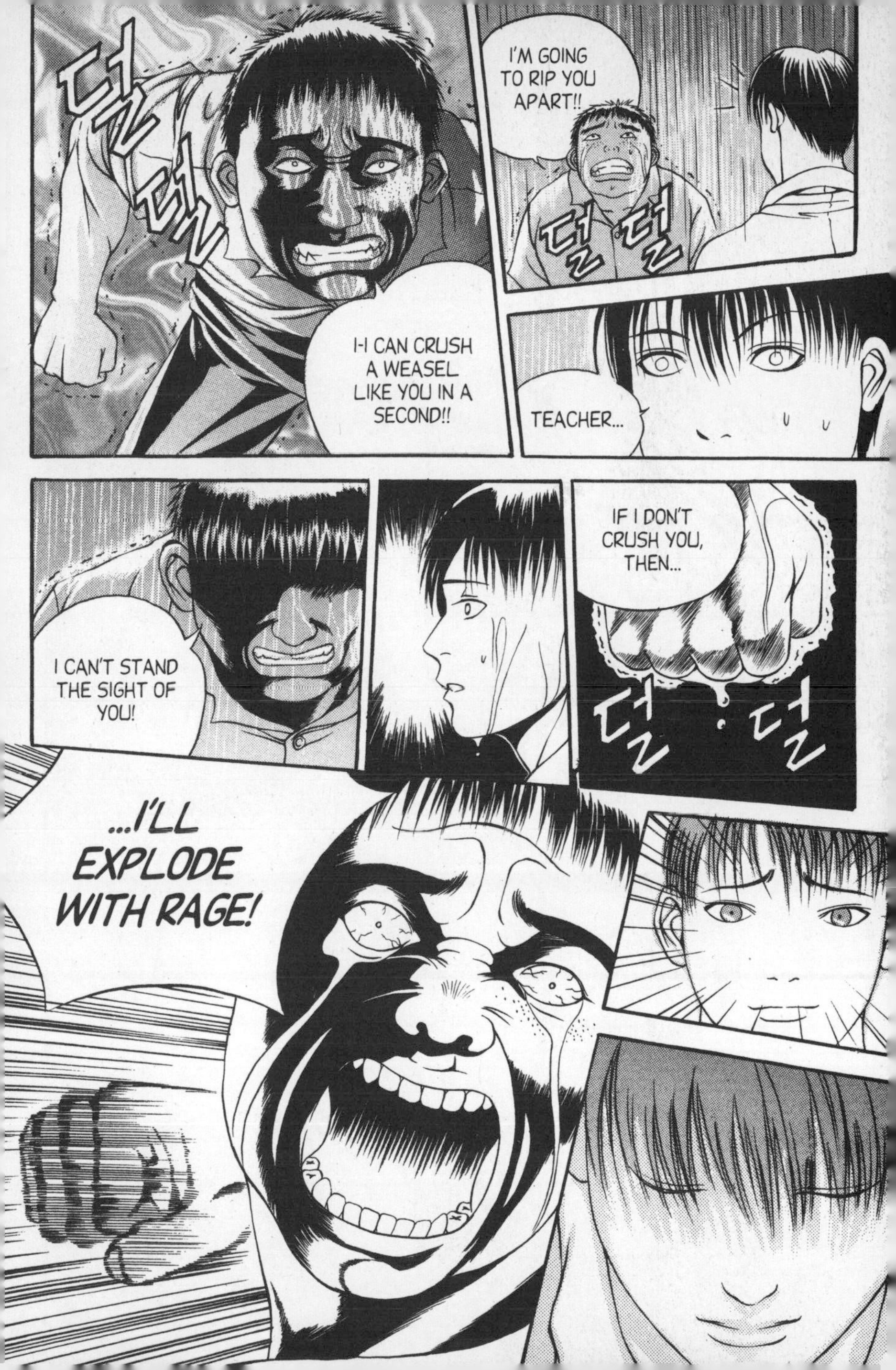
덜덜
I-I CAN CRUSH A WEASEL LIKE YOU IN A SECOND!!
I'M GOING TO RIP YOU APART!!
덜덜
TEACHER...
I CAN'T STAND THE SIGHT OF YOU!
IF I DON'T CRUSH YOU, THEN...
덜덜
...I'LL EXPLODE WITH RAGE!

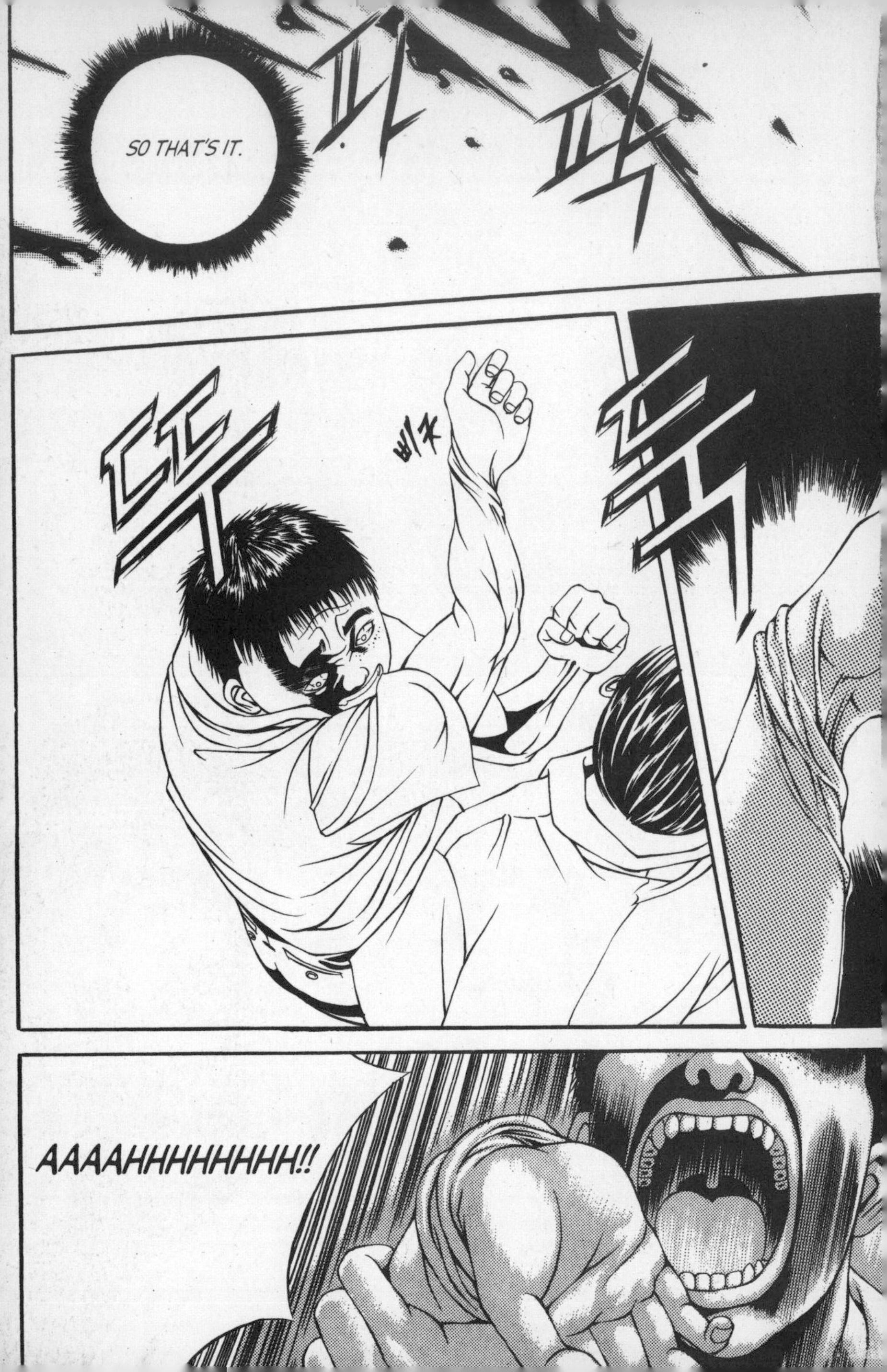
SO THAT'S IT.
AAAAHHHHHHHH!!

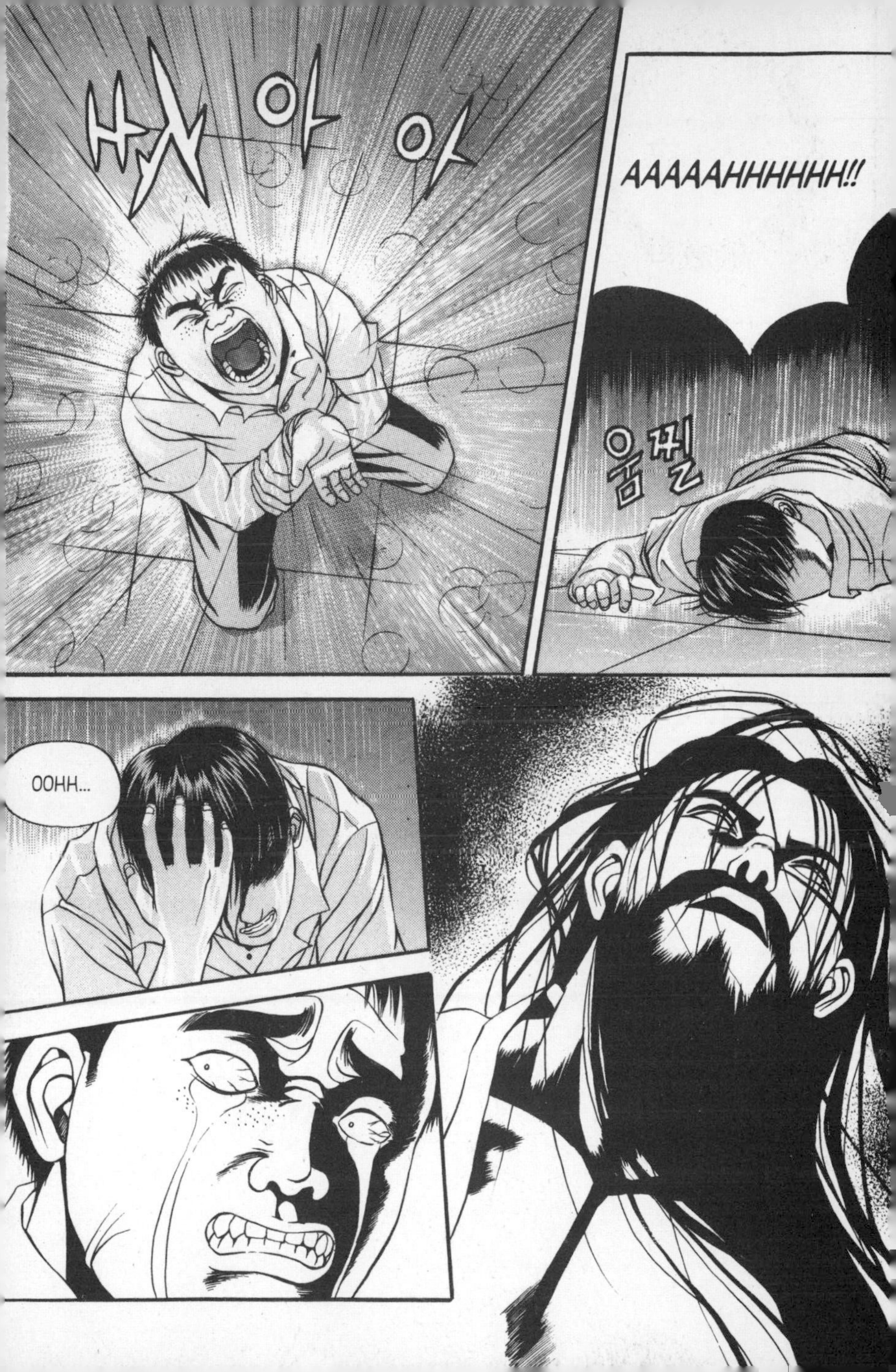
AAAAAHHHHHH!!
움찔
OOHH...

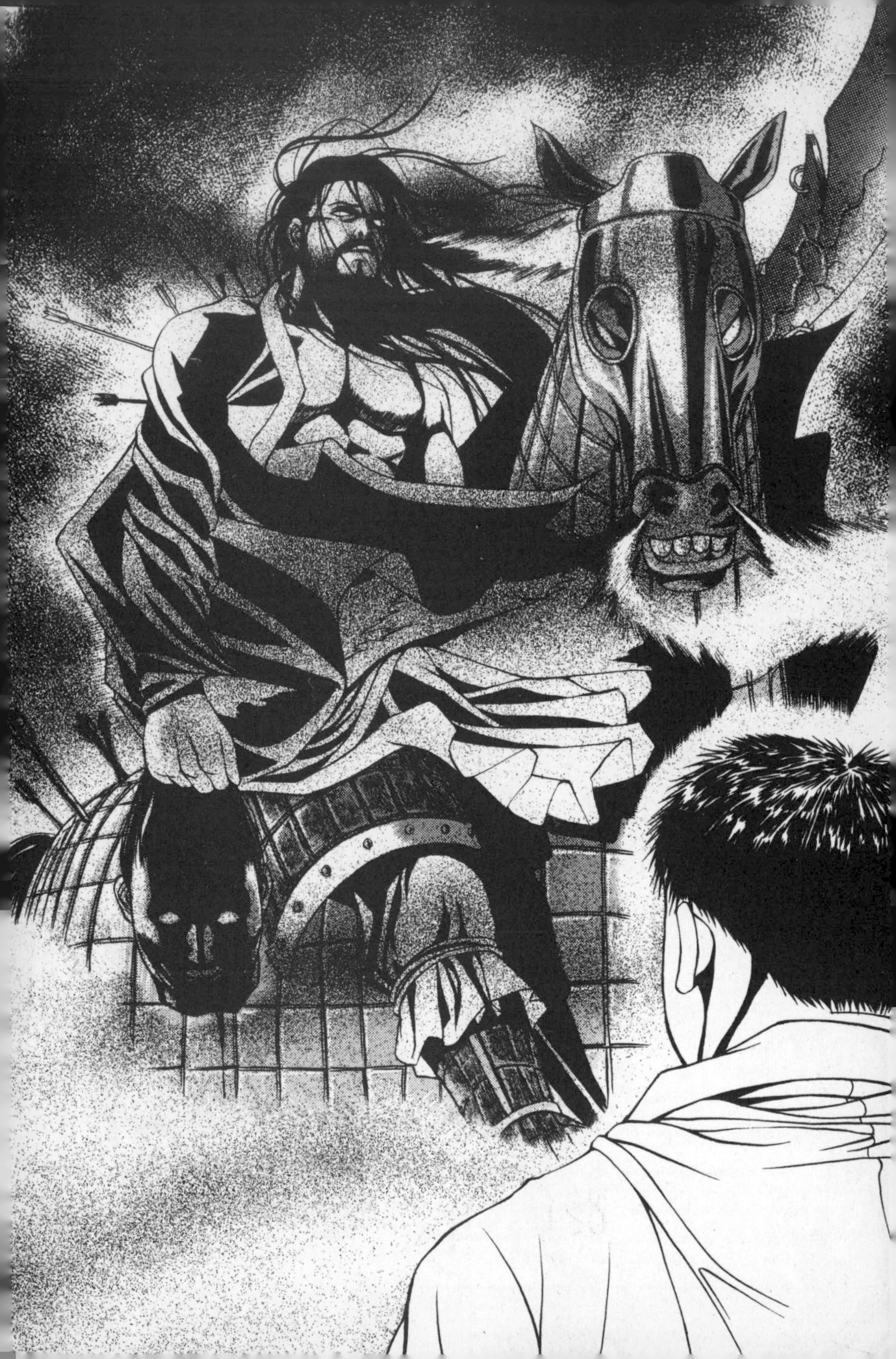

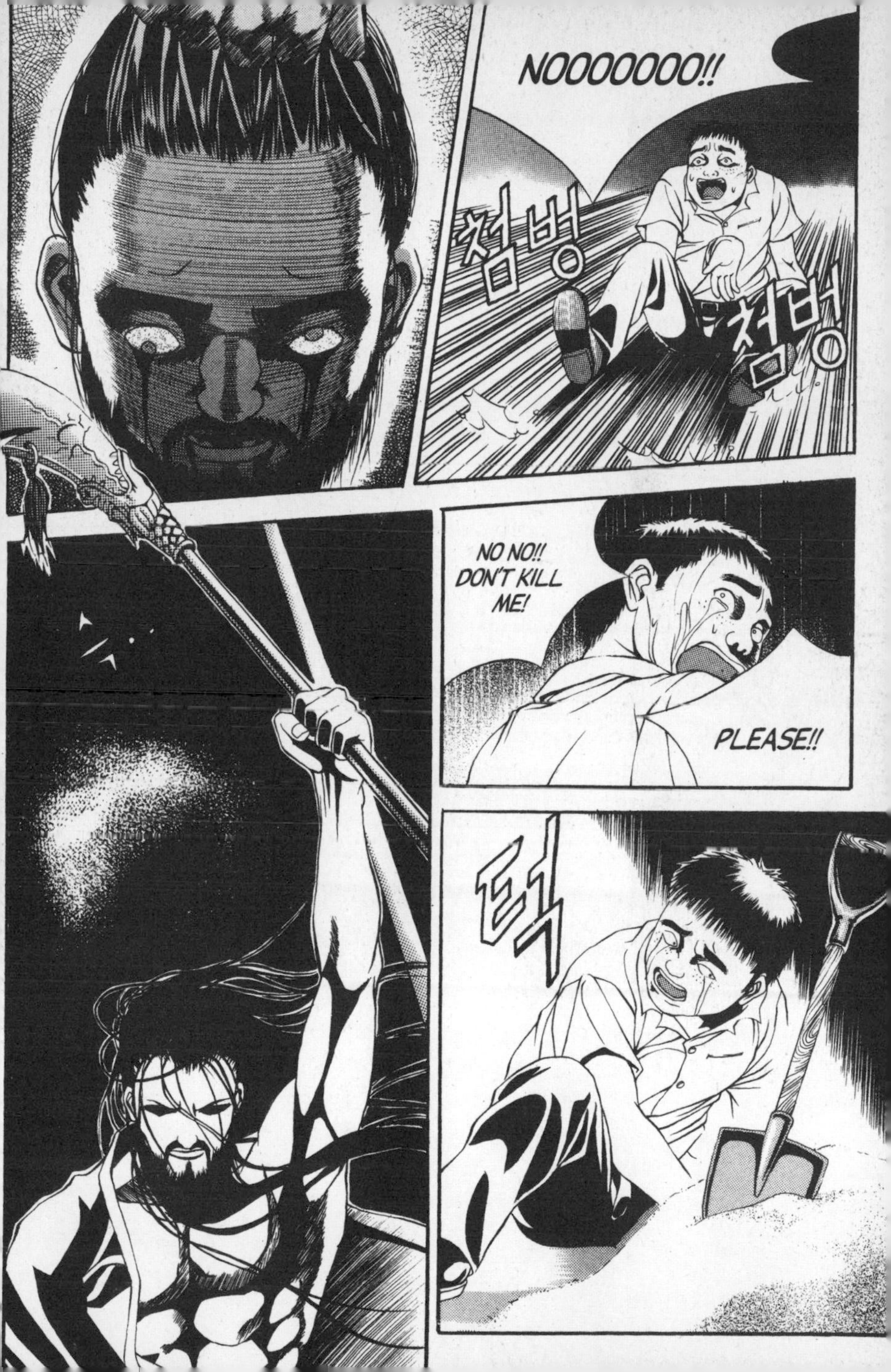
NOOOOOOO!!
첨벙
첨벙
NO NO!! DON'T KILL ME!
PLEASE!!
턱

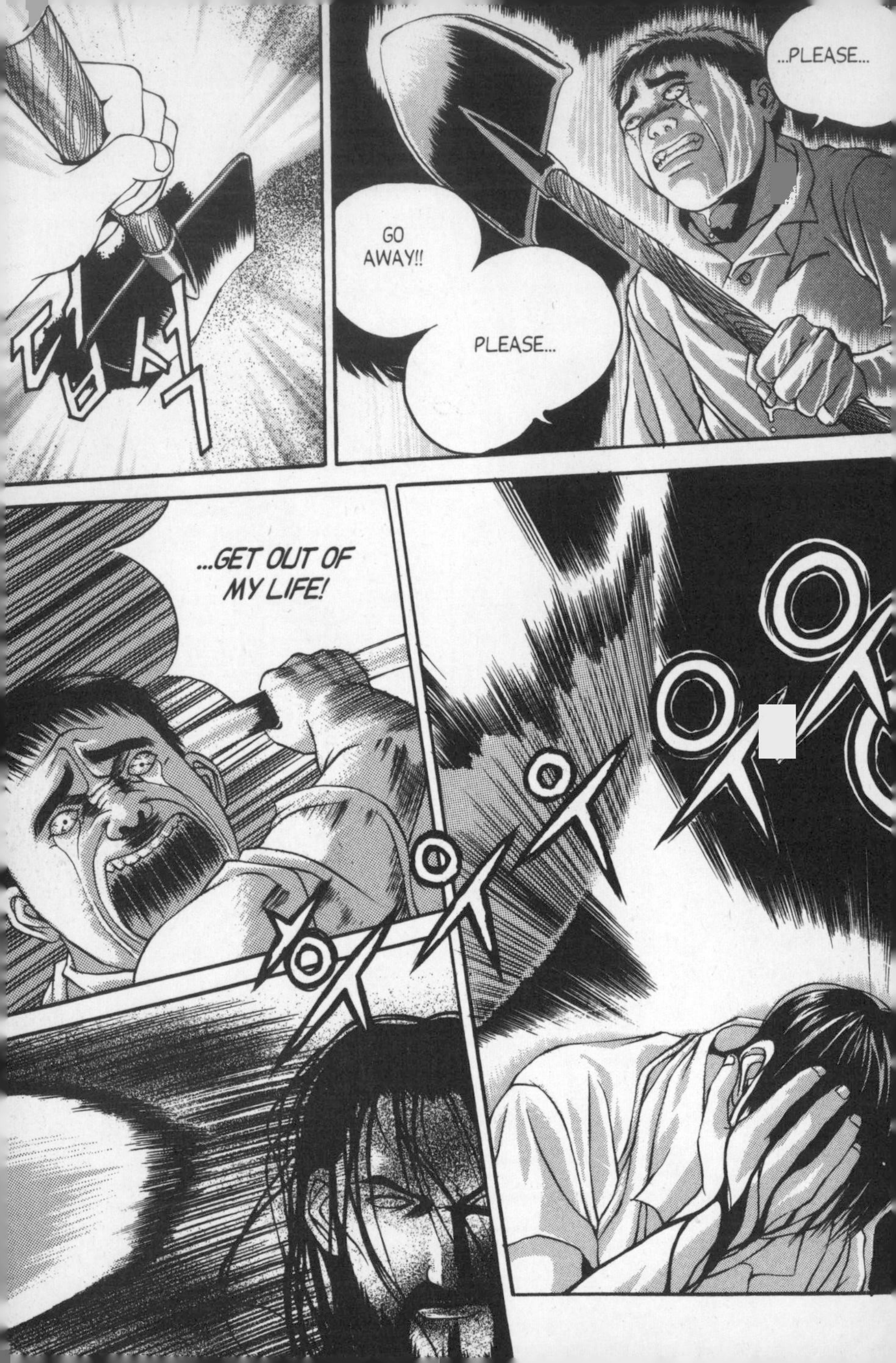
...PLEASE...
GO AWAY!!
PLEASE...
...GET OUT OF MY LIFE!

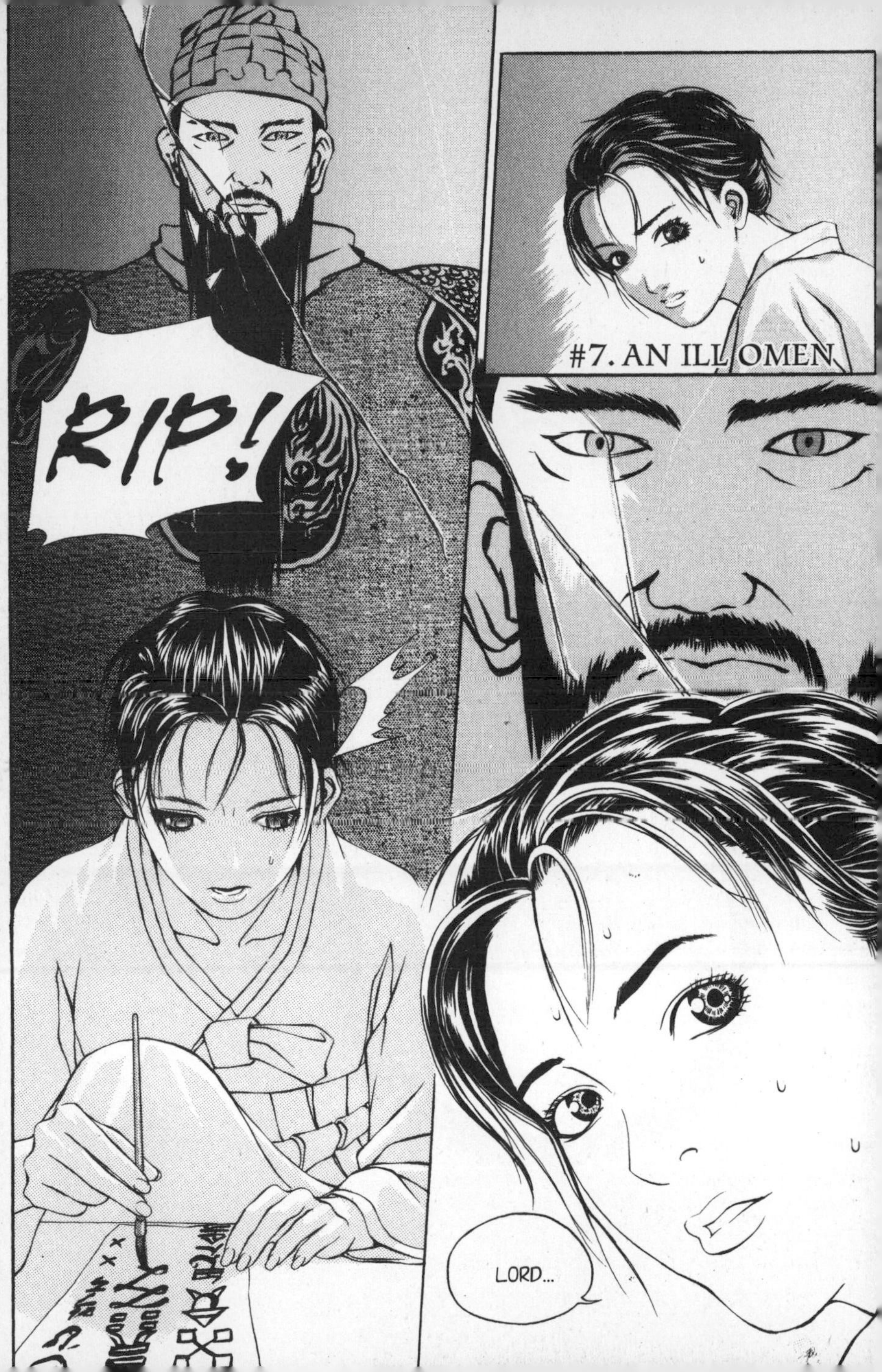

RIP!
#7. AN ILL OMEN
LORD...

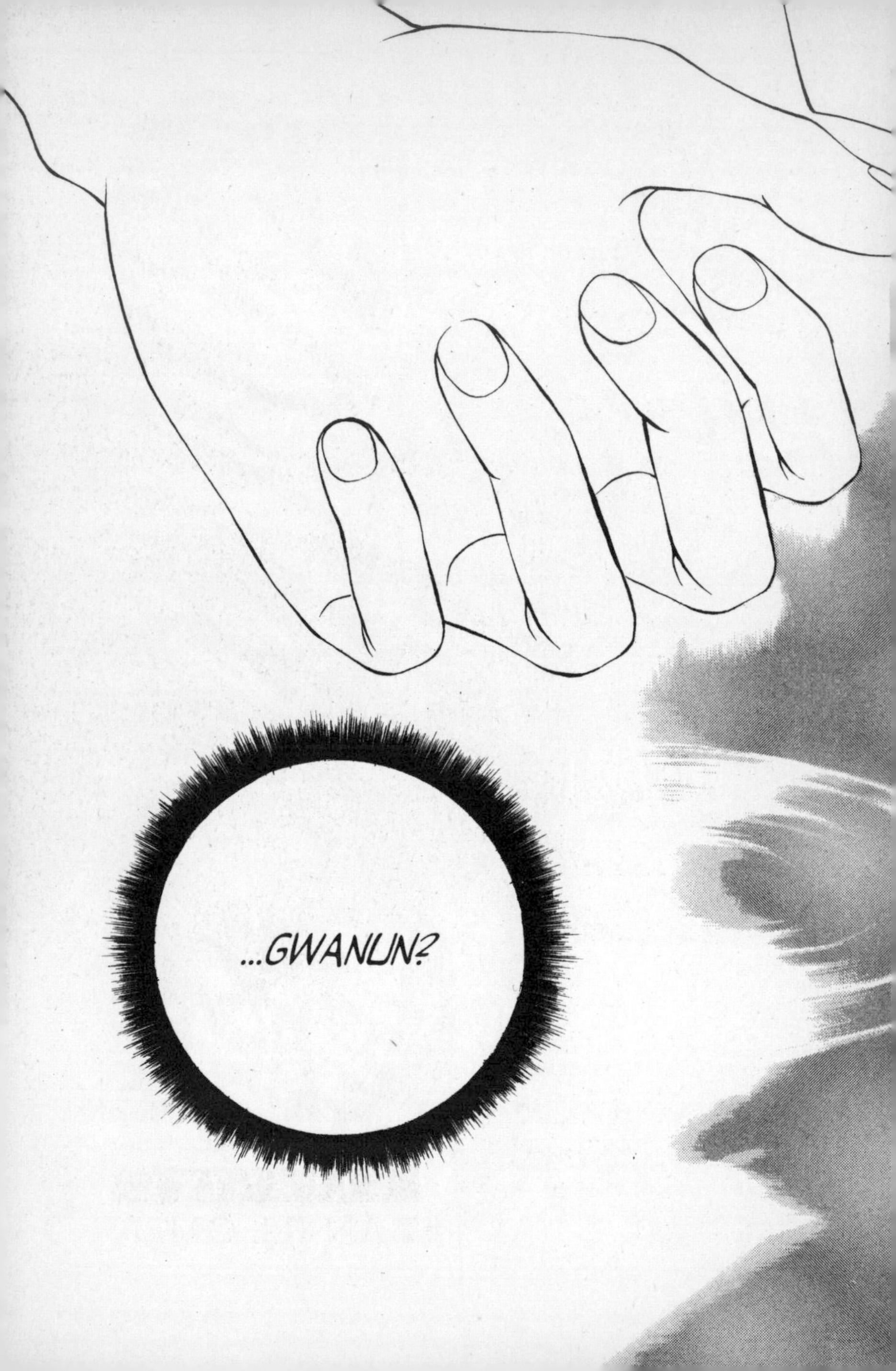
...GWANUN?

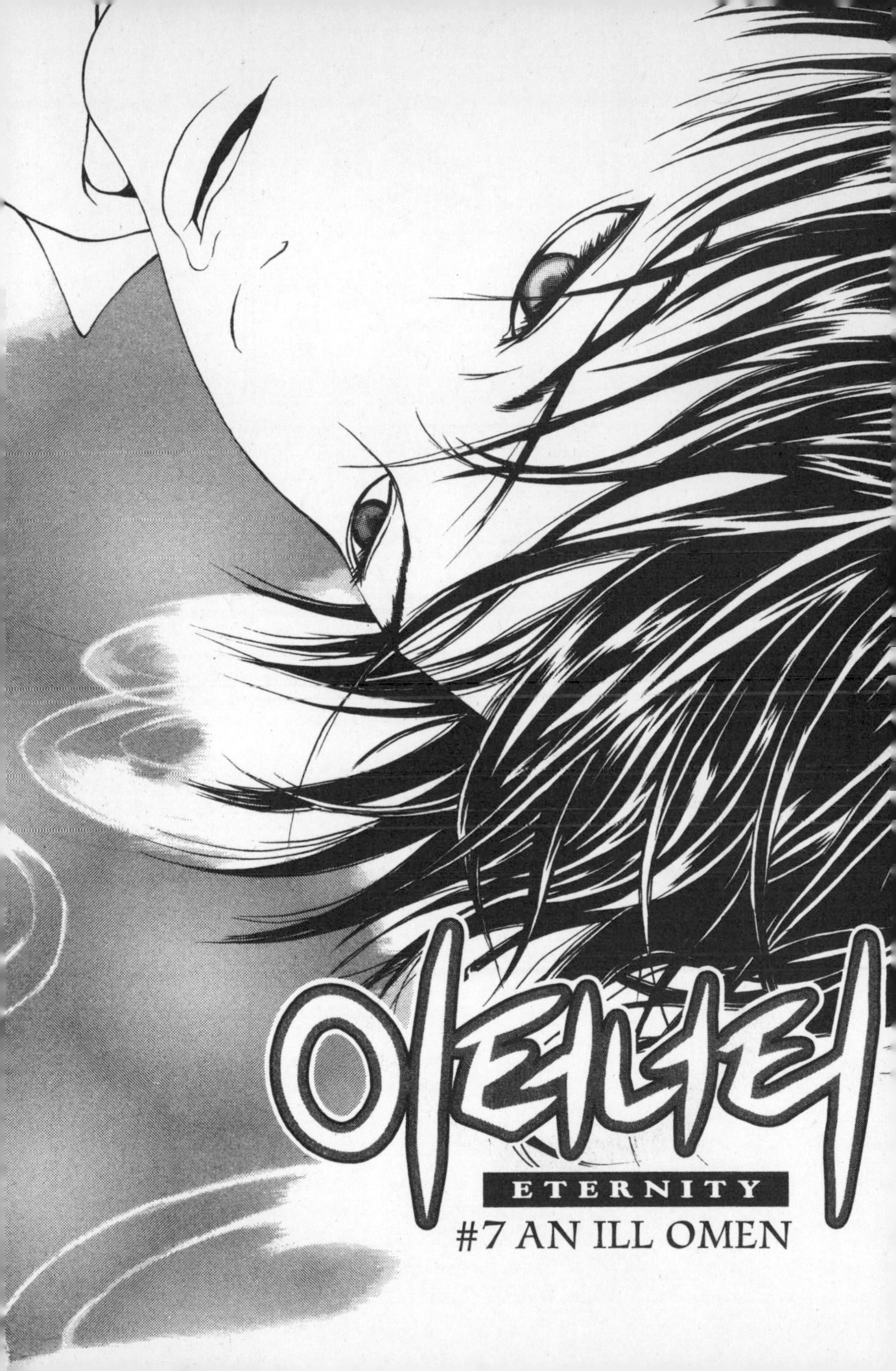
이터니티
ETERNITY
#7 AN ILL OMEN

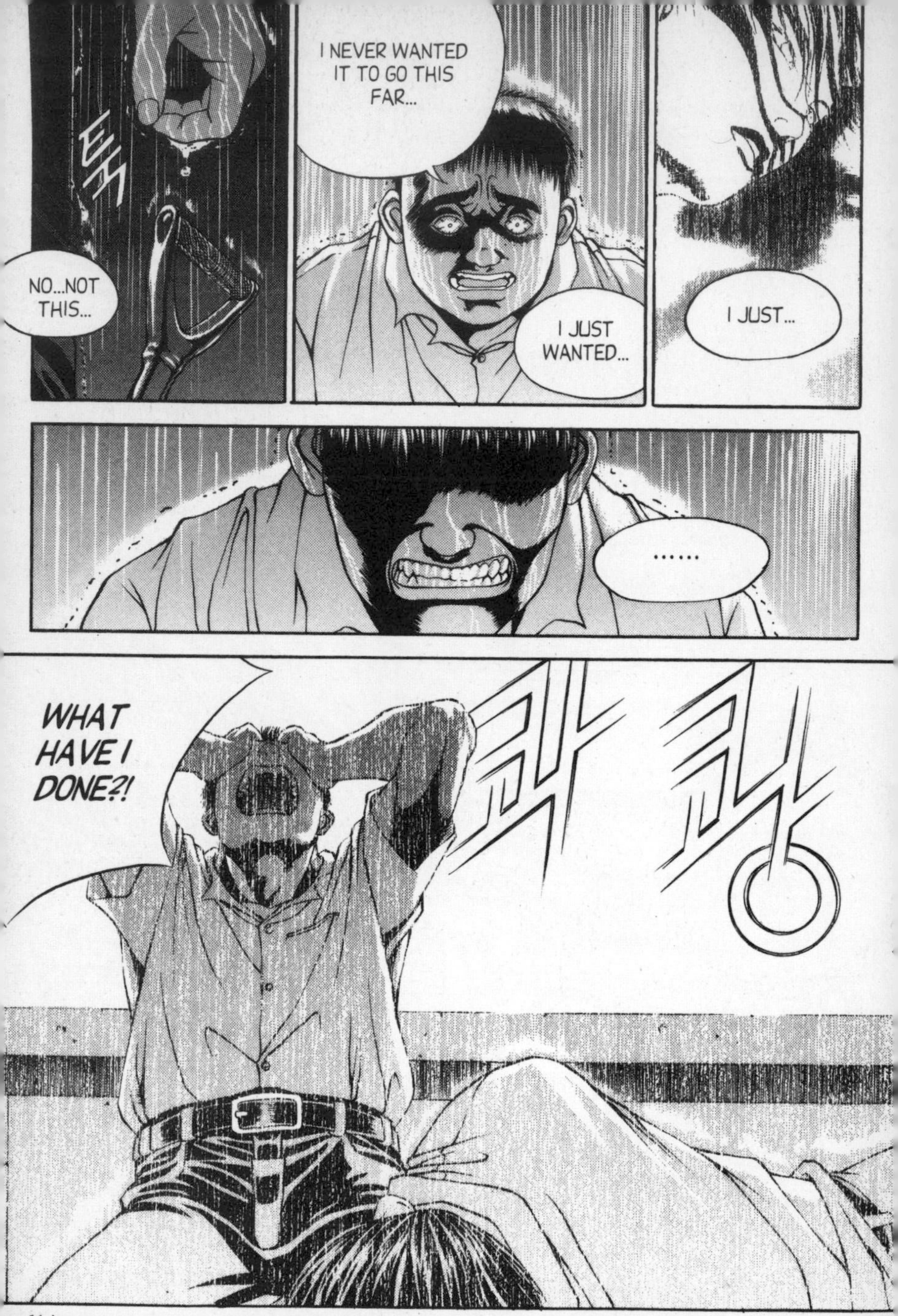
NO...NOT THIS...
I NEVER WANTED IT TO GO THIS FAR...
I JUST WANTED...
I JUST...
......
WHAT HAVE I DONE?!

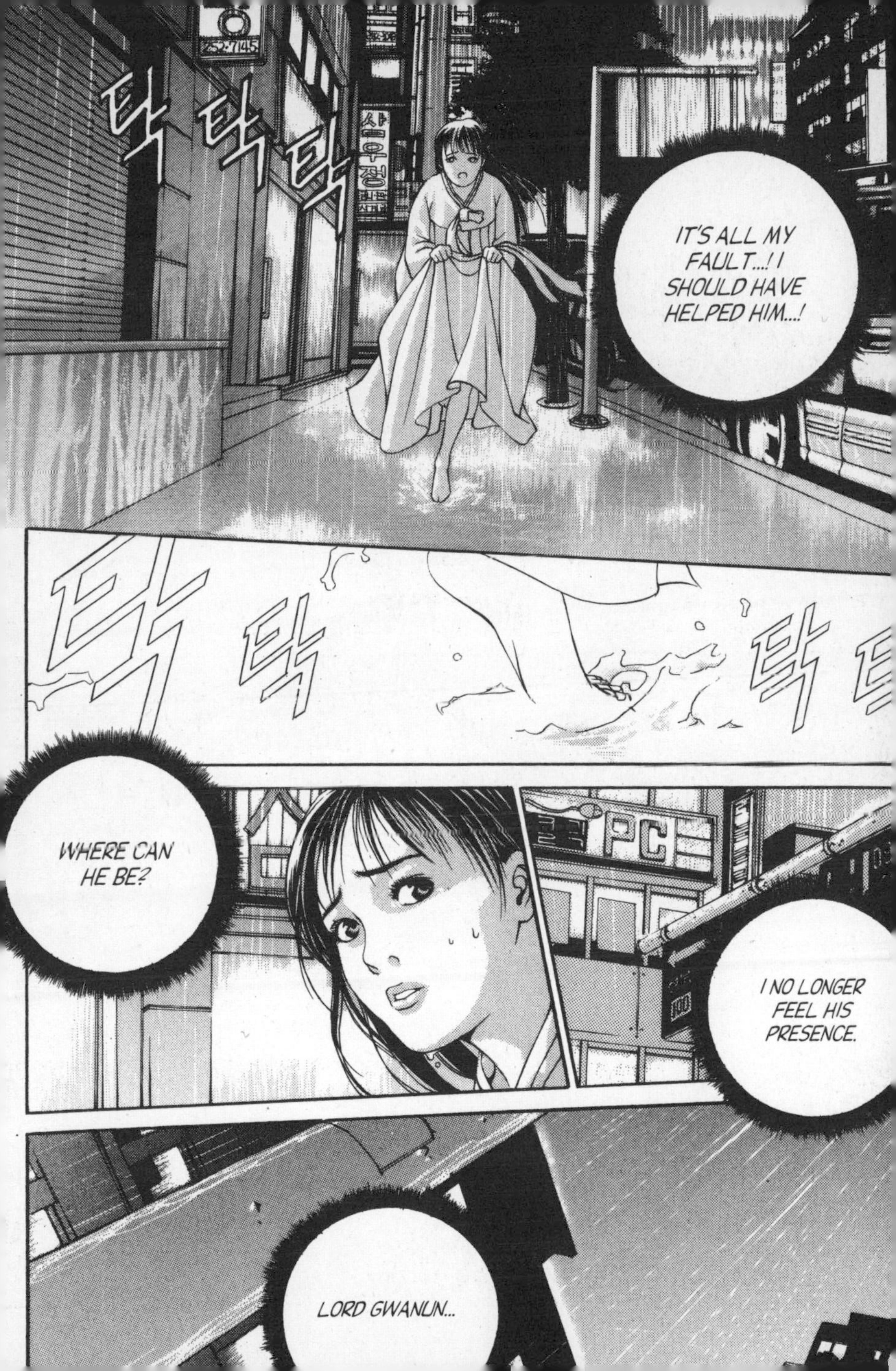
탁
탁
탁
IT'S ALL MY FAULT...! I SHOULD HAVE HELPED HIM...!
탁
탁
탁
WHERE CAN HE BE?
PC
I NO LONGER FEEL HIS PRESENCE.
LORD GWANUN...

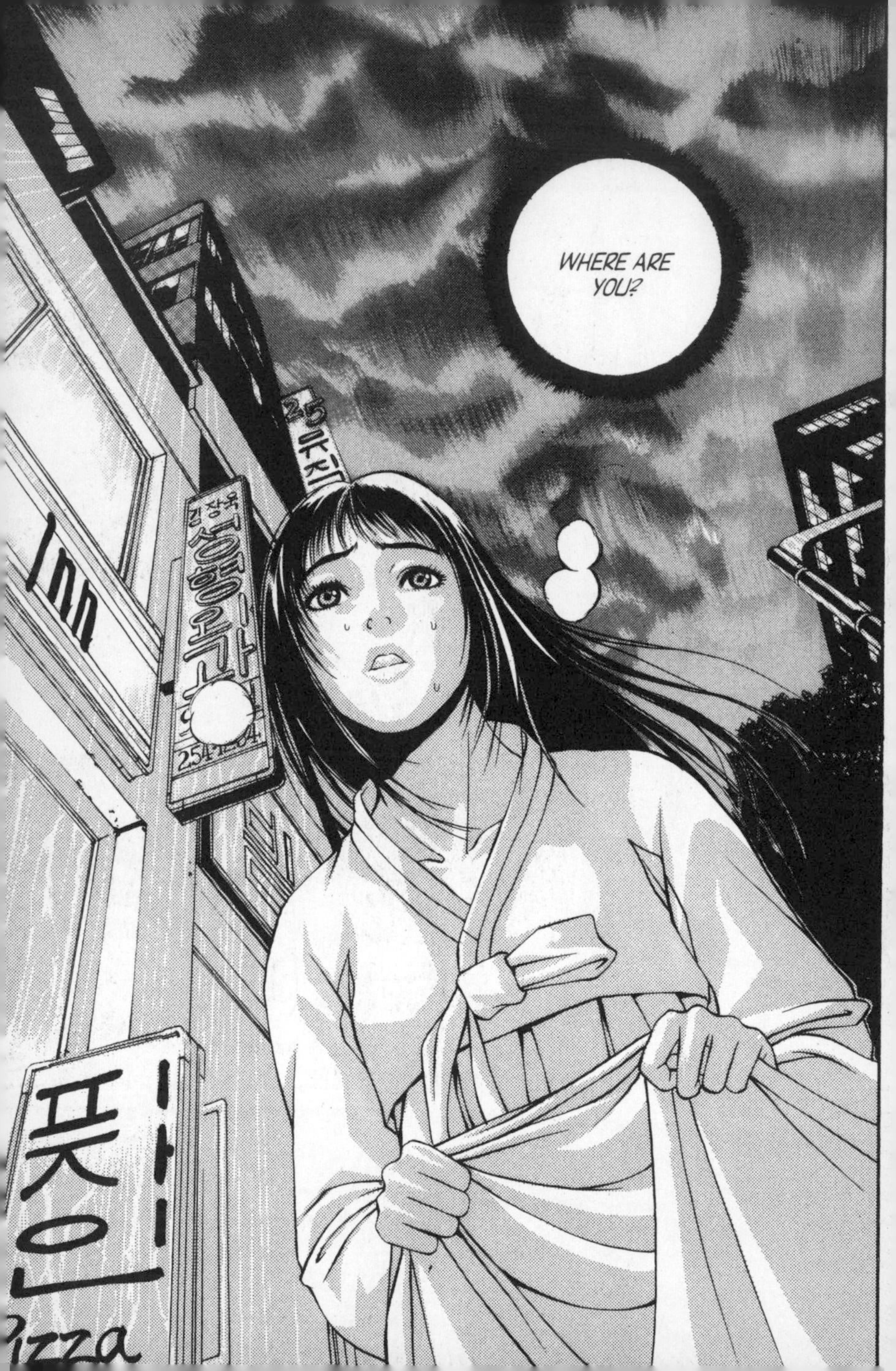
WHERE ARE YOU?
Inn

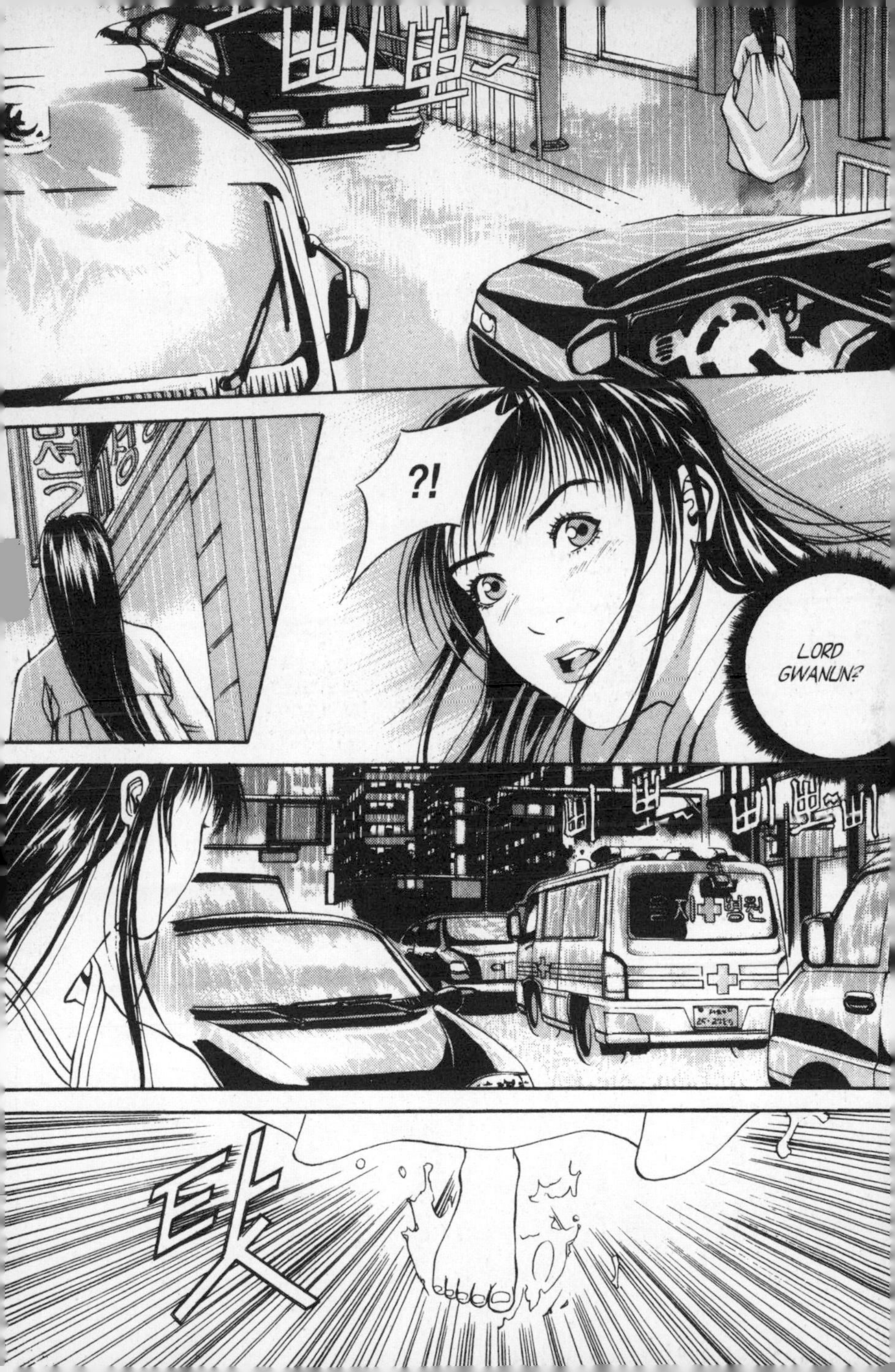
?!
LORD GWANUN?

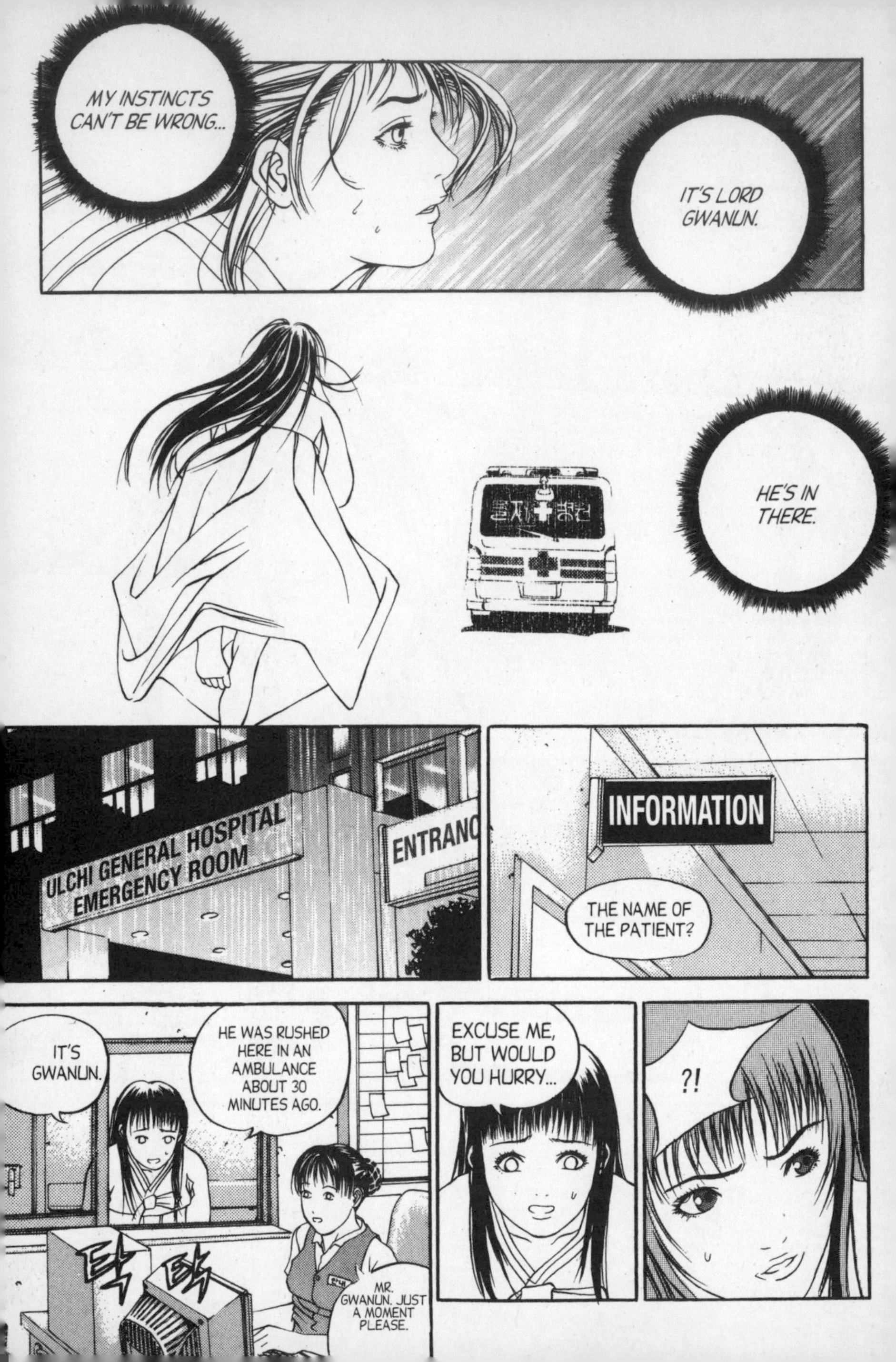
MY INSTINCTS CAN'T BE WRONG...
IT'S LORD GWANUN.
HE'S IN THERE.
ULCHI GENERAL HOSPITAL EMERGENCY ROOM
ENTRANC
INFORMATION
THE NAME OF THE PATIENT?
IT'S GWANUN.
HE WAS RUSHED HERE IN AN AMBULANCE ABOUT 30 MINUTES AGO.
MR. GWANUN. JUST A MOMENT PLEASE.
EXCUSE ME, BUT WOULD YOU HURRY...
?!

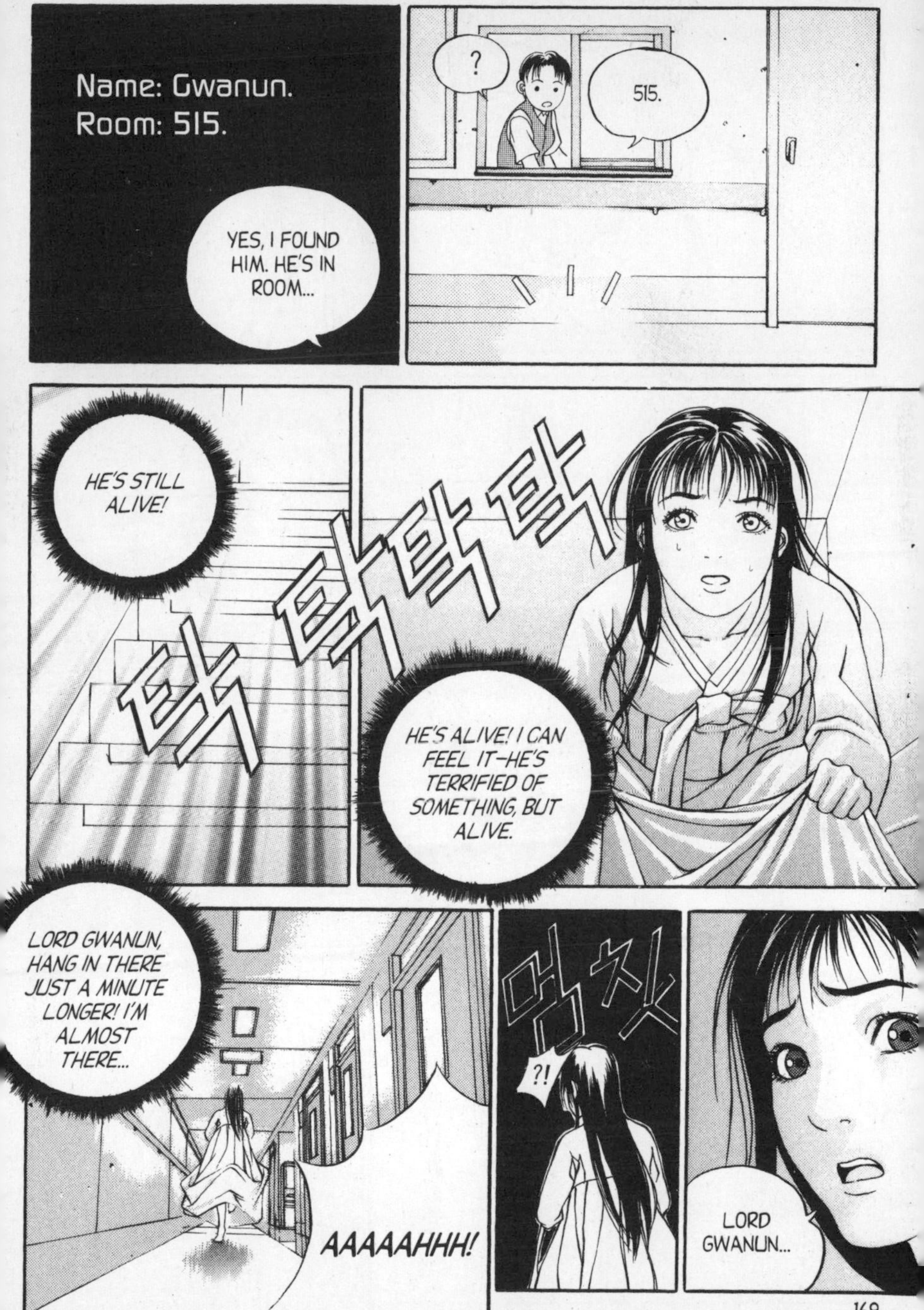
Name: Gwanun.
Room: 515.
YES, I FOUND HIM. HE'S IN ROOM...
?
515.
HE'S STILL ALIVE!
탁 탁탁 탁
HE'S ALIVE! I CAN FEEL IT—HE'S TERRIFIED OF SOMETHING, BUT ALIVE.
LORD GWANUN, HANG IN THERE JUST A MINUTE LONGER! I'M ALMOST THERE...
AAAAAHHH!
멈칫
?!
LORD GWANUN...

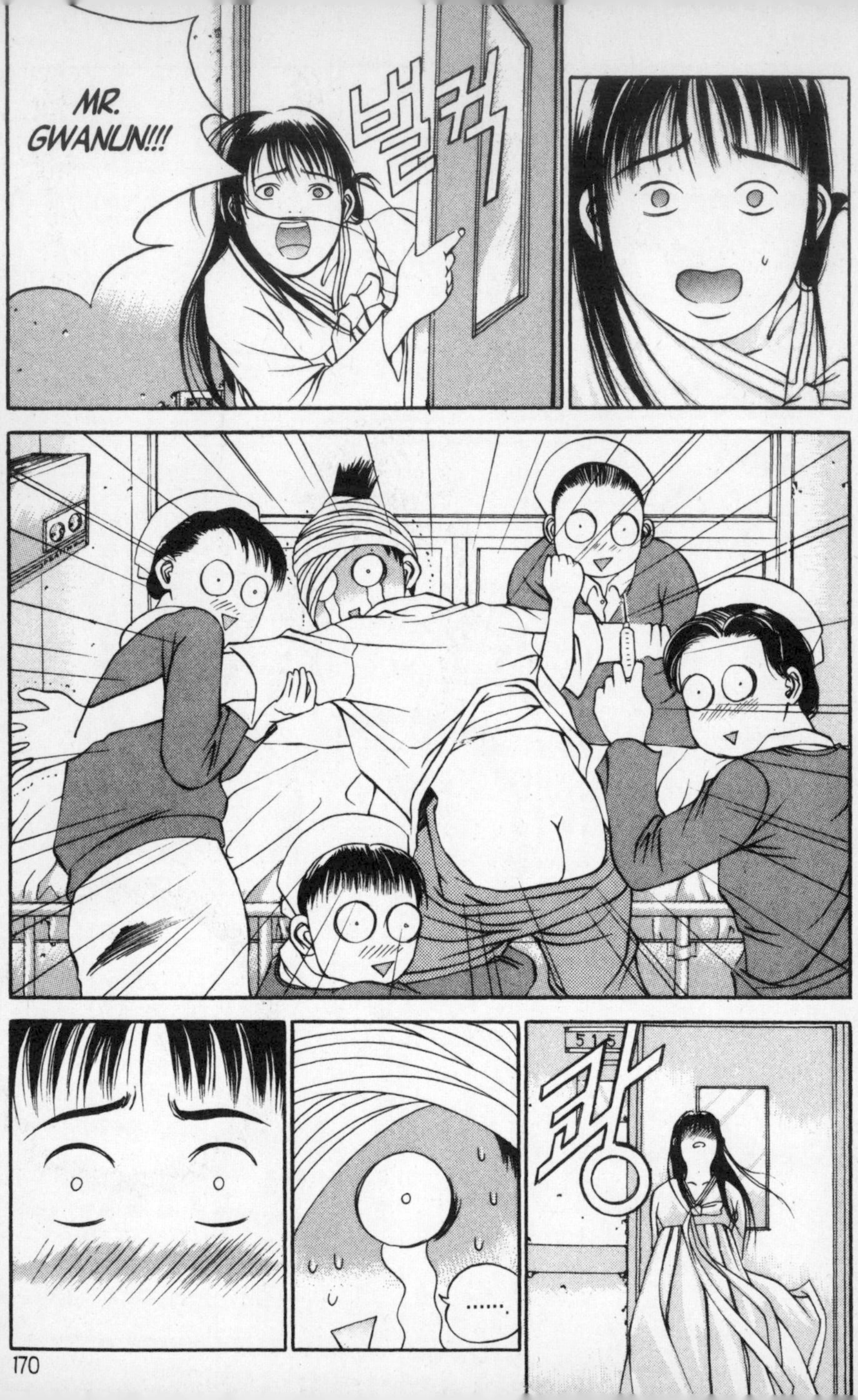
MR. GWANUN!!!
벌컥
......
515
쾅

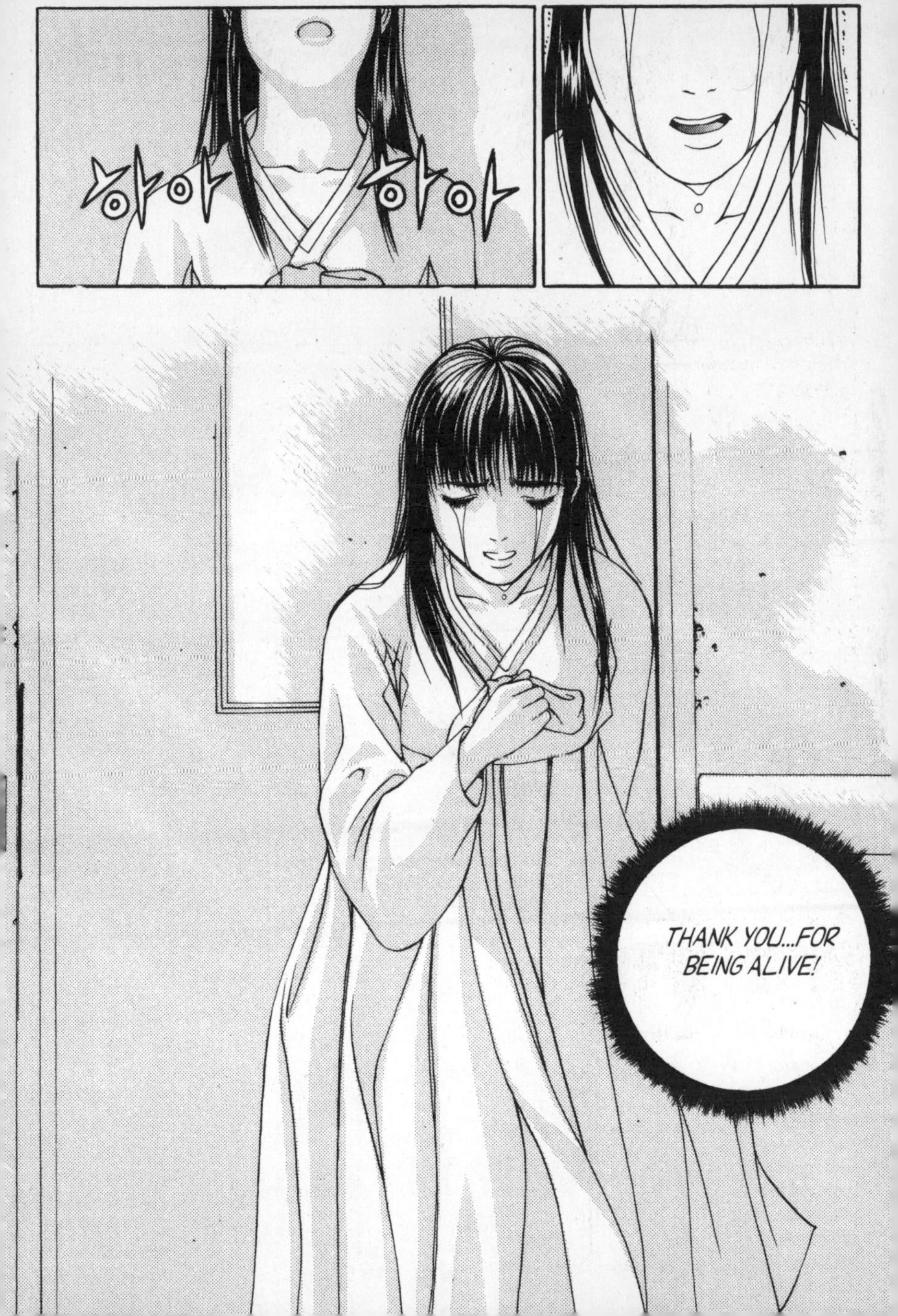
THANK YOU...FOR BEING ALIVE!

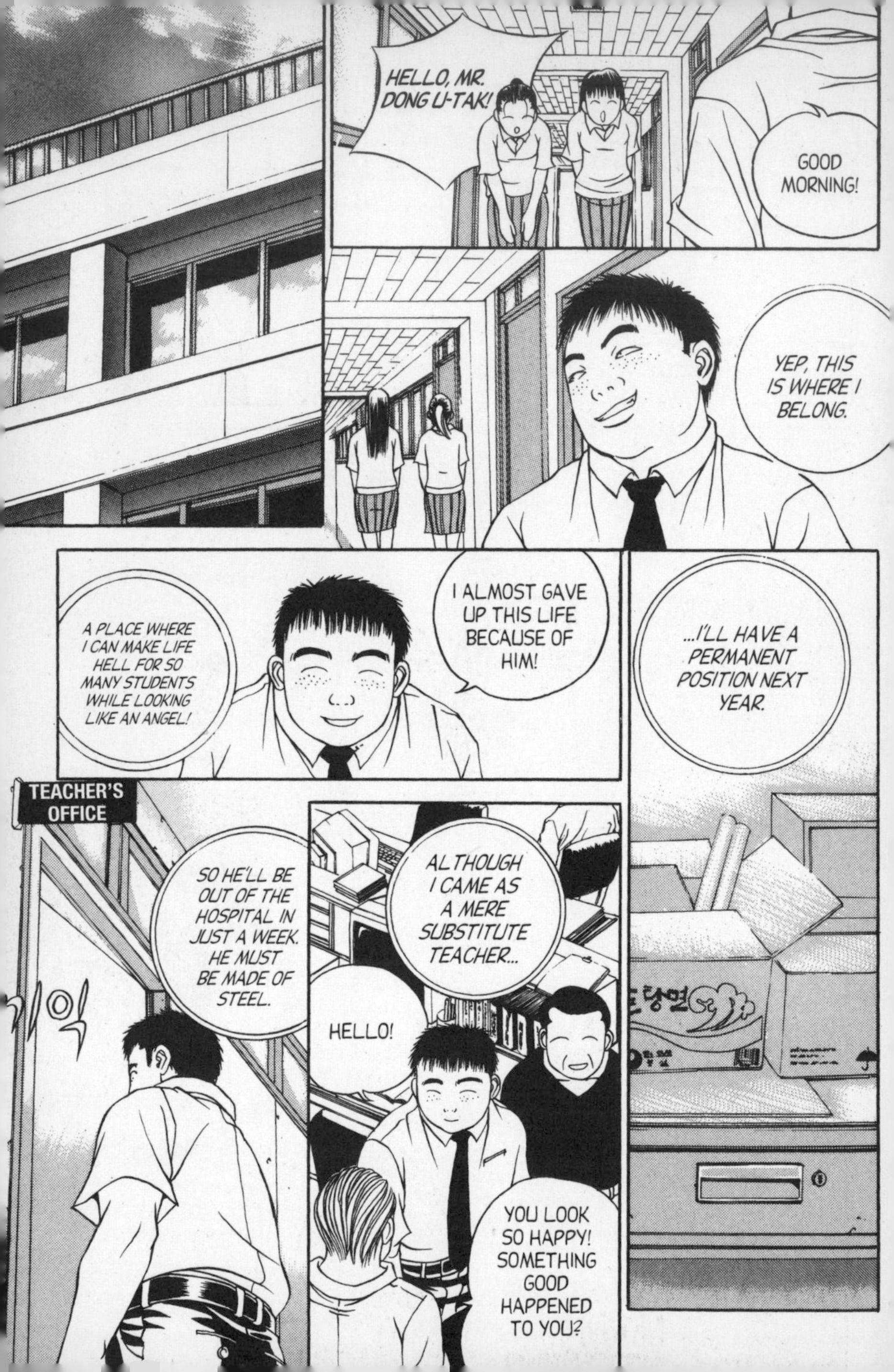
HELLO, MR. DONG U-TAK!
GOOD MORNING!
YEP, THIS IS WHERE I BELONG.
A PLACE WHERE I CAN MAKE LIFE HELL FOR SO MANY STUDENTS WHILE LOOKING LIKE AN ANGEL!
I ALMOST GAVE UP THIS LIFE BECAUSE OF HIM!
...I'LL HAVE A PERMANENT POSITION NEXT YEAR.
TEACHER'S OFFICE
끼익
SO HE'LL BE OUT OF THE HOSPITAL IN JUST A WEEK. HE MUST BE MADE OF STEEL.
ALTHOUGH I CAME AS A MERE SUBSTITUTE TEACHER...
HELLO!
YOU LOOK SO HAPPY! SOMETHING GOOD HAPPENED TO YOU?

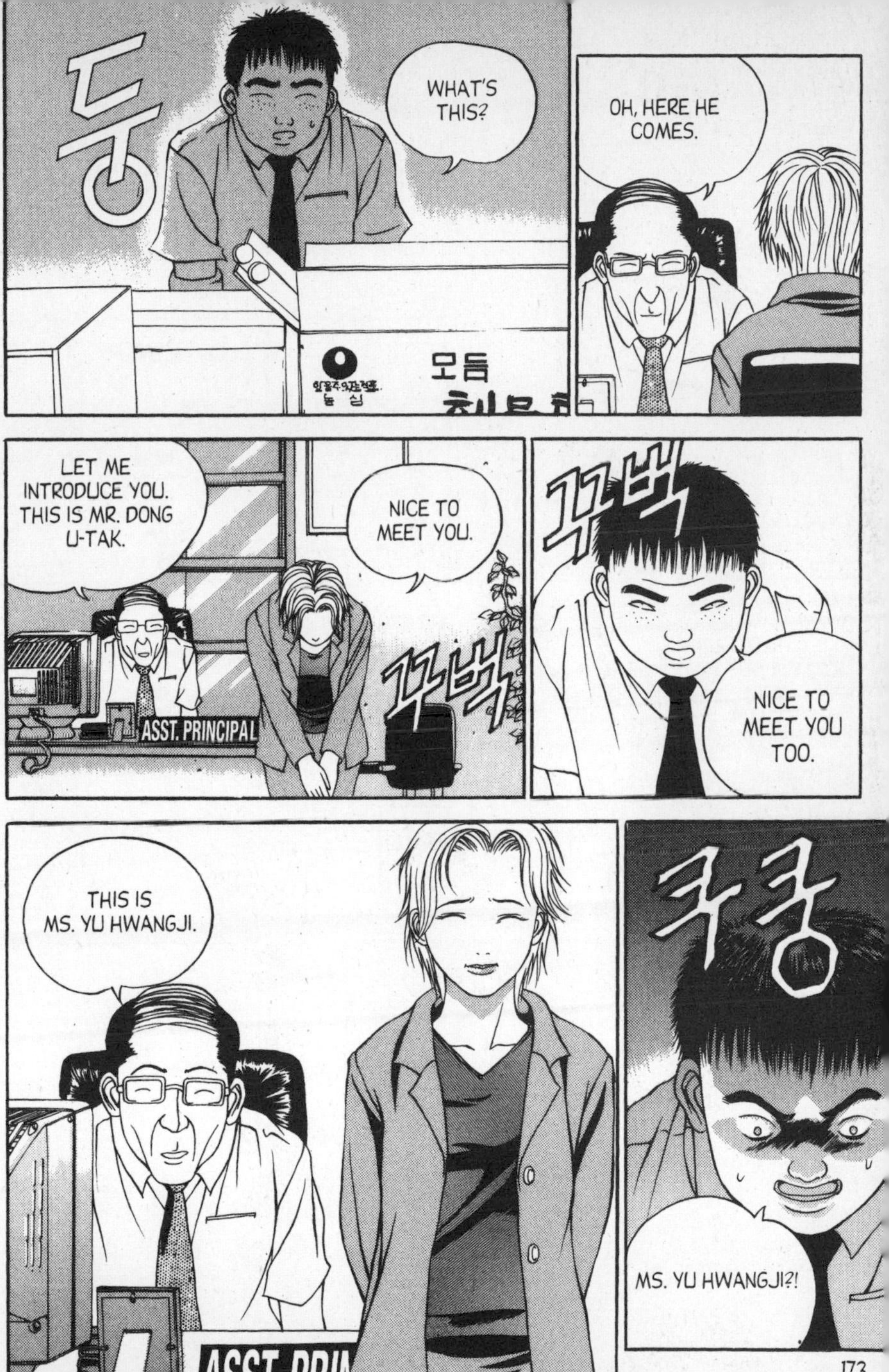

둥
WHAT'S THIS?
OH, HERE HE COMES.
LET ME INTRODUCE YOU. THIS IS MR. DONG U-TAK.
NICE TO MEET YOU.
꾸벅
ASST. PRINCIPAL
꾸벅
NICE TO MEET YOU TOO.
THIS IS MS. YU HWANGJI.
ASST. PRIN
쿠쿵
MS. YU HWANGJI?!

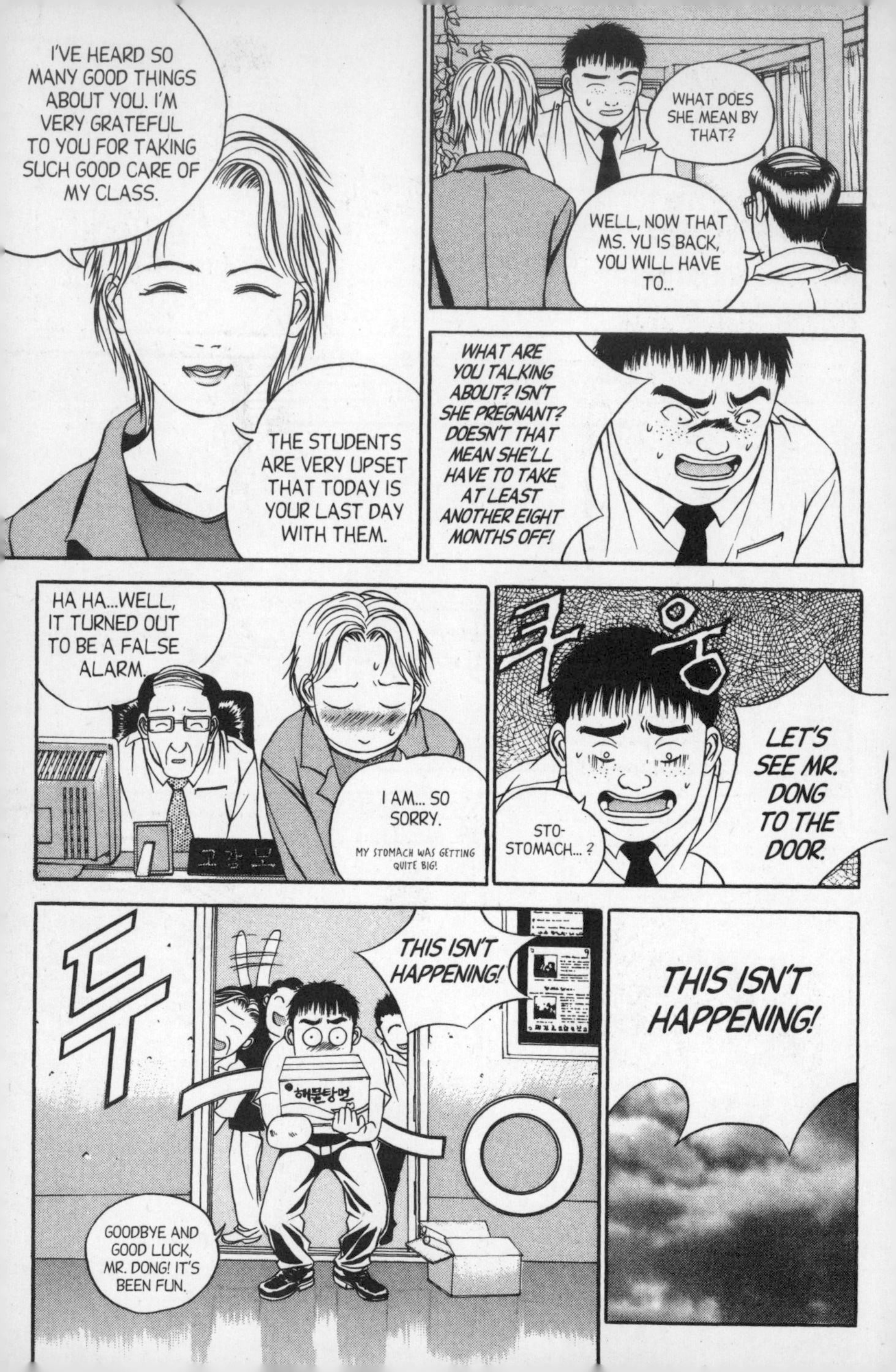
I'VE HEARD SO MANY GOOD THINGS ABOUT YOU. I'M VERY GRATEFUL TO YOU FOR TAKING SUCH GOOD CARE OF MY CLASS.
THE STUDENTS ARE VERY UPSET THAT TODAY IS YOUR LAST DAY WITH THEM.
WHAT DOES SHE MEAN BY THAT?
WELL, NOW THAT MS. YU IS BACK, YOU WILL HAVE TO...
WHAT ARE YOU TALKING ABOUT? ISN'T SHE PREGNANT? DOESN'T THAT MEAN SHE'LL HAVE TO TAKE AT LEAST ANOTHER EIGHT MONTHS OFF!
HA HA...WELL, IT TURNED OUT TO BE A FALSE ALARM.
I AM... SO SORRY.
MY STOMACH WAS GETTING QUITE BIG!
쿠웅
STO- STOMACH... ?
LET'S SEE MR. DONG TO THE DOOR.
THIS ISN'T HAPPENING!
GOODBYE AND GOOD LUCK, MR. DONG! IT'S BEEN FUN.
THIS ISN'T HAPPENING!

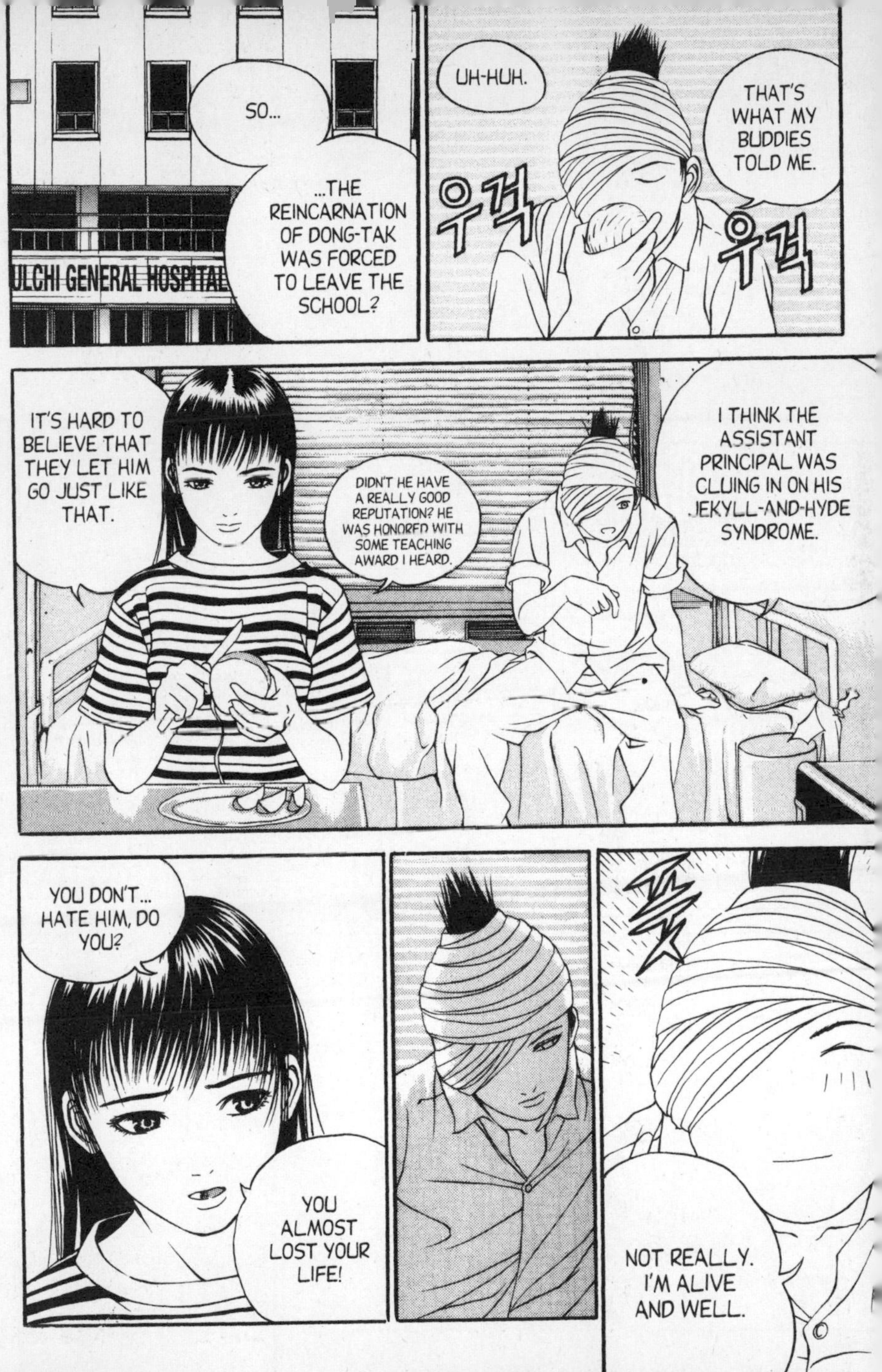
ULCHI GENERAL HOSPITAL
SO...
...THE REINCARNATION OF DONG-TAK WAS FORCED TO LEAVE THE SCHOOL?
UH-HUH.
우걱
THAT'S WHAT MY BUDDIES TOLD ME.
우걱
IT'S HARD TO BELIEVE THAT THEY LET HIM GO JUST LIKE THAT.
DIDN'T HE HAVE A REALLY GOOD REPUTATION? HE WAS HONORED WITH SOME TEACHING AWARD I HEARD.
I THINK THE ASSISTANT PRINCIPAL WAS CLUING IN ON HIS JEKYLL-AND-HYDE SYNDROME.
YOU DON'T... HATE HIM, DO YOU?
YOU ALMOST LOST YOUR LIFE!
NOT REALLY. I'M ALIVE AND WELL.

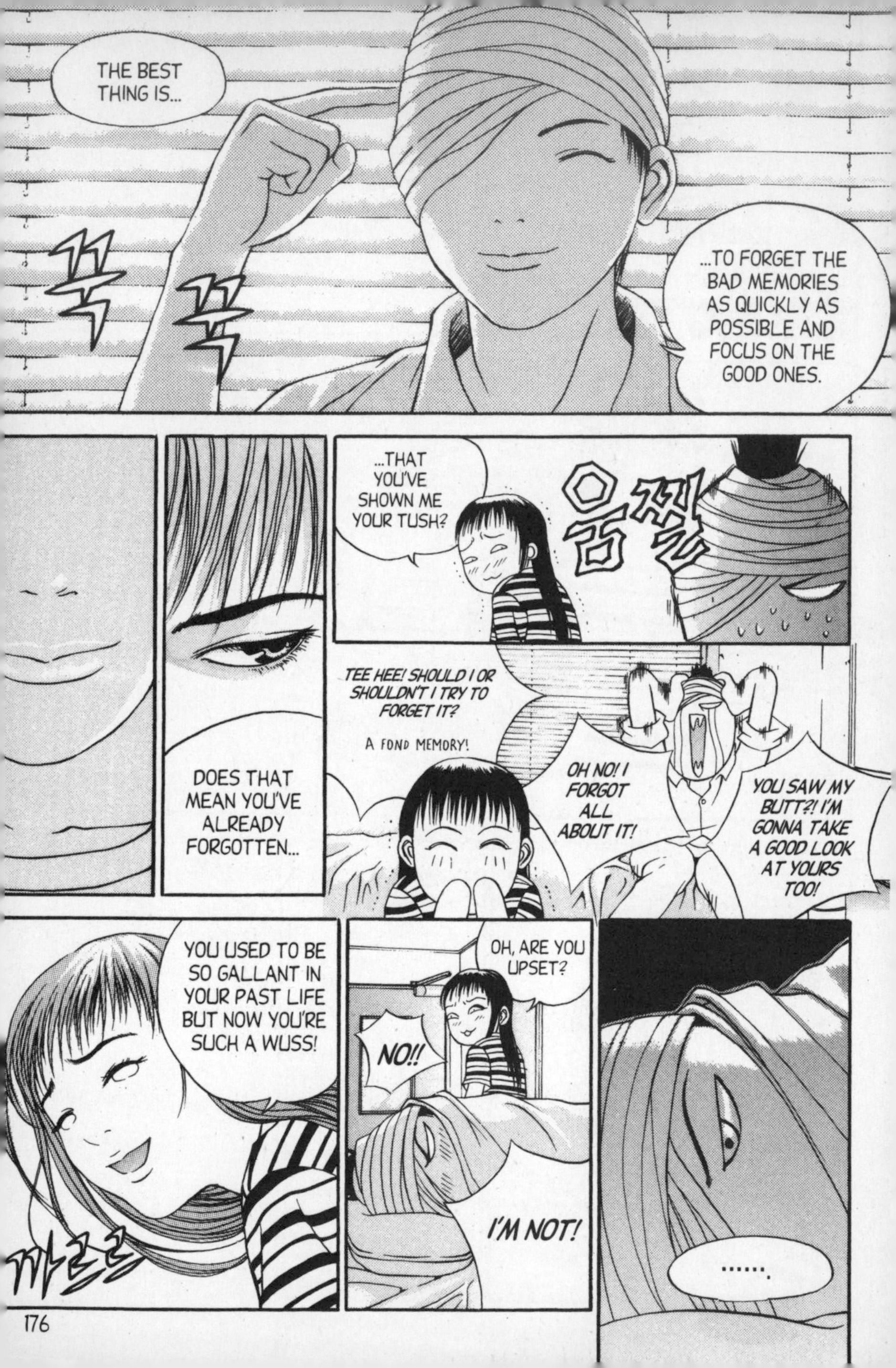
THE BEST THING IS...
꾹
꾹
...TO FORGET THE BAD MEMORIES AS QUICKLY AS POSSIBLE AND FOCUS ON THE GOOD ONES.
DOES THAT MEAN YOU'VE ALREADY FORGOTTEN...
...THAT YOU'VE SHOWN ME YOUR TUSH?
움찔
TEE HEE! SHOULD I OR SHOULDN'T I TRY TO FORGET IT?
A FOND MEMORY!
OH NO! I FORGOT ALL ABOUT IT!
YOU SAW MY BUTT?! I'M GONNA TAKE A GOOD LOOK AT YOURS TOO!
YOU USED TO BE SO GALLANT IN YOUR PAST LIFE BUT NOW YOU'RE SUCH A WUSS!
까르르
OH, ARE YOU UPSET?
NO!!
I'M NOT!
....

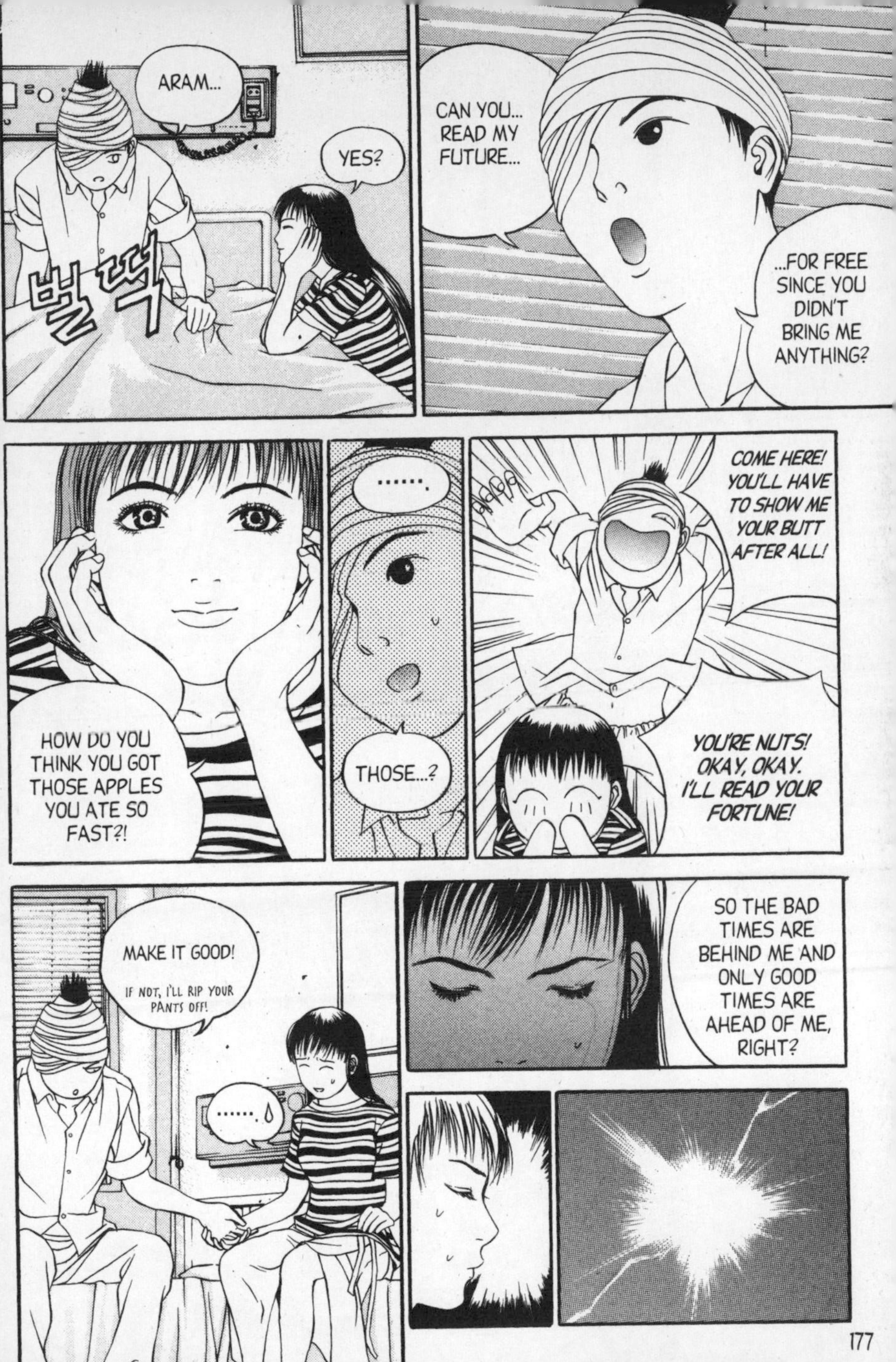

ARAM...
YES?
벌떡
CAN YOU... READ MY FUTURE...
...FOR FREE SINCE YOU DIDN'T BRING ME ANYTHING?
HOW DO YOU THINK YOU GOT THOSE APPLES YOU ATE SO FAST?!
....
THOSE...?
COME HERE! YOU'LL HAVE TO SHOW ME YOUR BUTT AFTER ALL!
YOU'RE NUTS! OKAY, OKAY. I'LL READ YOUR FORTUNE!
MAKE IT GOOD!
IF NOT, I'LL RIP YOUR PANTS OFF!
....
SO THE BAD TIMES ARE BEHIND ME AND ONLY GOOD TIMES ARE AHEAD OF ME, RIGHT?

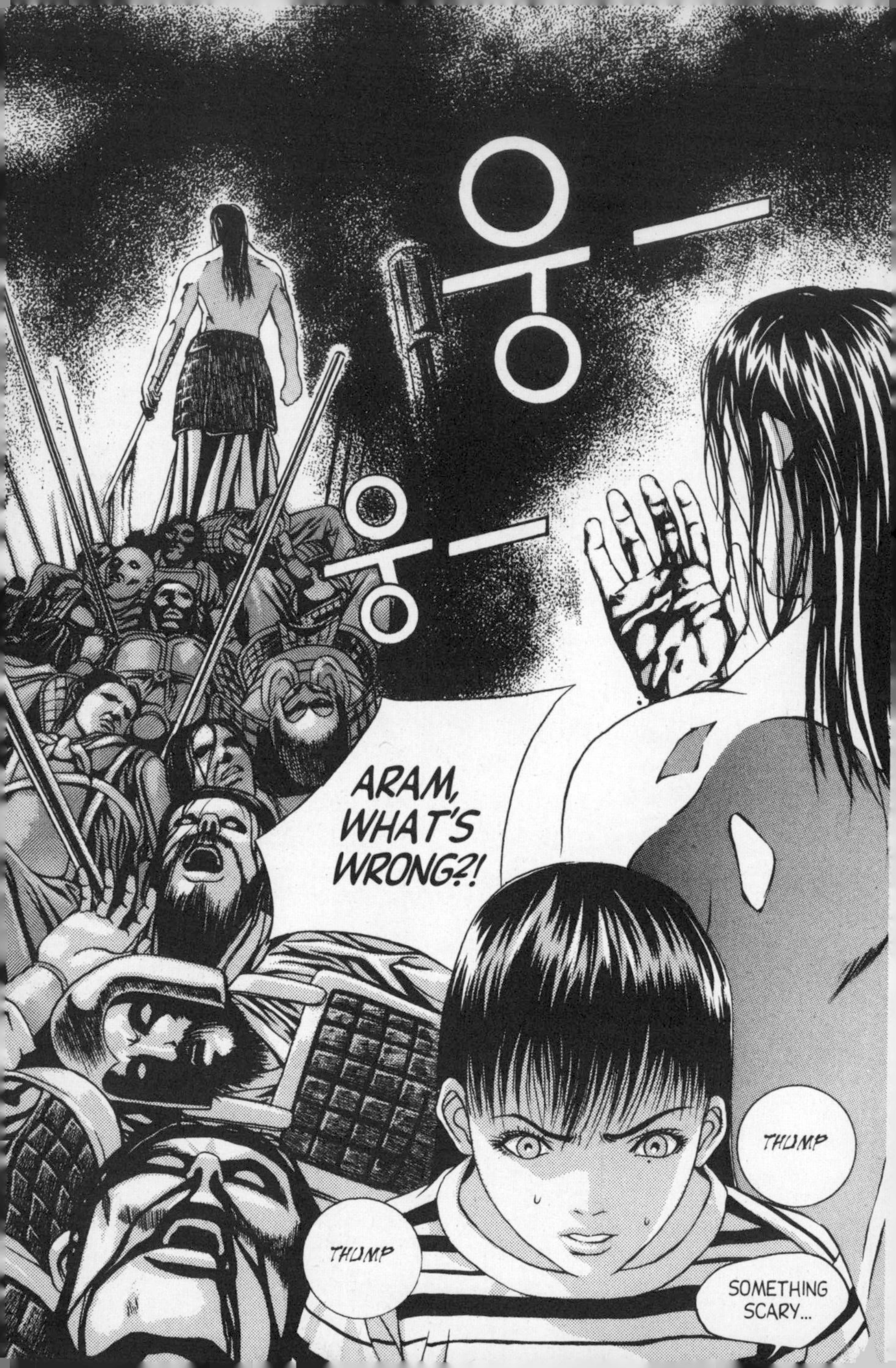
ARAM, WHAT'S WRONG?!
THUMP
THUMP
SOMETHING SCARY...

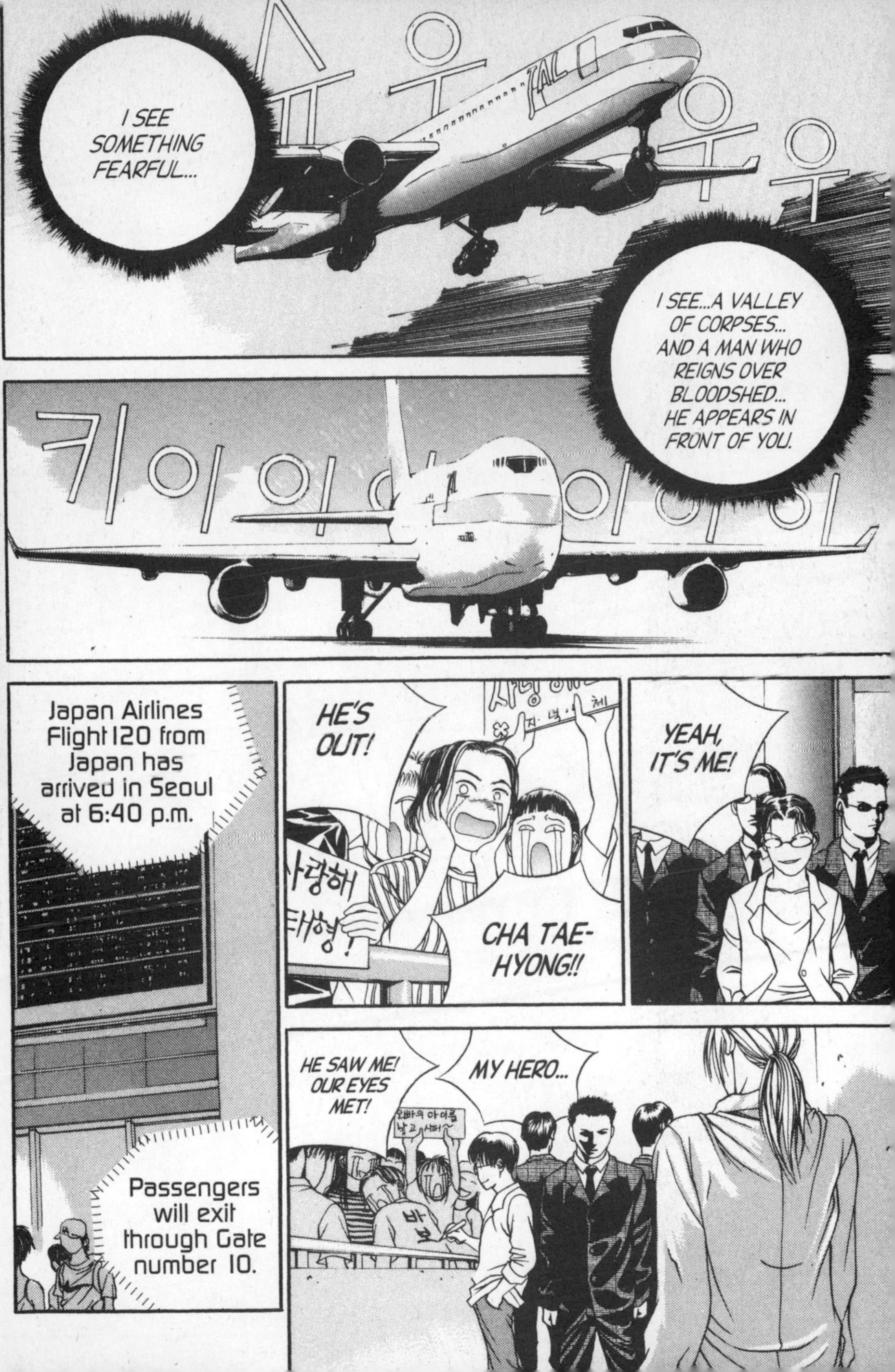
I SEE SOMETHING FEARFUL...
I SEE...A VALLEY OF CORPSES... AND A MAN WHO REIGNS OVER BLOODSHED... HE APPEARS IN FRONT OF YOU.
Japan Airlines Flight 120 from Japan has arrived in Seoul at 6:40 p.m.
Passengers will exit through Gate number 10.
HE'S OUT!
사랑해 태형!
CHA TAE-HYONG!!
YEAH, IT'S ME!
HE SAW ME! OUR EYES MET!
MY HERO...

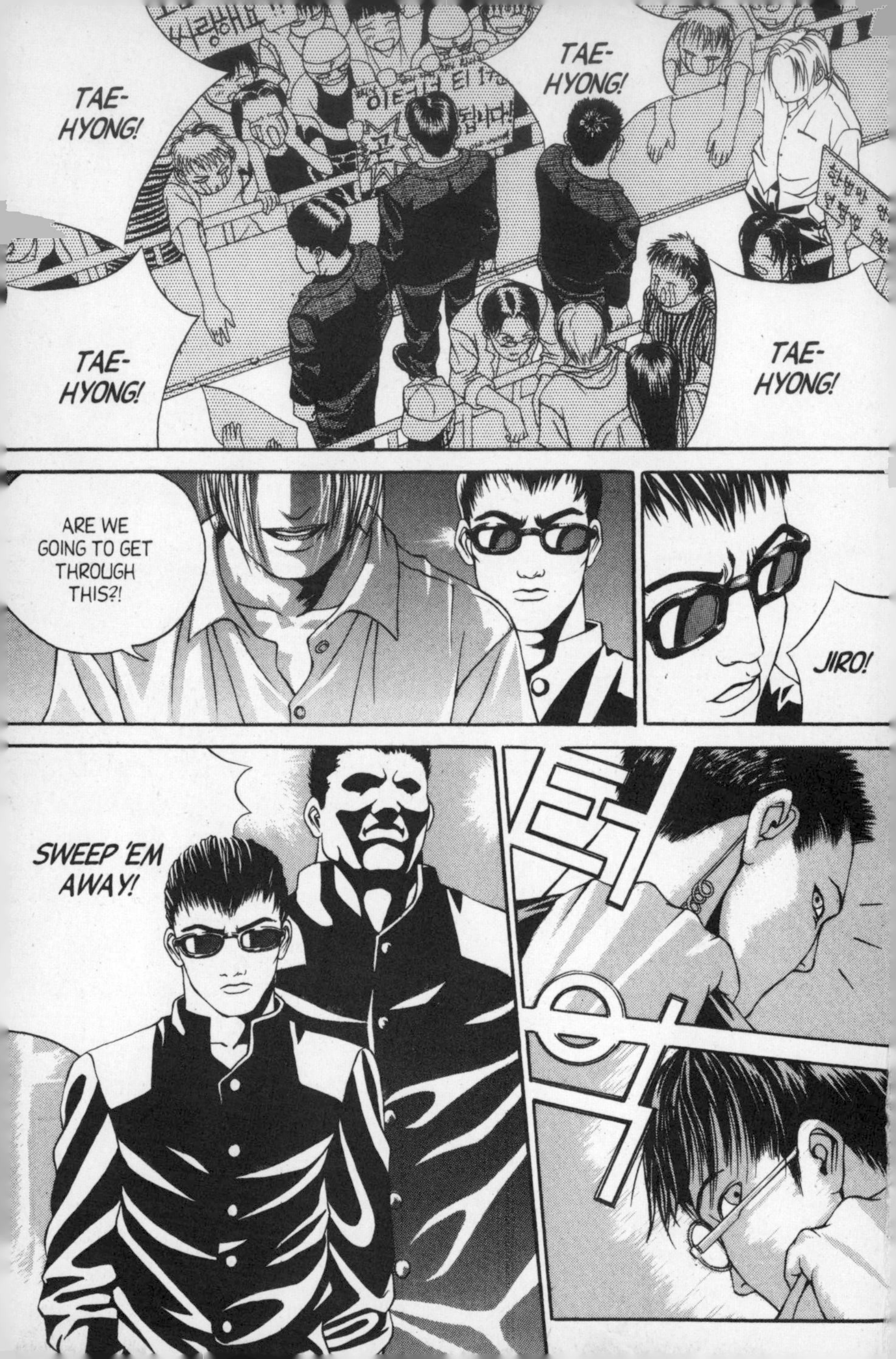
TAE-
HYONG!
TAE-
HYONG!
TAE-
HYONG!
TAE-
HYONG!
ARE WE GOING TO GET THROUGH THIS?!
JIRO!
SWEEP 'EM AWAY!

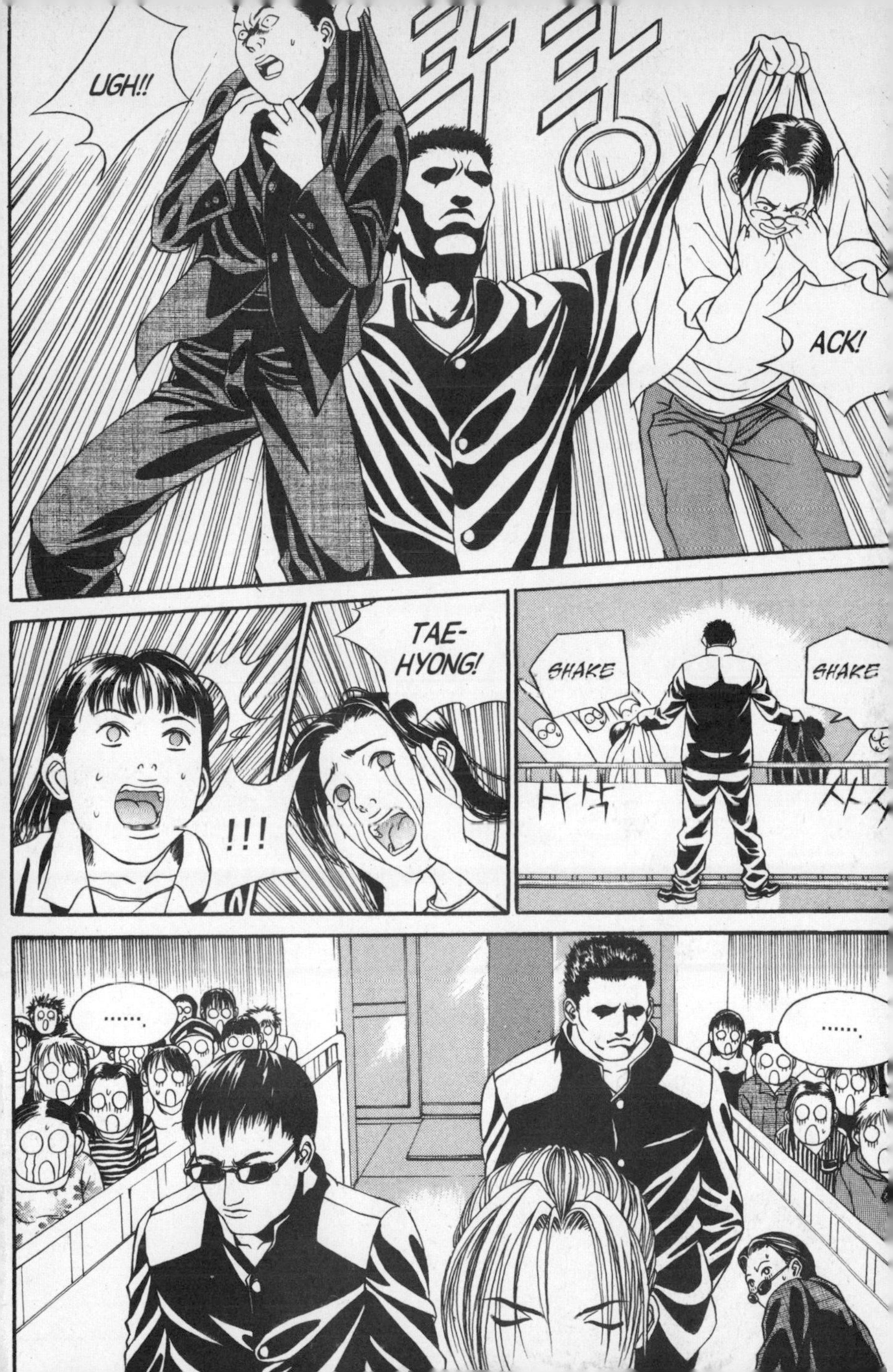
UGH!!
ACK!
TAE-HYONG!
!!!
SHAKE
SHAKE
....
....

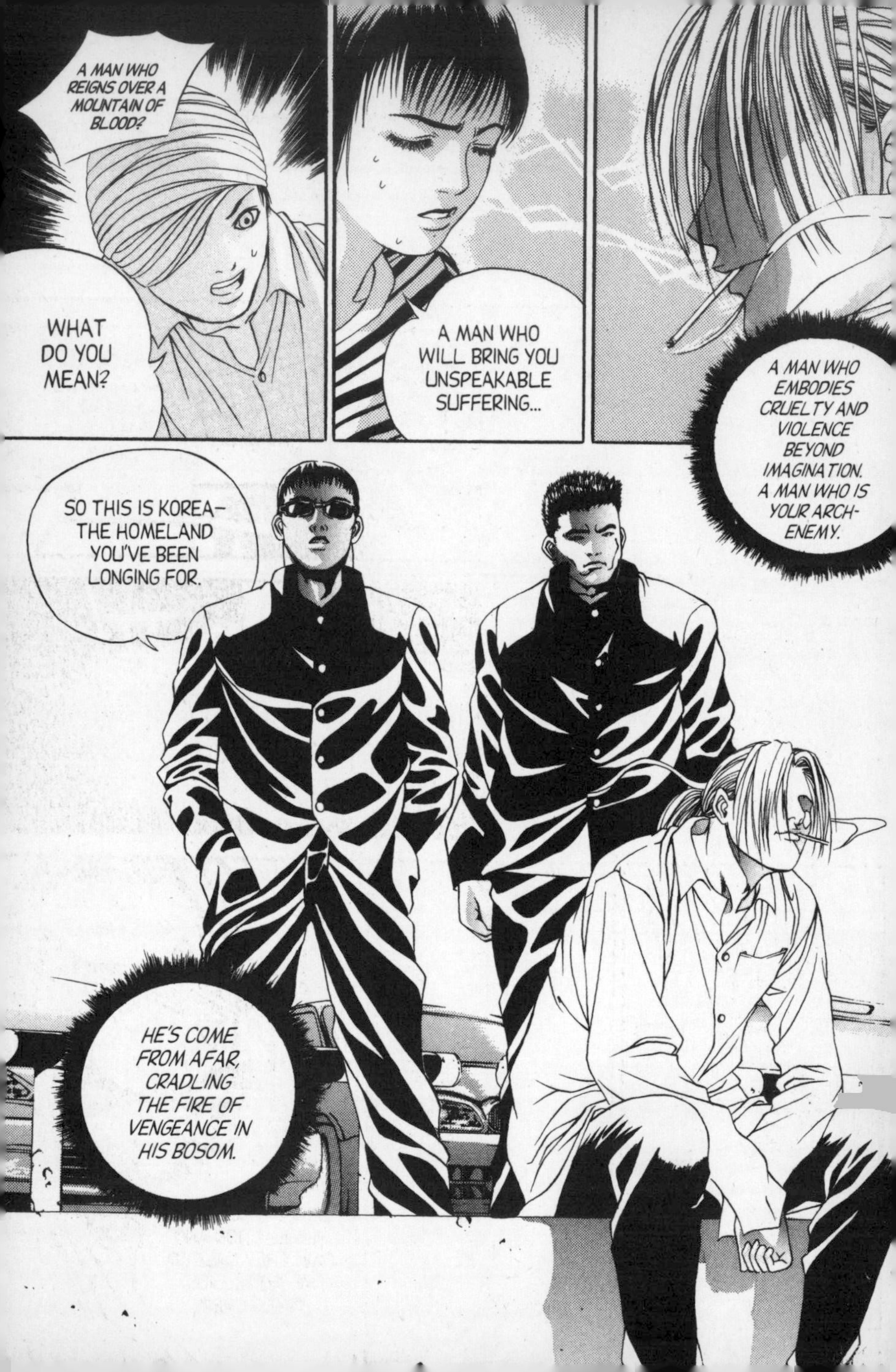
A MAN WHO REIGNS OVER A MOUNTAIN OF BLOOD?
WHAT DO YOU MEAN?
A MAN WHO WILL BRING YOU UNSPEAKABLE SUFFERING...
A MAN WHO EMBODIES CRUELTY AND VIOLENCE BEYOND IMAGINATION. A MAN WHO IS YOUR ARCH-ENEMY.
SO THIS IS KOREA–THE HOMELAND YOU'VE BEEN LONGING FOR.
HE'S COME FROM AFAR, CRADLING THE FIRE OF VENGEANCE IN HIS BOSOM.

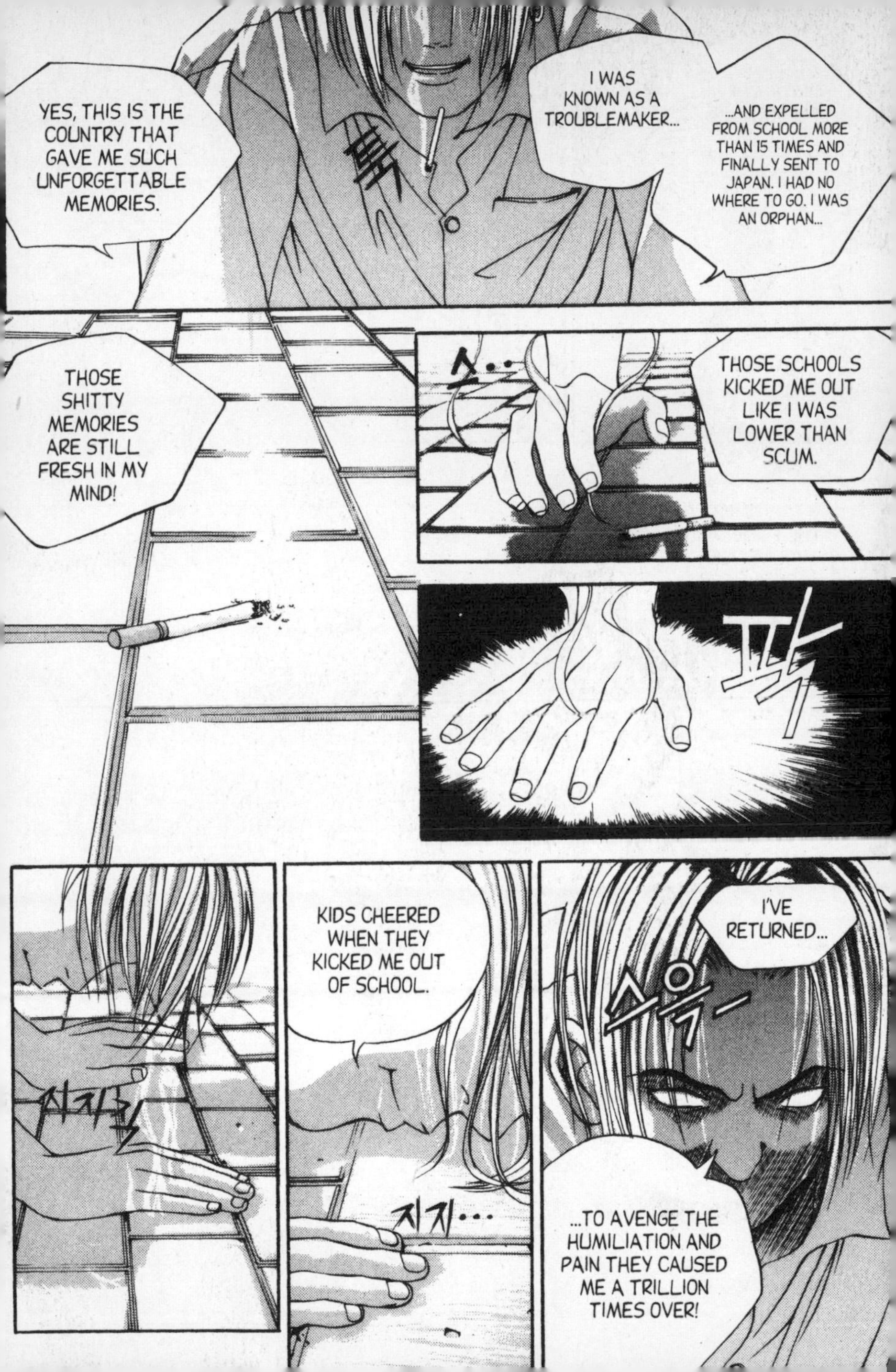
YES, THIS IS THE COUNTRY THAT GAVE ME SUCH UNFORGETTABLE MEMORIES.
I WAS KNOWN AS A TROUBLEMAKER...
...AND EXPELLED FROM SCHOOL MORE THAN 15 TIMES AND FINALLY SENT TO JAPAN. I HAD NO WHERE TO GO. I WAS AN ORPHAN...
THOSE SHITTY MEMORIES ARE STILL FRESH IN MY MIND!
THOSE SCHOOLS KICKED ME OUT LIKE I WAS LOWER THAN SCUM.
KIDS CHEERED WHEN THEY KICKED ME OUT OF SCHOOL.
I'VE RETURNED...
...TO AVENGE THE HUMILIATION AND PAIN THEY CAUSED ME A TRILLION TIMES OVER!

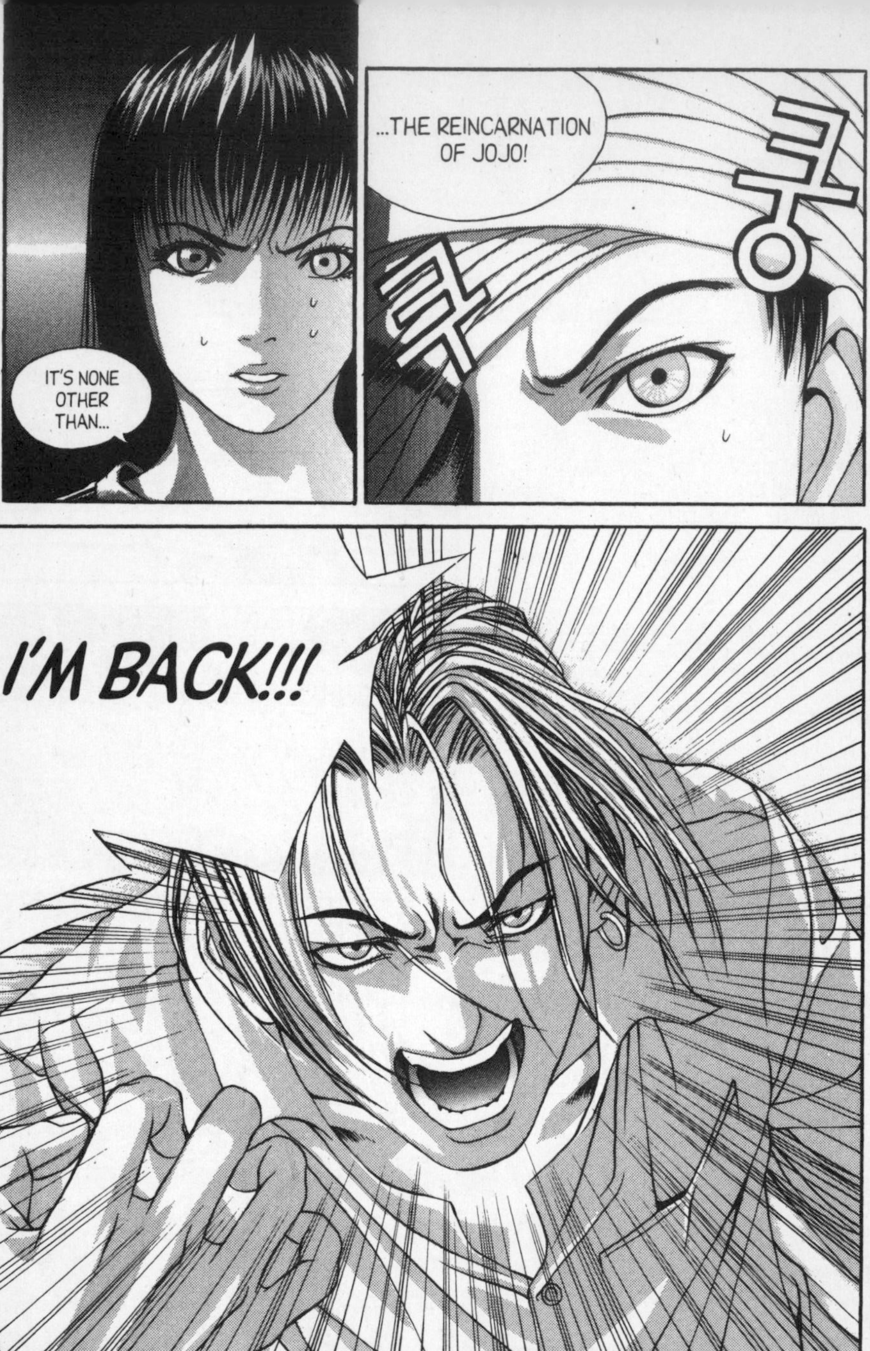
IT'S NONE OTHER THAN...
...THE REINCARNATION OF JOJO!
I'M BACK!!!

TO BE CONTINUED IN ETERNITY 2.

ETERNITY

PREVIEW

WITH JOJO BACK IN THE PICTURE, ARAM FEARS THAT HIS EVIL WAYS WILL INFLUENCE JANGBANG SO SHE RALLIES GWANUN TO COMB THE CITY STREETS LOOKING FOR HIM. WHEN JANGBANG'S PAST COMES BACK TO HAUNT HIM, HE DECIDES TO SETTLE THE SCORE WITH AN OLD "FRIEND." BUT WHEN HE GETS JUMPED BY A MOTORCYCLE GANG, HE CAN'T BELIEVE WHO SHOWS UP TO COVER HIS BACK! STAY TUNED FOR THE NEXT EPISODE OF ETERNITY!

SEE YOU IN VOLUME 2!

ALSO AVAILABLE FROM TOKYOPOP

MANGA

.HACK//LEGEND OF THE TWILIGHT
@LARGE
ABENOBASHI: MAGICAL SHOPPING ARCADE
A.I. LOVE YOU
AI YORI AOSHI
ANGELIC LAYER
ARM OF KANNON
BABY BIRTH
BATTLE ROYALE
BATTLE VIXENS
BRAIN POWERED
BRIGADOON
B'TX
CANDIDATE FOR GODDESS, THE
CARDCAPTOR SAKURA
CARDCAPTOR SAKURA - MASTER OF THE CLOW
CHOBITS
CHRONICLES OF THE CURSED SWORD
CLAMP SCHOOL DETECTIVES
CLOVER
COMIC PARTY
CONFIDENTIAL CONFESSIONS
CORRECTOR YUI
COWBOY BEBOP
COWBOY BEBOP: SHOOTING STAR
CRAZY LOVE STORY
CRESCENT MOON
CROSS
CULDCEPT
CYBORG 009
D•N•ANGEL
DEMON DIARY
DEMON ORORON, THE
DEUS VITAE
DIABOLO
DIGIMON
DIGIMON TAMERS
DIGIMON ZERO TWO
DOLL
DRAGON HUNTER
DRAGON KNIGHTS
DRAGON VOICE
DREAM SAGA
DUKLYON: CLAMP SCHOOL DEFENDERS
EERIE QUEERIE!
ERICA SAKURAZAWA: COLLECTED WORKS
ET CETERA
ETERNITY
EVIL'S RETURN
FAERIES' LANDING
FAKE
FLCL
FLOWER OF THE DEEP SLEEP
FORBIDDEN DANCE
FRUITS BASKET
G GUNDAM

GATEKEEPERS
GETBACKERS
GIRL GOT GAME
GIRLS' EDUCATIONAL CHARTER
GRAVITATION
GTO
GUNDAM BLUE DESTINY
GUNDAM SEED ASTRAY
GUNDAM WING
GUNDAM WING: BATTLEFIELD OF PACIFISTS
GUNDAM WING: ENDLESS WALTZ
GUNDAM WING: THE LAST OUTPOST (G-UNIT)
GUYS' GUIDE TO GIRLS
HANDS OFF!
HAPPY MANIA
HARLEM BEAT
HONEY MUSTARD
I.N.V.U.
IMMORTAL RAIN
INITIAL D
INSTANT TEEN: JUST ADD NUTS
ISLAND
JING: KING OF BANDITS
JING: KING OF BANDITS - TWILIGHT TALES
JULINE
KARE KANO
KILL ME, KISS ME
KINDAICHI CASE FILES, THE
KING OF HELL
KODOCHA: SANA'S STAGE
LAMENT OF THE LAMB
LEGAL DRUG
LEGEND OF CHUN HYANG, THE
LES BIJOUX
LOVE HINA
LUPIN III
LUPIN III: WORLD'S MOST WANTED
MAGIC KNIGHT RAYEARTH I
MAGIC KNIGHT RAYEARTH II
MAHOROMATIC: AUTOMATIC MAIDEN
MAN OF MANY FACES
MARMALADE BOY
MARS
MARS: HORSE WITH NO NAME
MINK
MIRACLE GIRLS
MIYUKI-CHAN IN WONDERLAND
MODEL
MY LOVE
NECK AND NECK
ONE
ONE I LOVE, THE
PARADISE KISS
PARASYTE
PASSION FRUIT
PEACH GIRL
PEACH GIRL: CHANGE OF HEART
PET SHOP OF HORRORS

03.30.04T

ALSO AVAILABLE FROM TOKYOPOP®

For more information visit www.TOKYOPOP.com

03.30.04T

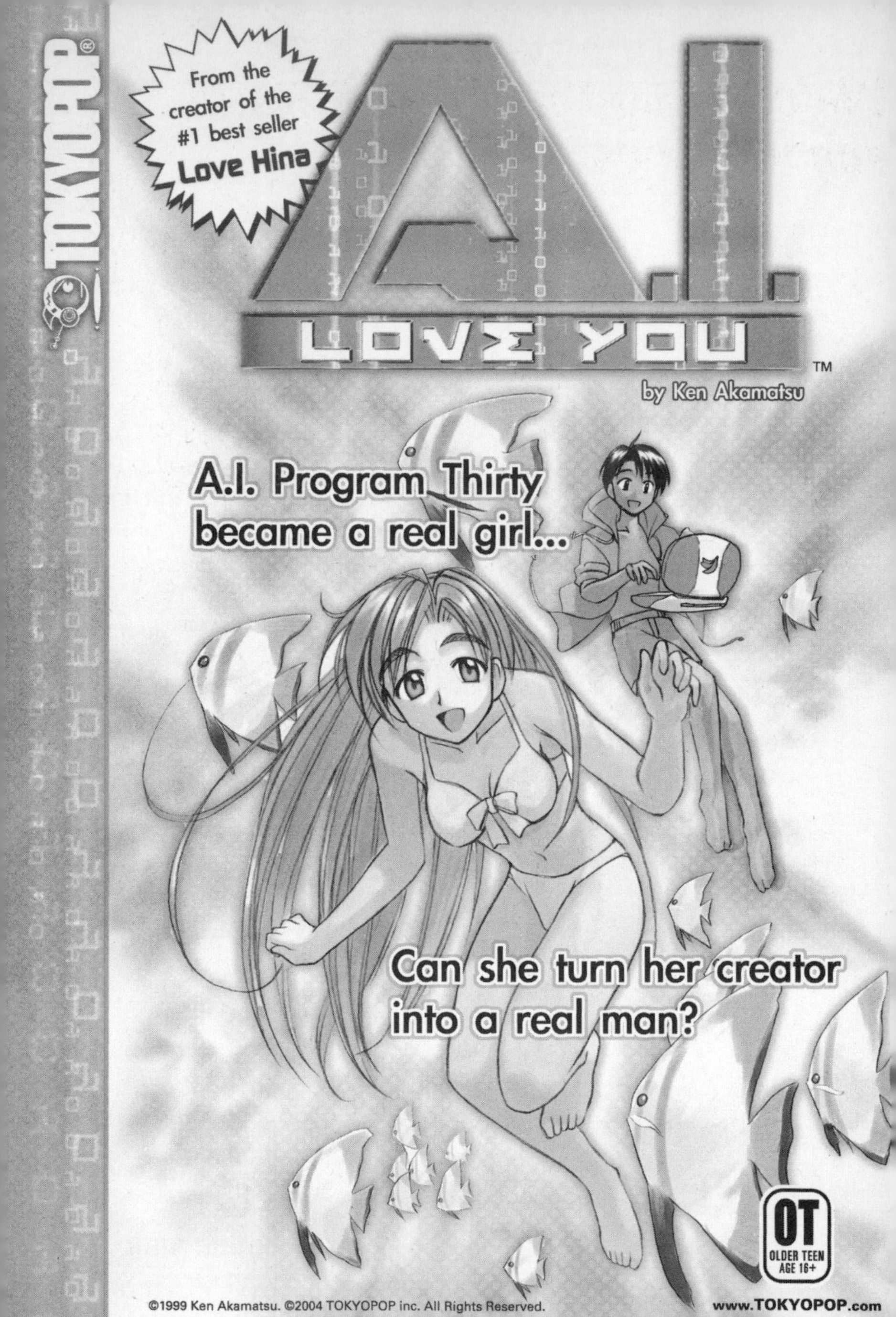
TOKYOPOP®
From the creator of the #1 best seller Love Hina
A.I. LOVE YOU™
by Ken Akamatsu
A.I. Program Thirty became a real girl...
Can she turn her creator into a real man?
OT
OLDER TEEN AGE 16+

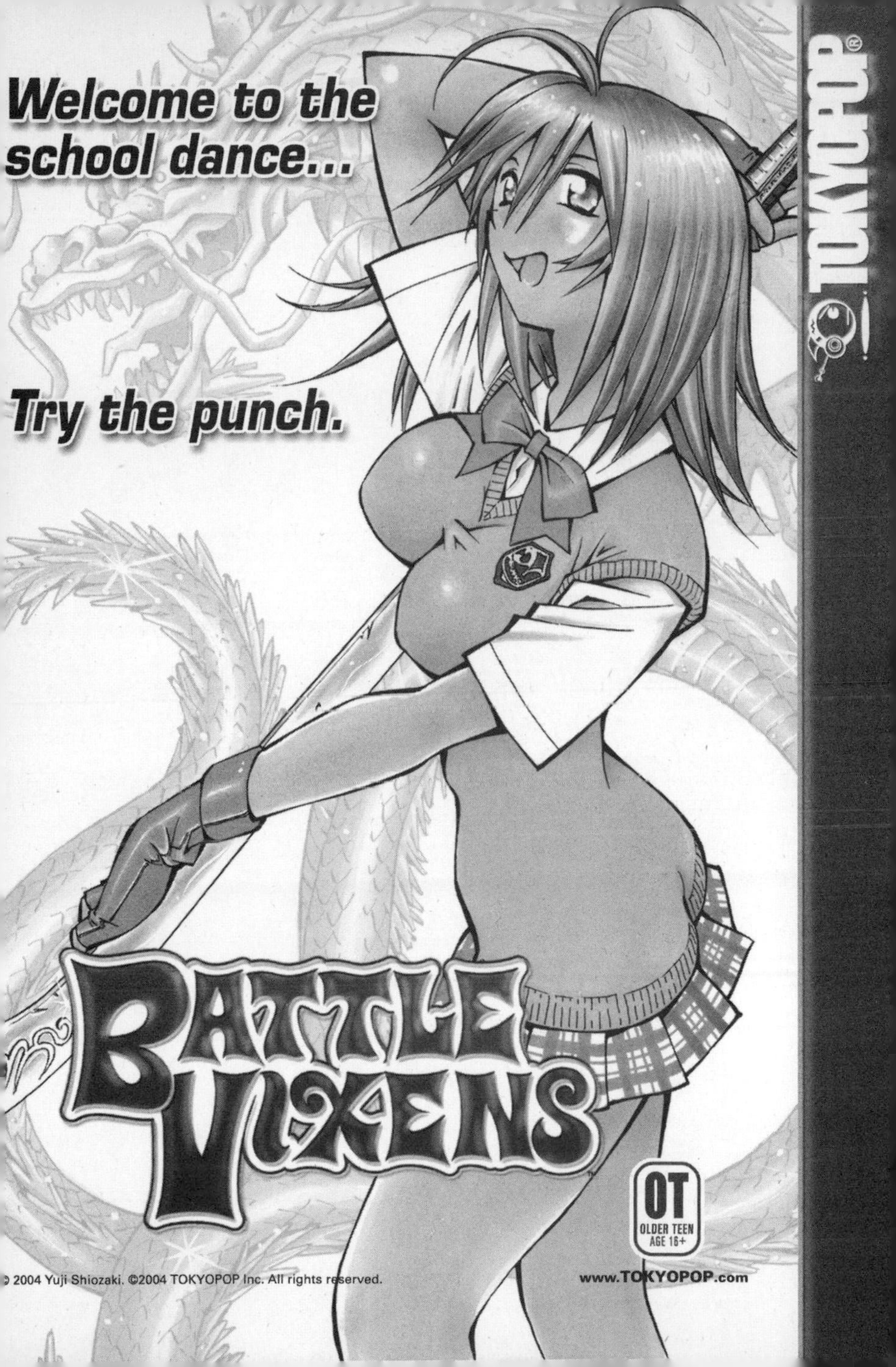
TOKYOPOP®
Welcome to the school dance...
Try the punch.
BATTLE VIXENS
OT
OLDER TEEN
AGE 16+
© 2004 Yuji Shiozaki. ©2004 TOKYOPOP Inc. All rights reserved.
www.TOKYOPOP.com

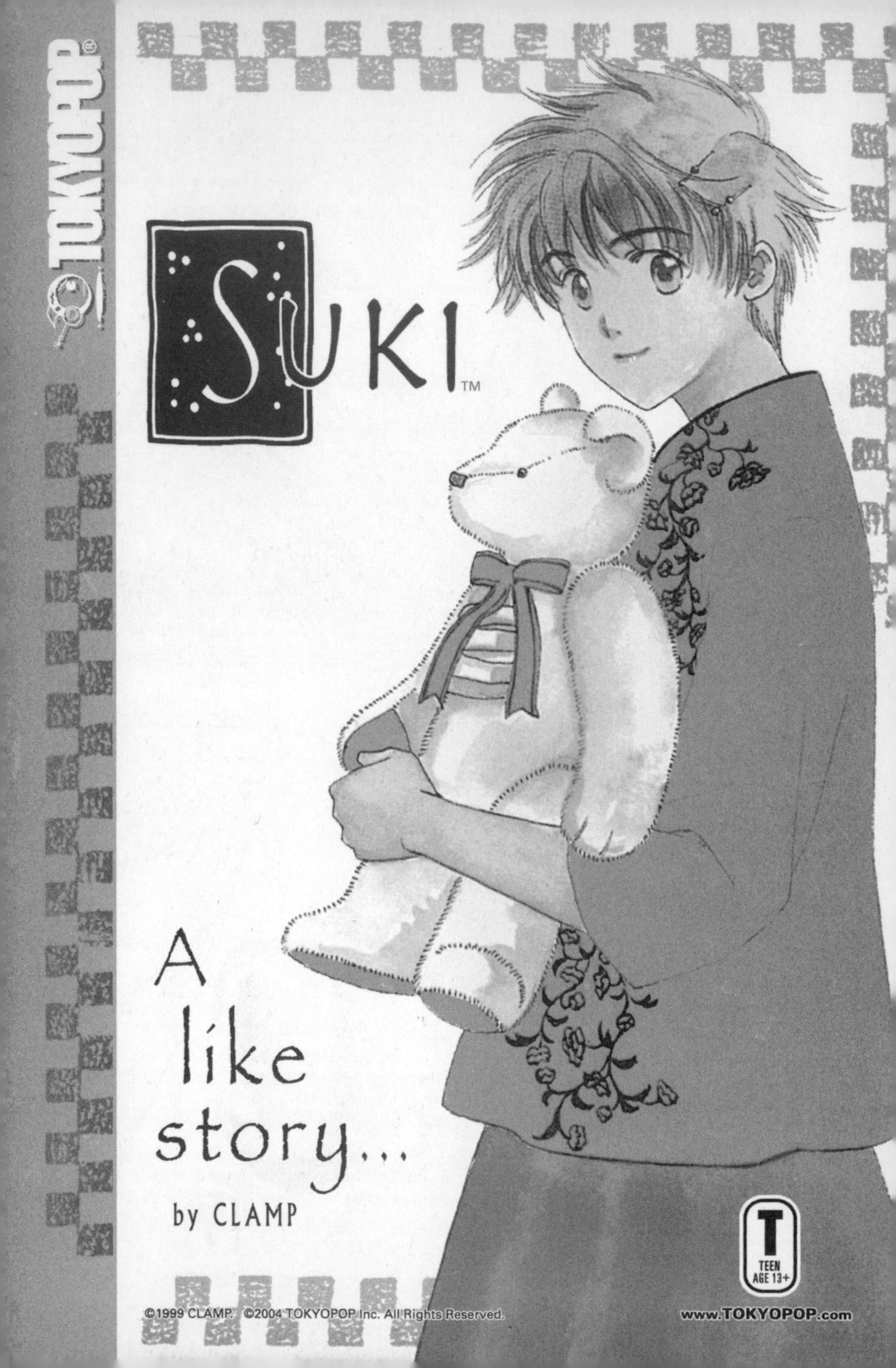
TOKYOPOP
SUKI™
A like story...
by CLAMP
T
TEEN AGE 13+
©1999 CLAMP. ©2004 TOKYOPOP Inc. All Rights Reserved.
www.TOKYOPOP.com

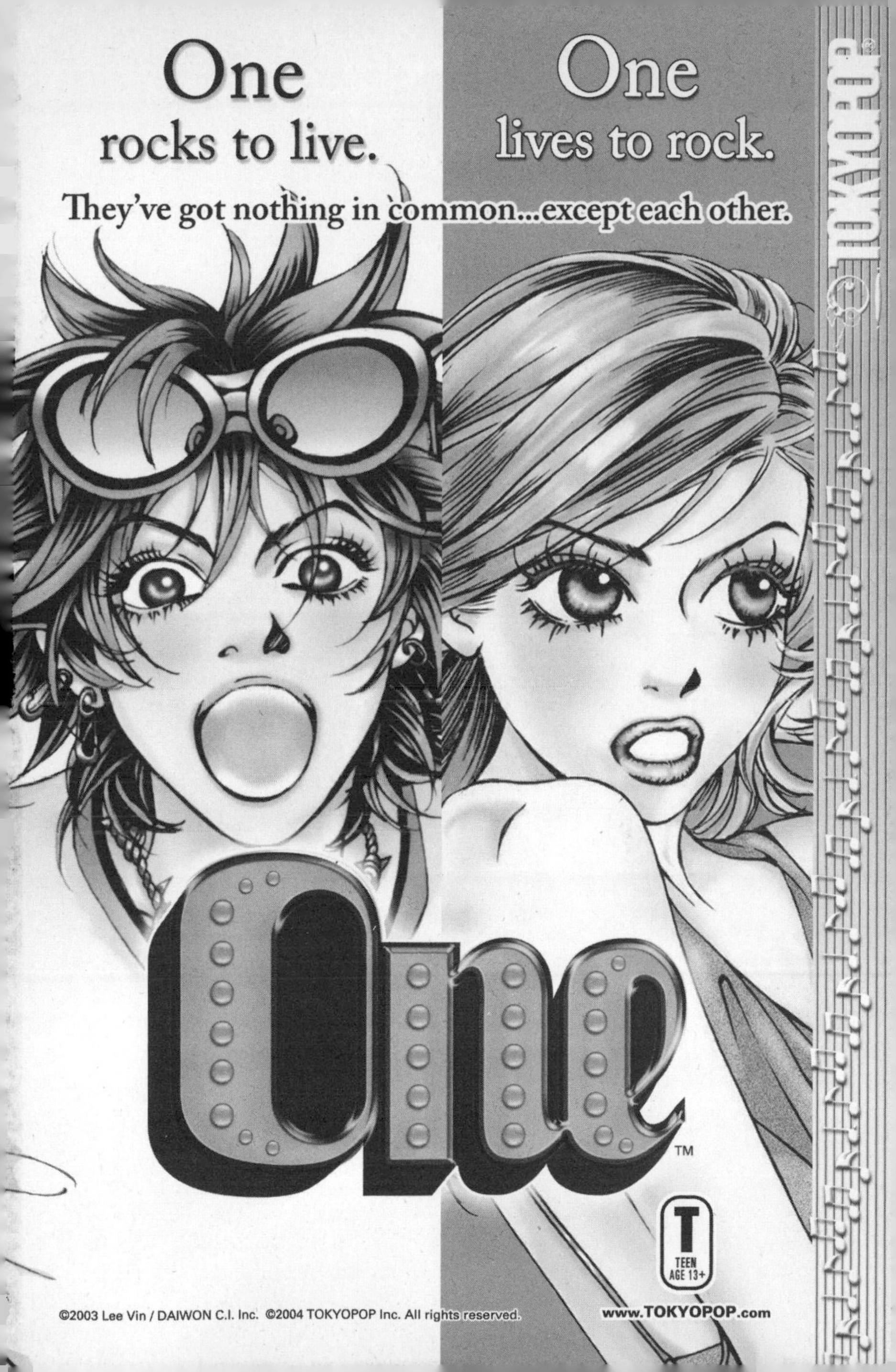

One
rocks to live.
One
lives to rock.
They've got nothing in common...except each other.
TOKYOPOP
One™
T
TEEN
AGE 13+
©2003 Lee Vin / DAIWON C.I. Inc. ©2004 TOKYOPOP Inc. All rights reserved.
www.TOKYOPOP.com

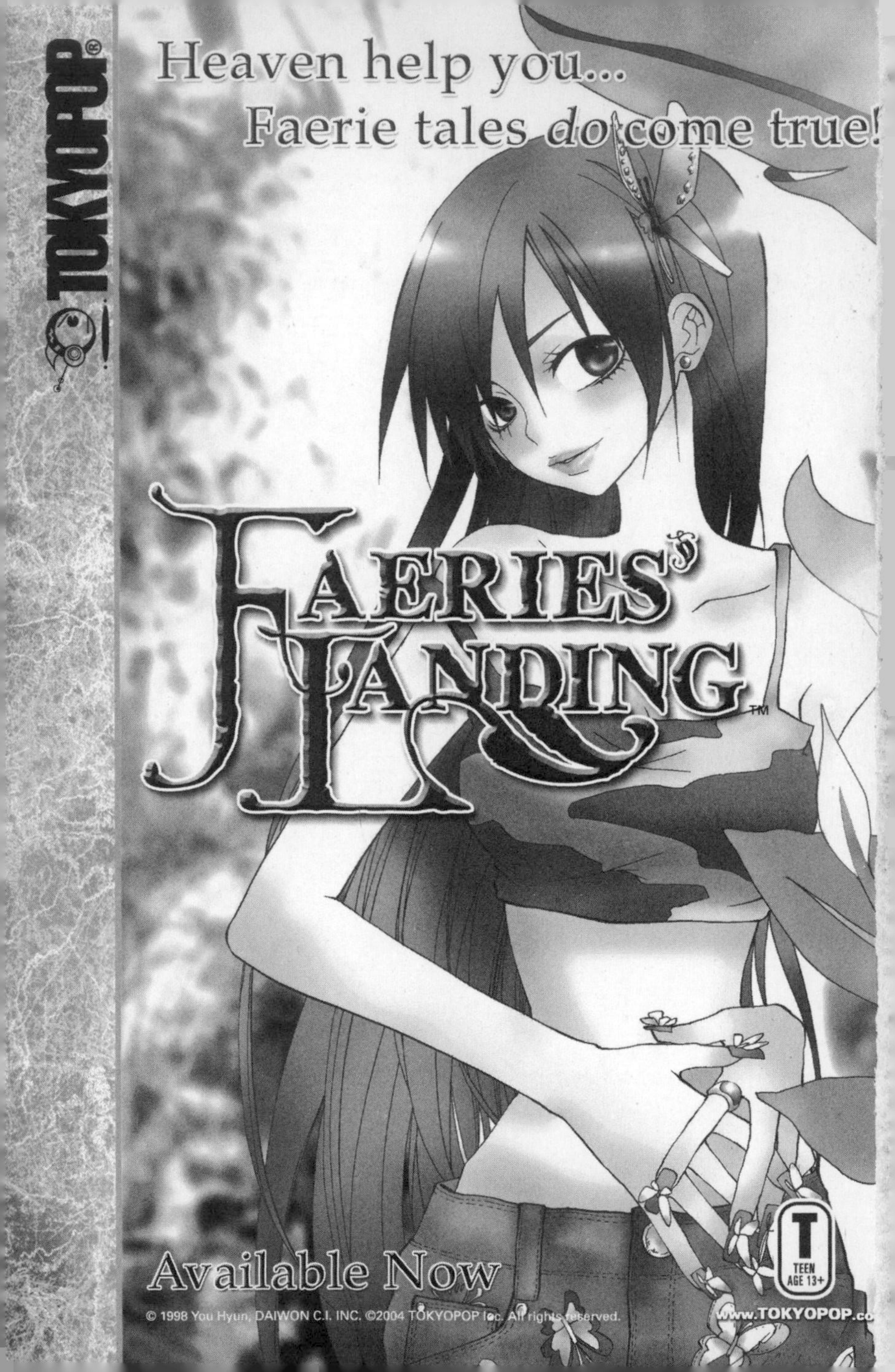
TOKYOPOP
Heaven help you...
Faerie tales *do* come true!
FAERIES' LANDING
Available Now
T
TEEN
AGE 13+
© 1998 You Hyun, DAIWON C.I. INC. ©2004 TOKYOPOP Inc. All rights reserved.
www.TOKYOPOP.co